Jewish Messianism and the History of Philosophy

Jewish Messianism and the History of Philosophy contests the ancient opposition between Athens and Jerusalem by retrieving the concept of meontology – the doctrine of nonbeing – from the Jewish philosophical and theological tradition. For Emmanuel Levinas, as well as for Franz Rosenzweig, Hermann Cohen, and Moses Maimonides, the Greek concept of nonbeing (understood as both lack and possibility) clarifies the meaning of Jewish life. These thinkers of "Jerusalem" use "Athens" for Jewish ends, justifying Jewish anticipation of a future messianic era, as well as portraying the subject's intellectual and ethical acts as central in accomplishing redemption. In addition, Kavka argues that this formal structure of messianic subjectivity is not simply an acculturating move of Judaism to modern or medieval philosophical values, but it can also be found in an earlier stratum of the Jewish tradition, particularly in an ancient midrashic text discussing a group that refers to itself as the Mourners of Zion.

This book envisions modern Jewish thought as an expression of the intimate relationship between Athens and Jerusalem. It also offers new readings of important figures in contemporary Continental philosophy, critiquing previous arguments about the role of lived religion in the thought of Jacques Derrida, the role of Plato in the thought of Emmanuel Levinas, and the centrality of ethics in the thought of Franz Rosenzweig.

Martin Kavka is an assistant professor of religion at Florida State University. He is the author of articles on philosophy of religion and modern Jewish thought appearing in *Religious Studies Review, Journal of Religious Ethics, Cross Currents,* and other leading journals.

Jewish Messianism and the History of Philosophy

MARTIN KAVKA

Florida State University

CAMBRIDGE
UNIVERSITY PRESS

PUBLISHED BY THE PRESS SYNDICATE OF THE UNIVERSITY OF CAMBRIDGE
The Pitt Building, Trumpington Street, Cambridge, United Kingdom

CAMBRIDGE UNIVERSITY PRESS
The Edinburgh Building, Cambridge CB2 2RU, UK
40 West 20th Street, New York, NY 10011-4211, USA
477 Williamstown Road, Port Melbourne, VIC 3207, Australia
Ruiz de Alarcón 13, 28014 Madrid, Spain
Dock House, The Waterfront, Cape Town 8001, South Africa

http://www.cambridge.org

First published 2004

Printed in the United States of America

Typeface ITC New Baskerville 10/12 pt.   *System* LATEX 2$_\varepsilon$ [TB]

A catalog record for this book is available from the British Library.

Library of Congress Cataloging in Publication Data
Kavka, Martin.
Jewish messianism and the history of philosophy / Martin Kavka.
p.   cm.
Includes bibliographical references and index.
ISBN 0-521-83103-2
1. Philosophy, Jewish – History.   2. Nonbeing.   3. Philosophy – History.
4. Lévinas, Emmanuel – Views on nonbeing.   5. Nonbeing – Religious aspects – Judaism.
6. Messiah – Judaism.   I. Title.
B5802.N65K38   2004
181′.06–dc22

2003061320

ISBN 0 521 83103 2 hardback

To Dan Casey, my *Maßiah,*
the measure which reflects the highest good
and thereby makes salvation possible

Contents

Acknowledgments

In the years that I have been working on the issue of negation in Jewish philosophy, I have had the benefit of support from numerous professors, colleagues, and friends. All of these individuals have been my teachers, and it will take me more than a lifetime to demonstrate my worthiness of the attention and care they have shown me.

My passion for this material is rooted in the inspiring pedagogical and intellectual gifts of Robert Gibbs, whom I encountered in a seminar at Princeton University in the fall of 1991. (The passion of the other seminar participants – including Jen Bajorek, Leora Batnitzky, Ruth Gerson, Elise Harris, Ariel Kaminer, and Viv Soni – was infectious.) Later, David Novak guided me toward refining the rigor of my thinking. He has since become a jewel of a conversation partner. And through her enigmatic nature and wily graciousness, Edith Wyschogrod made it possible for my years at Rice University to be challenging, productive, and happy beyond my wildest dreams.

I owe thanks also to Kamila Kavka, Misha Kavka and Stephen Turner, Cornel West, Victor Preller, Elaine Pagels, Malcolm Diamond z"l, Dmitry Gorenburg, Arun Sannuti, Mun Hou Lo, Robert Scharlemann, Michael Swartz, Larry Bouchard, Jamie Ferreira, Michael Satlow, Jennifer Geddes, Kyle Fedler, Clayton Crockett, Trent Pomplun, Willie Young, Laura Levitt, Susan Shapiro, Dave and Susannah Nix, Eric and Julie Boynton, Stephen Hood and Sdenka Aguilar-Hood, Shaul Magid, my big brother Zachary Braiterman, Brian Riedel, Andrea Frolic and Sheldon Smart, Steven Galt Crowell, Cynthia Freeland, Michael Weingrad, Diana Lobel, Gerald McKenny, Werner Kelber, David Nirenberg, Oona Ajzenstat, Willis Johnson, Judith Brown, Ann and Nicholas Willis, Caroline Willis, Misty Willis, Steve Kepnes, Claire Katz, Dana Hollander, Marc Lee Raphael, Gregory Kaplan, and Matthew LaGrone. Peter Ochs has shown me that my conversation partners are my family.

The friendship of Gene Rogers, Derek Krueger, Claire Kaplan, Leah Zahler z"l, Ned Brinkley, Bernard Mayes, and Mark Jordan has given me much-needed support at difficult times.

I owe special thanks to four women who have forever altered the categories of my understanding. Randi Rashkover has shown me that a life spent reading and writing Jewish theology is a life of great pleasure. Beth McManus has shown me how to live the patience and generosity that I admire on the page. Nancy Levene has shown me that brokenness need not be loneliness. Laurel Fulkerson has shown me how to be professional and fabulous at the same time. They have taught me to live and love more fully, and in so doing they have improved my thinking.

My wonderful friends and colleagues in Tallahassee are the most delightful of rewards: Shannon Burkes, John Corrigan and Sheila Curran, Bryan and Amanda Cuevas, Kathleen Erndl and Yakini Kemp, Aline Kalbian and Bob Cross, David Kangas and Inese Radzins, Nicole Kelley and Matt Day, John and Rita Kelsay, Amy Koehlinger and Charles Robinson, David and Cathy Levenson, Leo and Marvel Lou Sandon, and Barney and Pat Twiss. In the brief time I knew her, Tessa Bartholomeusz taught me many things. I miss her a great deal.

A draft of what eventually became Chapter 4 was read in 1999 at the annual meeting of the American Academy of Religion, and a preliminary version of the Conclusion was read in 2001 at the annual conference of the International Association of Philosophy and Literature. My thanks to those who gave me helpful criticisms, including Robert Gibbs, Peter Ochs, Zachary Braiterman, Barbara Galli, Dana Hollander, and Ferit Güven. Rewriting a previous draft of the Introduction as a letter to Dirk von der Horst was enormously helpful; I am grateful for the generosity of his response. Rewriting the Conclusion in its epistolary form was therapeutic; I hope its primary addressee knows who he is. Some of my previously published articles contain interpolations of this material into very different contexts. A small part of the Introduction appeared in "Recollection, *Zakhor, Anamnesis,*" *Cross Currents* 49, no. 4 (2000); part of Chapter 4 appeared in "Saying Kaddish for Gillian Rose," in *Secular Theology,* edited by Clayton Crockett (New York: Routledge, 2001), and part of the Conclusion appeared in "Textual Reasoning and Cultural Memory," in *Textual Reasonings,* edited by Nancy Levene and Peter Ochs (London: SCM Press, 2002).

In preparing this manuscript for publication, I had the good fortune to respond to comments and questions from Robert Gibbs, Oliver Davies, and Diana Lobel, all of whom read the manuscript with keen eyes and a warmth that invited me to push the limits of my ability to think through these issues. This book is far clearer as a result; the responsibility for its weaknesses and faults is mine alone. At Cambridge University Press, Andy Beck has been an exemplar of patient cool; he, Helen Wheeler, and Susan Greenberg make work fun. Bob Erlewine has provided an excellent index.

Finally, the man to whom this book is dedicated is the sine qua non of these words seeing print. The debt I owe him is the greatest of all.

Abbreviations

AE Emmanuel Levinas, *Autrement qu'être ou au-delà de l'essence.* The Hague: Martinus Nijhoff, 1974.
Emmanuel Levinas, *Otherwise than Being, or Beyond Essence.* Trans. Alphonso Lingis. Dordrecht: Kluwer Academic Publishers, 1991.

CEM Hermann Cohen, "Charakteristik der Ethik Maimunis." In *Jüdische Schriften,* vol. 3. Berlin: C. A. Schwetschke & Sohn, 1924: 221–89.

EE Emmanuel Levinas, *De l'existence à l'existent.* 2nd ed. Paris: Vrin, 1978.
Emmanuel Levinas, *Existence and Existents.* Trans. Alphonso Lingis. The Hague: Martinus Nijhoff, 1978.

EN Nicolas Abraham and Maria Torok, *L'écorce et le noyau.* 2nd ed. Paris: Aubier-Flammarion, 1987.
Nicolas Abraham and Maria Torok, *The Shell and the Kernel: Renewals of Psychoanalysis.* Trans. Nicholas Rand. Chicago: University of Chicago Press, 1994.

EY Moses Maimonides, *The Epistle to Yemen.* Trans. Joel Kraemer. In *Maimonides' Empire of Light.* Ed. Ralph Lerner. Chicago: University of Chicago Press, 2000.

G Moses Maimonides, *The Guide of the Perplexed.* Trans. Shlomo Pines. Chicago: University of Chicago Press, 1963.

I2 Edmund Husserl, *Ideen zu einer reinen Phänomenologie und phänomenologischen Philosophie. Zweites Buch: Phänomenologische Untersuchungen zur Konstitution.* Ed. Marly Biemel. The Hague: Martinus Nijhoff, 1952.

Edmund Husserl, *Ideas Pertaining to a Pure Phenomenology and to a Phenomenological Philosophy. Second Book: Studies in the Phenomenology of Constitution.* Trans. Richard Rojcewicz and André Schuwer. Dordrecht: Kluwer Academic Publishers, 1989.

LRE   Hermann Cohen, *Logik der reinen Erkenntnis.* 3rd ed. Berlin: Bruno Cassirer, 1922.

LU   Edmund Husserl, *Logische Untersuchungen.* 4th ed. Halle: Max Niemeyer, 1928.

Edmund Husserl, *Logical Investigations.* Trans. J. N. Findlay. New York: Humanities Press, 1970.

MH   Emil Fackenheim, "Metaphysics and Historicity." In *The God Within: Kant, Schelling and Historicity.* Ed. John Burbidge. Toronto: University of Toronto Press, 1996: 122–47, 215–27.

PIZ   Edmund Husserl, *Zur Phänomenologie des inneren Zeitbewusstseins (1893–1917).* Ed. Rudolf Boehm. The Hague: Martinus Nijhoff, 1969.

Edmund Husserl, *On the Phenomenology of the Consciousness of Internal Time (1893–1917).* Trans. John Barrett Brough. Dordrecht: Kluwer Academic Publishers, 1991.

RV   Hermann Cohen, *Religion der Vernunft aus den Quellen des Judentums.* 2nd ed. Köln: Joseph Melzer, 1928.

Hermann Cohen, *Religion of Reason out of the Sources of Judaism.* Trans. Simon Kaplan. New York: Frederick Ungar, 1972.

S   Franz Rosenzweig, *Der Stern der Erlösung.* 4th ed. The Hague: Martinus Nijhoff, 1976.

Franz Rosenzweig, *The Star of Redemption.* Trans. Rudolf Hallo. Notre Dame, Ind.: University of Notre Dame Press, 1985.

SM   Jacques Derrida, *Spectres de Marx.* Paris: Galilée, 1993.

Jacques Derrida, *Specters of Marx: The State of the Debt, the Work of Mourning, and the New International.* Trans. Peggy Kamuf. New York: Routledge, 1994.

TI   Emmanuel Levinas, *Totalité et l'infini.* The Hague: Martinus Nijhoff, 1961.

Emmanuel Levinas, *Totality and Infinity.* Trans. Alphonso Lingis. Pittsburgh: Duquesne University Press, 1969.

W   F. W. J. Schelling, *Die Weltalter.* In *Sämmtliche Werke.* Stuttgart and Augsburg: J. G. Cotta, 1856–61: vol. 8, 195–344. Reprinted with original pagination in *Schellings Werke,* vol. 4. Ed. Manfred Schröter. Munich: C. H. Beck, 1958.

F. W. J. Schelling, *The Ages of the World.* Trans. Jason Wirth. Albany: State University of New York Press, 2000.

On occasion, I have emended certain published translations. In dual citations, for example, AE 210/165, the first page reference is to the original-language edition and the second is to the English translation.

Introduction

From Athens to Jerusalem

D—— and others,

I write you anxious that these words will not be able to sustain our conversation.

After all, this is a book about meontology, literally the study of that which is not, of nonbeing (in Greek, *to mē on*). "Meontology" is not exactly a word that is on the tips of people's tongues at the moment. It perhaps only calls attention to its own obscurity, evidence for yet another scholar's ignorance of the real world, of body, of skin. If so, then our conversation will fall into nothingness – an event I cannot bear to face. In resistance against this possibility, I want to state, at the outset, as simply as possible, what is at stake in thinking about meontology, so that I can hear or read your response, which I so fervently desire. I imagine you (perhaps falsely) asking four questions about what I will describe in these pages as "the Jewish meontological tradition," and I offer four preliminary responses.

1. *What is not?* Everything that has not yet actualized its potential. Most viscerally, me.
2. *What is meontology?* The study of unmediated experiences of lack and privation. This study inaugurates self-critique and the realization that I live in a moment best described as not-yet. I thereby begin my path toward human perfection and toward God.
3. *How do I live in this not-yet?* In manic desire for what appears to me to be stable, for what displays a comfort in its own skin that I have never experienced. For you.
4. *What is the effect of this desire?* In the hope against hope that my desire will come to fulfillment, I keep you in mind, near me. I take care of you and work to engender political reforms that allow our conversation and relationship to perdure. I act to delay your death – even, perhaps, if this contributes to the skyrocketing proportion of the GDP taken up by the cost of medical care – and the death of your friends, and their

friends, ad infinitum. In these brief moments when I break free of my narcissistic chains, I act messianically and redeem the world that is responsible for your suffering and your death, which will always be premature for me. I engender a world that my tradition (and perhaps yours) says God engenders, and I articulate my resemblance to God.[1]

This argument makes a long journey from Athens to Jerusalem. It moves from a philosophy of nonbeing to the passionate faith in a redeemer still to come . . . whom I represent. Indeed, the notion of a redeemer to come – *the* difference between Judaism and Christianity – cannot be defended without turning back to the analysis of nonbeing in the Greek philosophical tradition. Without Athens, Jerusalem (Judaism) risks being unable to articulate the meaning of its own religious practices, becoming no more than a set of customs divorced from their ultimate source, a sedimented series of rote actions that can create an identity for its practitioners only through the profane category of "culture."

As a result, this book vigorously rejects the Athens–Jerusalem problem that has been our pet mosquito, sucking our lifeblood since the third century C.E. In its infancy, it was a problem for Christianity. It is first mentioned in the seventh chapter of the early Church father Tertullian's *de Praescriptione Hoereticorum* (*On the Prescription against Heretics*). To be sure, Tertullian credits Paul with posing the conflict in his command to the Colossians that "no one take you captive through philosophy and empty deception" (Col. 2:8). But it is Tertullian who first codifies the problem in geographical language: "What indeed has Athens to do with Jerusalem? What concord is there between the Academy and the Church? What between heretics and Christians? Away with all attempts to produce a mottled Christianity of Stoic, Platonic, and dialectic composition!"[2] Thus begins a long history of the fear of miscegenation, paralleled by rabbinic texts from the same time period that proscribe the learning of Greek wisdom.[3] But the Athens–Jerusalem problem is not only about the relationship between faith and the heresy of philosophy. In the modern period, it is about the relationship between Jewish faith and Western culture, which are perceived to be in necessary conflict. On the side of culture, the Orientalist Johann David Michaelis, writing in 1782 in Göttingen, claims that Jewish observance of the ceremonial law established Jews as being at cross-purposes with the laws of the German nation. Hence, "it will be impossible to grant the Jew the same freedoms [as

---

[1] In "The Absence Fetish," *Religious Studies Review* 29:3 (July 2003), 225–34, I argue that the fact that foundations are not accessible to human understanding necessitates an ethics that oscillates between narcissism and the sacrifice of that narcissism.

[2] Tertullian, "On the Prescription against Heretics," in *The Writings of Quintus Sept. Flor. Tertullianus*, vol. II [*Ante-Nicene Christian Library*, vol. XV], trans. Peter Holmes (Edinburgh: T & T Clark, 1870), 246.

[3] Cf. M. Sotah 9:14, B. Sotah 491, B. Menachot 64b.

German Christians], for he will never be a full citizen with respect to love for and pride in his country."⁴ On the side of Jewish faith, the argument of modern Jewish thinkers (including Moses Mendelssohn, Hermann Cohen, and Abraham Joshua Heschel) that Jews have a mission within the public rational sphere already appears to assume that the spheres of Jerusalem and Athens are different, that the mission is grounded in a text or culture different from that which grounds the nation-state.⁵ The either/or of the Athens–Jerusalem problem insidiously perseveres to this day, either in the move of the two Zions – Israel and America – to separate themselves from Europe, or in the need of contemporary Jews to articulate their cultural difference through means above and beyond the unique texts at the basis of study and prayer.

There is no reason why this either/or is necessary. In spite of the uneasy relationship with Athens displayed by the rabbis, some medieval Jewish philosophers refused to admit that there was any Athens–Jerusalem split. In a classic essay published in 1974, Herbert Davidson offers some religious motives for a Jewish intellectual in the medieval period to turn to Greek philosophy in the interest of gaining a better understanding of Judaism.⁶ Simply put, the Hebrew Bible commands knowledge of God. In the final four chapters of the *Guide of the Perplexed*, Maimonides cites at least four verses as prooftexts for his claim that divine worship has an intellectual dimension (G 620–21, G 636): Deut. 4:35 ("You have been shown, in order to know that the Lord is God"), Deut. 4:39 and Ps. 100:3 ("Know . . . that the Lord is God"), and Jer. 9:23 (then interpreted to mean "glory only in this, in intellectual understanding and knowledge" [*haskel ve-yado'a*]).⁷ This command to know God through studying Torah was expanded to include the requirement to learn the natural sciences and the Greek metaphysical tradition. For Maimonides, these are accounts of the ways God works in the created world. Maimonides connects this interpretation of the command to study natural science with the command to love God, when he writes in *Guide* III:28 that love of God "only becomes valid through the apprehension of the whole of being as it is and through the consideration of His wisdom as it is manifested in it" (G 512–13). He further claims that this holistic view of Torah is justified by the tradition itself. Bringing together Athens

---

4 Johann David Michaelis, excerpt from "Herr Ritter Michaelis Beurtheilung," reprinted in *The Jew in the Modern World*, 2nd ed., ed. Paul Mendes-Flohr and Jehuda Reinharz (Oxford: Oxford University Press, 1995), 43.

5 Cf. Moses Mendelssohn, *Jerusalem*, trans. Allan Arkush (Hanover, N.H.: Brandeis University Press, 1983), 118; RV 298/255; Abraham Joshua Heschel, *God in Search of Man* (New York: Noonday, 1955), 245.

6 Herbert A. Davidson, "The Study of Philosophy as a Religious Obligation," in *Religion in a Religious Age*, ed. S. D. Goitein (Cambridge, Mass.: Association for Jewish Studies, 1974), 53–68.

7 See ibid., 57–58.

and Jerusalem – in hindsight, having dual citizenship – becomes a means for working through elements of the tradition that are, on the surface, opaque and therefore open to challenge. "Greek philosophy highlights, for the medieval thinker, elements in the Jewish religion that were vague and problematical, and then provides him with the means for clarifying those problematic elements."[8]

Although this instinct to work through theological problems with the aid of philosophical texts appears organic in the texts of the medieval philosophers, it appears artificial in the texts of the modern Jewish philosophers. Here, Jewish philosophy has been stereotyped as an apologetic that seeks to defend Judaism as unopposed to the voice of secular reason, by redescribing Judaism in the foreign language of the Western philosophical canon.[9] This accusation is directed at the liberal Jewish tradition, stretching from Moses Mendelssohn in the eighteenth century to Emmanuel Levinas in the late twentieth (and his students today). These German Jews and their French heirs allegedly introduce some infectious agent into the tradition. In the eighteenth century, Mendelssohn used a Leibnizian-Wolffian framework; in the nineteenth century, Samuel Hirsch used Hegel while Hermann Cohen used Leibniz, Kant, and Plato; in the twentieth century, Franz Rosenzweig used Schelling while Emmanuel Levinas used a Platonic interpretation of the phenomenology of Edmund Husserl and Martin Heidegger. By using another culture's tools to examine Judaism, these supposed apologists risk a complete loss of the natural particularity of the Jewish tradition. And in an age in which any threat to the vitality of Judaism appears to run even a slight risk of granting Hitler a posthumous victory,[10] this simply will not do. Thus, as Arthur Green wrote about the nature of American Jewish theology in 1994, "[s]haken to our root by the experience of the Holocaust, our religious language took the predictable route of self-preservation by turning inward, setting aside this universalist agenda as non-essential to our own survival." For this reason, Green chooses to reject this entire Mendelssohn-to-Levinas tradition in favor of a neo-Hasidic stance based in Eastern European traditions, favoring the broad contours of the individual's religious experience and prayerful life. This has the effect of omitting all searches for justification of Judaism in the philosophical tradition of Western Europe.[11] The

---

[8] Ibid., 54.

[9] See Arthur Green, "New Directions in Jewish Theology in America," in *Contemporary Jewish Theology*, ed. Elliot N. Dorff and Louis E. Newman (Oxford: Oxford University Press, 1999), 488.

[10] The phrase is Emil Fackenheim's, and it can be found in several of his writings. One example is *God's Presence in History: Jewish Affirmations and Philosophical Reflections* (New York: Harper & Row, 1970), 84.

[11] Green, 493. While Green also states that "we find ourselves turning back to the interrupted work of our nascent Jewish universalists and theologicans of radical immanence" (493), it is clear that his universalism is radically different from that of the liberal Jewish philosophical tradition. Instead of a universalism in which different cultures gain self-understanding

post-Holocaust crisis of Jewish philosophy, then, should in Green's eyes lead to the dissolution of a tradition that extends back to the Hellenistic period and the writings of Philo in the first century C.E.

But with respect to Jewish philosophy, the dismissal is too hasty. What should now be the task of at least a subset of Jewish theology is to *retrieve* the modern Jewish philosophical tradition in a way that speaks to the particular needs (and the need for particularity) of the Jewish people. Only when it has been conclusively demonstrated that philosophy is a sham and of no aid to Jewish self-understanding can one accept Green's view. Davidson (and the entire field of medieval Jewish thought) has given the confidence necessary to retrieve modern Jewish thought in such a way that it serves not as an apologetic tool, but as a tool for deepening the relationship of contemporary Jews to core Jewish concepts.

THE THESIS AND TWO COROLLARIES

At this point, you may be expecting a hysterical assertion of the relevance of the liberal Jewish philosophical tradition despite recent history: "Don't forget that this is our past too!" But I will readily admit that Green is to some extent correct. Modern Jewish thought has indeed become somewhat sedimented as an era of Jewish history; we already see its theological elements drained off by intellectual historians.[12] When reconstructing these works of philosophy in terms of their cultural context, it is all too easy to read them either as cries to non-Jews to be serious about their acceptance of Jews in the political order, or as a series of melancholic consolations to Jews that acceptance from Gentile society will be easier if they understand themselves according to Jewish philosophy's refraction of the Jewish past. Why then not view modern Jewish thought as immaterial, as nothing?

But ironically enough, this focus on nothing in the Jewish philosophical tradition can end up having a reactivating effect on it.[13] In the chapters that follow, I will produce evidence that will show the possibility of invoking a different memory of the origin of modern Jewish thought, not as a desire to fit in to foreign empires or languages, but as an analysis of the nature of the world around us as nothing, as nonbeing, as unredeemed and deprived

through an exchange of languages, Green imagines a universalism in which particular cultures gain "a deeper and richer appreciation ... of our natural and earthly heritage" (493). This nature-mysticism, if rooted in traditional Jewish history as well as contemporary Jewish history, may well lead to political problems that can be solved only by a retreat from history to ahistorical concepts such as rationality. Cf. Richard L. Rubenstein, *After Auschwitz*, 2nd ed. (Baltimore: Johns Hopkins University Press, 1992), 232–33.

[12] Cf. Mark Lilla, "A Battle for Religion," *The New York Review of Books* 49:19 (December 5, 2002), 60–65.

[13] For the model for reactivating sedimented meanings, cf. Edmund Husserl, "The Origin of Geometry," in Jacques Derrida, *Edmund Husserl's* Origin of Geometry: *An Introduction*, trans. John P. Leavey, Jr. (Lincoln: University of Nebraska Press, 1989), 164ff.

of the fullness of God's presence. Therefore, it is the study of nonbeing and not-yet-being in some texts in this tradition (and in some texts that are key precursors of it) that will allow us to retrieve modern Jewish thought as something that can speak to our present cultural situation in which clarity has been exchanged for murkiness, and not as something that spoke only once upon a time.

Meontology plays a key – but understated – role in the strand of the Jewish philosophical tradition I analyze here. Although the term is used explicitly only in the writings of Emmanuel Levinas (and then, only sparingly), concepts that are thematically associated with it – privation, lack, not-yet – are important concerns in the writings of Maimonides, Hermann Cohen, and Franz Rosenzweig. These four thinkers participate in what I am forcefully naming "the Jewish meontological tradition," a tradition of Jewish thinkers who use either the explicit concept of nonbeing or implicit adjunct concepts as prisms for viewing the Jewish tradition. Further, I claim that the use of this Greek term for the purpose of Jewish theology, far from watering down the richness of Jewish life, expresses and clarifies it. All four thinkers argue for a teleological vector to existence, rendering history radically open, unfulfilled, and ungraspable. The nature of human being is to be not yet, to be deprived of the stasis of being, to hunger after it, and to work to engender it. This sets the stage for a view of the religious life as centered on messianic anticipation.

There are two corollaries to this main thesis. One is a claim about Levinas, or at least about current understandings of Levinas. Depending on one's view of deconstruction and the Jewishness of Jacques Derrida,[14] Levinas (1906–1995) is arguably the most recent representative of the Western Jewish philosophical strand rejected by Green. Trained under Edmund Husserl and Martin Heidegger, Levinas developed a phenomenology that uncovered an ethical and precognitive stratum at the base of experience, commanding us to let go of egoist tendencies and become responsible for others. In an important 1981 interview with Richard Kearney, Levinas described his ethics as "a meontology which affirms a meaning beyond Being, a primary mode of non-Being ($m\bar{e}$ on)."[15] Levinas's phenomenology of bodily expression belies an openness to the infinite that cannot be objectified in conceptual terms, and that therefore lies beyond that which is, exterior to the aegis of human knowing and willing, transcendent and hence belonging to religious discourse. Because of Levinas's antipathy to the later work

---

[14] Cf. Gideon Ofrat, *The Jewish Derrida*, trans. Peretz Kidron (Syracuse, N.Y.: Syracuse University Press, 2001).

[15] Richard Kearney, "Dialogue with Emmanuel Lévinas," in *Dialogues with Contemporary Continental Thinkers: The Phenomenological Heritage* (Manchester: Manchester University Press, 1984), 61 and 63. Reprinted in *Face to Face with Levinas*, ed. Richard Cohen (Albany: State University of New York Press, 1986), 25 and 27, and, as "Ethics of the Infinite," in Kearney, *States of Mind* (Manchester: Manchester University Perss, 1995), 190 and 192.

of Martin Heidegger, and because of Heidegger's sustained interaction with Greek philosophy throughout his career, many interpreters of Levinas within the discipline of modern Jewish thought associate his critique of the "Greek" philosophical tradition with a valorization of the "Jew" and remain trapped within Tertullian's distinction. Articles in which Levinas has claimed parallels between his phenomenology and various passages of Oral Torah have only made this trap more tempting. Reading Levinas's philosophy within what I draw to be the meontological tradition of Jewish theology allows one to see it as a species of Greek as well as Jewish thought, thereby sanctioning a critique of the very notion of a gap, no matter how oblique, between Athens and Jerusalem. For Green's claim that Jews must now turn inward assumes that they have been facing out before now, looking at someplace else, traveling to a different place. But if there is no gap between Athens and Jerusalem, then the call to turn inward can only be a call for Jewish philosophers to keep doing what they have been doing for centuries.

The second corollary of my main thesis is that while the Jewish meontological tradition centers on messianic anticipation, this anticipation has a double-edged quality, in which the Messiah I await is not external to myself. Traditionally, Jewish messianism refers not only to the general redemption of Israel and the world in the concrete sphere of historical and political reality but also to the anticipation of a particular figure who serves as the conduit of divine agency on earth. The anointed figure, whether seen as king or priest or holy person, manifests divine kingship in his association with Mount Zion (Ps. 2:6), the residence of God (Is. 8:18). Thus, anticipation of a messianic figure who brings peace and political autonomy to Israel is also anticipation of God's nearness to the nation, mediated through the human figure of the Messiah. In the Jewish meontological tradition, messianism expresses not only intimacy between the divine and a singular political or religious leader but the real possibility for *any* person to attain this perfection – if only for an ephemeral moment – through his or her teleological aim at human perfection. As Levinas writes in his first magnum opus, *Totality and Infinity*, the radically other-centered ethics for which he argues has the effect of conserving the self (TI 282/305) and ensuring my own redemption in messianic triumph (TI 261/285). It is difficult to pin down exactly who the messianic agent is, since redemption – both of the other person and of myself – is guaranteed through my own ethical action. In a radical sense, human agency has messianic force. I trace this idea back to Cohen, to a lesser extent to Rosenzweig, and further back into the rabbinic tradition. As Levinas formulates the view in one of his first Talmudic readings, "to be myself is to be the Messiah."[16] This "myself" [*moi*] is not the ego who lords

---

[16] Emmanuel Levinas, "Textes messianiques," in *Difficile liberté* (Paris: Albin Michel, 1984), 120, translated by Seán Hand as "Messianic Texts," in *Difficult Freedom* (Baltimore: Johns Hopkins University Press, 1990), 89.

power over others, but the ethical subject who gives up that power and takes responsibility for the suffering of others. In Levinas and Cohen, being the Messiah is synonymous with human moral perfection.

But there are less radical, yet still noteworthy, formulations of the association between human self-perfection and messianism in earlier strands of the tradition. In Maimonides' *Epistle to Yemen*, written in 1172, Maimonides subtly tells the embattled Jews of Yemen, who are responding to the possibility of forced conversion to Islam, that devoting themselves to rational perfection will prepare the way for (or even constitute) the arrival of the Messiah – a parallel to the path toward redemption that Maimonides will later lay out in the *Guide*. Also, in an ancient Jewish text, Pesikta Rabbati 34, an embattled group of Jews, who read Torah in a heterodox manner and refer to themselves as the Mourners of Zion, responds to the possibility of being ostracized by the majority of their community by arguing that their heterodox practice will facilitate messianic redemption. Furthermore, in what hindsight shows to be a blatant exercise of projection, they describe themselves in the same language in which they describe the messianic figure. This blurring of the boundary between the anticipated Messiah and the human striving for perfection in these texts is a heightened expression of the tradition's belief in the imminence of messianic advent.[17] Thus, while the openness of history associated with the interpretation of nonbeing in the Jewish meontological tradition rationally justifies Jews' anticipation of a future messianic figure and/or age, it is also the case that this tradition does not decide whether my process of intellectual perfection or my process of learning how to read Torah properly is a sign that messianic advent is really possible, or whether the messianic idea is only a code for the subject's own ethical or spiritual acts. Viewing the Jewish philosophical tradition as about nothing will lead us back to that concept at the core of the modern West, autonomy.

A PRELIMINARY SKETCH OF THE ARGUMENT

It would be possible for me to simply offer you a linear story about the concept of nonbeing in Jewish philosophy from Maimonides to the present, and in fact there are some pages that follow in which I explore questions of influence that would allow you to reconstruct such a narrative. But telling that story would fail to have the effect I desire. It would give the impression that Levinas has a nostalgia for a Maimonidean worldview that history has really passed by; you might then respond by saying that my narrative had persuaded you that history has passed Levinas by as well, and that we should relegate him to a curio in history of philosophy seminars. So it becomes duly important for me to tell you the story in as ahistorical a way as possible and

[17] Cf. B. Baba Metzia 85b, S 404/363 and 253/227.

have it still be coherent. In reading the following pages, you may be surprised to find sudden shifts in discourses, in figures, in time frames. You will wonder why Plato, Husserl, and Derrida are part of the cast of characters. But in order to show that there is no gap between Athens and Jerusalem, I must perform that proximity for you. To show that these texts are relevant today, to preserve their life, I must blast them out of their historical contexts.[18] And to persuade you that their life is in danger, I must show you first of all not only Green's desire to rid the Jewish philosophical tradition of its vitality but also how a first attempt to read this tradition in the light of nonbeing is fraught with difficulty.

Therefore, the first two chapters deal with what I call "the meontological conundrum," that is, the problem of defining meontology. This is not the clever problem of parsing sentences that begin with "nonbeing is..." Rather, the problem has to do with two different senses of "meontology" that are currently embedded in Jewish philosophy. Indeed, the two senses are diametrically opposed to one another. On the one hand, there is the Levinasian sense, which uses "nonbeing" to refer to that which transcends and is beyond being. On the other hand, Emil Fackenheim (1916–2003), in his 1961 lecture *Metaphysics and Historicity*, describes meontology as a dialectical process, a circular movement of self-making in which the self is established by integrating its own past history into its future projects. This history of the self, its existential situation including the structures and persons among and with whom it lives, is thus used as fuel for the construction of identity. As a result, Fackenheim's description of meontology involves a notion of otherness that is not beyond the realm of being – Fackenheim denies that his theology involves a notion of revelation[19] – but a mysterious otherness *within* being. Perhaps as a gift from being, otherness presents the self with options for other modes of living. This model of otherness risks losing the element of self-questioning found at such hyperbolic levels in Levinas's conception of alterity. Although Levinas does not offer an explicit critique of Fackenheim,[20] Fackenheim's notion of otherness might easily be the target of a Levinasian critique due to Fackenheim's attachment to Hegelian idealism. In a footnote to *Metaphysics and Historicity* (MH 221n. 23), Fackenheim writes that "the greatest attempt to explicate this kind of [meontological]

[18] The language of this sentence borrows from the seventeenth of Walter Benjamin's "Theses on the Philosophy of History," in Benjamin, *Illuminations*, ed. Hannah Arendt and trans. Harry Zohn (New York: Schocken, 1968), 263.

[19] Emil Fackenheim, "A Reply to My Critics: A Testament of Thought," in *Fackenheim: German Philosophy and Jewish Thought*, ed. Louis Greenspan and Graeme Nicholson (Toronto: University of Toronto Press, 1992), 268–69.

[20] Indeed, there is a paean to Fackenheim's *God's Presence in History* in Levinas's "La souffrance inutile," in *Entre nous* (Paris: Bernard Grasset, 1991), 115–18, translated by Michael B. Smith and Barbara Harshav as "Useless Suffering," in *Entre Nous* (New York: Columbia University Press, 1998), 97–100.

logic is beyond all doubt Hegel's *Science of Logic*." Yet for Hegel to be associated with meontology is anathema to Levinas. In Levinas's view, the drive to
comprehension and the concomitant predilection for violence that constitute Heideggerean method descend from Hegel. Sideswipes to Hegel occur
throughout Levinas's work in the cause of wresting the singularity of human
subjectivity from the universalist rhetoric of the vast majority of the philosophical tradition. This account of subjectivity is fundamentally opposed
to Hegel's language of a consciousness that bridges subject and substance,
erases the possibility of anything exterior to the self, and seeks to render different human existences commensurable with one another.[21] One might
therefore describe Hegel's philosophy as a heterophagy – a consumption of
the other person. In short, while meontology is Hegelian for Fackenheim,
it is completely anti-Hegelian for Levinas.

The possibility of finding a new account of the origin of the Jewish philosophical project through the category of nonbeing is threatened by this
conflict, and the conflict itself gives us no tools for adjudication. For this
reason, I turn in the second chapter to an early setting of the discussion
of *to mē on*, namely, Plato's *Sophist*. Here I critique Levinas's nostalgia for
middle-period Platonism and contextualize his meontology in a reading of
Husserl's *Logical Investigations*. Levinas's concept of ethical subjectivity is explicitly rooted in Plato's claim in the sixth book of the *Republic* (509b) that
the good beyond all being is the cause of truth (TI 76/103). Nevertheless,
Levinas's argument relies upon an uncritical understanding of the theory of
forms found in Plato's middle period, namely the argument that an object
has a property X because it participates in the form of that property. (For
example, one might say "Nathan is beautiful because he participates in the
Form of Beauty, in Beauty-itself.") Plato himself radically critiques this position in the *Parmenides*, through the voice of Parmenides who argues that it is
impossible for an object to be what it is in this manner, and ends up getting
the better of Socrates. An example: assume that both Nathan and Joan share
in Beauty-itself. They can either share in the entirety of the form, or each
can possess a part of the form, as a sail is spread over a group of people
(131b8). In each scenario, Parmenides claims that there is no longer one
form of Beauty, but two: either two separate but equal forms of Beauty in
the first scenario, or two parts of one form of Beauty in the second scenario.
In both cases, Parmenides has put forward a serious challenge to the theory
offered in the *Phaedo* and the *Republic* by which essences such as Beauty-itself
would necessarily be simplex, without composite parts. The *Sophist* attempts
to get past this impasse by delineating ways in which properties of an object
appear in the context of a network of interrelations between objects. It is
in this light that Plato introduces the concept of nonbeing, here defined
as otherness or difference. An object X is what it is by virtue of its being

[21] Cf. TI 193/217 and 250/272; AE 131/103.

different from (or other than) other objects. One can describe this notion of otherness in a loose sense as "horizontal"; it is fully divorced from the more "vertical," transcendent connotation of nonbeing and otherness in Levinas's work.

Hence Levinas's attempt to defend religion (and specifically Judaism) through a return to Plato would seem to be defeated on Platonic grounds.[22] I turn to the third of Husserl's *Logical Investigations* to resolve this problem. There, Husserl argues that when two objects are related to each other reciprocally (Husserl uses the term *unselbständig*, translated as "non-independent"), one has the right to posit a larger framework that includes them – a whole. Nevertheless, this whole is unnamable.[23] Since Plato's *Sophist* is an account of the way in which being and nonbeing belong together in the process of constructing meaning, one can conclude that the two are non-independent parts of a whole in the Husserlian sense. This authorizes Levinas's move of positing another kind of nonbeing – a "vertical" notion that transcends the Platonic distinction between being and otherness – as a mysterious and unnamable whole that provides the larger context behind the relationship between being and nonbeing. I thus show that Fackenheim's concept of meontology is grounded in Levinas's sense of the term.

The third and fourth chapters trace the appropriation of this double sense of meontology – of a process of self-making and stabilizing and a process of being destabilized and unmade – in the Jewish philosophical tradition from Maimonides through Levinas. My discussion shows the way Maimonides temporalizes the concept of nonbeing: in other words, nonbeing is not-yet-being. Examining Maimonides' use of nonbeing in the *Guide* and its influence upon Hermann Cohen's writings, I trace the movement from the analysis of nonbeing to the formulation of a messianic ethical teleology. From Aristotle, Maimonides associates nonbeing with privation of and potential for actuality;[24] from Plotinus, Maimonides associates this cluster of concepts with matter.[25] In addition, Maimonides appropriates the Plotinian notion that the distance between the soul's privation and the first cause awakens an erotic desire on the part of the embodied soul for this cause.[26] The desire institutes teleology as an ethical norm. Maimonides' echo of Plotinus here becomes apparent through an exploration of the

---

[22] When Levinas wrote the abstract of *Totality and Infinity* for submission as a thesis for his *Doctorat* from the University of Paris, he described the project as a return to Platonism. The thesis summary appears at the end of Adriaan Theodoor Peperzak, "The Platonism of Emmanuel Levinas," in *Platonic Transformations: With and After Hegel, Heidegger and Levinas* (Lanham, Md.: Rowman & Littlefield, 1997), 113–21.

[23] Cf. LU II/1 278–79/477, and Timothy J. Stapleton, *Husserl and Heidegger: The Question of a Phenomenological Beginning* (Albany: State University of New York Press, 1983), 60.

[24] Aristotle, *Physics* A.5–8.   [25] Plotinus, *Enneads* II.4, among other locations.

[26] Ibid., III.5.

Guide's literary structure. In *Guide* I:17–18, Maimonides passes from an analysis of privation to an examination of biblical verbs meaning "to approach" or "to draw near." In both cases, nonbeing as privation gives rise to a desire for the fullness of being.

Maimonides articulates the path of this erotic desire as a discipline of intellectual self-perfection. The desire for God is expressed through *imitatio Dei*, in which God is defined as pure intellect *in actu*, who cannot be reified into the language of substance and attribute. Maimonides argues that we can know only God's attributes of action; we cannot imitate who God is, but we can imitate what God does. One might read Maimonides as arguing that God has essential attributes that transcend the limits of human understanding. Against this view, I argue that there are no hidden attributes of God for Maimonides. Rather, Maimonides argues that God cannot have any qualities whatsoever. God is nothing outside of God's acting, because God's acts are God's essence – or in another formulation, God's essence is the actuality of God's life. There is thus no difference between intellectual perfection and practical perfection in Maimonides; I show that the divine attributes of loving-kindness, righteousness, and judgment are necessary corollaries of God's being an intellect *in actu*.[27] In other writings, Maimonides names the intellectual perfection that is the telos of religious life the world-to-come; it is defined as the soul's participation in the "supernal fellowship . . . with the existence of God the Creator."[28] Messianic anticipation plays a key role in this teleology, since the Messianic Era gives "powerful [assistance] for attaining the world-to-come."[29] But it is unclear whether contemporary readers of Maimonides are forced to think that this Messianic Era is fully exterior to the present time; a reading of Maimonides' *Epistle to Yemen* shows that we might see the analysis of the privative status of the world as inaugurating a path in which the process of rational self-perfection is also a process of messianic self-making.

A similar emphasis on nonbeing as opening up a path by which one might envision the end of the separation between the transcendent and the immanent, the infinite and the finite, is found in the work of Hermann Cohen. In his *Logik der reinen Erkenntnis* (1902), Cohen appropriates from Democritus the concept of nonbeing as the infinitesimal, presenting philosophy as a mode of calculus. In the same manner that the magnitude of an area under a curve is determined by integrating an infinite series of infinitesimals, the infinite origin (*Ursprung*) is determined as totality by taking a detour through the integration of an infinite series of relative nonbeings (spatiotemporal objects), each with its own conatus that propels thinking forward. Thinking

---

[27] Maimonides, *Guide of the Perplexed*, III:53.
[28] Maimonides, *Pereq Heleq*, trans. Arnold J. Wolf, in *A Maimonides Reader*, ed. Isadore Twersky (West Orange, N.J.: Behrman House, 1972), 412.
[29] Ibid., 416.

for Cohen thereby aims at the complete interpenetration of the infinite and the finite. Because of Cohen's claim that the methodologies of the social and natural sciences are grounded in mathematics – a systematic philosophy must be universally applicable – this framework can be transferred from the sphere of logic into those of religion and ethics. In the ethical context, the good becomes determinately real through the integration of persons into a community and a state, a process that involves ensuring that no one in the community suffers in exclusion from the community due to either poverty or intolerance. And referring to Maimonides' claim that God is the negation of all lack and privation, Cohen argues that since the infinite origin of this path of socioethical progress is God, this teleology is not only ethical but also messianic, insofar as it aims at the interpenetration of the divine and the mundane that broadly characterizes the Messianic Era.

Both Cohen and Maimonides postulate an intimacy between human being and God, between the nonbeing that is privation and the infinite that Cohen describes at some points as beyond being. The path toward perfection is an actualization of the individual's true essence, a bringing into relief of something that is already present in me.[30] Yet the individualist demeanor of this path opens itself up to ethical critique. Concern with the world is perhaps not genuine, only a means for the true goal of contemplation of God. Social action thereby might become merely a stepping-stone on the path toward my own redemption. This is more obviously the case for Maimonides, for whom the Messianic Era has no value in and of itself, but merely as a political aid to the aim of the world-to-come. For Cohen, the point is shadier. On the one hand, the other person undeniably has an intrinsic value. There is an imperative to know the other person in his or her particularity; one cannot integrate those who are suffering into the world without genuinely coming into relationship with them. On the other hand, there are sections in Cohen's writings in which the value of the other person is merely instrumental: "the knowledge of man becomes a means for the knowledge of God"(RV 127/109). This leads to a sizable ethical problem with trying to retrieve modern Jewish thought through the concept of meontology. Does not the grounding of the otherness of the other person in the otherness of God make ethics subservient to a theology that centers on the belief that the otherness of God is better than the otherness of the other person? If the goal of my ethical action is to know God, does not this ethics end up ultimately affirming nihilism, since it aspires to leave behind the realm of the human?[31]

---

[30] As Thomas Carlson shows, this is a fundamentally Hegelian move. Cf. Carlson, *Indiscretion: Finitude and the Naming of God* (Chicago: University of Chicago Press, 1999), 66–73.

[31] Martha Nussbaum expresses this concern in her writings, especially "Transcending Humanity," in *Love's Knowledge* (Oxford: Oxford University Press, 1990), 365–91, and *Upheavals of Thought* (Cambridge: Cambridge University Press, 2001).

In the fourth chapter, where I also continue a more traditional story of narrating the centrality of meontology in Rosenzweig and Levinas, this ethical question comes to the fore. Both Rosenzweig and Levinas assume the temporalization of the concept of nonbeing introduced by Maimonides. Their thought presents existence under the sign of the "not-yet" and thus justifies a structure of messianic or eschatological anticipation. Rosenzweig's presentation claims that the world is fundamentally unfinished (as *mē on*) until persons transform the world from the status of mere creature or substance to something endowed with subjectivity, something "animated with a soul" (S 267/241). Levinas's presentation is rooted in a phenomenology of sensibility or eros in which the inability to cognize the thing or person that I sense inaugurates an "intentionality of search" and the description of the present moment as "not yet," as subservient to the future (TI 235/258). But contrary to current interpretations of Levinas and Rosenzweig as kindred spirits, my interpretation draws a sharp distinction between their two methods. Rosenzweig has more Maimonidean elements; his analysis of the privation of the world (either as created or as relative to the individual believer's experience of revelation) leads to a desire for the eternity that transcends the world. This desire, operative in Rosenzweig's account of interpersonal relations, has the effect of making neighbor-love utilitarian; Rosenzweig's descriptions of the others I encounter in the religious community are too abstract to correspond to any structure of concrete life.

In contrast, Levinas's analysis of the created world offers an account of the created objects of the world both as deprived of fullness – as not yet – and as vehicles of revelation that give evidence of transcendence. This is due, I claim, to Levinas's phenomenological heritage, and I outline the ways in which evidence for transcendence is contained within the phenomenality of the other person. Using arguments rooted in Husserl's *Ideas II* and his lectures on time-consciousness, Levinas demonstrates that I cannot understand another person even on the simplest level without positing that the Other precedes me.[32] My consciousness of my own corporeality is grounded in the prior bodily and spatial expression of others. Self-consciousness is not self-originating, but is predicated upon the existence of others in the world. As a result, other persons in the world cannot be contained in any concept of my consciousness. From my perspective, they are infinite, calling my self-sufficiency into question. For Levinas, this argument grounds an ethics in which the neighbor is seen as intrinsically good.

---

[32] Levinas is clearest on this point in the 1965 essay "Intentionalité et Sensation," in *En découvrant l'existence avec Hasserl et Heidegger*, 3rd ed. (Paris: Vrin, 1994), 145–62, translated by Richard A. Cohen and Michael B. Smith as "Intentionality and Sensation," in *Discovering Existence in Husserl* (Evanston, Ill.: Northwestern University Press, 1998), 135–50.

Telling the story of meontology in modern Jewish philosophy in this manner allows me not only to save it from the ashbin of history but to save it by emphasizing the way in which Levinasian meontology is also a Fackenheimian story of self-making (and vice versa). For Levinas, the non-being that lies beyond being and beyond history announces itself within history, within time (AE 36/28). This does not happen directly in a reve-latory unveiling, but in "indirect ways" (AE 19/16), through phenomeno-logical analyses of time, body, and skin. Through these indirect ways, I can come to know that God takes place in time (AE 187/147). I can also come to know that I have been unconsciously performing this knowledge in my bodily acts all along, and that I can, through ethics, engender this truth, this occurrence of God, in the world. Far from being unmade by the im-possibility of discovering a present foundation for the world, Levinasian meontology allows me to express this foundation in messianic action, in the social and political relationships of life. As I claim at the end of Chapter 4, there is no reason why a believer should not imbue in these relationships the same modality of religious experience that Green imbues primarily in nature-mysticism, since the phenomenological work demonstrates that our experiences in the social and political realms are already modes of religious experience.

Nevertheless, I am all too aware that these claims might still appear to you – or, if not to you personally, at least to a rabbi who might be reading these pages – as yet another example of a modernist imposition of philoso-phy upon Judaism. The messianic idea that is rationally justifiable does not necessarily have to resemble any of the variants of the messianic idea in the Jewish tradition. And so it is incumbent upon me to show that this philosoph-ical understanding of messianism is not entirely foreign to the tradition. In the concluding chapter, I turn to the rabbinic text mentioned earlier, Pesikta Rabbati 34, and its treatment of the Mourners of Zion. I argue that the mes-sianic posture of this sect, insofar as it straddles positions of awaiting redemp-tion and asserting the sect's own redemptive power, is meontological, since it speaks to the belonging-together of the infinite and the finite that flows from the analyses of Cohen and Levinas. Phenomenologically speaking, this text displays a reduction (*epochē*) of the Messiah; it abstracts the concept from the presuppositions of the tradition and views the Messiah in terms of the believer's intentional relation to the idea. I use this text to argue against re-cent anti-meontological writings of Jacques Derrida (SM 236/148, 102/59), which claim that the authentically messianic – that is, a phenomenologically reduced and thereby completely abstract messianism – cannot possibly be found in any of the Western monotheisms. With this example, I bring the Jewish meontological tradition, which Green alleges to have only apolo-getic force, to bear on a classical Jewish text for decidedly nonapologetic ends.

A NOTE ON GENDER

Someone – was it my sister? – described this argument as "hysterically butch." This would not be the case simply because the argument revels in arcane aspects of Husserl or in teasing out the reasons why Cohen cites Democritus and Leibniz. The argument may go through these motions as a nervous tic, to avoid having to come face-to-face with nonbeing and its lack. (This tic may also express itself in an epistolary conceit that verges on melodrama or camp.) The focus on messianism, the desire to relieve this lack, may belie a deep-seated discomfort with the concept of nonbeing, a desire for presence and a desire to *be* present. These foci and these desires have been typically associated with the masculinist imaginary. As Diane Jonte-Pace has pointed out, "the insight of psychoanalytic theory lies in its description of the way that the religious and metaphysical language of presence and absence [of being and nonbeing] in Western culture is/has become the language of gender."[33] Isn't the perseverance of the desire for absence to become messianically present playing into classically hegemonic power structures? Isn't Levinas's view of life, constituted by desire for being to relieve nonbeing, for the beyond-being to stop being beyond and to finally *be*, ultimately otherworldly?

Sharon Welch offers a trenchant critique of Tillich's view of nonbeing that cuts to the core of my attempt to reconstruct meontology.

Tillich's description of the power of Being as that which "eternally conquer[s] its own nonbeing" seems plausible and innocuous until we realize what he means by nonbeing. While Tillich rarely defines nonbeing, his description of one central aspect of nonbeing in *The Courage to Be* is revealing. He sees as a threat and as something to be conquered the constituent elements of human life: our belonging to history and place and our dependence on a world that is itself changing and interdependent... Tillich interprets our interdependence as a threat.[34]

Yes – our interdependence is a threat. I could not cry with you in your pain if this were not the case. But is meontology really this masculinist? I will argue that meontology does not await the transformation of a world encoded by lack into one encoded by plenitude, or from "woman" into "man." It does not await the conquering army of being, courageously riding in to conquer the threats of everyday existence and the risks of friendship and love. It does not await a presence that will bring us to a truer life than this one, which would in comparison be marked by death. Rather, it discloses the

---

33 Diane Jonte-Pace, "Situating Kristeva Differently," in *Body/Text in Julia Kristeva: Religion, Women, Psychoanalysis*, ed. David Crownfield (Albany: State University of New York Press, 1992), 21.

34 Sharon D. Welch, "Sporting Power: American Feminism, French Feminisms, and an Ethic of Conflict," in *Transfigurations: Theology and the French Feminists*, ed. C. W. Maggie Kim, Susan M. St. Ville, and Susan M. Simonaitis (Minneapolis: Fortress Press, 1993), 178. Also see Welch, *A Feminist Ethic of Risk* (Minneapolis: Fortress Press, 1990), 117–22. For Tillich's own words, see, for example, *The Courage to Be* (New Haven, Conn.: Yale University Press, 1952), 45.

potential, the possibility, the power of nonbeings – the power of we who are not yet – to reconstitute the world. Our task, in the phenomenological view I adopt in the pages that follow, is both announced and accomplished through the faculty of touch, the contact between persons, through a skin that is essentially nongendered, nongenital, and nonsexed. The task cannot be accomplished unless I remain constituted by lack, unless the desire to touch you and relate to you perdures within me. Only nonbeing can ground our ability to transform the world and make salvation possible.

Welch moves closer toward this point when she celebrates Mary Daly's *Pure Lust* as "unadulterated, absolute, simple sheer striving for abundance of be-ing ... unlimited, unlimiting desire/fire." "Be-ing" here departs from ontology insofar as it is constituted by waves of desire moving in different directions in different moments and is "fluid, dynamic, and changing."[35] Meontology opens on to this erotic direction – Daly's "be-ing" may be the same as the nonbeing of the Jewish meontological tradition. I have my suspicions, though. Touching you does not bring me into communion with the elemental nature of the earth, as Daly believes.[36] Instead, touching you places me face-to-face with the limits of my understanding, with the fact that I am not yet actual or actualized, a fact that puts all my attempts to commune with you under the necessary risk of failure. To make this relation happen, I must pull away from the relation, be silent and let you speak. At that point, I must wend my way back into the conversation somehow, and I have lost my own way as I began to listen to you. I am not sure whether Daly or Welch would agree with the central idea of a non-Tillichean meontology: the desire of the not-yet perseveres because my attempts to save us will always miss their mark. I will never extirpate my lack, and for this reason I act again, asking you how I can refine my messianic nature.

But I cannot say any of this for certain until you respond.

---

[35] Welch, "Sporting Power," 190.
[36] Mary Daly, *Pure Lust* (Boston: Beacon Press, 1984), 3 and 356–57.

1

The Meontological Conundrum

Emmanuel Levinas and Emil Fackenheim on the Athens–Jerusalem Conflict

Any argument that meontology can resolve the conflict between Athens and Jerusalem, between reason and revelation, must naturally begin with a survey of how this conflict is currently sedimented in philosophy. For even the two serious approaches to the conflict, both of which use the term "meontology" explicitly, contradict each other. I term the first of these two approaches *critical.* According to this type of thinking, whose representative here is Emmanuel Levinas, the faith that defines "Jerusalem" is not only a valid approach to answering the perennial questions raised by "Athens," it is perhaps the best approach to these questions themselves. Levinas claims that "Athens" necessarily announces a realm beyond the order of being and the rationally necessary laws that constitute it; "Athens" commands faith. Levinas therefore appears as a philosopher in the Kantian spirit. Kant offered a critical inquiry into the nature of reason, showing that the a priori principles of reason limited the "pretensions to transcendent insight" of dogmatism and speculative metaphysics, and concluded that it was "necessary to deny knowledge in order to make room for faith."[1] While it is admittedly possible to overstate the overlap between Kant and Levinas,[2] there is nothing that prohibits the reader from noting a family resemblance

[1] Immanuel Kant, *Critique of Pure Reason,* trans. Norman Kemp Smith (New York: St. Martin's Press, 1929), B xxx.
[2] Levinas announces his deep opposition to Kant in a 1988 interview: "The essential theme of my research is the deformalization of the notion of time, [which] Kant says is the form of all experience." Cf. Levinas, "L'autre, Utopie et Justice," in *Entre nous* (Paris: Bernard Grasset, 1991), 263, translated by Michael B. Smith and Barbara Harshav as "The Other, Utopia, and Justice" in *Entre Nous* (New York: Columbia University Press, 1998), 232. Nevertheless, in an earlier article Levinas describes "the exaltation of theoretical reason in practical reason in Kant" as an example of the "questioning of the Same by the Other." Cf. Levinas, "La philosophie et l'éveil" in *Entre nous,* 105, translated by Michael B. Smith and Barbara Harshav as "Philosophy and Awakening," in *Entre Nous,* 89.

between Levinas and the Kantian methodologies. Both seek to hollow out a space within philosophy for faith through a limitation of philosophy's proper aegis.

The other serious approach to the conflict is *dialectical.* In opposition to the Kantian move that limits philosophical consciousness, it is indebted to a Hegelian account of consciousness as always going beyond its limits, as always transcending itself, coming to self-consciousness through recognizing itself in other particularities.[3] Yet just as Levinas is only Kantian in a methodological sense, so this approach is only Hegelian in a methodological sense. Here represented by the German-Canadian philosopher Emil Fackenheim, the dialectical approach to the Athens–Jerusalem conflict does not admit of an easy peace. Nevertheless, in taking each pole to the maximum of its strength, in the assumption that Jerusalem can come to a richer self-consciousness by passing through Athens (and vice versa), philosophy and politics can use the polemic between Athens and Jerusalem to fuel an uneasy peace: a fulfilling and deep account of religious existence that speaks to the hesitance of millennial times. This model of "Jerusalem" is one that attentively passes through Athens, but not in order to be swallowed up therein. Rather, in a building up of Athens, the vulnerabilities of Jerusalem are eliminated, and Jewish practice can truly become valid. Faith is here the height of Hegelian dialectic.

Therefore, we have two opposite approaches. The critical approach – what I will from here on refer to as "critical meontology" – strengthens Jerusalem by limiting the strength of Athens, while the dialectical approach ("dialectical meontology") strengthens Jerusalem by strengthening Athens, its other. This opposition is reflected in how the two approaches understand the nonbeing about which meontology speaks. On the one hand, critical meontology understands nonbeing as beyond the ontological order, as beyond what speculative metaphysics can grasp. On the other hand, dialectical meontology sees nonbeing as the other being whom I understand and through whom I come to understand myself. One would think that one of the two approaches has to be wrong. Meontology cannot both hollow out and build up Athens; it is logically impossible. *Someone* has to be using the term in an unreflective manner. The conundrum arising from this *Auseinandersetzung* threatens both sides' resolutions of the conflict. It hints at the distressing possibility that there is no resolution of the crisis-filled relationship between faith and philosophy – and, by extension, that Judaism can never make itself understood by a secularized culture. In this chapter, I allow the conflict to deepen before moving to a resolution in Chapter 2.

---

[3] G. W. F. Hegel, *Phenomenology of Spirit*, trans. A. V. Miller (Oxford: Oxford University Press, 1977), par. 80.

CRITICAL MEONTOLOGY: EMMANUEL LEVINAS

One would expect that a survey of the Levinasian approach to the Athens–Jerusalem conflict would begin with an account of Levinas's Talmudic commentaries. This is by now the traditional approach of the secondary literature.[4] I do not take this approach here. This does not reflect any decision made in advance for Athens over and above Jerusalem; rather, it reflects problems that can arise when philosophers do text-study. At times, Levinas's inability to treat issues of redaction disturbs his readings. For example, Levinas implies that the central characteristic of Judaism is the Israelites' response of "doing [the commands revealed by God from Mt. Sinai] before hearing [*na'aseh ve-nishma'*]" spoken at Ex. 24:7; this perversion of "Athenian" rational deliberation is a secret of the angels, Levinas claims, in his reading of B. Shabbat 88.[5] But this is not necessarily a good thing. The *very next page* of the tractate explains in great detail why the Torah is meant for humans and not angels; it portrays angels as imps who have a tension-filled relationship with humans, both competing for God's attention. This portrayal is widespread in rabbinic literature.[6] Thus, for persons to take on any angelic secret would itself be a risky departure from Torah as divine revelation to human beings. Furthermore, while the Talmudic readings indeed show a correspondence between Jewish texts and Levinas's phenomenological arguments, this correspondence suggests no more than a *right* to faith. To make the stronger statement that Levinasian phenomenology *requires* faith as a logical decision demands an internal analysis of Levinas's phenomenological arguments.

To my knowledge, the word "meontology" appears on only four occasions in the writings of Emmanuel Levinas. Two of these can be found in the 1981 interview with Richard Kearney that has appeared in a variety of collections.[7] Here, the word is used to describe both ethical action ("ethics is not derived

---

4 Cf. Annette Aronowicz, "Translator's Introduction," in Emmanuel Levinas, *Nine Talmudic Readings*, ed. and trans. Annette Aronowicz (Bloomington: Indiana University Press, 1990), ix–xxxix; Jill Robbins, *Prodigal Son/Elder Brother* (Chicago: University of Chicago Press, 1991), 122–28; Susan Handelman, *Fragments of Redemption* (Bloomington: Indiana University Press, 1991), 263–336; Robert Gibbs, *Correlations in Rosenzweig and Levinas* (Princeton, N.J.: Princeton University Press, 1992), 155–75.

5 Levinas, "La tentation de tentation," in *Quatre lectures talmudiques* (Paris: Minuit, 1968), 98, translated by Annette Aronowicz as "The Temptation of Temptation," in *Nine Talmudic Readings*, 45.

6 Cf. Peter Schäfer, *Rivalität zwischen Engeln und Menschen* (New York: de Gruyter, 1975).

7 Levinas and Richard Kearney, "Dialogue with Emmanuel Lévinas," in *Dialogues with Contemporary Continental Thinkers*, ed. Richard Kearney (Manchester: Manchester University Press, 1984), 47–70; reprinted without Kearney's introduction and bibliography in *Face to Face with Levinas*, ed. Richard Cohen (Albany: State University of New York Press, 1986), 13–33, and once again with Kearney's introduction and bibliography but now under its original subtitle "Ethics of the Infinite," in *States of Mind*, ed. Richard Kearney (Manchester: Manchester University Press, 1995), 177–99.

from an ontology of nature; it is its opposite, a meontology which affirms a meaning beyond Being, a primary mode of non-Being [*mē-on*]") and an anti-idealist notion of subjectivity ("traditional ontological versions of subjectivity have nothing to do with the meontological version of subjectivity that I put forward in *Autrement qu'être*").[8] The other two occurrences date from 1968. One appears in the essay "A Man-God?":

Through this solicitation of the beggar, and of the homeless without a place to lay his head – at the mercy of the bidding of the one who welcomes – humility disturbs absolutely; it is not of the world. Humility and poverty are a bearing *within being* – an ontological (or meontological) mode – and not a social condition.[9]

Levinas's words here give the appearance of contradicting the sense of meontology given in the Kearney interview. There, meontology is associated with what lies beyond being; here, it is associated with the realm of being itself. This hints at a belonging-together between the realm of privation (poverty and humility as the privation of the self, and thus as modes of *to mē on* for Levinas) and the realm of the transcendent that will be more fully articulated in Chapter 4. The fourth and most complete occurrence of "meontology" amplifies the Kearney interview and is found in the 1968 essay "Substitution":

It is in a *responsibility that is justified by no prior commitment*, in the responsibility for another – in an ethical situation – that the meontological and metalogical structure of this anarchy takes form, undoing the logos in which the apology by which consciousness always regains its self-control, and commands, is inserted. This passion is absolute in that it takes hold without any a priori.[10]

It is not immediately apparent that from four isolated quotes from a highly prolific writer, one can immediately conclude that "meontology" is a blanket term for Levinasian thinking. Indeed, when "Substitution" was republished in *Otherwise than Being* in 1974, Levinas changed "meontological" to "meta-ontological" (AE 129/102). I assume that the change is relatively unimportant and merely clarifies the sense of the term for the reader. Certainly, "meta-ontological" in 1974 means the same as "meontological" in the 1981 interview; if the distinction between the two were substantive, I assume that Levinas would have used "meta-ontological" in conversation with Kearney. In addition, because Levinas does not begin to use the word "meontology"

---

[8] Quotations are from this interview as it appears in Kearney, *Dialogues* (1984), 61 and 63; *Face to Face* (1986), 25 and 27; *States of Mind* (1995), 190 and 192.

[9] Levinas, "Un Homme-Dieu?" in *Entre Nous*, translated by Michael B. Smith and Barbara Harshav as "A Man-God?" in *Entre Nous*, 55.

[10] Levinas, "Substitution," *Revue philosophique de Louvain* 66 (1968), 489, translated by Peter Atterton, Simon Critchley, and Graham Noctor in Levinas, *Basic Philosophical Writings*, ed. Adriaan T. Peperzak, Simon Critchley, and Robert Bernasconi (Bloomington: Indiana University Press, 1996), 82.

until 1968, one might conclude that it speaks only to various structures analyzed in the later writings typified by *Otherwise than Being*, writings that may come after a Heidegger-like turn in Levinas's oeuvre. However, Levinas himself has denied that there is any such shift,[11] and *Otherwise than Being* makes several references to Levinas's phenomenological writings of the 1940s.

To make a claim for the importance of meontology to Levinasian thinking, it is important to make links between the characteristics of meontology given in the quotations just noted and broader Levinasian themes. In the first quotation cited from the Kearney interview, Levinas appears to define meontology as any attestation to a beyond-being, and this is certainly in line with the elucidation of a philosophy of the infinite in the early writings. But the ground of the philosophy of the infinite, in my view, appears in the anti-idealist notion of the self, described as "meontological" in the second quotation from the Kearney interview. This view of selfhood bears much in common with the analysis of the self in writings as early as *Existence and Existents*, originally published in 1947. It is to the meontological elements in this early work – the refusal of static identity, the refusal to say what the telos of human existence is – that I now turn, not only because they help to unpack the comments Levinas made to Kearney but also because *Existence and Existents* is an exemplary case of how Levinas limits Athens to make room for Jerusalem.

In short, the argument of *Existence and Existents*, rooted in a phenomenology of forced labor, is as follows:

A. Because forced labor discloses a fatigue that is my fatigue of existence itself, selfhood is essentially dipolar, composed of a Heideggerean I that transcends itself in its projects, and a prior self that does not transcend but "ex-cends," burdens and lags behind the I in a wearied sluggishness.

B. This lagging-behind leads to a conception of the relationship between the self and the world as constituted by the desire to bridge the distance between two apparently opposite poles, not by any immediate "givenness."

C. Because sluggishness (or "lassitude") is an essential aspect of existence and can never be eliminated from selfhood, effort must always appear in fits and stops.

D. Effort can appear in this manner if and only if time is punctiform, a series of separate points that do not flow into each other.

E. The ephemerality of the punctiform instant precludes sating the self's desire to extirpate fatigue. Only the absolute otherness of messianic salvation can fulfill this hope.

---

[11] In a 1982 interview with Edith Wyschogrod, "he remarked with *un clin d'œil* (a wink), '*Je ne suis pas Heidegger.*'" Edith Wyschogrod, *Emmanuel Levinas: The Problem of Ethical Metaphysics*, 2nd ed. (New York: Fordham University Press, 2000), ix.

F. Because desire is an essential aspect of selfhood, the object of this desire must be really possible in the Kantian sense, and messianic hope (including the religious practice in which this hope is exercised) is therefore authorized.

This analysis is, to a certain degree, in harmony with that of Heidegger. In "Martin Heidegger and Ontology," originally published in 1932, Levinas admirably summarizes the first book of Heidegger's *Being and Time*:

Being, for *Dasein*, is the understanding of being. To understand being is to exist in such a manner that "existence itself is at stake." "Existence itself is at stake" is "Being-in-the-world." "Being in the world is to transcend oneself." The whole paradox of this structure, in which existence in view of itself presents itself as essentially ecstatic, is the very paradox of existence and time.[12]

Approximately a decade later, when writing *Existence and Existents*, Levinas still agrees with the first three sentences of the preceding passage. The essence of human *Dasein* is still existence in a world that is disclosed to it in a certain manner. However, whereas Heidegger understands "Being-in-the-world" as a certain way of understanding one's possibilities, one's ability to "do this or that,"[13] Levinas's phenomenological explorations point to ways in which we can understand being through modes of existence that are not precisely ones in which we do any "this or that," in which we come to understand the limitations of one's possibilities in a more nuanced manner than the existential limit of absolute nonbeing qua death. Levinas moves from Heidegger's freely appropriated death to his own concept of an enforced dying. The different picture of being that comes from these ontic clues reveals a fundamental disagreement with Heidegger on the issues of temporality and the ecstatic essence of existence.

For Levinas, the phenomenological elements of enforced labor – indolence, fatigue, and insomnia – reveal that time is not "a continual birth, understood as a distinct operation by which an existent makes itself master over its existence," such as that in which *Dasein* can resolutely be ready for future moments of anxiety (EE 31/23).[14] Rather, time is given as discontinuous, unflowing, and always punctiform,[15] a series of stop-and-go lurches that the self can make continuous only through the struggle of effort. But insofar as this is a struggle, there is also revealed an ability to give up, to

---

[12] Levinas, "Martin Heidegger et l'ontologie," in *En découvrant l'existence avec Husserl et Heidegger*, 3rd ed. (Paris: Vrin, 1994), 66. Translated by the Committee of Public Safety as "Martin Heidegger and Ontology," *diacritics* 26:1 (1996), 22.

[13] Ibid.

[14] Cf. Martin Heidegger, *Being and Time*, trans. John McQuarrie and Edward Robinson (San Francisco: Harper & Row, 1962), §59.

[15] For an analysis of the distinction between punctiform and stretched time, see Edith Wyschogrod, *An Ethics of Remembering: History, Heterology, and the Nameless Others* (Chicago: University of Chicago Press, 1998), ch. 5.

withdraw from the world and let dying take over. The two possibilities for selfhood show that the self is double: the ability to withdraw shows that the self can be absorbed by the world, objectified by it, whereas the self who succeeds in effort remains separate from the world of mere objects. In struggle, these two possibilities coalesce into one, and this structure remains constant throughout Levinas's writings: the doubleness of the "*on s'est*" (EE 38/28), in which the use of the middle voice communicates selfhood as being both the subject of the world and an object in it, reappears as the separated "psychism" (TI 23/54) that relates to the exterior (TI 195/220), and the hostage who wills his or her own ethical responsibility to the captor (AE 163/127).

To unpack this further: the doubleness of the self is part and parcel of the phenomenology of forced labor. The possibility of indolence – the perpetual delay of action that ordinarily goes by the name of "laziness" – shows that action does not progress straightforwardly from the body. Rather, the action must jump across some sort of synaptic gap of effort before it can be exercised. The will to act does not always hit its target; rather, in indolence and fatigue the self acts as an anchoring weight that inhibits and drags down action. Thus, the I is not simply one that understands itself in its projects; the I also possesses itself as a companion, dancing partner, or shadow (EE 38/28). This desire often successfully burdens the I into existing as nothing more than a pure inwardness, a selfhood that is not for anything, not directed toward the world at all, but is purely ateleological matter. Thus, even in the desire to delay the movements of its essential existence, the possibility of falling back into bare selfhood reveals that the "relationship" with existence is unavoidable. I indeed exist as being-in-the-world, but I *also* exist as the accusative object of my effort to act (AE 107/85). In successful action, the gap between the subject-I and the object-self can be bridged, hiding the double dimension of existence. Yet in the hesitation to act, the momentary impossibility of action shows that selfhood is essentially a duality between an outward willing I of Heideggerean transcendence and an inward burdensome self who is "excendent" (EE 9/15), who lies to the side of the general frame of existence. As "a being fatigued by the future" (EE 39/29), by the thought of any further moments in the world, the self that struggles with great effort to exist does not anticipate the future from a sea of pacific inner strength, but fitfully oscillates between transcendent and excendent movements, "dashes forward out of fatigue and falls back upon it" (EE 44/31). The notion of subjectivity here is complex without being dialectical: successful action does not incorporate the object-self in a way that would end the possibility of fatigue at any future time. The subject is simply "disjointed [*désarticulé*]" (EE 50/35), schizoid, tied around itself in a knot (AE 32/25).

Levinasian phenomenology is oriented toward privative experiences; this is what makes it meontological. In *Existence and Existents*, the privative phenomenon that is fatigue reveals that the ontological study of the self is never a study of any single being (*to on*), but of something that does not even have the strength to be, and is thus perhaps best described as a nonbeing (*to mē on*). Thus, if effort in fatigue discloses a movement in which a shadow self catches up to the autonomous self-transcending ego that has lurched ahead, then it must be the case that all action depends upon a similar duality between transcendence and excendence, of a similar movement in which the prior existent catches up to existence.

There is a fundamental lag time to existing. Classical phenomenology would state that "objects are destined for me; they are for me" (EE 73/47), immediately given to my consciousness. However, the disclosure of lag time forces us to rearticulate the "for me" as a desire for the object that I do not yet possess. (There can be no phenomenology of desire, such as that which inaugurates Levinas's *Totality and Infinity*, without the concept of the dual present, lagging behind itself, that grounds desire. *Existence and Existents* demonstrates that, whether we know it or not, all of our desires are metaphysical because we are not unified selves.) This desire cannot be thought unless one asserts that existence is teleological and posits "a time ahead of me."

Yet this is no ordinary teleology; it is radically unachievable by any human project and thereby crosses the line into eschatology. Levinas asserts that "we are separated from objects by a distance, which can indeed be traversed, but remains a distance" (EE 72/46). The argument for the first clause of this is the by-now familiar phenomenon of fatigue; the argument for the last clause is less clear, since one might pose the question of whether indolence or fatigue could possibly be conquered by a kind of resoluteness. This question, however, forgets the punctiform structure of time revealed in the phenomenology of forced labor. Time's essential structure is one of discrete instants, ephemeral moments of successful effort that are interstices between moments of falling back into fatigue. The present is always ephemeral; successful effort is always a heterogeneous and singular instant. Once my aim has come to pass in the world, this success cannot perdure; time passes, and the world moves on without me. The desire of the indolent I for a pure beginning can never be sated; all hope is thus necessarily hope for "the Messiah, or salvation" (EE 156/91). The phenomenological examination of fatigued and indolent *Dasein* is shown to rationally allow messianic hope. Being announces itself as merely doxic, subordinate to that which is beyond being (*epekeina tēs ousias*). Knowledge has made room for faith.

But messianic salvation cannot really be possible unless there are already structures of experience in which alterity (like that of the Messiah) can appear in the world. These structures are guaranteed by the punctiformity of time. If the I is to reappear in successive instants, then somehow "its death in the empty interval will have been the condition for a new birth" (EE 157/92). In the passage of time, in each lurching forward, the I – always new, always other than before – is resurrected across the gap that exists between instants.[16] The passage of time is thus a miraculous response to the salvific hope of the self. Each present instant is exigent – not merely insofar as it issues an exacting demand for a subsequent instant but also insofar as the present is literally exigent (from the Latin *ex-agere*), since the object-self is driven out of itself (in ex-cendance). It is exigency that constitutes subjectivity, an exigency of some otherness to come and guarantee future instants by "unravelling the knot" (EE 159/93) of the transcendent and excendent dimensions of existence. In the passage of time, this otherness appears insofar as the resurrected I "re-commences as other" (EE 159/93), insofar as this instant has no relation whatsoever to the previous one.

But the ego cannot save itself by itself. Rather, any alleged act of self-redemption is always only a self-nearing to those structures in which alterity comes to the subject. Alterity can arrive only insofar as the other person remains distant – for alterity to arrive completely, to become present-at-hand, would cancel its otherness (EE 163/95): the "absence of the other is precisely her presence qua other."[17] It must relate to the future in such a manner that is true to the futural essence of fatigue, in which the future can never be recuperated by the present due to the eternal possibility of fatigue and lassitude. This openness to the eternality of the future (as opposed to a static eternity that might arrive at some futural point) is *messianic anticipation.* This is not only the case according to the language of *Existence and Existents; Totality and Infinity* explicitly regards its project as a securing of the real possibility of "messianic triumph" (TI 261/285), an exchange of the wars of history for "the eschatology of messianic peace" (TI x/22),[18] while *Otherwise than Being* posits a prophetic "mission towards one another [*vers Autrui*] in the glory of the Infinite" (AE 194/152).

---

[16] Thus, contra a recent essay by John Milbank ("The Ethics of Self-Sacrifice," *First Things* 91 [March 1999], 33–38), the phenomenological evidence for resurrection does not need to point to a claim of a singular historical resurrection in 33 c.e. Rather, the cycle of death and resurrection symbolized in the New Testament is more primordially woven into the very structure of temporality.

[17] The Lingis translation reads "his" here; of course, the French possessive pronoun does not resolve this issue. For heterosexual men, the erotic Other will be feminine; for others, this may vary.

[18] In the Kearney interview, Levinas rejects the word "eschatology" on the grounds that it posits a final moment, an end that would reinscribe a teleology and a consciousness into anticipation. And even in EE, it is the notion of "end" that is most closely associated with the Heideggerean climate that Levinas wants to leave. In the 1972 essay "Meaning and Sense," however, Levinas implies a differentiation between an eschatology *tout court* and an "eschatology without hope for oneself," which seems to be near to the notion of the eschatology that uproots the self from the universality of the historical order. Cf. Levinas, "La signification et le sens," in *Humanisme de l'autre homme* (Montpellier: Fata Morgana, 1972), 45, translated by Alphonso Lingis, Simon Critchley, and Adrian Peperzak as "Meaning and Sense," in Levinas, *Basic Philosophical Writings*, 50.

Levinas presents two possible paths of becoming endowed with or affected by alterity, one of private eros between a lover and the beloved, and the other the maintenance of asymmetrical I–You relationships within the social realm. The former inaugurates time in the birth of my children, who continue to exist (as mine) after my death. The latter buys time in delaying the death of the Other through various modes of sacrifice. The relationship with alterity is in general erotic, since the enduring of separation in a relationship with another leads to a Platonic mania, a heightening of desire. The touch of sensibility – associated with the caress in *Totality and Infinity* (TI 235/257) – escapes representation. Nothing is given except *this* skin, *this* face. It cannot be turned into a universal by the operations of consciousness. The contact made in the touch of one person cannot be converted into the touch of an entire audience; when politicians or rock stars shake a row of hands, there is no caress, and there is no relationship that traverses the skin.

In both cases, Levinasian meontology is an analysis of the privation of stable subjectivity. The insufficiency of the self leads to a need to tarry with the Other in the manic yet fruitless search for the stability that comes with the sense that one is not at the mercy of the world. Trapped within my own interiority, I have no basis for the conclusion that other individuals share my bifurcation. Beginning from my radical aloneness discovered in the privacy of labor or eros, the others whom I encounter in the social realm appear to me only as unified selves, and thus as completely different from myself: the Other of the social realm "is what I am not" (EE 162/95) and hence transcends me in a way that I am unable to transcend myself. As such, whether in the guise of the destitute or the powerful, as Levinas makes clear here, the Other is able to command me. As transcendent, this alterity cannot be murdered even if this murder is my greatest desire: the force of the other's command is of a higher order than is my desire to kill.

Yet I have good reason to obey this command; in delaying the death of the Other, I buy time, I trade futures of Time Incorporated, I trade myself for the future of time incorporated in the Other's flesh: "The mortal will can escape violence by driving violence and murder from the world, that is, by profiting from time to delay always further the hours of expiration [*les échéances*]" (TI 219/242). Temporal profit, irreducible to an economic model, is the motive for my breaking with the feeling of lassitude. This is not a profit that I can capitalize on, however; rather, the break with real lassitude must be performed by a move to a correlate lassitude, in which I still feel the exterior binding upon me. The correlate lassitude is an ethical lassitude; the I is not bound over to the self of the *on s'est*, but is bound over to the Other. Once the Other has been located as the arena in which I buy future instants and once I use my freedom to sacrifice freedom in responsibility for the Other (the postponement of her death) in a "positing of the self as a deposing of the ego" (AE 75/58), my being hostage to myself in real lassitude expresses itself on the ethical stratum as my being hostage to the

Other. As a hostage bound to myself, out of joint or "dephased by" myself (AE 147/115), I am consumed by guilt, remorse, and "gnaw away" at those vestiges of identity that still remain in the way of life that has called to me. It is not that I find myself free and then abjure freedom; rather, autonomy and heteronomy are simultaneous strata within Levinas's phenomenology of selfhood that appear together as "a torsion and a restlessness" within the self, the recurrence of "identity in breaking up the limits of identity" (AE 136/107).

This admittedly brief account of Levinas's work is sufficient for noting that the meontological announcement of that which lies beyond being correlates with the formulation of a meontological subjectivity grounded in a phenomenology of privative modes of existence. However, it is prudent to make some observations on an ambiguity in Levinas's notion of nonbeing. On one hand, Levinas argues in the Kearney interview that the ethical announcement of a beyond being is also the announcement of a primary mode of nonbeing. This announcement is purportedly based in the arguments of *Otherwise than Being*, and one can cite here a passage in which Levinas's analysis of substitution leads to the conclusion that "being is transcended" (AE 149/117). On the other hand, one also notes on the opening page of the first chapter of this same text that the beyond-being would seem to transcend *both* being *and* nonbeing: "being and not-being [*ne-pas-être*] illuminate one another, and unfold a speculative dialectic which is a determination of being . . . Being's essence dominates not-being itself" (AE 3/3). What is beyond essence is here not a primary mode of nonbeing but "an excluded middle between being and non-being" (AE 37/29).[19] Even if one interprets the "not-being" of AE 3 as not-being only in the ordinary sense, as death (certainly the primary meaning suggested by the context of the passage), the language of "excluded middle" at AE 37 is still confusing. Here it seems that even the word "meontology" can be recuperated in a dialectical move. How can there be a meontology between being and nonbeing? How did *two* notions of nonbeing (one the subject of Levinasian meontology, the other that which Levinasian meontology transcends) suddenly come on the scene? Where was nonbeing's shadow hiding? One notes here the traces of an ambiguity that is seen in the early writings as well, namely the ambiguity between negation in its dialectic and absolute senses. When Levinas writes that "Transcendence Is Not Negativity" (TI 11/40) or that "it is not negativity, still wholly correlate with being, that will have sufficed to signify the *other than being*" (AE 10/9), the type of negation Levinas is invoking is thoroughly dialectical, always posterior to a unitary self. Nonbeing understood in this sense is not-I and depends upon a previous consciousness that

---

[19] There is similar language in AE 17/14, 58/45 (where Levinas speaks of *non–être*), and 229/181.

knows itself through a sort of Fichtean intellectual intuition: "If any ∼A is to be posited, an A must be posited."[20] This dialectical sort of negation is predicated upon a theory of consciousness that Levinas associates with the egology that reduces the singular to the general. But more importantly, the Fichtean account of selfhood, in which the self is the ground of statements about the world, can no longer be valid after the phenomenology of labor, which discloses a world in which it is impossible for the self to exist and have projects. For Levinas, there can be no such thing as a dialectical meontology. The type of nonbeing that Levinasian meontology invokes refers not to another being, but to an inability to be, the privation of being. This privation in turn discloses transcendence, a realm "other than being" that is a nonbeing beyond (and hence more fundamental than) the dialectical notion of "not-being" mentioned in the opening pages of *Otherwise than Being.*

Levinas's turn to faith as messianic anticipation is not the sign of an irrationalist thinker. His critical meontology is rooted in the philosophical techniques that have sustained the ontologies of previous thinkers. Yet in the move to certain pieces of phenomenological evidence (fatigue, labor, etc.), ontology shows itself to be inadequate, in need of a messianic faith as its supplement.

DIALECTICAL MEONTOLOGY: EMIL FACKENHEIM

Emil Fackenheim's solution to the Athens–Jerusalem problem is most succinctly expressed in a reply to a group of essays written in his honor. During a moment in history (the Persian Gulf conflict) when Jewish existence appeared to him to be threatened, Fackenheim writes:

A rabbinic legend has Plato go to school with Moses: what made the rabbis invent it? A deep question, but less relevant in the present Jerusalem – post-Holocaust, non-metaphorical, physical, Jewish – than its opposite. The rabbis tell the tale of a Torah prior to Creation, preworldly and known to God but – needless to add – revealed also to Moses: what made the rabbis let Moses go to school with Plato?

A Jew of today, I open the Book of Isaiah for an answer. Athens is universal. In Isaiah's second chapter – all nations flowing unto Mount Zion, so as to unlearn war – Jewish Jerusalem reaches a universalism of its own. The Jewish urge to get to that chapter is great, greater today, perhaps, at this time of my writing than ever before: yet just now a Jew cannot, it seems, get beyond Isaiah's first chapter, with Jerusalem a "besieged city" (Isa. 1:8), and its people – compared to the multitude laying the siege – "a small remnant" (Isa. 1:9). Perhaps such is a time when a Jew, holding fast to a Torah vulnerable below – never letting go of that "below" – needs support from

---

[20] J. G. Fichte, *Science of Knowledge*, trans. Peter Heath and John Lachs (Cambridge: Cambridge University Press, 1982), 105.

a preworldly Torah, unassailable above. Perhaps such is a time for Moses to go to school with Plato.[21]

We see here an example of Fackenheim's philosophical appropriation of midrash as a literary medium capable of speaking to a post-Holocaust existence, which – like midrash – is simultaneously "fragmentary and whole."[22] It is fragmented due to the cataclysm of the Holocaust, but whole because to leave the fragments as fragments would be to violate the so-called 614th commandment against granting Hitler a posthumous victory. But we also see Fackenheim's Hegelianism: the opposition between Judaism ("Torah below") and Athens ("Torah above") is simultaneously an identity – both are Torah, after all – and this strongly echoes the theme of the developmental growth of spirit in Hegel. The last sentence of the preceding quotation can be read as suggesting "perhaps it is time that Judaism dialectically generate itself anew. Indeed, history shows that it is already occurring in one fashion, as Netanyahu goes on CNN wearing a gas mask." Fackenheim always remains rooted in Hegel. Even when (as in his book of constructive post-Holocaust thought, *To Mend the World*) he shows how history has revealed the failure of Hegelian dialectic, Fackenheim nevertheless maintains that this failure is part of the dialectic of history, which has dialectical results.[23] Hegel's conclusions may be wrong; Hegelian method is not.[24] The entire corpus of Fackenheim's writings attempts to set out both what a life in the Hegelian middle – between comprehensive conceptuality and embodied experience – might be and how Hegelian method might guarantee that such a life is genuinely possible. To write of Moses going to school with Plato, of Jerusalem using Athens as a bulwark against hostile forces, is to write of how to be a "Hegelian-after-Hegel."[25]

This project is most notably undertaken in *To Mend the World*, but its contours appear in Fackenheim's earlier writings as well. Fackenheim first makes an attempt to systematize his post-Hegelian philosophy in *Metaphysics and Historicity* (written in 1961); importantly for the purposes of this chapter, he briefly shows that a theory of alterity is part and parcel of this project. This essay is an extremely complicated argument as to whether and how it is possible to agree on eternal truths in an age in which those very truths are understood to be historically constituted. The two positions – metaphysics

[21] Emil Fackenheim, "A Reply to My Critics: A Testament of Thought," in *Fackenheim: German Philosophy and Jewish Thought*, ed. Louis Greenspan and Graeme Nicholson (Toronto: University of Toronto Press, 1992), 297.

[22] This is Fackenheim's description of midrash in *God's Presence in History* (New York: Harper & Row, 1970), 20.

[23] Fackenheim, *To Mend the World* (New York: Schocken, 1982), 120.

[24] Zachary Braiterman, in his (*God*) *After Auschwitz* (Princeton, N.J.: Princeton University Press, 1998), 144ff., shows how Hegelian method is retained in *To Mend the World* in Fackenheim's reduction of Spinoza and Rosenzweig to "Hegelian signifiers."

[25] Fackenheim, "Reply," 278.

and historicity, respectively – are fundamentally opposed. The timeless truth of the metaphysician is shown by later thinkers to be simply the result of a certain historical perspective upon the world. Truth is reduced to a world-view, and philosophy is reduced to the history of ideas, none of which can be shown to be truer than others (MH 137). Fackenheim is made nervous by this historicist position (MH 123); it entails the risk of justifying totalitarian ideologies that cannot be assured of the rightness of their worldview without violently stamping it upon the rest of the world.[26] Historicism is immune to ethical critique. However, Fackenheim by no means assumes that historicism *necessarily* collapses into relativism. He wants to respect the truth of humanity's historical situatedness. But how can one talk about historicity without falling into the ethical abyss of historicism? Fackenheim's essay is an answer to this question, and he turns explicitly to meontology as a way of articulating this response. As I shall claim, this meontology also undergirds the discussion of history in *To Mend the World*.

There are two assumptions of historicity with which Fackenheim agrees: human freedom introduces a distinction between the order of history in which humankind acts and the order of nature in which humankind is acted upon, and the essence and laws of beings are always in flux. The first assumption expresses the view that, by virtue of natural (biological, chemical, psychological) processes, I am able to project myself into the world and break out of my shell, be part of the public realm called "history." The second assumption rests on the fact that my actions change over time; this is the true sign of freedom and demonstrates that the agents of history are not merely automata. Fackenheim concludes from these principles that "human being, then, is a self-making or self-constituting process" (MH 128).

Being is thus the result, and not the condition, of action. Process is primary; there is no independent being (no *to on*) in selfhood outside of the historical sphere. Fackenheim grounds this account of human self-making in an account of the divine, understood not as being (*to on*), but as self-making, as process. Fackenheim describes this as "meontological metaphysics" (MH 129). But meontology here means something different than it does for Levinas. For Levinas, as we saw earlier, meontology points to a place beyond being that is truly the ultimate, yet is also *totaliter aliter* (wholly other) than human being and hence cannot be spoken. For Fackenheim, the relation between human being and the ultimate is more dialectical; God is the speculative expression of the process of self-making. The ultimate can

---

[26] Michael Morgan makes this point in "Philosophy, History, and the Jewish Thinker," both in *Fackenheim: German Philosophy and Jewish Thought*, 161n. 25, and *Dilemmas in Modern Jewish Thought* (Bloomington: Indiana University Press, 1992), 174n. 26. It is here in MH that Fackenheim obliquely points to the anxieties of post-Holocaust Jewish life. Also see his "Holocaust and *Weltanschauung*: Philosophical Reflections on Why They Did It," in Fackenhein's *The God Within: Kant, Schelling and Historicity*, ed. John Burbidge (Toronto: University of Toronto Press, 1996), 172–85.

easily be spoken ("self-making"), and although it might not make any sense from the ontological point of view in which being is the basis of action, "meontological logic" generates a logic of its own (MH 130) and has roots in the history of philosophy (for example, John Scot Eriugena, Jacob Boehme, Friedrich Schelling, and Nicolas Berdyaev).

The God of meontological metaphysics would have to be described as a process which (i) because it is pure *making*, proceeds from the indifference of sheer possibility of nothingness (*mē on*) into the differentiation of actuality – *ex nihilo in aliquid*; (ii) because it is *self*-making, established its own identity throughout this process by returning upon itself; or, otherwise put, proceeds into otherness, yet cancels this otherness and in so doing establishes itself; (iii) because it is *absolute* self-making, actualizes *ex nihilo* the totality of possibilities. (MH 129)

The circularity apparent in the logic of meontological process is necessary precisely because self-making is predicated upon a forward movement that also returns upon itself, which establishes itself by integrating its own past history into its projection of future possibilities.[27]

Fackenheim stays with the theme of meontology for only four paragraphs; he departs from it by adding that "We cannot here further describe this kind of logic" (MH 130). This sentence is attached to the following footnote: "It may be observed in passing, however, that the greatest attempt to explicate this kind of logic is beyond all doubt Hegel's work by that name" (MH 130). This makes a certain kind of sense: after all, if the meontological tradition indeed practices the type of dialectic described earlier, in which an individual strives to recognize him- or herself within the historical sphere, it will doubtlessly be Hegelian. Nevertheless, at this point, the reader schooled in French postphenomenological thinking may very well fall into shock, or at least break a pencil in a rush of mad scribbling. The possibility that Hegel might be associated with meontology is anathema to Levinasian thinking. The logic of totality and its inherent violence to which Levinas proposes his meontological response was, in Levinas's view, begun by Hegel. Levinas's opposition to Hegel is already apparent in the preface to *Totality and Infinity*, which posits an eschatology that would be "beyond history" (TI xi/22), and the negative references to Hegel never cease. More often than not, they are mere sound bites. Hegel's universal is one of the "insidious forms of the impersonal" (TI 250/272); the Hegelian identification of will and reason "is opposed by the entire pathos-filled [*pathétique*] experience of humanity" (TI 193/217). But these remarks represent a thoroughgoing opposition. The singularity of human existence that Levinas describes throughout his work is fundamentally opposed to the very language of "consciousness" that reduces persons to voiceless objects. But in the modern era, philosophy

---

[27] Fackenheim is not completely averse to this Heideggerean language. Cf. MH 131–32, 227–28n.45; and Fackenheim, "The Historicity and Transcendence of Philosophical Truth," in *The God Within*, 148–63.

has in Levinas's eyes been nothing but philosophy of consciousness "which since Hegel has been trying to overcome the duality of being and thought, by identifying, under different figures, substance and subject" (AE 131/103). When Levinas describes his work as a meontology, this is an anti-Hegelian rallying cry. When Fackenheim does it, it is a Hegelian rallying cry.

Yet Fackenheim is still able to derive a theory of alterity from his version of meontology. When the meontological concept of a self-making God is used to analyze the nature of human historical self-making, it becomes clear that although divine self-making is always and everywhere absolute, human self-making is always "fragmented by the loss of a past which it cannot recapture, and by the refractoriness of a future which refuses to be subdued into presentness. It is, in short, a returning-upon-itself within the limits of a *situation*" (MH 132). In a situation, both human and historical, there are limits placed upon humans by nature or by sociopolitical contexts. In this manner, otherness enters the historical analysis, since the relation between the self and its situation is dialectical. The self projects its possibilities on the basis of its situation and incorporates the situation into its self-making process, but the situation is also the absolutely distinct ground of the self-making process. The element of otherness in the situation is maintained, but because human existence cannot wholly transcend its situation, the dialectic is insurmountable. It is the struggle of reason itself.

While metaphysics cannot trump the fact of historical situatedness, it is also the case that historicism cannot trump metaphysics and its eternal truths, since on historicism's terms it – like the metaphysics it counters – is itself is part of the self-making process. The distinction between historicism and history collapses (MH 136). What is needed, Fackenheim claims, is a historical-metaphysical doctrine that expresses this struggle by way of a theory of self-making in which historicity can make room for "transhistorical possibilities of self-making . . . [in which] the transhistorical integrate[s] itself with the historical, and thus itself become[s] infected with historicity" (MH 139, 137), all the while dialectically maintaining its nature as transhistorical. In "The Historicity and Transcendence of Philosophical Truth," Fackenheim describes this elegantly:

The philosopher may be unable to escape from the cave of history. He does find, however, that a light from beyond the cave shines into the cave itself, and that it lights up both the lives of men who must live in history and the philosophic thought which seeks to understand it.[28]

For such an understanding to take place, Fackenheim argues that the Hegelian speculative language about the struggle of self-making must pass over into an existentialist language, and that the concept of historical situation must be expanded into that of the human situation. This latter concept

---

[28] Fackenheim, "Historicity and Transcendence," 163.

lets us speculate that the otherness of the natural and historical situations never allows for a wholly autonomous self-making process. The finitude of the situation does not simply show the logical possibility of my self-making (as the natural situation does) or even give me determinate concrete options for this self-making. It reveals the human condition universally as one in which these limits and opportunities exist. These are no longer my objective limits and opportunities, but are part and parcel of a recognition "that all history is a conjunction of compulsion and freedom, and that to be subject to one and to be challenged to realize the other is universally part of the human condition" (MH 142).

Fackenheim openly invokes Kierkegaard and Heidegger here (MH 226–31nn. 43–48), but his distillation of these existentialist positions in this context is not his final position on the matter. While existentialist interpretations of both Heidegger and Kierkegaard seek to present themselves as anti-Hegelian and as having left speculative thought behind, their claim to do so is specious. After all, this claim is itself grounded in speculation (MH 146). Thus Fackenheim wants to dialectically integrate Hegel and existentialism into a position that maintains the irreducibility of both poles and allows for the human recognition of metaphysical truths about self-making without having these metaphysical truths succumb to the very doctrine of self-making. This integration or mediation, however, is written in the language neither of Hegel nor of Kierkegaard. Fackenheim's final position (MH 144) turns out to be something that appears remarkably Levinasian, given the gulf between Fackenheim and Levinas on the issue of the proper role of idealism in thinking.

For what situates man humanly is not produced by man but on the contrary is the condition of all human producing. And in rising to metaphysics man recognizes this fact; but in recognizing it he recognizes the otherness of the Other that situates him. This Other is the Other *par excellence*.

In this recognition the Other must, and yet cannot, remain wholly unknown. It must remain unknown, for if human being were to know it it would cease to be situated by It. . . . And yet this Other cannot remain wholly unknown. For to know its otherness is to have passed beyond simple ignorance. We have seen that existential metaphysics originates in the recognition of man's human situation as a dialectical mystery. We now see that this metaphysics culminates in pointing, as to a vastly greater mystery, to the ultimate Other which situates man humanly. And this pointing-to is itself dialectical. It expresses an ignorance which knows the grounds of this ignorance, or a knowledge which knows that it is ignorant, and why. The Other that is pointed to thus remains undefined, and is yet given names. But the names express Mystery. They do not disclose It.

Fackenheim's resolution of the impasse between metaphysics and historicity is thus a dialectical meditation on "the ultimate Other"; the impasse between Hegel and Kierkegaard leads to a point of view that is religious, an awareness of being situated by an agent that transcends all human agency.

Whether or not the ultimate Other is given the name of God is a point on which Fackenheim himself is oblique. Yet there are two reasons why we should read these paragraphs as statements about God. First, in the elliptical epilogue to the essay, Fackenheim invokes a marginal note by Coleridge written in a volume of Schelling. Schelling writes, "I am because I am," and Coleridge responds "I am because God made me." And second, in the footnote accompanying the passage just quoted at length, Fackenheim briefly and tentatively (and, I believe, without argumentative support) extends his conclusion from one in which the otherness of the world expresses God as creator to one that expresses God as revealer. It is true that, late in his career, Fackenheim himself stated that he no longer subscribes to a concept of revelation in his thinking.[29] However, the general thrust of *Metaphysics and Historicity* suggests that the impasse between metaphysics and historicity prevents Fackenheim from remaining wholly in the sphere of thought, divorced from life: "Pointing-to-the-Other, the last achievement of unaided philosophical thought, need not be regarded in existential thought as necessarily the last achievement of man: if the Other is God who reveals Himself" (MH 231n. 50). This would mark a smooth transition from *Metaphysics and Historicity* to Fackenheim's later *The Religious Dimension in Hegel's Thought*, which argues that only religion can be the mediating bridge between life and thought.[30]

Although both Levinas and Fackenheim pass from analyses of human finitude to mysterious evocations of the divine, the distinction between critical and dialectical meontology should not immediately be regretted. There is something definitely odd in Fackenheim from the Levinasian point of view. In spite of the common emphasis on a quasi-religious otherness as the transcendental condition of selfhood, the mystery of otherness in Fackenheim is not anything specifically "phenomenal," such as the face or touch. Rather, it is the dialectic, resulting from reflection upon the nature of history, which is the engine producing alterity. In *Metaphysics and Historicity*, Fackenheim almost completely leaves the situations of concrete history behind. For Fackenheim, it is metaphysics that points to the "Other *par excellence*." For Levinas, what produces alterity as a philosophical category is the transcendental analysis of phenomena, an analysis that occurs without regard for any and all Hegelian "shapes of consciousness" that are culturally constituted.[31] It would indeed be valid to object that there is little space in the constricted lecture format of *Metaphysics and Historicity* to describe how the philosopheme of "the Other who situates me" dialectically passes into life.

[29] Fackenheim, "Reply," 268.
[30] Fackenheim, *The Religious Dimension in Hegel's Thought* (Bloomington: Indiana University Press, 1967), 117ff.
[31] Cf. Michael N. Forster, *Hegel's Idea of a Phenomenology of Spirit* (Chicago: University of Chicago Press, 1998), 119ff.

Indeed, the majority of Fackenheim's writings after 1961, centering on the Holocaust, perform this dialectical turn and demonstrate that Fackenheim actually does accept the 1961 meontological theory of historicity that he had then described as merely a hypothesis. Fackenheim's "Jewish writings" are an outgrowth of the theories developed in his "philosophical writings," thus preventing an easy distinction between the two.[32] Yet in these later writings, the "Other *par excellence*" disappears.

God's Presence in History and *To Mend the World* are predicated upon the claim that there is a new human situation after the Holocaust, since belief in a God who acts either as progress or providence is no longer feasible. Therefore, this new situation offers up new metaphysical truths, even if this runs the risk of becoming "a negative natural theology."[33] Indeed, this claim is the wedge that separates Fackenheim from other contemporary Jewish thinkers. Fackenheim is unable to accept either Michael Wyschogrod's view that a radically contingent history has no recourse to critique a transcendent God, or Richard Rubenstein's argument that the Shoah calls for the rejection of the God of history.[34] This is not simply for personal reasons or even for theological ones, but for Hegelian ones. On the Hegelian assumption that life is dialectically related to thought, that history expresses metaphysical positions, the Shoah must be perceived as making a theological or a philosophical claim. Wyschogrod claims that Fackenheim's first mistake is to view the Shoah "from the human point of view,"[35] but for a Hegelian the human reflection on life that propels philosophical self-understanding is necessarily bound up with this viewpoint. However, to follow the path Rubenstein does in confronting the Holocaust – to make a clean break with the long-lasting historical idea of God's acting in human history – is, as in Wyschogrod, to make a turn to pure and simple thought that, because it does not relate to all events in history, cannot relate at all to the category of history.

If the task of post-Holocaust self-making is important, it is necessary to appropriate the Holocaust in the context of its historical situation: not the context of mechanization and antisemitism that led up to the Holocaust, but the context of past Jewish historical actualities that the Holocaust threatens.

---

[32] Michael Morgan has edited two books of Fackenheim's "Jewish thought": *The Jewish Thought of Emil Fackenheim* (Detroit: Wayne State University Press, 1987), and *Jewish Philosophers and Jewish Philosophy* (Bloomington: Indiana University Press, 1996). These titles give the appearance of a strict opposition between Jewish and non-Jewish thought in Fackenheim's work (even if a passage from MH is excerpted in the 1987 volume). Nevertheless, as John Burbidge implies in his preface to *The God Within* (ix–xiii, esp. xi), Fackenheim's later Jewish thought cannot be divorced from, and is indebted to, Fackenheim's earlier studies of German idealism.

[33] Michael Wyschogrod, "Faith and the Holocaust," *Judaism* 20:3 (1971), 288.

[34] Fackenheim, *God's Presence in History*, 30–31. Cf. Richard Rubenstein, *After Auschwitz*, 2nd ed. (Baltimore: Johns Hopkins University Press, 1992).

[35] M. Wyschogrod, "Faith and the Holocaust," 286.

This can occur only when the past that fragments my present appropriation is itself thematized as fragmentary (MH 132).[36] For history to have a more ontologically positive valence than "fragment" would imply that human self-making can be as absolute and self-enclosed as is divine self-making and would thus ignore the fact that the post-Holocaust situation is situat*ing*, insofar as it determines human projects. If history must be fragmentary according to Fackenheim's logic, it makes sense that he will subsume Jewish history under the rubric of its "midrashic framework," the framework of the very fragmentariness of Jewish history.

The midrashic framework is both light and heavy for Fackenheim. It is light because the tensions between the fragments allow us to reject some of them; Fackenheim thus has no problem rejecting various theodicies formulated in the rabbinic period.[37] Yet it is heavy because Jewish history cannot be reintegrated by Jews of today into a seamless fabric. The dialectical turns that the post-Holocaust situation inaugurates cannot be overcome, but their contradictions multiply and grow as each turn retains the features of the previous one. Thus, in *God's Presence in History*, the collapse of religious theodicies after the Holocaust determines a turn from faith to Jewish secularism. Yet this collapse itself collapses insofar as Jewish secularism is shown, in its affirmation of Jewishness, to be an acceptance of a certain kind of election, a type of being-singled-out. The election of the secular Jew has its origin in an Other *par excellence* that can only be described as the Commanding Voice of Auschwitz, "as truly *other* than man-made ideals – an imperative as truly *given* – as was the Voice of Sinai."[38] This stage of post-Holocaust self-making, in making the turn back to an uneasy faith that unites faith and secularism within it while maintaining the difference between the two, marks the pinnacle of the integration of the fragmentariness of the post-Holocaust human situation into the general fragmented midrashic framework of Judaism. Jewish existence can continue in the post-Holocaust human situation because the thought of Judaism can still possess a dialectical relation to the life of both the victims and the survivors. The past narratives of witnessing God as Other at Sinai are at one with, but simultaneously ruptured by, narratives in which Otherness is witnessed at Auschwitz. The best example of this is Fackenheim's frequent citation of Pelagia Lewinska's "I felt under orders to live" in *To Mend the World*, a citation in which Fackenheim refuses to speculate on who or what issued the command.[39] These narratives are gathered into present imperatives that determine future action ("survive!"). Yet this

---

36 It should be noted that Fackenheim's fragmentation of historical actualities is not limited to Jewish history. It is a constant hermeneutical technique, which extends also to the reading of the incarnation narrative given in *To Mend the World*, 281ff., and to the reduction of Spinoza and Rosenzweig to "Hegelian signifiers."

37 Fackenheim, *God's Presence in History*, 73–79.   38 Ibid., 83.

39 Fackenheim, *To Mend the World*, 25, 217–19, 229, 248, and esp. 302. Also cf. Braiterman, *(God) After Auschwitz*, 148–50.

gathering does not have the absolute character of a Heideggerean *Versamm-lung*, which would gather being as it is itself; here, Fackenheim makes his dialectical-meontological move both outside of being and within it, a move to a rupture in being whose fragments we cannot transcend. Fackenheim stresses that the demands of the Commanding Voice of Auschwitz – the four fragments of witness, survival, hope, and acceptance of the commanding power of the divine presence – cannot be united into any calm maxims of will. Bearing witness to the Holocaust does not exactly breed hope. Yet all must be maintained in the uneasy *Aufhebung* of these commands. Thus, the argument from *Metaphysics and Historicity* that the doctrine of self-making, if accepted, authorizes only limited integrations of the historical into my future plans, appears pari passu in the last two sentences of *God's Presence in History*: "Jews after Auschwitz will never understand the longing, defiance, endurance of the Jews at Auschwitz. But so far as is humanly possible they must make them their own as they carry the whole Jewish past into a future yet unknown."[40] As Fackenheim describes it, implicit within the commands at Auschwitz is the idea of historicity. And as in *Metaphysics and Historicity*, the dialectic of the post-Holocaust human situation leads to an inability to express that which transcends as anything more than a voice. Even the term "voice," situated as it is within the midrashic framework, cannot have any ontological referent that can be gleaned by human understanding. Certainly not God.[41]

In such a manner the transhistorical enters the order of the historical. Thus, when William Dray points out in his own article on *Metaphysics and Historicity* that Fackenheim never answers the question of whether the transhistorical must necessarily become infected with historicity,[42] we can counter by pointing out that *God's Presence in History* is engaged in nothing less than the elucidation of a positive answer to this question. It should be duly noted that this is not Fackenheim's own response to Dray. Fackenheim looks back at *Metaphysics and Historicity* "with a disbelief engendered in retrospect" and chastises his younger self for a romantic attachment to Mozart (!) and for the error of describing the Holocaust only as an example of "ideological

[40] Fackenheim, *God's Presence in History*, 98.

[41] It is true that Levinas cites a long passage from Fackenheim's *God's Presence in History* in the 1982 essay "Useless Suffering." But Levinas is wrong in the way he glosses Fackenheim's argument: "Auschwitz would paradoxically entail a revelation from the very God who nevertheless was silent at Auschwitz." This expression of the paradox, which Levinas then extends to argue for an imperative to "continue to live out Sacred History," saps the dialectical tension between the historical and the metaphysical elements in Fackenheim's work. Levinas's citation of Fackenheim in "Useless Suffering" is thus evidence for the discrepancy between their views, all appearances to the contrary. Cf. Emmanuel Levinas, "La souffrance inutile," in *Entre Nous*, 117, translated by Michael B. Smith and Barbara Harshav as "Useless Suffering," in *Entre Nous*, 99–100.

[42] W. H. Dray, "Historicity, Historicism, and Self-Making," in *Fackenheim: German Philosophy and Jewish Thought*, 125.

fanaticism," and not as the overwhelming of the human situation that it was.[43] While this may be true of MH taken on its own, I believe that, when read as part of Fackenheim's entire corpus, it calls forth a dialectical turn from thought into life that Fackenheim makes in his future work.

To Mend the World renames the dialectic of *God's Presence in History* as the "dialectic of *teshuvah* [repentance]." This move further integrates the post-Holocaust human situation into the fabric of the Jewish tradition. The dialectic finds its fruition in an uneasy maintenance of historical polarities, what Fackenheim here defines as *tikkun*, "mending." Fackenheim appropriates this concept from the medieval system of Jewish mysticism developed by Isaac Luria. However, in its Lurianic context, *tikkun* is a total mending of a total rupture; the two movements are folded into an "at-oneness of God and men" in the exile of the Shekhinah (the divine presence) along with Israel. The rupture that is exile is accompanied by the mending that is God's presence with the Jewish people, a presence that grounds an anticipated redemption. Fackenheim's appropriation of *tikkun* maintains this paradox: after the Holocaust, "the impossible *tikkun* is also necessary."[44] Nevertheless, Fackenhim, in his notion of *tikkun*, claims on dialectical grounds that the *tikkun* can be only fragmentary, "both ever-incomplete and ever-laden with risk."[45] Israel is this fragment, yet it also becomes dialectically folded into a post-Holocaust *tikkun* through its prayer on Yom Kippur (a prayer that for Fackenheim binds together religious and secular Jews). On this day in the calendar year, Israel turns from a questioning of the why of existence into an acknowledgment of its feeling of being-elected, of being-singled-out: "And in this returning – a Messianic moment, a messianic fragment – Israel, Torah, and God are one."[46] The Other *par excellence* crosses the boundaries between these three entities; and their oneness is, in my opinion, the clearest formulation of "the vastly greater mystery" to which Fackenheim refers in *Metaphysics and Historicity* as the implied consequence of articulating meontological metaphysics. The mystery is not God alone, but rather the Hegelian interweaving of subjects and worldly substance in an absolute self-transcending motion. Here, the structure of the mystery – the way in which this interpenetration comes to be – is indeed not disclosed. But the mystery itself can be easily named – *amcha*, literally "your people," the people who survive by affirming themselves as the people of Israel.[47] A mystery

---

43 Fackenheim, "Reply," 293–96.
44 All preceding ideas and quotations in this paragraph are from Fackenheim, *To Mend the World*, 252–54.
45 Ibid., 310.   46 Ibid., 329.
47 As Braiterman shows in his analysis of Fackenheim in (*God*) *After Auschwitz*, 147, the word *amcha* is a key element in the Fackenheimian dialectic. Indeed, Fackenheim at "Reply," 287, uses the word in the context of a brief rejoinder to Michael Wyschogrod: "In elementary – nay, survival – necessities, I have learned over the years, *amcha* is more to be trusted than its professors."

it must be, or else *teshuvah* would be an exhaustive answer to the Holocaust and the Holocaust would no longer be a rupture in history. In a sense, this is the mystery of otherness itself: how does my recognition of something as other, insofar as it passes beyond mere ignorance, retain the otherness of that which I recognize?

While the deconstruction of biblical revelation is common to both *God's Presence in History* and *To Mend the World*, there is a slight shift in ideas between the two works. In the fourth chapter of the latter work, Fackenheim for the first time proves that the command of *teshuvah* is possible within life and can ground post-Holocaust existence without that existence collapsing into madness, even if that madness is also forbidden. In *God's Presence in History*, the testimony of those who did and those who did not survive the Holocaust is invoked only to testify to the complete discontinuity in the human situation that the Holocaust marked. In *To Mend the World*, this testimony – a resistance that passes from thought into life – is shown to be a way of being, "an ontological category." One wonders, then, whether the rupture in Fackenheim's own writing in 1967 – the turn that ends his treatment of German philosophy and Jewish thought as separate arenas – also marks a turn away from the theory of meontology developed in *Metaphysics and Historicity*. The answer to this question must be a negative one. For the description of self-making in 1961 reappears not only in *God's Presence in History*, as already seen, but also in *To Mend the World*. Fackenheim defines *tikkun* as a recovery of past tradition that, in its fragmentariness, determines the riskiness of the Jewish future.[48] *Tikkun* is hence meontological through and through. John Burbidge points this out when he describes *tikkun* as a type of (post-)Hegelian dialectic, a "double representation" in which thought and life are distinct yet related. Burbidge takes the concept of *tikkun* further than Fackenheim is willing; it is meontological insofar as it moves backward and forward along the historical axis by its hearkening back to past narratives and issuing new imperatives for the future.[49]

Because *tikkun*, as Fackenheim describes it, is the only possible mode of action in the post-Holocaust human situation, and because it rests upon a certain understanding of the world that is rooted in German idealism, it is the epitome of Fackenheim's formulation of "Moses going to school with Plato." The Torah's ineluctable bond to the order of history carries with it the risk of being negated by certain historical situations and so needs the "unassailable preworldly Torah" that is "Athens," which for Fackenheim is typified by Hegelian dialectic. But when Hegelian dialectic buttresses the Torah, it makes Torah the product of an Athens–Jerusalem dialectic. Fackenheim's meontological resolution of the Athens–Jerusalem

---

[48] Fackenheim, *To Mend the World*, 310.
[49] John Burbidge, "Reason and Existence in Schelling and Fackenheim," in *Fackenheim: German Philosophy and Jewish Thought*, 90–117, esp. 109–10.

problematic is thoroughly dialectical. For Fackenheim, "Jerusalem" is a combination of "Greek" thought with the traditional Jerusalem in which both seek each other and flee from each other. Jerusalem needs Athens in order to survive the post-Holocaust human situation, but not so much that the essential meontological determination of being-singled-out by the Other *par excellence* is threatened.[50]

The two thinkers discussed in this chapter resolve the Athens–Jerusalem problem through the delineation of a type of thinking they both name "meontology," broadly centered on the theme of nonbeing. Yet the recourse to this term is, in and of itself, philosophically murky, because Levinas and Fackeneim have opposite understandings of the relationship between meontology and ontology. In surface readings of Levinas, there is no relation between the order of being and what lies beyond being. The ontological tradition of philosophy has simply thought incorrectly. But for Fackenheim, meontology is a type of ontology. Insofar as self-making determines being, the question of being can still be answered – for Fackenheim by the State of Israel – even if there are some mysterious elements that remain in this answer. Despite the similar theory of alterity in both Levinas and Fackenheim, and despite the two philosophers' mutual opposition to certain aspects of Heideggerean thought, we find that there can be no mediation between critical and dialectical meontology. Critical meontology views *to mē on* as totally other than being; dialectical meontology views *to mē on* as simply another being or another way of being. Hegel blocks any mediation here. Levinas wants to inoculate the transhistorical against history; the coming-to-pass of the Infinite in the ethical relation cannot be narrated in a traditional history that reduces singular persons to members of classes or tribes. Of what use is this concept if one cannot even answer the question of what meontology is? To speak of "meontology" in Judaism as a resolution of the Athens–Jerusalem problem is to invoke a conundrum; unless this puzzle is solved, it is all too tempting to agree with Tertullian and ghettoize Jerusalem.

One could try to resolve the question by turning to an analysis of Hegel, and determining whether Fackenheim is or is not more correct than Levinas in his view of Hegel as the meontologist *par excellence*. However, this does not guard against the possibility that Hegel himself has misunderstood meontology. In order to resolve the meontological conundrum, it is necessary to go back to the Platonic teaching of *to mē on*, to reawaken the idea in its original guise.

---

[50] Thus, I agree with Michael Morgan's assessment in "Philosophy, History, and the Jewish Thinker" that *To Mend the World* belongs to Athens and Jerusalem and that Fackenheim's life informs this style of thinking – this is only good post-Hegelian Hegelianism. Nevertheless, the dialectic relationship between Athens and Jerusalem in Fackenheim's thought prevents any interpretation of Fackenheim as a "fanatic" or "militant" Jewish thinker, as Fackenheim himself argues. Whether Fackenheim's Zionism constitutes a blind spot in this matter is for the reader to decide. Cf. Morgan, *Dilemmas*, 122; Fackenheim, "Reply," 277–78.

2

Beyond "Beyond Being"

Nonbeing in Plato and Husserl

Near the close of the sixth book of Plato's *Republic* (508d–509c), Socrates declares that the idea of the good is the cause of all truth and explicates this statement by drawing an analogy between the good and the sun. As the sun provides for the "coming to be, growth, and nourishment"[1] of visible objects but is not itself any of these processes of becoming, so the good is the source of both existence and being without being either of these. Indeed, the good is defined as beyond being (*epekeina tēs ousias*, 509b). By stating that the good is superior to being, Plato leaves the *Republic* open to an interpretation that holds that discussions of the good – ethics – are superior to epistemological or metaphysical discussions. This view that "ethics is first philosophy" is perhaps the most common distillation of Levinas's thought. It appears throughout Levinas's writings, with specific reference to this section of the *Republic*. In *Totality and Infinity*, Levinas writes that "the Place of the Good above every essence is the most profound teaching – the definitive teaching – not of theology, but of philosophy" (TI 76/103). In the précis of the argument of *Otherwise than Being*, Levinas continues along these lines by asserting that the humanist reduction of the person to the historical fact is a forgetting of "what is better than being, that is, the Good" (AE 23/19).

Now it is clear that Levinas is not a thoroughgoing Platonist. The very analogy of the sun in *Republic* VI is contrary to Levinas's conception of appearance as an enigmatic shadow.[2] Furthermore, the transcendental necessity

---

[1] All citations from Plato will be from the translations found in *Plato: Complete Works*, ed. John M. Cooper (Indianapolis: Hackett, 1997).

[2] Cf. Levinas, "La réalité et son ombre," *Les temps modernes* 38 (1948), 771–89, esp. 777–81, translated by Alphonso Lingis as "Reality and Its Shadow" in *Collected Philosophical Papers* (Dordrecht: Martinus Nijhoff, 1987), 1–13, esp. 5–8; Levinas, "Enigme et phénomène," in *En découvrant l'existence avec Husserl et Heidegger*, 3rd ed. (Paris: Vrin, 1994), 203–16, esp. 207–9, translated by Alphonso Lingis, Robert Bernasconi, and Simon Critchley as "Enigma and Phenomenon," in Levinas, *Basic Philosophical Writings*, ed. Adriaan T. Peperzak, Simon Critchley, and Robert Bernasconi (Bloomington: Indiana University Press, 1996), 66–77, esp. 69–70.

Levinas ascribes to the life of separation and its economic order (because there can be no ethics without separation; TI 195/220) is used in *Time and the Other* to criticize the Platonic distrust of pleasure.[3] Thus, one should interpret Levinas's acceptance of Platonic doctrine at *Republic* VI as predicated not on an acceptance of Platonic metaphysics and epistemology *tout court*, but on Levinas's resolution of problems in the Husserlian and Heideggerean theories of intuition and appearance. It seems that the most that can be said about Levinas's Platonism is that there is broad agreement between Levinas and the "interrelational" view of Platonic epistemology: the (form of the) good is not an *ousia* but an organizing teleological structure, and knowledge of a thing involves being able to relate it to the teleological structure of goodness.[4]

Nevertheless, I claim that we should even go as far as to question Levinas's acceptance – indeed, anyone's acceptance – of the good beyond being.[5] There are problems with the theory of the Good as it is laid out in the *Republic*. Indeed, it seems very possible that Plato intends that the reader question Socrates; immediately after Socrates' claim that the good transcends being, Plato describes Glaucon's response: "And Glaucon comically said: By Apollo, what a dæmonic superiority!" (509c).[6] The comic element cannot be a judgment on the validity of Glaucon's comment, since Socrates immediately responds by blaming Glaucon for forcing him to give a definition in the first place. If Glaucon were not to be taken seriously, there would be no reason for Socrates to chastise him. Rather, what is comic is the hyperessential language Glaucon forces upon Socrates, language that is ultimately useless and that implies that the inconceivability of the good (509a) would be better reflected if the good were left unspoken. And indeed, the analogy of the Divided Line (509d–511e), which follows this comic interlude, fails to mention the form of the Good, as is often noted in the secondary literature.[7]

3 Levinas, *Le temps et l'autre* (Paris: Presses Universitaires de France, 1989), 46 and 91–92n. 3, translated by Richard A. Cohen as *Time and the Other* (Pittsburgh: Duquesne University Press, 1985), 64n. 38.
4 Cf. Gail Fine, "Knowledge and Belief in *Republic* V–VII," in *Plato: Critical Assessments*, ed. Nicholas D. Smith (London: Routledge, 1998), 2:235–65, esp. 245–46; also cf. Alexander Nehamas, *"Episteme* and *Logos* in Plato's Later Thought," *Archiv für Geschichte der Philosophie* 66 (1984), 11–36, esp. 20–21 and 33–36.
5 Indeed, Russ Dancy writes that "the natural reading of his unnatural text gives an outright contradiction, and it stands in splendid isolation on this score. I suspect Plato came to wish he had not written it." R. M. Dancy, "Ancient Non-Beings: Speusippus and Others," in *Two Studies in the Early Academy* (Albany: State University of New York Press, 1991), 96.
6 For another interpretation of Glaucon's response to Socrates, cf. Jacques Derrida, "Comment ne pas parler: Dénégations," in *Psyché: Inventions de l'autre* (Paris: Galilée, 1987), 565, translated by Ken Frieden as "How to Avoid Speaking: Denials," in *Derrida and Negative Theology*, ed. Harold Coward and Toby Foshay (Albany: State University of New York Press, 1992), 103.
7 For example, Julia Annas, *An Introduction to Plato's* Republic (Oxford: Clarendon, 1981), 250.

Although the good is mentioned once again in the analogy of the cave in *Republic* VII, it remains unspoken in later Platonic dialogues such as the *Sophist* and *Statesman*. Moreover, in a very late dialogue, we get a completely different definition of the Good from the one given at *Republic* VI. At *Philebus* 65a, we read:

Well, then, if we cannot capture the good in *one* form [*ousia*], we will have to take hold of it in a conjunction of three: beauty, proportion, and truth. Let us affirm that these three should by right be treated as a unity and be held responsible for what is in the mixture, for its goodness is what makes the mixture itself a good one.

Here we find an outright rejection of the hyperessential language of the *Republic.* The good is no longer beyond being, but is now a mixture of three forms. And goodness is not the source of the being of objects, as Socrates asserts in *Republic* 509; in the *Philebus*, goodness is the result of a good mixture, with proper proportion or measure. Goodness is achieved through a skill in measuring, a *technē*. Indeed, if goodness exists only because of the unity of the three forms listed in the passage just quoted, then (as Kenneth Sayre argues from this passage) for the late Plato, the good can be defined as unity itself. It is no longer the case that something is good because it participates in the form of the Good (as one would assume from the theory of forms given in the *Phaedo*); something is good because it participates in unity.[8]

This is puzzling. If Levinas is right in his assertion that middle-period Plato represents "the most profound teaching of philosophy," why on earth should someone of Plato's acuity leave it behind? If we are to trust Levinas, then it becomes necessary to construct some notion of "being" that would harmonize the different definitions of the good in the *Republic* and the *Philebus* by showing that the later definition fits the criterion of "beyond being" given in the earlier definition. This is not impossible. For if the good cannot be determined under a single form, one must construct a theory of value around the unity of disparate features: whether of beauty, proportion, and truth, or of the one and many (as mentioned in *Philebus* 15d), or of limit and unlimitedness (as in *Philebus* 16cd). In this unity there would be something of the character of beyond essence, insofar as the unity would not be a pure and indivisible unity. What it would mean to be a form, to be the essence of a thing, would be beyond a primitive monological or unifaceted definition of *ousia* that is the basis of the definition of the good given in the *Republic.* In short, I propose a rereading of "the good is beyond being" as "the good is beyond being$_M$," where "being$_M$" stands for the middle-period unifaceted understanding of being. Being$_M$ is insufficiently reflective. In the words of the visitor from Elea at *Sophist* 218c (in another context), it is

---

[8] Kenneth M. Sayre, *Plato's Late Ontology* (Princeton, N.J.: Princeton University Press, 1983), 173.

"content to use the same word without formulating what it means." In the late dialogues, the answer to the question "what is X?" is no longer unitary.

This all might be fairly unimpressive were it not for the fact that the move from a simple to a composite understanding of *ousia* is described by Plato as a move away from pure ontology. It is only through the analysis of nonbeing in the *Sophist* – in other words, the meontological analysis – that the unity of disparate features becomes theoretically possible. There, in the sections detailing the battle between the giants and the gods – the gigantomachia – and the blending of the five highest kinds, Plato takes steps toward a new definition of *ousia* that depends upon a theory of blending (*symplokē*).[9] This theory of blending becomes possible only through an analysis of nonbeing as difference or otherness. It thus becomes possible to say that for the late Plato there is no knowledge of being as something meaningful without an elucidation of the concept of alterity. But what kind of alterity? Is it the alterity of the other being, the "not" of dialectical meontology seen in the analysis of Emil Fackenheim's work in the previous chapter? Or is it a more Levinasian notion of alterity, one that would point to the other-than-being, the "not" of critical meontology?

In this chapter, I will argue the following: in the *Sophist*, Plato asserts that being and alterity are *non-independent*, in the sense Husserl gives this phrase in the third of the *Logical Investigations*.[10] While it is possible to read the *Sophist* in such a manner as to conclude that being is primary, that alterity is merely a path to a surer and more stable ontology, I present an account of the *Sophist* in which both being and alterity, that which is and that which is not, are *moments-of-*... By focusing on the absence of a philosophical right to ontologically define an alleged larger structure, indicated through the ellipsis, this locution brings the notion of alterity typified by critical meontology – the other-than-being – within a framework previously thought

---

9 This analysis assumes that the discussion of the gigantomachia is commensurable with the following section on the five highest kinds, even though the gigantomachia speaks of *ousia* whereas it is *to on* that is one of the five highest kinds (cf. 255b). Scholars appear to be divided on the issue of their equivalence. Stanley Rosen asserts that *ousia* is a more general term than *to on*, and cites the previously noted passage from *Republic* VI ("*to einai te kai ten ousian*") as evidence. That there is no occurrence of the phrase *ta mē ousia* in the *Sophist* provides more striking evidence for Rosen's point. Nevertheless, Lesley Brown is equally adamant that the two terms are used interchangeably and cites a use of each to refer to the subject matter of the gigantomachia (at 248c2 and 247d6). Both sides are compelling, and the argument may well have no resolution. Nevertheless, because the discussion of the five kinds serves as a dramatic resolution to the problems on each side of the gigantomachia, equivalence can be accepted for the purposes that follow. Cf. Stanley Rosen, *Plato's* Sophist: *The Drama of Original and Image* (New Haven, Conn.: Yale University Press, 1983), 212; Lesley Brown, "Being in the *Sophist*: A Syntactical Inquiry," *Oxford Studies in Ancient Philosophy* 4 (1986), 63.

10 For a brief reference to Husserl's concept of non-independence in Levinas, cf. "Totalité et totalisation," in *Altérité et transcendance* (Montpellier: Fata Morgana, 1995), 61, translated by Michael B. Smith as "Totality and Totalization," in *Alterity and Transcendence* (New York: Columbia University Press, 1999), 43–44.

by scholars to be inhabited only by dialectical meontology, the other being. The title of this chapter therefore has a double meaning. It refers to a move *back* from the Levinasian notion of the beyond-being, which fails to do justice to the way in which an account of nonbeing is imbricated in a supposedly purely ontological account. Simultaneously, it refers to a move *forward* that follows Levinas in elucidating the structure of the beyond-being, and how beings lie in its traces.

Obviously, one cannot jump head-first into this argument without some preparatory work. This chapter will thereby adhere to the following structure. First, I will give an overview of the problems concomitant with the theory of forms set forth in the *Phaedo* and the *Republic*, according to the later interpretation of middle Platonism we find in the *Parmenides*. Second, I will relate the arguments against unifaceted definition in the sections of the *Sophist* that give the details of a "gigantomachia," a struggle between gods and giants over the meaning of being. Third, I will present Plato's argument that nonbeing should be conceived not as nothingness (as Parmenides thought), but as otherness. A being's difference from other beings, its aspect as nonbeing, makes it possible for consciousness to ascribe essential properties to that object. Plato thus clearly opts for a dialectical view that being and alterity are always and everywhere co-said. Fourth, I show that there is a problem of foundationalism in the *Sophist*, a problem that I believe can be clarified only by a turn to phenomenology. Here, I lay out certain Husserlian theories necessary for this clarification – foundation, categorial intuition, and the distinction between parts and moments – and show how a phenomenological examination of these issues discloses the truth of middle Platonism. An otherness beyond being and being's others grounds the dialectical turns between being and alterity found in the *Sophist*.

THE PROBLEMS OF MIDDLE PLATONISM

The primary characteristic of the Platonic forms as they appear in the *Phaedo* and the *Republic* is their complete separation from objects.[11] Beauty does not need beautiful objects in order to be Beauty; Largeness does not need large objects in order to be Largeness. At *Phaedo* 78d5, Socrates states that each form is *auto kath'hauto*, existing "itself by itself." Key passages in Plato's

---

[11] The following analysis of middle Platonism is indebted to the numerous texts, including: Sayre, *Plato's Late Ontology*, 16–27; Sayre, *Parmenides' Lesson* (Notre Dame, Ind.: University of Notre Dame Press, 1996), 57–97; Sayre, "The Role of the *Timaeus* in the Development of Plato's Late Ontology," *Ancient Philosophy* 18 (1998), 93–124; Constance Meinwald, *Plato's Parmenides* (Oxford: Oxford University Press, 1991), 3–19; Lloyd Gerson, "A Distinction in Plato's *Sophist*," in *Plato: Critical Assessments* 4:125–41; Gregory Vlastos, "Degrees of Reality in Plato," in *Plato: Critical Assessments*, 2:219–34; S. Marc Cohen, "The Logic of the Third Man," in *Plato: Critical Assessments* 4:28–50; William J. Prior, *Unity and Development in Plato's Metaphysics* (La Salle, Ill.: Open Court, 1985), 1–50.

dialogues depend upon this theory of forms. Glaucon uses the same phrase near the opening of *Republic* II (358d2-3) in his desire to hear Socrates praise justice "itself by itself," in contrast to the elenchic arguments Socrates posed against Thrasymachus' defense of injustice. Diotima describes beauty in this matter at *Symposium* 211b; many more examples could be cited. The aspect of forms as *kath'hauto* means that forms are simplex, noncomposite (*Phaedo* 78c), without parts, "entirely free from what they are not."[12] The partial features of sensible objects can never be free from their opposites: an object might have one beautiful feature and another ugly one, or its degree of beauty might change depending on its spatial position or the quality of lighting. Sensible objects can thus be both beautiful and ugly simultaneously (*Symposium* 211a) or tall and short simultaneously (*Phaedo* 102bc) and are thus never *auto kath'hauto* as forms are. The fact that sensible objects can be characterized simultaneously by opposite predicates leads to an epistemological denigration of the visible. Because of the separation between forms and visible objects, forms are always only *intelligible*. The claim that the forms are "intelligible but not visible" is made in the analogy of the Sun (507b8) and is predicated upon arguments made in the *Phaedo* for the superiority of the intelligible over the visible in the same manner that the soul is superior to the body. These arguments are nicely summarized at *Phaedo* 66a:

> Then he will do this [grasp the forms] most perfectly who approaches the object with thought alone, without associating any sight with his thought, or dragging in any sense-perception with his reasoning, but who, using pure thought [*dianoia*] alone, tries to track down each reality pure and by itself, freeing himself as far as possible from eyes and ears, and in a word, from the whole body, because the body confuses the soul and does not allow it to acquire truth and wisdom whenever it is associated with it.

It is not only the body that "confuses the soul," it is worldly reality in general. Even when the soul focuses on worldly objects that are constituted by becoming and change (as opposed to focusing on forms, which are really real), the soul "seems bereft of understanding" and thus gives up the possibility of epistemic knowledge in its ability to formulate only doxic opinions about the world, opinions that are never stable, but that are "changing this way and that" (*Republic* 508d). Furthermore, forms are a type of cause (*Phaedo* 100e), a ground of our predications about sensible objects: "it is through Beauty that beautiful things are made beautiful." This early attempt at forming a language of essences is further developed in the analogy of the Sun in the *Republic* (507b5-7). Here, Socrates states that the forms such as "beauty itself and good itself" are observed in terms of their "single form" (*mia idea*), and that this is the ontological essence of the many beautiful and good objects.

---

[12] Sayre, "The Role of the *Timaeus*," 95.

The being of the object is seen to have the same character as the beings that exhibit this essence. Forms predicate themselves (*Phaedo* 102e): "Tallness, being tall, cannot venture to be small."

In the *Parmenides*, this understanding of forms is threatened with collapse. During a dialogue between Socrates and Parmenides, Socrates and the middle-period theory of forms are subjected to a number of damning criticisms from Parmenides. When Socrates explains the relationships between sensible objects and forms as one of participation (*methexis*) or sharing-in (*metalepsis*) – the large object participates in the form of Largeness, the beautiful man has a share in the form of Beauty – Parmenides turns the tables on him (131ac). Making the proper logical assumption that if this model is true, the sensible object must share either in the whole form or in part of it, Parmenides comes to the conclusion that neither of these options is possible, and middle Platonism is therefore not a viable path of thinking. If the object shares in the whole form, then the whole form is present in many objects, and is thus itself many and no longer single, not simply transcendentally separated from objects but indeed "separated from itself" (131b2). Yet if the object shares in a smaller part of the form, like a sail spread over a group of people (131b8) – and this scenario is particularly odd in the case of Largeness, for which "small parts" is an oxymoron – then the form can no longer be simplex.

Another problem, which has been known since Aristotle as the "Third Man" Problem (see *Metaphysics* 990b17, 1039a2-3), arises at *Parmenides* 132ab as a logical consequence of the theory of the self-predication of forms. Since Largeness itself cannot be the condition of our knowing that Largeness is large, it becomes necessary to posit a $Largeness_2$ to explain how Largeness and large objects are large. But since $Largeness_2$ also predicates itself (it too is large), we must explain how we know it to be large by positing the existence of a $Largeness_3$. This becomes an infinite regress, and the boundary between forms and objective appearances becomes blurred; forms can no longer be *auto kath'hauto*. A similar regress occurs when Socrates suggests to Parmenides that forms are patterns in nature that sensible objects resemble. Parmenides points out, quite reasonably, that such resemblance must be symmetrical; again forms and sensible objects must partake of a higher-order common genus that organizes them, and again the resemblance of the forms to the sensible objects means that forms cannot be rigorously thought as *auto kath'hauto*. Furthermore, the intelligibility of forms is also at odds with the basic account of participation. If sensible objects participate in nonsensible forms, which Socrates describes to Parmenides as "thoughts" (132b5), then the thought-structure of forms must be spread out along sensible objects in some manner. This would lead to the odd conclusion that things are composed of thoughts.

In short, there is a tension between the transcendence and immanence of forms that grounds middle Platonism. On the one hand, there is the structure of the forms themselves: they must be *auto kath'hauto* in order to have the explanatory power that they do. Nevertheless, this very fact can be cognized only if forms show themselves in some manner, in some particular arrangement of sensible objects. And in this moment of realizing the necessity of the relationship between forms and particular objects, forms instantly cease to be *auto kath'hauto*. Thus Parmenides points out that the main logical consequence of the forms being *auto kath'hauto* is that they are "necessarily unknowable": if the forms are not "in us" (as Parmenides describes the situation at 133c7), if they are not phenomenally apparent, then the very form of knowledge by which we would putatively know these forms can never be accessible to humankind. Yet Parmenides is not arguing for a two-world hypothesis, in which we know particulars by virtue of "the truth that belongs to our world" (134a12), whereas the world of generals and its truth remain forever unknowable. For without *some* theory of forms, thought (135b10–c1) "doesn't allow that for each thing there is a character that is always the same."

What is needed, then, is a reinterpretation of how the one form can come to appear in many objects and not itself be changed as a result. This necessitates nothing less than a sweeping revision of the ontology of the *Republic*. This revision begins in the *Parmenides*, continues through the *Sophist* and *Statesman*, and ends tentatively in the *Philebus*. Constance Meinwald has already described this change in terms of what one might call a deconstruction of the form–particular binarism, since forms are now said to be like particulars insofar as they are "rolling around as intermediates between what is not and what purely is."[13] But being and nonbeing are two victims of this redefinition of forms. Being and nonbeing no longer rest on a stable bedrock of number (their oneness) or self-sufficiency *kath'hauto*. Rather, the stability of being and nonbeing – like that of every form – is now rooted in their blending with other forms, including one another.

THE INADEQUACY OF UNIFACETED DEFINITION

On the surface, Plato's *Sophist* recounts the successful attempt to define sophistry, performed by the mathematician and Academy member Theaetetus and a visitor (*xenos*) from Elea. The first two-fifths of the dialogue show attempts to define the sophist using a method of collection and division that Plato had previously outlined at *Phaedrus* 265d–266c. After seven attempts

---

[13] Meinwald, *Plato's Pamenides* 167. For Meinwald's account of why there is no Third Man Problem for late-Platonic ontology, cf. 155–57, and Meinwald, "Good-bye to the Third Man," in *The Cambridge Companion to Plato*, ed. Richard Kraut (Cambridge: Cambridge University Press, 1992), 365–96. For a critique of Meinwald's position, as well as for an alternate account of the relation between middle-period and late-period Platonism, cf. Samuel C. Rickless, "How Parmenides Saved the Theory of Forms," *The Philosophical Review* 107:4 (1998), 501–54.

at defining the sophist in this manner, Theaetetus and the visitor give up (236de). The difficulty is ascribed to the fact that the sophist makes false statements, and the assertion of this fact rests on the assumption that false statements *are*. However, this is an anti-Parmenidean assumption, one that is especially "difficult" for a philosopher who, like the visitor, hails from the same city as Parmenides (236e1). Since false statements state what is not the case, or more generally what is not (*mē on*), the analysis of false statements rests on the assumption that "that which is not is" (*to mē on einai*). Otherwise, it would be impossible even to utter falsehoods. Yet this goes against the Parmenidean command that philosophy should never take on this very thought, the thought that what is not is (237a8, 258d2). What thus becomes necessary for the visitor, in the interest of truth, is a parricide (241d3) that begins from the realization that Parmenides has blindly failed to recognize a fundamental confusion about the meanings of "is" and "is not" (243c).

The first problem of being (243b–246d) is a quantitative one: the position of the *diakribologoumenoi* (245e7) – those who claim to give a precise account of the proper number of being by assigning it a numerical value – is untenable.[14] Parmenidean monism successfully deals with problems in pre-Socratic dualism. Although one might say that all things are either hot or cold, a better foundationalism would be rooted in the fact that both heat and cold *are* – being is one. But this monism collapses in an uncritical synonymy of being and wholeness. Whereas being cannot participate in wholeness (because a form cannot have parts), wholeness participates in being (because wholeness is). By substitution, one reaches the odd conclusion that being cannot participate in itself, which the visitor interprets as the paradoxical statement that, on this account, being will not be being (245c5: *ouk on estai to on*). A model that is open to both unity and plurality is necessary for any justified true account of the nature of being.[15]

After the visitor has disposed of the *diakribologoumenoi*, he goes on to reexamine the difficulty of defining being from the point of view of competing nonnumerical views of the nature of *ousia*. This quarrel is described as a "gigantomachia," a battle between gods and giants. On one side of the quarrel are the giants, who state that being is always embodied (246ab); on the other are those "friends of forms" (248a), who argue that true being (*ousia*) has no body whatsoever (246b). The giants have views similar to Democritus and the atomists; the gods have views similar to middle-period

---

[14] The word *diakribologoumenoi* does not in and of itself refer to a numerical definition of being as either one, two, or three; it simply means "those who give a precise/exact/detailed (*akribes*) account." However, the context at 245e1–2 makes it clear that this precision relates to whether being is one or two, and thus the exactness/*akribeia* of the account/*logos* is a numerical exactness.

[15] Also cf. the deduction of number in *Parmenides* 143, which proceeds along similar grounds. For readers who find the arguments about naming in this section suspicious if not specious, it might be suggestive to think of them as primitive attempts at a Quinean critique of synonymy.

Platonism (cf. *Phaedo* 66a). The visitor argues against the giants by forcing them to admit that not only souls but also abstract entities such as wisdom and justice exist, since the just soul can only become just if the abstract quality of justice is genuinely present in it. Once they admit that being must consist of both embodied and bodiless entities (247c11), the giants are at a loss to determine what these two types of beings have in common, and their materialist position collapses.

At this point, the visitor attempts to give a description of being (*to on*) as possessing power (*dynamis*) to affect or be affected. There has been much speculation as to what this *dynamis* might actually be; for the purposes of this chapter, it is sufficient to note that the visitor refers to power as a description (*horos*) of beings and not a defining account (*logos*).[16] The power to affect and be affected is not a definition of what it is to be a being, but only a *mark* of being's character, which does not exhaust its nature. If this were to be a definition, it would be difficult to reconcile with the attack on Parmenides and the other *diakribologoumenoi* that the visitor has made fewer than three pages earlier. The effect of the visitor's alleged definition of being as power seems to give *dynamis* the supreme status of the Parmenidean One that had just been overthrown. Whether all is one or all is power, the argument for an imprecise account of being that allows plurality and unity to simultaneously characterize *to on* nevertheless stands. No defining account of being can be uniform or unifaceted.[17]

The critique of unifaceted definition continues in the discussion of the friends of forms. Like the Socrates of the *Phaedo*, this group makes a distinction between the variable realm of becoming and the realm of unchanging being. The visitor's objection is that the epistemology of this group, centered on a theory of consciousness's intercourse (*koinōnia*) with objects of becoming (through sense) or with being (through reflection), depends upon a strict separation between being and becoming that makes knowledge impossible. The friends of forms reject the argument that any dialectic of

---

[16] Cf. Francis M. Cornford, *Plato's Theory of Knowledge* (New York: Harcourt Brace & Co., 1935), 238n. 3, who correctly stresses this point.

[17] In his lectures on the *Sophist*, Martin Heidegger suggests that the visitor's claim that the mark of beings is power is part of a very sophisticated pun occurring in these lines, which can and should be read as an anticipation of the model of interrelation between forms that appears later in the dialogue. For it is necessary to read closely the words with which the visitor leaves the giants (247e8). After Theaetetus represents the giants as accepting the visitor's mark of being, the visitor says, "That will do, for later on both they and we perhaps may change our minds [*kalos isos gar an eis husteron hēmin te kai toutois heteron an phaneiē*]." Not only is the language of otherness (*heteron*) significant here as a hope for an actual definition of being, but one can also read this as a hope that otherness *itself* will occur later within the dialogue, to alleviate the problems of unifaceted definition. This indeed is the case when difference is introduced as one of the five highest forms. Martin Heidegger, *Platon: Sophistes* (Frankfurt am Main: Vittorio Klostermann, 1992), 476, translated by André Schuwer and Richard Rojcewicz as *Plato's* Sophist (Bloomington: Indiana University Press, 1997), 329.

affecting or being-affected occurs in the knowledge of being. Yet the visitor
counters (248e):

> If knowing is doing something, then necessarily what is known has something done
> to it. When being is known by knowledge, according to this account, then insofar
> as it's known it's changed by having something done to it – which we say wouldn't
> happen to something that's at rest.

The problem is once again the knowability of forms. It is not a problem of
the logical right to claim that forms exist; the argument against the giants
tells us this much. Rather it is an issue of the incommensurability that results
when a strict dichotomy is drawn between becoming and being in an argument that would state that they exist in different realms. How can forms be
known when the knower/soul exists within the realm of change and becoming, and the forms lie within the realm of unchanging being? Nevertheless,
like Parmenides' admission that the theory of forms is in some way necessary,
the visitor asks "for heaven's sake" (*pros Dios*; 248e8) whether it is so easy to
be convinced that change and other characteristics of becoming (life, soul,
mind, etc.) have no place within the realm of being. Theaetetus answers that
to admit such a radical separation would be "admitting something frightening" (249a3) despite the fact that such a doctrine is the centerpiece of
the *Phaedo* and *Republic*. Theaetetus' fear is allayed by the visitor's argument
that since it is strange not to ascribe mind (*nous*) to absolute being, the
properties of mobile/sensible objects such as life and soul must be drawn
back into the picture. There is no *nous* without life, no life without soul, no
soul without change. Thus, the narrow definition of being (*ousia*) given by
the friends of forms collapses and must be broadened to include the realm
of change (249b2-3): "we must admit that what changes and change itself
are real things [*onta*]."

This is not a return to a quasi-materialistic notion of being. Rather, the
closing exchanges of the gigantomachia imply that neither side – neither
materialism nor idealism – is valid. Instead, they must unite into a more
coherent theory. Either pole alone is untenable; *both* are necessary. The
visitor states that if all is changeless – if the friends of forms are correct – then
nothing is knowable and the quest for knowledge is fruitless. Yet if all is only
flux, then the abstract notions by which we ground our lives are destroyed;
without things that "abide constant in the same condition and in the same
respect" there is no stable thing that could possibly be known. In conclusion,
as the visitor states at 249e2-4, "now we are wholly in the dark about it [being;
to on], though we fancy we are talking good sense." This tension is expressed
quite wittily in the speech at 249c10-d4 in which the visitor asserts that the
knowledge-valuing philosopher must refuse the position of both sides, but
simultaneously urges the philosopher to *accept* both sides (249d3-4): "he
must declare that reality or the sum of things is both at once – all that is
unchangeable and all that is in change." It is the nature of this "both at

once" – which the visitor describes as childlike (249d2) – that marks the final rejection of unifaceted definition and grounds the expansion of the interrelational model of knowledge to include the forms themselves. Here, the definition of nonbeing as otherness is key, for it explains how forms can possibly relate.

NONBEING, OTHERNESS, AND THE COHERENCE
OF DISPARATE ELEMENTS

The gigantomachia has been nothing less than an argument against a style of definition that de facto excludes all things different than it from the object being defined. Being cannot be captured in monism or dualism, materialism or idealism. Combination between forms is thus to be the principle of discourse; we know this from the "ordinary language" of such a proposition as "The person is good" in which the form of personhood combines with the form of the good to make the proposition meaningful (251b). In addition, if there is no combination between forms, there can be no discourse of any kind; we would not be able to speak of rest and movement if they were not allowed to combine with existence (252a). Even phrases such as "apart from the others," when used to describe the separation of forms *auto kath'hauto*, invoke a model of combination (between movement, being, distance, and otherness) that is alien to this middle-Platonic position (252c). Yet this does not mean that the opposite tack is to be taken. If all forms combine, then the distinction between movement and rest becomes utterly meaningless (252d). So it remains to draw a map of which forms blend with which others, as well as to demonstrate how this blending is possible at all.

Five highest forms (*megista genē*) are put forth in 254d-255e: motion, rest, existence (i.e., that which is, being), sameness, and difference. (Again, it is worth noting that goodness is *not* part of this group.) It is difference or otherness that is most important in this section. Only the account of difference allows the visitor to solve the problem of the specific being of nonbeing by stating that beings that are not are other-than (241d) and, indeed, to explain the false statements of sophistry as statements that *are not* insofar as they are other than the truth. However, even though difference is the fulcrum of the new arguments about forms, at this point we cannot conclude that Plato is claiming otherness to be the most supreme of these five forms, and thus more primary than existence. Rather, the account of difference is an account of how being and nonbeing belong *together* as partners in all of our claims of how forms and things interrelate. At best, one might say that since the understanding of nonbeing serves as a precondition for the fuller understanding of being, it makes sense to say that all our epistemic claims are meontological in this guarded sense.

The visitor first broaches the relation between being and otherness in the discussion of whether any of the five highest kinds are the same as one another. He asks first whether otherness and being might simply be two names for one form (255c8–10); given the nature of the visitor's argument against the *diakribologoumenoi*, the reader should already be suspicious. And indeed, a wedge between being and difference is discovered, with the help of the distinction between those things that are said or predicated *auta kath'hauta* ("by themselves") and those that are *pros alla* ("in relation to other things"). Constance Meinwald has convincingly interpreted this distinction in predication as the great theme of late Platonism. (It first appears in the *Parmenides*, where the distinction is written as one between predication *pros heautō* and predication *pros ta alla*, but with the same meaning as the distinction in the *Sophist*.) Predication *kath'hauto* or *pros heautō* is grounded in "the structure of the nature in question"; the predicate is part of what it means to be the subject. Hence, examples of such nonrelational sentences include "Triangularity is three-sided" and "The Just is virtuous," since "being virtuous is part of what it is to be just." Predications *pros* (*ta*) *alla*, on the other hand, are more ordinary relational predicates dealing with the display of features by individuals: "Ruth Ginsburg is just," "Fluffy is a cat," "The sweater is puce," and so on.[18] This predicative distinction is used to argue for a strict difference between *to on* and *to thateron* at 255d1-8, on the grounds that while *to on* can be spoken of as being both *kath'hauto* and *pros allo*, difference is always said *pros alla*. To speak of difference, it is necessary to speak of at least two differentia; difference is always difference-from-something-else.

Quickly the distinction between otherness and being becomes more difficult. Since the relation of otherness is always one between objects other than one another, *to on*, the nature of the object itself, has been momentarily pushed out of the picture. When the visitor speaks of otherness itself, he is no longer speaking explicitly of being but of something else in which all objects participate that is utterly different from being. The nature of this participation is explained at 255e3–6:

And we're going to say that it [difference/otherness] pervades [*dielēluthuian*, lit., passes through] all of them [the highest forms], since each of them is different from

---

[18] Meinwald, "Good-bye to the Third Man," 378–81, and *Plato's Parmenides*, 46–75. In addition, this distinction between self-relation and other-relation has been the cause of almost all secondary literature on the *Sophist* – a debate (between G. E. L. Owen and Michael Frede on one side, with Stanley Rosen, David Bostock, and Lesley Brown on the other) over whether this represents a distinction between an existential and a predicative use of "is." A partial list: G. E. L. Owen, "Plato on Not-Being," in *Plato I*, ed. Gregory Vlastos (New York: Anchor, 1971), 223–67; Michael Frede, "Plato's *Sophist* on False Statements," in *The Cambridge Companion to Plato*, 397–424; Rosen, *Plato's Sophist*; David Bostock, "Plato on 'Is Not,'" *Oxford Studies in Ancient Philosophy* 2 (1984), 89–119; L. Brown, 49–70. For an approach to the dialogue that argues that this debate is not useful and that it ignores the cosmological contexts of the dialogue, see Jean Roberts, "The Problem about Being in the *Sophist*," in *Plato: Critical Assessments*, 4:143–57.

the others, not because of its own nature, but because of participating [*metechein*] in the type of the different [*thaterou*].

If otherness pervades every form, then it would be fair to assume that no form can come to be understood as the form that it is without its being situated in a cluster of forms that are other than it. This does *not* automatically mean that being is essentially otherness in a strong sense, or that no object can display properties on its own. The nature of an object is not otherness. But the preceding passage does mean that a list of characteristics that would define the nature of an object could have meaning for us only insofar as these differ from other characteristics that would be displayed by other objects. The nature of objects, when pervaded by otherness, allows this nature to be comprehended more fully.

And how is participation in the preceding passage to be interpreted? J. L. Ackrill claims that *metechei thaterou* here performs a nonidentity function: "(1) where *estin* ['is'] is being used as copula it gets replaced in the philosopher's version by *metechei*; (2) the philosopher's version of *ouk estin* ['is not'], when the *estin* is not the copula but the identity-sign, is not *ou metechei* ['does not participate'], but *metechei thaterou pros* ['participates in otherness with regard to']."[19] But when this analysis is combined with the visitor's insistence that being and otherness are radically different, both of Ackrill's statements turn out to be both true and false, though in different senses. For the only way by which the assertion that "being and otherness are not the same as each other" can be understood is through the common participation of being and difference in difference and being. It is this common perception that allows being and otherness to be predicated of each other (being is other-than, otherness is). One does not have priority over the other. Every nonidentity necessarily implies a copula – if Theaetetus is not flying, he *is* not-flying. As a result, the natures of Ackrill's *estin* and *ouk estin* are so closely related that his argument for the separation between the existential and the predicative "is" is threatened. The fact that simplex forms cannot be known *auto kath'hauto* (as the *Parmenides* showed) necessitates that as far as the requirements of knowledge are concerned, the essence of an object is known through its clusters of relations with other objects.[20] The object's participation in being has no meaning without its participation in otherness with regard to other objects.

What we have here, then, is the beginnings of a rethinking of *ousia* by the visitor in which otherness becomes part of the account of being. This is a new model of participation; in the middle dialogues, participation was always about the nature of the object. (For example, in a middle-Platonic view, a bouncer at a local club might instantiate the forms of Beauty and Largeness.) But the new model is strange in that the pervasion of otherness

[19] J. L. Ackrill, "Plato and the Copula: *Sophist* 251–9," in Vlastos, *Plato I*, 212–13.
[20] Cf. Fine, 2:235–65, and Nehamas, 11–36.

accounts only for relations and multiplicity. The immunity of otherness from being able to make claims about the proper predicates of an object has given it a strange phantom identity. As a result, the question of whether difference and existence are two or one has become rather complicated. The argument for their strict difference, rooted in the distinction between two types of predication, is valid; however, epistemological necessities related to the knowability of objects complicate the picture. There is an echo here of the visitor's earlier critique of the attempt to determine the number of being, an exchange that called for a simultaneous thinking of unity and plurality. This thinking begins with the parceling out of difference and continues with the analysis of the blending (*koinōnia*) of forms.

Each of the five highest kinds blends both positively and negatively with sameness and difference. Motion is the same (as itself); it is not the same (as sameness). Motion is different (from difference), but it is not difference itself. Motion *is*, but it is not the form of being. The visitor concludes that for each of the forms "being is many, and not-being is unlimited [*polu men esto to on, apeiron de plēthei to mē on*]" (256e6-7). All forms both are and are not, depending on the type of predication involved. This applies even to being (*to on*). This is not a very radical position; it is consistent with what Gail Fine has called the "interrelation" model of knowledge in Plato, in which "nothing can be known in itself, but only as an element occupying a particular place within a structured field, knowledge of which is involved in knowing all its elements."[21]

Nevertheless, certain of the visitor's statements are stronger than this, and they make it tempting to construct a notion of otherness that goes beyond Plato's hesitance in guarding it from claims that an object is properly thought of as other. At 256d10-e4, the visitor expresses the interrelation model in a baldly contradictory manner. For each form, "the nature of otherness makes each other than being and therefore a thing that is not." If the reader uses being (*to on*) as an example here, he or she would have to come to the conclusion that the visitor's statement implies that being is not being, that *to on ouk on esti*.[22] Not only would being be other than other kinds, as such it would not be being. Otherness would thus take over the domain of being, and interrelation would then not be solely between different kinds but within each kind itself.[23] This second kind of otherness is not a *thateron pros*, but

---

[21] This is Alexander Nehamas's summary of Fine's position. Nehamas, 20.

[22] To be sure, the visitor uses both *mē* and *ou* to express otherness at 257b12; nevertheless, this formulation is strange when *metechei tou mē ontos* could have been used instead.

[23] It is usually taken to be the case that being is exempted from this argument because of the contradiction that ensues. Cf. Frede, 403. Yet Plato never says this explicitly. Indeed, difference has to pervade being in order to make the argument that, for example, being is not the same as sameness. Insofar as being is different from other *genē*, being is not, and thus participates in notbeing (as Frede seems to note on 404). Denis O'Brien (*Le Non-Être: Deux Études sur le* Sophiste *de Platon* [Sankt Augustin: Academia Verlag, 1995], 53–56 and

is hypostasized. This second meontology is not dialectical, but critical. The 256de passage says not simply that being needs to be other *pros ta alla* – that a form of otherness is needed in order to explain how being and motion can differ – but that being needs to be other *pros heautō*, that otherness is part of the meaning of being in a manner just as virtue is part of the meaning of justice.

This is not sophistry. Rather, this reading points to the fact that the relational account of nonbeing as difference does not resolve the issues raised by the visitor at 251bc, namely, the proposition "the man is good." For although 257b–260c solves the problem of how certain *types* of predication are possible, it does not directly resolve the problem of how predication and meaning *themselves* are possible. For this, it is necessary to have a stronger notion of otherness as a predicate of forms *pros heautō*, in order to give birth to *meaningful* forms. For example, the proposition "My phlegm is green" is not meaningful unless it already implies that phlegm is not greenness. Otherwise the sentence would be a simple analytic judgment. Predication by its very nature is otherness pervading the realm of being, breaking it apart in order to create meaningful propositions such as "Fluffy is white." Without otherness speaking always and everywhere throughout language in the sense of *to on ouk on* implied at 256e, there is no way that a field of possible predicates could be set off apart from the object for the purpose of linkage to it. Otherwise, only self-predication would be possible, and the problems of middle Platonism return. Otherness *gives* being to consciousness, not simply insofar as (the) being is different from other forms or other objects are different from each other, but in the sense that otherness is the condition for the object's knowability.

At this point we can return to the question of whether otherness and being constitute separate forms. And in line with the philosopher-child's demand at the close of the gigantomachia, it becomes possible to have it both ways. If difference and being were two names for a single kind, it would be impossible to argue that predication could take place, since none of the forms could blend. However, as argued earlier, it seems that otherness, in its pervading of being, marks epistemological territory in the realm of being in order to fulfill the standard functions of language. We are able to assert "S is p" propositions only by linking two disparate kinds, and we are able to make "negative" predicates (such as shortness, equalness, plainness, ugliness, unjustness) only through the parceling of otherness across being. Through the introduction of difference and the concomitant possibility of the coherence of disparate kinds within a single unitary structure, it has

177), argues that being does not participate in otherness in relation to the being of each object – this would institute a contrary relation between being and nonbeing that is the very trap from which the visitor seeks extrication – but does participate in otherness in relation to the objects themselves.

become difficult for the philosophical eye "to keep its gaze fixed" (254b1) in the face of all this shifting around between being and nonbeing. And since all forms, including being and nonbeing, engage in this rolling around and blending, the argument of the *Republic* that forms just don't behave in such a slatternly manner collapses.

Thus, Plato has gone beyond the fundamental presuppositions of the accounts of being given in the gigantomachia. The analysis of otherness has led dialectic beyond being (*epekeina tēs ousias*), and it is tempting to conclude from this that otherness therefore constitutes goodness. Yet one must not give in to this temptation. It would certainly be a mistake to say that otherness *by itself* is *epekeina tēs ousias*. To do so would revert to the very model of unifaceted definition that the visitor consistently critiques in the gigantomachia and in the arguments against the *diakribologoumenoi.* For if being (*to on*) has become constituted in part by otherness, then the symmetrical relation holds as well. Otherness is dialectically pervaded in a strong sense by being.[24] Thus it would be more proper to say that it is in the argument for the intimate coupling of being and nonbeing/otherness that the account of *ousia* in the *Sophist* moves beyond that of the *Republic.*

PHENOMENOLOGY AND MEONTOLOGY

The problem of nonbeing therefore opens up a problem of foundation or grounding. It is the intimate relationship between being and nonbeing – the way in which being is other than other forms and thus *is not*, and the way in which nonbeing qua otherness *is* – that enables us to understand the nature of sensible objects. Yet at the same time, it is the sensation of objects that founds our knowledge that this relationship is foundational. A turn to the phenomenological concept of categorial intuition – the way in which the intuition of an object's being-white serves as a precondition for the statement "X is white" – is natural. Or, at least, a turn to the concept of categorial intuition – to aid working out the meaning of being and the relationship between the sensible and the intelligible – has been made before. In the 1963 account of "My Way to Phenomenology," Heidegger specifically singles out the Sixth Logical Investigation, in which Husserl first develops an account of categorial intuition, as an influence upon his thinking insofar as "the distinction which is worked out there between sensuous and categorial intuition revealed itself to me in its scope for the determination of the 'manifold meaning of being.'"[25] This is not a backhanded statement of

---

[24] Ackrill points out that "motion exists" is obviously not the same as "existence moves," but he allows that symmetry does have its place within *symploke*, especially where difference is involved. Cf. Ackrill, 217–18.

[25] Heidegger, "Mein Weg in die Phänomenologie," in *Zur Sache des Denkens* (Tübingen: Niemeyer, 1969), 86, translated by Joan Stambaugh as "My Way to Phenomenology," in *On Time and Being* (New York: Harper & Row, 1972), 78.

praise, made in hindsight. Heidegger also singles out categorial intuition as a fundamental discovery of phenomenology in the lecture course he gave at the University of Marburg in the summer semester of 1925, later published as *History of the Concept of Time*.[26] As I will argue, it is in the turn to categorial intuition that the link between the sensible object and the intelligible form appears at its most complex and enables an understanding of the apparently contrary positions of Fackenheim and Levinas seen in the previous chapter.

How does the issue of categorial intuition arise? In the sixth of the *Logical Investigations*, Husserl argues that a distinction between sensuous and categorial intuition is necessary, since sensuous perception can never be sufficient for consciousness' understanding of a percept. In the course of analyzing a perceptual statement such as "Fluffy is on the bed, eating some food and ruining my fuchsia sheets"[27] (this example is not Husserl's), the question of how my perception has been fulfilled, of how I come to recognize the identity of the perceived object with the object I sense in my consciousness, comes to the fore. The confirmation of the nouns in the preceding statement – the issue of whether "Fluffy" refers to my cat or to my leather-clad spouse with whom I am playing a game – is clear enough. But how is it possible to fulfill such logical particles as "and," "is," "some," and so on, elements that are not included in simple sensuous intuition (LU II/2 128–29/773–74)? One cannot simply lay eyes upon the forms of quantity or union. The problem of fulfillment raises problems even for apparently simple percepts such as "fuchsia sheets." When I say "fuchsia sheets," I am not only referring to the two fuchsia-sheet objects that lie in front of my eyes. "Fuchsia" also refers to the category of being-fuchsia. In other words, my perception of "fuchsia sheets" is inherently predicative; it is ineluctably intertwined with the sentence "the sheets are fuchsia," since fuchsia sheets are sheets that *are* fuchsia (LU II/2 131/775).[28] Thus, I must have a concept of the category of being-fuchsia that accompanies the sensuous intuition of food strewn throughout my bedroom. But there is no such sensible thing there as being-fuchsia; there are only the sheets. "Being-fuchsia" is not simply an ontological category; it is also a relational one. As Husserl points out in §42 of the Sixth Investigation (and as Heidegger summarizes in *History of the Concept of Time*),[29] the intuition of something such as being-fuchsia implies a synthesis of the relata ("sheets" and "fuchsia") into a totality that

[26] Heidegger, *Prolegomena zur Geschichte des Zeitbegriffs* (Frankfurt am Main: Vittorio Klostermann, 1979), 63–99, translated by Theodore Kisiel as *History of the Concept of Time* (Bloomington: Indiana University Press, 1985), 47–72.

[27] References to Fluffy throughout this chapter are made in gratitude to Cynthia Freeland and her cat Fluffy. Fluffy's participation in many classroom examples has allowed me to come to a better understanding of the material of this chapter.

[28] "White paper is paper which *is* white." (*Weißes, das bedeutet weiß seiendes Papier.*)

[29] Heidegger, *Prolegomena*, 72–73; Heidegger, *History*, 54.

takes the structure of "S is p" (LU II/2 135/779). This totality is not real; to use the language of the Third Investigation, being-fuchsia is not a *piece* of the sheets themselves that could be cut off and displayed independently (LU II/1 266ff./467ff.). Rather, the relation is ideal. The abstract nature of being-fuchsia renders it non-independent, and hence a *moment* of the sheets. The category is always needy, requiring the S-is-p structure of the state of affairs (*Sachverhalt*) in order to come to presence.[30]

Thus, the intention of the word "fuchsia," as Husserl writes, "only partially coincides with the color-aspect of the apparent object; a surplus of meaning remains over, a form which finds nothing in the appearance itself to confirm it" (LU II/2 131/775). Whence this excess? Husserl is forced to posit the existence of another type of intuition, one that pertains to categories (and other formal particles of language) and specifically the category of being, as opposed to sensibilia. Being is given to consciousness in categorial intuition (LU II/2 141/784) "if based on an act which at least sets some individual instance of it imaginatively before our eyes."[31]

The order of intuition in general, as laid out through the distinction between sensuous and categorial moments, is awkward. In §46, Husserl argues that sensuous intuition precedes categorial intuition. I cannot have an intuition of being-fuchsia in the earlier example without the sight of the food-spattered bedding. As the most straightforward example of intuition, sensuous intuition comes first temporally and serves as the *foundation* for other perceptive levels and acts. Categorial intuitions are always founded in sensuous intuitions. Husserl defines foundation in the Third Investigation as a need for supplementation: "if a law of essence means that an A cannot as such exist except in a more comprehensive unity which associates it with an M, we say that an A as such requires foundation by an M or also that an A as such needs to be supplemented by an M" (LU II/1 261/463). Something is founded if it needs something else in order to come to presence; hence, for something to be founded is nothing other than for it to be a non-independent moment. Categorial intuitions are non-independent because I cannot sensibly intuit being, quantity, and so forth; they require supplementation by the stuff of sensuous intuition. Hence the categorial act is always founded upon the act of sensuous perception (LU II/2 137/780–81). The

---

[30] The key sentence from LU on the difference between pieces and moments (II/1 266/467) reads as follows: "We first perform a fundamental division of the concept 'part' [*Teil*] into 'pieces' [*Stücke*], or parts in the narrowest sense, and into moments or abstract parts of the whole. Each part that is independent relatively to a whole W we call a piece, each part that is non-independent relative to W we call a moment (an abstract part) of this same whole W." Robert Sokolowski, in his discussion of parts and wholes in *Husserlian Meditations* (Evanston, Ill.: Northwestern University Press, 1974), 8–17, gives helpful examples (9): leaves, branches, and roots are pieces of a tree, while loudness, timbre, and pitch are moments of a sound.
[31] Cf. Immanuel Kant, *Critique of Pure Reason*, trans. Norman Kemp Smith (New York: St. Martin's Press, 1929), B 626 ff.

temporal succession between sensuous and categorial perception is clear: consciousness moves from the particular to the general.

What we have are acts which constitute new objects, acts in which something appears as actual and self-given – something which was not yet (and could not have been) given in these foundational acts alone as what it now appears to be. On the other hand, the new objects are based on the older ones, they refer to what appears in the founding acts [*Grundakte*]. Their manner of appearance is essentially determined by this relationship. We are here dealing with a sphere of objects, which can only show themselves 'in person' in such founded acts. In such founded acts we have the categorial element in intuition and knowledge. In them assertive thought, functioning expressively, finds fulfillment. (LU II/2 146–47/787–88)

Sensuous perception precedes categorial intuition in the process of knowledge. Yet at the same time, it is clear from the example of the fuchsia sheets that I cannot *say* "fuchsia sheets" unless the categorial intuition is prior in some manner. How can I be sure in my attribution of being-fuchsia or being-sheet to this object before me if I have not already some intuition of being-fuchsia or being-sheet? Although I have to see the sheets before I say "fuchsia sheets," the question arises of whether what I see has any meaning to me without the categorial intuition. Husserl's description of categorial intuition as manifesting itself as a "surplus of meaning" is thereby threatened by his subsequent splitting of intuition into sensuous and categorial moments, which make the founded act transcendentally prior to the founding act. When we make explicit the categorial element in intuition – that is, when we turn to the analysis of predicative statements about perception – the relationship of foundation becomes complicated. Although "the matter seems quite the same" to Husserl when he turns from perception to language (LU II/2 130/775), it has become anything but that. If my statement expresses what I see with "precise adequacy," and if this statement is already imbricated in categorial acts, then the categorial act is transcendentally prior (but not temporally prior) to perception. Even when I quickly glance at a blank computer monitor,[32] I still see it as dark, and this seeing is still imbricated in intuitions of being-dark; the issue is one of whether I could ever isolate an unarticulated perception that would be free from imbrication in categorial acts.

What comes to the fore is that categorial intuitions *constitute*, or give sense to, sensuous intuitions by giving them objectivity, by generating the meaning of objectivity as something broader than the mere ontic reality of bare perception. In *History of the Concept of Time*, Heidegger points out that the act of synthesis that makes a state of affairs such as "the sheets are fuchsia" present, although dependent upon the material sheets, "occurs so that this matter and this alone shows itself explicitly in the state of affairs [and thus] gives

---

[32] The example (but not the conclusion) is Steven Crowell's, from personal correspondence.

something which is inconceivable through simple perception as such."[33] In this higher-order phenomenological analysis of the object beyond the level of simple perception, Heidegger appears to realize that categorial intuitions need to be ontologically prior to sensuous intuition if the category is not to be a subjectivist philosophical construct. Thus, Heidegger writes that "concrete intuition expressly giving its object is never an isolated, single-layered sense perception, but is always a multi-layered intuition, that is, a categorially specified intuition"[34] As Jacques Taminiaux writes, "perception . . . is universalizing from the outset,"[35] and this seems to be a moment at which Heidegger has to make an anti-Husserlian argument in the process of performing a rigorous science of categorial intuition.

To elucidate this structure on the ontological level, the Heideggerean focus on the importance of categorial intuition on phenomenology demonstrates that being is always and everywhere in beings. Being is at issue in all our assertions but cannot be shown to be at issue without the evidence of those assertions themselves: "each concrete apprehending thus also already includes the ideal unity of the species, although not explicitly."[36] However, the way in which this mutual relation comes about remains a mystery and can be explained only through some sort of dynamic nature in being as well as concrete beings. This dynamic nature, as Heidegger explains in the lecture course on the *Sophist* (given in the winter semester of 1924–25), is nonbeing. Only in a relationship of reciprocal foundedness between being and nonbeing, *to on* and *to mē on*, in which isolating one from the other is senseless and in which no larger whole encompasses them, can the relationship between being and beings (categorial intuition) be explained.

For Heidegger, it is in the notness of nonbeing that we find the possibility for understanding an object, not simply as something other than some other sensible object but also as the being that is other than being. Nonbeing brings the ontological difference to light. This is the conclusion to be drawn from the following passage that appears at §78aα of the lecture course:

Putting it sharply, the Being of the "not" [*das Sein des Nicht*], the *mē*, is nothing else than the *dynamis* of the *pros ti*, the presence of the Being-in-relation-to. This is only a more precise formulation given to our interpretation of the idea of *koinōnia*. The Being of the "not," the *mē* in the sense of the *heteron* is the *dynamis* of the *pros ti*. Plato does not exhibit this as such, but it is implicit in the idea of *koinōnia*.[37]

For Heidegger, being *always* appears *pros ti*, in relation to an object. It is only in the equiprimordiality of being with beings that the equiprimordiality of the universal and the particular (which Heidegger teases out of Aristotle in

---

33 Heidegger, *Prolegomena*, 87; Heidegger, *History*, 64.

34 Heidegger, *Prolegomena*, 93; Heidegger, *History*, 68.

35 Jacques Taminiaux, "From One Idea of Phenomenology to the Other," in *Heidegger and the Project of Fundamental Ontology* (Albany: State University of New York Press, 1991), 31.

36 Heidegger, *Prolegomena*, 91; Heidegger, *History*, 67.

37 Heidegger, *Platon: Sophistes*, 558; Heidegger, *Plato's* Sophist, 386–87.

the opening half of the lecture course) is possible. But if this relationality is due to nonbeing, as Heidegger claims in the preceding passage, then Heidegger's lesson to the reader of the *Sophist* is that being can never properly be thought without its "not," the *mē* of *to mē on*. Being and nonbeing are also equiprimordial. *To mē on* is constitutive; it is the precondition for a being to be seen as the being that it is, and Heidegger recognizes nonbeing as such. Thus, the phenomenological seeing of being that Heidegger has performed in his analysis of the *Sophist* is just as much meontology as it is ontology. To draw a hierarchy here in which the *mē on* is more supreme than the *on* would be ultimately useless and would mark a return to the false position of the *diakribologoumenoi*. Thus, when Heidegger states later in the lectures at §78bβ that *to mē on* is like *to on* and that "Plato acquires *mē on* as *on*,"[38] it is incumbent upon the readers of Heidegger to take this passage in conjunction with the previous statements on the being of the *mē* at §78aα and to realize that this can only stress the equal *koinōnia* between being and nonbeing.

This is not a kinder, gentler interpretation of Heidegger, made with the benefit of hindsight, or with trepidation about muscular ontologies. Rather, this equiprimordiality is part of the Husserlian heritage that Heidegger is appropriating and articulating here.[39] At this point, a return to Husserl is in order. In the Third Logical Investigation, Husserl spends some time speaking of reciprocal foundedness. In his definition of the phrase, Husserl writes that "their relative lack of independence is unquestionable, as is the case, e.g., in the unity of Quality and Place" (LU II/1 265/466). In addition, for these non-independent moments, Husserl writes that these parts need not be incorporated into a higher unity that binds them. The reciprocal relation of foundedness is for Husserl a sufficient bond that obviates the addition of a supernumerary whole: "for this reason they require no chains and bonds to chain or tie them together, or to bring them to one another" (LU II/1 279/477). Indeed, in these relations, there is "simply *no* unifying form." But this relationship can apply only to situations in which the parts are inseparable moments, not in which they are pieces, separately presentable from each other.[40]

Since the *Sophist* demonstrates that one cannot intuit being without the intuition of nonbeing as well, that is, being and nonbeing blend with each other, we can describe being and nonbeing as concepts that are not

[38] Heidegger, *Platon: Sophistes*, 566; Heidegger, *Plato's Sophist*, 392.
[39] Again, this approach follows that of Jacques Taminiaux. See "From One Idea of Phenomenology to the Other," 1–54, esp. 25–45, and "Heidegger and Husserl's *Logical Investigations*: In Remembrance of Heidegger's Last Seminar," in Taminiaux, *Dialectic and Difference: Modern Thought and the Sense of Human Limits* (Atlantic Highlands, N.J.: Humanities Press, 1990), 91–114, esp. 106ff.
[40] Timothy J. Stapleton, *Husserl and Heidegger* (Albany: State University of New York Press, 1983), 60: "Those wholes whose parts are moments, essentially dependent, require no external bond."

separately presentable. Thus, their relation is non-independent. They are not pieces of some X, but moments. If this relation is non-independent, then by Husserl's argument in the Third Logical Investigation, one has a right to ask why any overarching whole should be posited to explain their relationship. One might read Heidegger's "Plato acquires nonbeing as a type of being" as a foreshadowing of a muscular ontology based on an always implicit comprehension of the meaning of being that awaits only to be articulated in a form of life – a form of life that would punish those who happen not to share this comprehension. But this would repeat certain idealist moves that Husserl himself claims are unnecessary. Husserl tells us that there is no need to name this overarching and unifying form; on a Husserlian reading of the *Sophist*, we must be willing to let the dialectic relationship between being and nonbeing remain foundational. And there is a corollary benefit to the Husserlian approach that should persuade that the critique of Heidegger is not simply politically motivated: for Heidegger's understanding of the relationship between being and nonbeing as disclosive of a more fundamental ontological understanding leads to a Third Man Problem. If a being can come to have meaning only by rolling around with its other in a reciprocal or dialectical relationship of affecting and being affected, and if this rolling around instantiates the dynamic of being-itself, it is all too easy to recreate Parmenides' critique of middle Platonism and aim it at ontology. Could not one say that being-itself too must roll around with its other to be knowable? What will happen then? Should one then posit a still higher order of being – being$_2$ – to serve as a unifying whole that encompasses this relationship? And what about that being? Would we then need to posit a being$_3$? Would this not continue ad infinitum? The most that one can say is that meaning is constituted through the intercrossing[41] of being and non-being. While *to on* and *to mē on* are non-independent moments of a larger whole, to give a name to this whole would engender a series of inextricable philosophical problems. Being and nonbeing are moments-of-...

In the refusal to name, we gain a philosophical right to be critical meontologists and posit that which is situated beyond being. But we should be aware that it was dialectical meontology, the exploration of the way in which being and nonbeing interpenetrate, that gave us this right. If the critical notion of nonbeing (the unnamable Other that lies at the origin) serves as the condition for the possibility of the dialectical notion of nonbeing, then one can indeed say that a Hegelian trip to the broken middle, of the kind that Fackenheim wants to make, is false. Indeed, Fackenheim should leave Hegel behind, charter a boat on the Mediterranean, and make the move from Athens to Jerusalem. Nevertheless, it is equally important to point out that one cannot *know* to make this move without an engagement in the dialectical relations of otherness. I come to know the unnamable Other

---

[41] *Durcheinanderlaufen.* Heidegger, *Platon: Sophistes*, 461; Heidegger, *Plato's* Sophist, 319.

through tarrying with the named others of my existential situation (Fluffy, for example). In addition, if I perceive this other as *not* me, then according to the model of Platonic epistemology that Gail Fine lays out, then I also come to know *myself* better in this process. In the next two chapters, I lay out a history of these crossings between religious and ethical attunements to alterity, and between other-regard and self-cultivation. This is the lesson of the Jewish meontological tradition: the Other beyond being and the other being are correlate to each other, and the realization of this correlation engenders my ability to redeem the world.

3

Nonbeing as Not-Yet-Being

Meontology in Maimonides and Hermann Cohen

In the previous chapter, I argued that Levinas misinterpreted the Platonic arguments he uses to justify his critical meontology; Plato cannot get past the dialectical meontology in which otherness can refer only to other objects, and not to a transcendent realm. Nevertheless, there are phenomenological arguments, notably from the third of Husserl's *Logical Investigations*, that can justify the Levinasian view of nonbeing as absolute otherness. These arguments, however, do not give evidence for critical meontology over and above dialectical meontology; it is not the case that Husserl proves Levinas to be true and Fackenheim to be false. Rather, they argue for a correlation of the two kinds of meontology; the two kinds of nonbeing are shown to be non-independent. The otherness beyond being announces itself in the other being that is not me.

In this chapter, I will show that in Maimonides and Cohen, nonbeing refers to the material realm, which is deprived of a perfect form – the realm of privation is *to mē on*. Human existence begins in the nonbeing that is lack, and its task is to near (as fully as possible) the nonbeing that is fullness, the nonbeing above being. Given that teleology is part of the natural structure of existence, meontology opens up a realm of futurity and the process of approaching the telos is given normative value. Meontology necessitates ethics. Nevertheless, I also offer critiques of both Maimonidean and Cohenian ethics. The value of the telos, in both thinkers (although to different degrees) risks completely overshadowing the value of those whom I encounter on my teleological path. For Maimonides, ethical actions are only instrumental; I carry them out for the sake of my own process of self-perfection and to attain the world-to-come (*'olam ha-ba'*). Cohen is more torn on this issue. There are passages in his writings in which ethical acts are viewed as good in and of themselves – since he argues that the self cannot gain anything from the ethical affect of compassion (*Mitleid*) – but there are others in which he formulates a more instrumentalist position.

Cohen understands his concept of nonbeing to be strictly Maimonidean. But Cohen's filial piety to Maimonides (and indeed, to many philosophers) is at times difficult to establish. Therefore, I begin this chapter with a brief analysis of the mention of meontology in Hermann Cohen's *Religion of Reason out of the Sources of Judaism*, and mark out the necessity of the return to Maimonides. Using both the *Guide* and the *Epistle to Yemen*, I argue that Maimonides' notion of nonbeing is always temporalized – nonbeing, existence in the realm of privation and contingency, is being on the way to being, not-yet-being – and gives a philosophical right to speak of messianic anticipation. However, since the teleological path is the subject's own, achieved through his or her own actions, one discovers a tension between the anticipation of a future Messiah and the subject's own redemptive actions. This structure is equivalent to one we find in the writings of Hermann Cohen: thought is on its way to an interpenetration of the infinite and finite, and this teleological path is encoded in messianic language; yet in Cohen as well, we find a tension between the subject's awaiting the Messiah and the subject's accomplishing messianism.

RETURN

There is a fascinating passage, occurring relatively early in Cohen's posthumously published (1918) *Religion of Reason* (RV 71–74/62–64), in which Cohen asserts that his concept of the *Ursprung* – the originative causal principle that Cohen understands to be God – is indebted to Maimonides' development of the thematic of *to mē on* as privation in the *Guide of the Perplexed*. Maimonides, for Cohen, develops the theological stakes of the development of meontology in ancient Greek thought. According to Cohen, in pre-Socratic Greek culture, thanks to the deceptions of oratory and sophistry, the difference between the Greek negative particles *ou* and *mē* had disappeared. Democritus and Plato renew this distinction in stringent form, between simple negation (*ou*) and privation (*mē*).[1] Meontology, a mode

---

[1] Whether this distinction actually exists in this way in Greek philosophy is indeed a matter of debate. According to the Liddell-Scott lexicon, *mē* is used in dependent clauses with a subjunctive or optative verbal mood, and *ou* is used in independent clauses with an indicative: "*mē* expresses that one *thinks* a thing *is not, ou* that it *is not*." The definitions, however, do not speak to the negation of nonparticiple nouns such as *to mē on*. Despite the lexical problems, the distinction is strong in the history of philosophy in other thinkers besides Hermann Cohen. Paul Tillich takes it for granted in the first volume of his *Systematic Theology*, vol. 1 (Chicago: University of Chicago Press, 1951), 188ff.; the distinction seems to be rooted in Schelling and Schelling's interpretation of Jakob Boehme but not in Greek thought itself. To see it reflected in Cohen, then, is rather strange, since Cohen associates Schellingian ontology with pantheism. A full explication of this problem would involve carefully reconstructing Cohen's relationship to idealism in the Trendelenburg–Fischer debate. Cf. Henry Liddell and Robert Scott, *Greek-English Lexicon*, abr. ed. (Oxford: Oxford University Press, 1994), 442, 504; Robert F. Brown, *The Later Philosophy of Schelling* (Lewisburg, Penn.: Bucknell University Press,

of thought oriented around the evidence of privation, serves "to endow affirmation with its ground" (RV 71/162). In other words, privation (lack) is
dialectically linked to a notion of fullness – infinite, hyperessential, and
beyond the simple ontology that lies behind ordinary affirmations and
negations. Meontology is indispensable for Cohen, insofar as it is the only
philosophical argument he marshals in the *Religion of Reason* for his demythologized concepts of God and creation. It is Maimonidean in spirit.
Maimonides, according to Cohen, has taken over the Platonic distinction
of negation and privation. Cohen's evidence is *Guide* I:58, in which (Cohen
claims) Maimonides makes the following argument: since privation exists,
there must be a negation of that privation that is completely one, unique,
and serves as the ground of all activity by humans, who are deprived of that
essential oneness. If God is the negation of the set of all objects that are
relatively inert, then God is the *Ursprung* of activity, absolute originary act.
Hence, God's existence suffices for the existence of creatures, and there is
a logical right to speak of God as Creator.

But this is the final, and not the only, appearance of this idea in Cohen's
writings. Cohen's analyses of *to mē on* appear at least as early as his 1902 *Logik
der reinen Erkenntnis*, and Cohen explicitly links meontology and Maimonides
in 1908, in the essay "Charakteristik der Ethik Maimunis." Here, Cohen
reads his own devotion to Maimonides as a reaction against Aristotelian
materialism. Cohen charges Aristotle with reinaugurating a historical disap-
pearance of the *ou/mη* distinction (CEM 250) and interprets Maimonides
as a thoroughgoing Platonist who only plays at being an Aristotelian within
medieval culture at large. But Cohen's view of Aristotle in this essay seems
anachronistic to the modern reader. Today, Aristotelian ethics is dominant,
either as "virtue ethics" in the work of Alasdair MacIntyre or as a statement of self-insufficiency and the need for others in the work of Martha
Nussbaum.[2] Still, Cohen describes Aristotle's thought as "hostility against
the idea, against the idea of the Good . . . if the Idea is generally of no value,
then the idea of the Good cannot have value either" (CEM 239). Almost a
century later, we can read this description as being too extreme. We know

1977), 127, 164; Andrea Poma, *The Critical Philosophy of Hermann Cohen*, trans. John Denton
(Albany: State University of New York Press, 1997), 73–78; Klaus Köhnke, *The Rise of Neo-
Kantianism: German Academic Philosophy between Idealism and Positivism*, trans. R. J. Hollingdale
(Cambridge: Cambridge University Press, 1991), 170–78, 267.
[2] Cf. Alasdair MacIntyre, *After Virtue*, 2nd ed. (Notre Dame, Ind.: University of Notre Dame
Press, 1984), 277: "It scarcely needs repeating that it is the central thesis of *After Virtue*
that the Aristotelian moral tradition is the best example we possess of a tradition whose
adherents are rationally entitled to a high measure of confidence in its epistemological and
moral resources." Also cf. Martha Nussbaum, *The Fragility of Goodness* (Cambridge: Cambridge
University Press, 1986), 20: the advantage of Aristotelian philosophy over Plato's emphasis on
self-sufficiency is that Aristotelian philosophy offers "a kind of human worth that is inseparable from vulnerability, an excellence that is in its nature other-related and social . . . in whose
values openness, receptivity, and wonder play an important part."

that Aristotelian and Neoplatonic themes share an uneasy togetherness in the *Guide*; we know that Aristotle is *not* an enemy of the concept of goodness *tout court*, but only of *Cohen's* idealized concept of goodness derived from the sixth book of Plato's *Republic*.

Nevertheless, the section of Cohen's "Charakteristik" on the relation between privation and negation does serve two important purposes for our preliminary observations on what is at stake in meontological thinking. First, Cohen is clearer here than in the *Religion of Reason* on the unique nature of Maimonides' doctrine of the "so-called" negative attributes (CEM 248). What Maimonides is doing is not negative theology, which would simply be a learned ignorance of God or a realization that this essence is unknowable. Cohen argues that God's essence is indeed knowable for Maimonides. Through the meontological technique of describing God as the negation of the multiple privations of the created world, the true nature of God as ethical comes into view: "the purpose of the increase in negations is to help Maimonides towards the increase in the true, fruitful, that is to say the ethical, knowledge of God" (CEM 254). In Cohen's eyes, then, the *Guide* offers no such thing as negative theology, even though Maimonides places limits on the language that one can use to describe God. Second, Cohen argues that the Maimonidean doctrine of creation, rooted in meontological principles, contains a temporal element that governs the teleological path of the *Guide*. The created realm is one of privation and possibility, but the definition of possibility is for Cohen dialectically related to a future actuality. The "not" of creation qua realm of privation is future-oriented: "that which is possible is that which is *not yet* actual" (CEM 254). Created existence is never without a propulsive longing to realize itself. For Cohen, the path engendered by this propulsion is Torah, a gradual coming-to-be of actuality and passing-away of privation.

It is all too easy to argue against Cohen's reading of Maimonides. From whom is Maimonides supposed to have gotten his Platonic orientation? In the *Guide*, the only Platonic dialogue mentioned is the *Timaeus*, whereas Cohen's reading of the Plato–Maimonides relationship depends on the assumption that Maimonides is familiar with the arguments of the *Parmenides* and *Sophist*. Furthermore, Cohen's argument is a reductive syllogism: (1) Aristotle is an enemy of the good; (2) Plato is a friend of the good; (3) Maimonides is a friend of the good; (4) Maimonides is a friend of Plato and not Aristotle. Indeed, a cynic would charge Cohen with misreading Maimonides in order to delineate a history within the Jewish tradition of Cohen's own theory of correlation between humankind and God, in which humankind depends upon God for existence, and God depends upon humans for the actualization and unfolding of God's being.[3] Yet this theory is apparently controverted by Maimonides himself in *Guide* I:52, in which he states that

[3] Cf. RV 102–3/88.

"it is clear at first glance that there is no correlation between Him and the things created by Him" (G 117).[4] The Arabic term used by Maimonides for "correlation" here, *idafa*, refers rather specifically to a relation between two terms that cannot be conceived separately in the mind, such as parent and child.[5] To posit a correlation between humans and God in this framework would mean that God could not be a completely independent entity. God would no longer be the necessary existent that Maimonides defines God to be. God would be contingent, and God and humanity would in some way be interdependent. For this reason, Maimonides' refusal at chapter I:52 of the *Guide* to posit a correlation between God and humans is grounded in the claim that "He has a necessary existence while that which is other than He has a possible/contingent existence" (G 117). If God is in need of anything from humankind, we can no longer speak of God as the negation of privation. If God needs humankind in order to actually be, as Cohen indeed thinks – "It is as if God's being were actual *[aktuell]* in man's knowledge only" (RV 103/88) – then God is deprived of something that God should, by God's very nature as the negation of all privation, possess. And if we introduce privation into the God-idea here, we lose the philosophical right to protect God from other privations, other expressions of finitude, such as corporeality. As a result, it is necessary to return strictly to the framework of the *Guide* to establish whether Cohen is being as faithful to Maimonidean meontology as he claims. One must forge a Maimonidean map of privation and negation, matter and form, the human moral path and death.

MAIMONIDEAN MEONTOLOGY

The first mention of privation – what Cohen understands to be *to mē on* – in Maimonides' *Guide of the Perplexed* appears at *Guide* I:17 (G 43). I have divided it into sections for handier analysis.

1. Now you know that the principles of the existents subject to generation and corruption are three: Matter, Form, and Particularized Privation, which is always connected *[muqarin]*[6] with matter.

---

4 It should be noted that the most sustained effort to rehabilitate Cohen for a postmodern age, by Almut Sh. Bruckstein, is cognizant of Cohen's misreadings of the tradition and therefore attempts to make other arguments for his conclusions. Cf. "Hermann Cohen's 'Charakteristik der Ethik Maimunis': A Reconstructive Reading of Maimonides' Ethics" (Ph.D. diss., Temple University, 1992); Bruckstein, "On Jewish Hermeneutics: Maimonides and Bachya as Vectors in Cohen's Philosophy of Origin," in *Hermann Cohen's Philosophy of Religion*, ed. Stéphane Mosès and Hartwig Wiedebach (Hildesheim: Olms, 1997); Bruckstein, "Joining the Narrators: A Philosophy of Talmudic Hermeneutics," in *Reasoning after Revelation*, ed. Peter Ochs, Robert Gibbs, and Steven Kepnes (Boulder, Colo.: Westview Press, 1998), 105–21.
5 Edward William Lane, *Lexicon of the Arabic Language* (Cambridge: Islam Texts Society, 1984). I thank Diana Lobel for assistance with the nuances of Arabic vocabulary here.
6 The alteration of Shlomo Pines's translation of the *Guide* here is Diana Lobel's.

2. For, were it not for this connection with Privation, Matter would not receive Form. It is in this sense that Privation is to be considered as one of the principles.

3. However, when a form is achieved, the particular privation in question, I mean the privation of the form that is achieved, disappears, and another privation is conjoined with matter; and this goes on for ever, as has been made clear in natural science.

4. Now as even those upon whom the charge of corruption would not be laid in the event of clear exposition used terms figuratively and resorted to teaching in similes, how much all the more is it incumbent upon us, the community of those adhering to Law, not to state explicitly a matter that is either remote from the understanding of the multitude or the truth of which as it appears to the imagination of these people is different from what is intended by us. Know this also.

Guide I:17 progresses from an aping of Aristotelian arguments toward a complete embracing of the Plotinian worldview. The section I have identified as (1) is almost a carbon copy of Aristotle's *Metaphysics* 1069b32–34, which states that the principles of the beings that come to be and pass away are matter, form, and privation. If Maimonides were explicitly adhering to a Plotinian worldview, then presumably he would have stated that there are only two principles, form and matter (as Plotinus does at *Enneads* II.4). However, the second half of (1), that is, the statement that matter is always and everywhere "connected" with privation, is closer to a Plotinian argument, since Plotinus explicitly equates matter and privation. (Plotinus states that Aristotle's definition of privation as a quality – for example, a blind individual has the quality of blindness – is inaccurate. Rather, "privation is certainly not quality or qualified, but lack of quality or of something else, as soundlessness does not belong to sound or anything else [positive]; for privation is a taking away [*arsis*], but qualification is a matter of positive assertion.")[7] But Maimonides is not explicitly separating matter and privation as Aristotle does. The language of "connection" skirts the question of whether the number of principles is actually two or three. Thus it appears that, in (1), Maimonides' position is stretched between that of Aristotle and that of Plotinus.

When we turn to (2), the un-Aristotelian tone is brought into further relief. Maimonides here argues that the inclusion of privation as one of the three principles is necessary in order to explain how matter can receive form. The language of reception is rather un-Aristotelian; although both Aristotle and Plotinus see form as being in matter, only Plotinus uses the strong language of reception (cf. *Enneads* III.4.1.15). Finally, the claim in

---

7 *Enneads* II.4.13.21–23. The translation is A. H. Armstrong's, from *Enneads* (Cambridge, Mass.: Harvard University Press, 1966–88).

statement (3) of the eternal conjunction of matter with privation is decidedly un-Aristotelian. Maimonides is here claiming that every object X will
always be marked under the sign of the privative "not" (for if an X not-Y
object becomes Y, it is now not-X, not to mention not-Z, etc.). This does not
correspond with Aristotle at all; if a blind individual regains sight, Aristotle
does not describe his or her faculty of vision as the privation of blindness.
Maimonides here seems to be defining matter in terms of an eternal connection with the category of privation, closer to the view found in the
Enneads. For Maimonides, privation says something about what it means
to exist within the material world; this is true of Plotinus but not true of
Aristotle.

What is at stake in this Maimonidean account of privation that I have used
to argue for a Plotinian meontology in the *Guide*? The answer to this question
is literary. Plotinus does not have a strict argument leading from the nature
of nonbeing to the desire of the soul for the One; rather, the empirical
observation of the desire to turn toward pleasure and away from pain is
associated with the nature of nonbeing. Plotinus implies, at *Enneads* III.5.1,
that the distance between the embodied individual and the One leads to
a relationship of the most intimate and fervent desire. The soul's desire
for the One is the desire to replace the pain associated with the evil of the
material world with the pleasure of seeing beauty and is contingent upon
recognizing the world of matter as evil. This association finds a parallel in
the *Guide* in the literary transition from I:17 to I:18. It is only in recognizing
the privative state of embodied existence that we come to realize that the
soul's desire is a desire for God, and come to wish to articulate this desire
in terms of a path that will bring one nearer to God.

Leo Strauss has previously noticed the oddness of *Guide* I:17. In "How to
Begin to Study *The Guide of the Perplexed*" (G xxx), Strauss notes a striking
interruption of the continuity of the argument in the sudden shift from
the previous lexicographical chapters (i.e., analyses of the various semantic
meanings of words that appear in the Bible) to the discussion of the prohibition of the masses' education in divine and natural science. Although
Strauss claims that I:17 and the other nonlexicographic chapters (i.e., those
that do not perform semantic analyses) of the first part of the *Guide* "are
subtly interwoven with the chapters preceding and following them," the primary conclusion he draws from I:17 is not about this interweaving per se.
Instead, the reader comes upon musings on the role of the numeral 17
in Maimonidean numerology: "17 stands for nature." Strauss's analysis is
simultaneously tantalizing and frustrating, and invites a wrestling with the
relationship between the lexicographic and nonlexicographic sections of
the first part of the *Guide*. It would not be an overstatement to say that
Maimonides' crafting skills come to the fore at I:17. The sudden insertion of
a nonlexicographic section into the first part of the *Guide* serves as a wake-
up call, which guides the reader to further reflection upon the thematic

connection between the metaphysical discussion and the equivocal language analyzed in the subsequent section.

Guide I:17 is thus not only Maimonides' reminder to his disciple. Joseph of basic metaphysics; neither is it only an esoteric argument for Plotinus over and above Aristotle. It is a signal that leads the reader to pay special attention to the citations and analyses of biblical texts that follow. The reader's concentration is already heightened when the reader returns to lexicographical analysis in *Guide* I:18, which deals with senses of "approach" or "drawing near" in the Bible. In the literary structure of the *Guide*, the brief discussion of privation calls forth a discussion of nearing and, as the context of I:18 makes clear, a discussion of what it means to near God. As nonbeing in Plotinus gives rise to the desire for its contrary and the discipline necessary for eliminating it from the soul, the discussion of privation in Maimonides gives rise to a discussion of how to conquer privation by nearing God through cognitive apprehension, that is, through prophecy.

Even as a member of the list of equivocal terms, "nearing" is by no means clear in the *Guide*. There is no firm answer to the question of whether the goal of nearing is union with the telos, or whether nearness to God is in itself the goal. At the opening of I:18, Maimonides writes that approach and nearing refer in the figurative sense to "the union of cognition with what is cognized, which is, as it were, similar to the proximity of one body to another" (G 44). Spatial nearness thus seems to be a code for cognitive union. There are certain points in the *Guide* at which Maimonides seems to define all cognition as unitive. At I:68 Maimonides argues from the example of cognizing as a piece of wood an object within the field of vision:

The thing that is intellectually cognized is the abstract form of the piece of wood, that this form is identical with the intellect realized *in actu*, and that these are not two things – intellect and the intellectually cognized form of the piece of wood . . . Whenever, therefore, you assume that an intellect exists *in actu*, that intellect is identical with the apprehension of what has been intellectually cognized. (G 164)

Maimonides takes the Aristotelian view, found most readily at *De Anima* III:5 (430a17–18) that when the mind successfully apprehends an object, its essence is its act: "the act of the intellect, which is its apprehension, is the true reality and the essence of the intellect" (G 164). The cognizing subject is nothing outside of its acts of apprehension. Yet this apprehension is nothing else than *poiēsis*, the creation as representation within mind of the pure abstract form of the cognized object, stripped away from its material substrate. If the intellecting subject is no more than the content of its acts of intellectual apprehension, and if the content of each act of apprehension is the formal nature of the cognized object, then by syllogistic reasoning, successful cognition is the union of subject and object.

Yet I:18 at certain points moves away from the unitive model of I:68. The figurative meaning of drawing near is later described as "union in/of knowledge and drawing near through apprehension" (G 44).[8] If knowledge is nothing outside of its acts of apprehension, as I:68 tells us, then the reader should rightly ask, "Which is it: union or drawing near?" Presumably, it cannot be both. The situation is further complicated by Maimonides' use of phrases such as "nearness through cognition, I mean cognitive apprehension" and the condemnation of all such spatial vocabulary in the name of the nonspatial nature of the cognitive relationship: "there is no nearness and proximity, and no remoteness, no union and no separation, no contact and no succession" (G 44). At the same time that the unitive model is decried as linguistically falling short of the mark, the spatial language is still necessary, given that Maimonides claims that "there are very many gradations in being near to or far away from Him [in respect of apprehension]" (G 45). While this most probably simply means that every actual cognition of God contains the potential for a more complete cognition of God, this statement raises the disturbing corollary that this more complete cognition would involve the cognition of another part of God – and God, as absolutely simplex, cannot have parts.

I stated earlier that a literary analysis of the *Guide* reveals that the discussion of privation calls forth a discussion of nearing God. This does not mean that Maimonides has no argumentation to back this up; it simply means that this argumentation is not to be found in I:17 or I:18. Instead, it is necessary to turn to I:55. There Maimonides makes the claim, common to both Aristotle and Plotinus, that "privation is necessarily attached to all potentiality" (G 45). Potentiality contains within it its teleological vector; potentiality is always potentiality-for-something-actual. But what is this actuality in the case of the self mired in the prison house of the material world? In I:18 Maimonides claims that nearing God is the answer to the question of what constitutes the human's passage from potentiality to actuality. Yet in this very answer, Maimonides once again reveals his Plotinian colors. As stated in the earlier analysis of I:17, Maimonides views the realm of generation and corruption as a realm eternally deprived of form at least in some respect. As long as an object possesses matter, it will stand essentially opposed to the form that is intellection in actuality. True enough, some of my potentialities may become actual. I may start moving, and thus actualize the potentiality of rest; I may even cognize a piece of wood. Nevertheless, in Maimonides' view the self can never become pure actuality. Actuality is the province of God: "all His perfections must exist in actuality, and nothing may belong to Him that exists potentially in any respect whatever" (G 128). The privation of

---

[8] The same uneasy cohabitation of the rhetoric of nearness and union can be found in Neoplatonic writings. At *The Life of Plotinus* 23.15–16, Porphyry writes that Plotinus' "end and goal was to be united to, to approach (*henothemai kai pelasai*) the God who is over all things."

actuality is the province of humankind and the material world. The central claim of Maimonides' "negative theology" in *Guide* I:58 – that in discussing divine attributes, any attribute signifies "the negation of the privation of the attribute in question" (G 136) – is a further corollary of the claim in I:55 that "one must likewise of necessity deny, with reference to Him, His being similar to any existing thing." God and humankind could not be more different.

Existing things – including humans – are thus completely dissimilar from God. In the exploration of Maimonides' appropriation of the Greek doctrine of *to mē on*, one conclusion cannot be avoided. Maimonides follows Greek thinking to the utmost insofar as meontology is not a study of God. *To mē on* is not opposed to being in the same sense as Levinas's beyond-being. For Maimonides, God is in no sense deprived of being, but is being in its most pure actuality. God's essence is hyperessential with respect to what goes by the name of essence in the material world;[9] God's existence is hyperessential with respect to what goes by the name of existence in the material world. Meontology in Aristotle, Plotinus, and Maimonides is a study of the world as utterly deprived of being in any meaningful – that is, absolute – sense. For any philosopher who uses God as the yardstick of being, there is no choice but to look upon the material world as meontological, as inferior if not evil. Insofar as this is the case, Maimonides follows standard Plotinian accounts of matter as concomitant with *to mē on* and hence "evil" insofar as it is not completely actualized.[10]

At the opening of the discussion of providence in the third part of the *Guide*, Maimonides affirms other philosophers' belief that "matter is a strong veil preventing the apprehension of that which is separate from matter as it truly is. It does this even if it is the matter of the heavenly spheres" (III:9; G 436). Matter is always associated with privation: the nature of the matter created by God "consists in matter always being a concomitant of privation, as is known" (III:10; G 440). And "all evils are privations," as Maimonides writes earlier in the same chapter (G 439), because evils have no essence of their own but are evils only in privative relation to some good. Thus, matter and evil share a strong family resemblance. Insofar as human existence is material existence, it would seem to be as separate as possible from the goodness Maimonides associates with God.

Nevertheless, these claims cannot be all-encompassing. What is important in the denial of attributes of relation (for this would place God and

---

9 Cf. Alfred L. Ivry, "Maimonides on Creation," in *Creation and the End of Days: Judaism and Scientific Cosmology*, ed. David Novak and Norbert Samuelson (Lanham, Md.: University Press of America, 1986), 191–92.

10 Cf. Harry A. Wolfson, "The Meaning of *Ex Nihilo* in the Church Fathers, Arabic and Hebrew Philosophy, and St. Thomas," in *Studies in the History of Philosophy and Religion*, ed. Isidore Twersky and George H. Williams (Cambridge, Mass.: Harvard University Press, 1973), 1: 212.

humankind in the same species), or in the claims of I:52 and I:55 that God is not similar to creatures, is not the denial of similarity *tout court*, but the denial of similarity to a *thing*, that is, to a substance. If it is possible to think of certain of God's creatures in non-spatiotemporal ways, then the language of similarity can creep back into the *Guide* in another fashion. This is not very difficult; a human individual is more than simply material substance, and even more than formal qualities existing within or imposed onto material substance. The similarity between God and humankind lies on a completely different axis than that of substance: that of act.[11]

Maimonides defines God at I:68 as pure intellect, divorced from the spatiotemporal world. Intellect here is not reified; for Maimonides, the definition of God as pure self-apprehension is a description of life: "life and knowledge form in this case one notion" (G 122).[12] God does not possess knowledge as some sort of faculty, but simply knows; God is not the knower but knowing. God does not possess life, but is simply living. God does not possess intellect, but is simply intelligencing. To define God as intellect is to define God as pure actuality and acting. To define God as intellect is to highlight the difference between God and God's creatures by refusing to stain God with the language of reification of substance. Kenneth Seeskin has recently written that "to say that God cannot be defined [as Maimonides does in *Guide* I:52] is to say that even claims like 'God is pure intellect' or 'God is pure activity,' though helpful up to a point, are misleading...for they still try to make God fall within conceptual boundaries, to condition the unconditioned."[13] However, in no way does my analysis of Maimonides' language conceptualize God; I make no claim to understand the mechanism of God's intellecting activity. Indeed, I have no rich knowledge of what the concept of "pure intellect" and "pure activity" mean. Although I can argue that God can and must be defined by these terms, I cannot make any substantive claims on the basis of these definitions that would condition God in any manner.

To speak of God as "pure activity" echoes what is now commonplace within studies of Maimonidean "negative theology": the only attributes allowed of God are attributes of action; we cannot speak of what God is – as when we say that John Doe is a weaver – but only of what God does – as when we say that Mr. Doe is he who miraculously quickly handwove these 1, 000-thread-count sheets. To speak of God as, for example, a weaver is not only to attribute ontological multiplicity to God (for God would thus have

---

[11] I am greatly indebted to Diana Lobel, "'Silence Is Praise to You': Maimonides on Negative Theology, Looseness of Expression, and Religious Experience," *American Catholic Philosophical Quarterly* 76:1 (2002), 25–49, for the conclusions that follow.

[12] Cf. Aristotle, *Metaphysics*, trans. Apostle, Λ.7, 1072b26–27: "Life belongs to God, for the actuality (*energeia*) of the intellect is life, and God is actuality."

[13] Kenneth Seeskin, *Searching for a Distant God: The Legacy of Maimonides* (New York: Oxford University Press, 2000), 33.

qualities/properties and no longer be simplex) but also to introduce motion and hence embodiment into our language.[14] When we speak about humans in terms of attributes of action, we speak in terms of attributes that are "remote from the essence of the thing" of which said attributes are predicated (G 119). Thus, Maimonides gives the example in I:52 of Zayd as a carpenter. This refers to Zayd's action of, for example, door making, while his essence as a man remains hidden behind this action. Knowing that Zayd made the door tells us nothing about what it means for Zayd to be a rational animal. By analogy, one would conclude that knowing God's actions tells us nothing about God's supposed essential attributes. Arthur Hyman gives the following example:

Suppose that (*a*) a being *X* exists in an otherwise empty room; (*b*) wood, nails, and other materials are introduced into the room; (*c*) nothing miraculous happens in the room; and (*d*) after some time a finished table is handed out of the room. From these conditions we can infer that *X* has the ability to make a table, though we do not gain any knowledge of what kind of being *X* is or of any property that enables *X* to make a table.[15]

This is an apt description of what Maimonides is aiming at when he writes at I:58 that God is not a creator but that "His existence suffices for the bringing into existence of things other than He" (G 136).

However, Hyman's and Seeskin's arguments assume that God's essence or properties remain hidden behind our material veil, whereas Maimonides asserts many times in the *Guide* that God cannot have any properties whatsoever because the language of quality with reference to God introduces ontological multiplicity. This would also have to include hidden properties. The essence of God is *not* hidden to humans; Maimonides baldly tells the reader at I:58 that the essence of God is existence (G 136).[16] This is the only "property" that God has, and an analysis of the divine life (existence) leads to certain claims about divine knowledge, divine eternality, creation, and so forth. It would therefore seem that the limiting of divine attributes to attributes of action does not posit a set of hidden divine attributes that our finite minds cannot know. Rather, to speak in terms of attributes of action is a consequence of the great extent of our knowledge, because this language reflects our knowledge that only for God are essence and existence one.

[14] Cf. Arthur Hyman, "Maimonides on Religious Language," in Kraemer, *Perspective on Maimonides*, ed. Joel L. Kraemer (Oxford: Oxford University Press, 1991), 185–86, esp. 186n. 33.

[15] Ibid., 186.

[16] This is the starting point of Alexander Altmann's "Essence and Existence in Maimonides," in *Studies in Religious Philosophy and Mysticism* (Ithaca, N.Y.: Cornell University Press, 1969), 108–27. Yet Altmann does not apply this to the issue of Maimonidean "negative theology." On the other hand, Charles Manekin, "Belief, Certainty, and Divine Attributes in the *Guide of the Perplexed*," *Maimonidean Studies* 1 (1990), 117–41, esp. 136, moves in this direction, although Manekin does not cite Altmann's essay.

In speaking of God's actions instead of God's properties, theology is more precise because God's "being" is nothing outside of God's acting.[17]

This interpretation of I:58 is, on the surface, at odds with direct claims that Maimonides makes at I:54, primarily the pithy statement that "His essence cannot be grasped as it really is" (G 123). Maimonides bolsters this claim through narrating the conversation between Moses and God at Ex. 33:20–23. Here, Moses asks to see the divine glory, which Maimonides interprets to be identical to the divine essence; God responds by both assenting only to Moses' request from Ex. 33:13 to see God's ways and rebuffing the request for vision of God's essence, informing Moses that God's face cannot be seen.[18] Nevertheless, it may be the case that the contradiction between I:54 and I:58 is only apparent. Alexander Altmann has noted that Maimonides oscillates between two notions of essence in the *Guide*. On one hand, essence can refer to the true reality of an object and be expressed in the language of a definition that notes the genus and the specific differentiae of an object. On the other hand, there is the essence of God that is God's existence, as expressed in the name of God of Ex. 3:14 *'ehyeh asher 'ehyeh*, "I am that I am."[19] Thus, when God responds to Moses' request to see the divine essence by showing Moses God's ways – by which Maimonides understands the totality of the beings that are the result of the act of creation – this does not contradict Moses' request to see God's essence, if "essence" is understood in the sense in which it applies to God. Moses asks to see God's essence. God responds by showing Moses God's existence – God's life of intellecting action that creates and maintains the world and its creatures (III:21; G 485), for created things "follow upon His knowledge, which preceded and established them as they are." This is not to say that one can imagine how God is that which God is; one cannot map out the mechanism by which thought in and of itself is creative. If "you cannot see my face" means anything, it is this. Such would appear to be the upshot of Maimonides' statement in III:21:

For through knowing the true reality of His own immutable essence, He also knows the totality of what necessarily derives from all His acts. For us to desire to have an intellectual cognition of the way this comes about is as if we desired that we be He and our apprehension be His apprehension. He who studies true reality equitable ought accordingly to believe that nothing is hidden in any way from Him, may He be exalted, but that, on the contrary, everything is revealed to His knowledge, which is His essence, and that it is impossible for us to know in any way this kind of

---

[17] Likewise, Philo associated the properties of God with his actions. Philo argues that this must be the case because God's properties must be simplex, as he is, and actions cannot be converted into the language of substance and attribute that threatens the noncomposite nature of God. Cf. Harry Wolfson, *Philo: Foundations of Religious Philosophy in Judaism, Christianity, and Islam* (Cambridge, Mass.: Harvard University Press, 1947), 130ff.

[18] There are similar interpretations of this conversation at I:21 (G 48) and I:37 (G 86).

[19] Altmann, "Essence and Existence in Maimonides," 110.

apprehension. If we knew how it comes about, we would have an intellect in virtue of which an apprehension of this kind might be had.

But that is not to say that we cannot know the facts *that* God's essence is action and *that* creation of the world is the result of divine self-apprehension. To deny this would be to deny that the descriptions of God's actions in the Torah give us any insight into God's existence, and would undermine the very project of the *Guide* – to reconcile the Torah with philosophy. Maimonides means to say only that we cannot know *how* God is that which God is; to describe this "how" would require a recourse to language that is mechanistic and material – since machines are material – and therefore entirely unsuited to God's immaterial and simplex nature.

Intellect qua action is the axis on which theology is allowed to posit similarities between God and humankind. It is in this sense that Maimonides, in the opening chapter of the *Guide*, explains that the relationship of image between man and God – as expressed in Gen. 1:26, "Let us make man in our image" – is one of intellect. Gen. 1:26 speaks the way that it does "because of the divine intellect conjoined with man" (G 23). If image, in the Bible, refers to "the true reality of the thing in so far as the latter is that particular being" (G 22), then the true reality of humanity is intellect. However, this is veiled by the material shape in which this intellect lies. Intellect is thus the most perfect part of human nature – it is the divine part of human nature – but the language of intellect in Maimonides is a language of action, of intellecting. The intellect is not a thing, as the brain is, because its essence is action: "And it has become clear that the act of every intellect, which act consists in its being intellectually cognizing is identical with the essence of that intellect" (I:68; G 164). And this is true for both humans (G 164) and God (G 165).

The evidence examined thus far points to a bifurcation in the essence of humankind. On one axis, as already seen, humankind is material and God is not, and never the twain shall meet. God and the human are infinitely distant, and God is absolutely transcendent. To threaten this supreme distance in any way would be to imagine God as a body, which would be both heretical and false. On the other axis, God and humankind are both intellectual. God and the human are infinitesimally close and exist in some sort of intimate relationship. This double viewpoint is suggested by Simon Rawidowicz: "Maimonides envisaged *both* the maximum of remoteness and the infinite[simal] nearness between God and man."[20]

This bifurcation is at stake in much of the secondary literature on Maimonides in the last fifty years, which has dealt with the extent of the role

[20] Simon Rawidowicz, "Knowledge of God: A Study in Maimonides' Philosophy of Religion," in *Studies in Jewish Thought*, ed. Nahum Glatzer (Philadelphia: Jewish Publication Society, 1974), 269–304. The quoted passage is on 271; I read "infinitesimal" for "infinite" here, since "infinite nearness" is an awkward phrase.

of the intellect in the description of the human telos in Maimonides. Is human perfection intellectual perfection, or moral perfection? Given the equivalence that Maimonides draws between intellect and act, I am puzzled as to why this has to be a choice. In any case, the fact of this choice has long been taken for granted, and it lies at the bottom of the debate between Shlomo Pines and Alexander Altmann on the nature of ultimate human perfection in the *Guide*.[21] For Pines, the ontological gap between the completely transcendent God and the finite individual is never bridged in the least. The divide between the two poles is so great for Pines that he argues that Maimonides is fundamentally anti-Aristotelian on the issue of human perfection. Whereas for Aristotle in the final book of the *Nicomachean Ethics* the perfectly human life is a life of theory, for Maimonides human perfection is oriented toward the practical, and primarily political, life. Pines's argumentation from within the material of the *Guide* itself is primarily twofold. First, Pines cites the passage from III:9 in which Maimonides makes a blanket statement about the limitations of human reason in all contexts, since matter "is a strong veil preventing the apprehension of that which is separate" from the material world (G 436). Second, Pines gives a strong reading of Maimonides' doctrine of negative attributes, so that any knowledge of God is eliminated and knowledge is limited to "the natural phenomena and their causes,"[22] that is, natural processes. Altmann does not argue against

---

[21] Shlomo Pines, "The Limitations of Human Knowledge According to al-Farabi, ibn Bajja, and Maimonides," in *Studies in Medieval Jewish History and Literature*, ed. Isadore Twersky (Cambridge, Mass.: Harvard University Press, 1979), 82–109; Alexander Altmann, "Maimonides on the Intellect and Scope of Metaphysics," in *Von der mittelalterlichen zur modernen Aufklärung* (Tübingen: J. C. B. Mohr, 1987), 60–129. An excellent survey of the issues can be found in Menachem Kellner, *Maimonides on Human Perfection* (Atlanta: Scholars Press, 1990); I disagree with Kellner's conclusion (64) that the *Guide* is "a guide leading us from the view of God as intellect to the view of God as active in the world." I do not see any reason why these views should be regarded as mutually exclusive.

[22] Pines, 98. Recently, Pines's view has been defended and expanded by Josef Stern, in "Maimonides' Demonstrations: Principles and Practice," *Medieval Philosophy and Theology* 10 (2001), 47–84, and Stern, "Maimonides on Language and the Science of Language," in *Maimonides and the Sciences*, ed. R. S. Cohen and H. Levine (Dordrecht: Kluwer Academic Publishers, 2000), 173–226. Stern's argument rests on a claim that all language necessarily fails when it tries to describe God, since God's noncomposite nature cannot be spoken of in the subject-predicate limitations of human language ("Language," 206ff.) Because of this failure, Maimonides states that "we are only able to apprehend the fact that He is (*'anniyya*) and cannot apprehend His quiddity (*mahiyya*)" (G 135). For Stern, Maimonides' avoidance of using the predicate "existence" (*wujud*) tells the reader of the *Guide* that "we cannot even apprehend that God *exists*, only the fact that He is" ("Demonstrations," 71). Nevertheless, although we can know the fact that God is, Maimonides seems to be clear that we can also make further conclusions. For example, we can say that God governs the world through an overflow that emanates from God to the Active Intellect (G 275). Apprehension of this "fact" is not the same as apprehending that "existence" is a predicate to be attributed to God and does not constitute any apprehension of God's quiddity. Knowledge of acts, granted in an account of God as intellect without knowing the mechanism of how this works, seems

Pines that there are no limitations to human knowledge – for example, Altmann asserts that Maimonides does not believe in the possible conjunction of the human intellect with the Active Intellect (the intellect that governs the tenth and lowest sphere, according to medieval cosmology)[23] – yet he does argue that there is a theoretical perfection that is described in Maimonides' theory of the actualized "acquired" human intellect. This perfection is, in Altmann's view, a state of similarity to the Active Intellect. This perspective, unlike Pines's, allows for humans to have some metaphysical knowledge by achieving perfection in divine science. Because there is some apprehension of the divine in the *Guide* according to Altmann, one can describe his viewpoint as positing a greater degree of ontological intimacy between the human and the divine than the interpretation of Pines.

The range of views on what constitutes human perfection for Maimonides is due in great part to the difficulty of III:54, the final section of the *Guide*, in which Maimonides describes human perfection in apparently opposing manners. In a sequential ranking of four perfections, the fourth and highest perfection

> is the true human perfection; it consists in the acquisition of the rational virtues – I refer to the conception of intelligibles, which teach true opinions concerning divine things. This is in true reality the ultimate end; this is what gives the individual true perfection, a perfection belonging to him alone; and it gives him permanent perdurance; through it man is man. (G 635)

Intellectual perfection is the perfection of humankind's essence, and it lies higher than moral perfection, Maimonides' third perfection. This stance resonates with many passages in the *Guide*, particularly III:27, where Maimonides flatly asserts that human "perfection is to become rational *in actu*" (G 511), and III:51, where Maimonides describes the exalted ranks of the Patriarchs and Moses within Jewish tradition as due to "the union of their intellects [with God] through apprehension of Him" (G 623). Yet shortly after this passage – almost at the very end of the *Guide* – Maimonides seems to change his mind and reverse the hierarchy of perfections to one in which moral or practical perfection is superior to intellectual perfection. Using Jer. 9:23 as a prooftext, Maimonides claims that devotion to God is not merely an intellectual delight but also a delight in God's attributes of action (G 637–38). The way of life of this truly perfect individual "will always have in view loving-kindness, righteousness and judgment, through assimilation to His actions, may He be exalted, just as we have explained several times in this treatise." Here it does seem, as Cohen will argue, that morality is the essence of God.

---

to me to stake out a middle ground between mere knowledge of the fact that God is and metaphysical knowledge of God's quiddity.

[23] Altmann, "Maimonides on Metaphysics," 84.

But to view the poles of this dichotomy as mutually exclusive would be a mistake. In III:53 (G 632), the divine actional attributes of loving-kindness, righteousness, and judgment are described in intellectualist terms, thus forestalling any distinction that commentators might want to make between the theoretical and the practical.

When refuting the doctrine of divine attributes, we have already explained that every attribute by which God is described in the books of the prophets is an attribute of action. Accordingly He is described as *chasid* [one possessing loving-kindness] because He has brought the all into being; as *tzaddiq* [righteous] because of His mercy toward the weak – I refer to the providence[24] of the living being by means of its forces; and as *shophet* [Judge] because of the occurrence in the world of relative good things and of relative great calamities, necessitated by judgment that is consequent upon wisdom.

It is true that in this description, only the actional attribute of *mishpat* (judgment) is described in explicitly intellectualist terms; judgment is consequent upon the wisdom that constitutes God's essence as self-intellecting existence. Yet the description of the other two attributes can also be recast into intellectualist language; to do so, it is necessary to follow Maimonides' advice to his student Joseph that "if you wish to grasp the totality of what this Treatise contains, then you must connect its chapters one with another" (G 15). Here in III:53, the divine *ḥesed*, or loving-kindness, is expressed through God's creation of the world. Thus we have a link between a *practical* perfection and creation. However, in the first part of the *Guide*, in the discussion of the divine attributes to which Maimonides directs his reader (I:58; G 136), Maimonides interprets creation to be a necessary corollary of God's essence described as *intellectual* perfection, a consequence of God's being described as the negation of all privations associated with the material realm. Thus when God is described as "powerful," this means that God is the negation of all privations associated with powerlessness. For Maimonides, this entails that God is ultimately powerful, that "His existence suffices for the bringing into existence of things other than He."

The chain of reasoning is thus as follows. First, Maimonides states in I:68 that "it has been demonstrated that God is an intellect *in actu.*" Second, it is necessary to describe this intellect through the language of "negation of privation," as Maimonides claims in I:58. Since privation is always concomitant with matter; it is necessary to protect the transcendence of God by protecting our conception of God from the material realm. Third, the language of "negation of privation" necessitates our speaking of God as Creator, not only because God is sufficiently powerful to create but also because the actuality of divine self-apprehension entails creation. Here it is important to cite the enigmatic passage from III:21 in which Maimonides describes God as

[24] The translation here follows Kellner, 34.

knowing things into being: "through knowing the true reality of His own immutable essence, He also knows the totality of what necessarily derives from His acts" (G 485). But God's acts are God's intellectual apprehensions; God is an intellect *in actu* (G 165), which essentially is its acts of apprehension (G 164). The creation of the world is thus a corollary of God's ultimate intellectual perfection; there is no difference between cognition and action when speaking of God. With regard to divine *tzedaqah*/righteousness, one can construct a similar chain of reasoning reflecting the collapse of the distinction between cognition and action in the Godhead, as Maimonides links righteousness to divine providence, which he describes as an intellectual overflow from God: "According to me, as I consider the matter, divine providence is consequent upon the divine overflow, and the species with which this intellectual overflow is united . . . is the one accompanied by divine providence" (G 471–72).

Thus, while it is correct to speak of an intellectualist element to Maimonidean teleology, it is also the case that the intellectual perfection at which an individual aims will involve worldly acts. As God's intellectual perfection is performed through action, so our aim at intellectual perfection to the best of our capacity must also be performed in acts, situated within a social, political, and moral context. True intellectual worship of God has an actional component; mere contemplation cannot achieve imitation of God. Each politically or ethically wise human action in this world is a step on a path of nearing God.

To conclude, Maimonides opens up a teleological path toward the actualization of human intellect; political and/or moral action is part of this path. The privation that constitutes matter is a privation of intellect, and we can speak of this privation as the absence of something that belongs to humankind naturally and essentially. The God–human relationship in the *Guide*, described eloquently by Rawidowicz, is a new expression of the meontological conundrum. There is a relationship of infinite distance: God is the opposite of humankind, the negation of all meontological privations associated with human materiality. And there is a relationship of infinitesimal nearness: the analysis of meontology as potentiality shows the hidden essence of intellect, shared with God, that humans must actualize on their teleological path.

In the following section, I shall demonstrate that when Maimonides transfers teleology from the individual case of intellectual perfection to the broader communal sphere – to the telos for the Jewish community, which is redemption – the intellectualist nature of the teleological path remains. This has two consequences. First, the intellectualist path toward redemption abjures the realm of contingency – matter and passions – with the consequence that, because of their material dimension, the embodied persons in my community are not seen as intrinsically good. Second, my striving for intellectual perfection allows me to bypass the need to await a redeemer, giving me the freedom to live a life of Torah without fear of reprisal from other communities.

THE EXTIRPATION OF THE PASSIONS IN MAIMONIDES

There is rampant debate in the secondary literature over the extent to which Maimonides approves of an extirpation of physical and passionate desire. Much of this debate is rooted in the appearance of two contradictory arguments in *Hilkhot Déot* ("Laws of Psychological Characteristics"), an early section in the *Mishneh Torah*, the summary of Jewish law that Maimonides wrote ten to fifteen years before writing the *Guide of the Perplexed*. On the one hand, Maimonides is completely Aristotelian with regard to the emotions, saying that the good life is one that cultivates a disposition that lies at the mean between two extremes.[25] Thus, concerning anger, Maimonides writes that "a man should not be choleric, easily moved to anger, nor be like the dead without feeling, but should aim at a happy medium: be angry only for a grave cause that rightly calls for indignation, so that the like shall not be done again."[26] On the other hand, there are passages that could be described as Stoic, insofar as they argue for the extirpation of all passions.[27] What is most confusing is that the passages that express the Stoic view are proximate to those of the more Aristotelian tenor. In the very next chapter of *Hilkhot Déot*,[28] Maimonides writes that "anger, too, is an extremely bad passion, and one should avoid it to the extreme. . . . The sages charged us that anger should be avoided to such a degree that one should train oneself to be unmoved by things that naturally would provoke anger; and this is the good way." These two opposing attitudes can be found in the *Guide* as well.[29]

However we might try to solve this problem within the corpus of Maimonides itself, the fact remains that the Stoic aspects of Maimonides' ethics are not easily dismissed; indeed, commentators usually transform these

---

[25] Maimonides' account here adheres to that of the *Shemonah Peraqim* (Eight Chapters), the section of his *Commentary on the Mishnah* (c. 1168) that deals with the tractate *Pirqei Avot*. There, Maimonides writes that the goal of Torah is "for man to be natural by following the middle way." Cf. *Ethical Writings of Maimonides*, ed. and trans. Raymond L. Weiss, with Charles Butterworth (New York: New York University Press, 1975), 70.

[26] *Hilkhot De'ot* I:4; trans. Moses Hyamson in *A Maimonides Reader*, ed. Isadore Twersky (West Orange, N.J.: Behrman House, 1972), 52.

[27] This distinction should not be drawn too solidly. In *De Ira* 1.1.3, Seneca claims that his account of anger is quite close to Aristotle's. Nevertheless, Maimonides' distinction in *Hilkhot De'ot* I:5 between the mesotic ideal of the wise man (*hakham*) and the supererogatory ideal of the pious man (*chasid*) involves a contrast in the role of the passions in decision making similar to that between Aristotle and the Stoics.

[28] *Hilkhot De'ot* II:3; *A Maimonides Reader*, 54–55.

[29] The Aristotelian viewpoint can be found in II:39; the Stoic in III:8. Cf. Herbert A. Davidson, "The Middle Way in Maimonides' Ethics," *Proceedings of the American Academy for Jewish Research* 54 (1987), 46–52.

passages into an argument that the Stoic ethic of supererogation is nearer to actual rabbinic teaching than the Aristotelian ethic that is its bedfellow.[30] Yet at the same time, current readers of Maimonides should question whether the extirpation of the passions is truly part of a good life, Jewish or non-Jewish, in this world. Martha Nussbaum, in *The Therapy of Desire*, has severely critiqued the Stoic radical detachment from the world, a detachment "that greets slavery and even torture with equanimity."[31] She writes:

The state that Seneca describes is indeed called joy. But consider how he describes it. It is like a child that is born inside of one and never leaves the womb to go out into the world. it has no commerce with laughter and elation. For wise people, we know, are harshly astringent . . . [and] intolerant of idle pleasure in themselves and in others. [The shift from the Aristotelian to the Stoic account of joy] is the change from suspense and elation to solid self-absorption; from surprise and spontaneity to measured watchfulness; from wonder at the separate and external to security in that which is oneself and one's own.[32]

Maimonides' account in the final chapters of the *Guide* of the intellectual love of God marks no departure from the Stoic account of joy described here. For intellectual love is rooted in the actualization of the human intellect, that which is essential to the human, properly "one's own." One can restate Nussbaum's critique in a more theological fashion: the inward idealist move of Maimonidean teleology is a move that regards the created realm only as the necessary framing environment in which God's revelation takes place. It refuses to see the external world as intrinsically good. It does not know how to make the argument that if God is essentially goodness, then that which God creates (whether or not it is endowed with reason) must also have an essence that is essentially good. Rather, the world is seen as good only insofar as it is good-for: good for the individual who is on the path of actualizing his or her intellect and performing those actions that advance the individual along that path. The world is seen only through the lens of *utility*, as that which my intellect transcends, the necessary precondition for a future felicity that will be commensurate with God's goodness. While one might argue that this critique reads a medieval text through the filter

---

[30] See Marvin Fox, "The Doctrine of the Mean in Aristotle and Maimonides: A Comparative Study," in *Interpreting Maimonides: Studies in Methodology, Metaphysics, and Moral Philosophy* (Chicago: University of Chicago Press, 1990), 93–123; Daniel Frank, "Humility as a Virtue: A Maimonidean Critique of Aristotle's Ethics," in *Moses Maimonides and His Time*, ed. Eric L. Ormsby (Washington, D.C.: Catholic University of America Press, 1989), 89–99; Steven Schwarzschild, "Moral Radicalism and 'Middlingness' in the Ethics of Maimonides," in *The Pursuit of the Ideal*, ed. Menachem Kellner (Albany: State University of New York Press, 1990), 137–60.

[31] Martha Nussbaum, *The Therapy of Desire* (Princeton, N.J.: Princeton University Press, 1994), 363.

[32] Ibid., 400–401.

of modern sensibilities, contemporary readers nevertheless must come to terms with the ethical force of the critique.

Maimonides' tendency toward a utilitarian view of the world comes sharply into focus when one examines the relation in his writings, particularly the *Epistle to Yemen*, between the Messianic Era and the world-to-come. Maimonides' utilitarianism displays itself as a denigration of the messianic idea, at least to the extent that the Messiah is a person other than one's own intellectually perfected self.

Maimonides always draws a strict distinction between the Messianic Era and the world-to-come. The essence of the distinction is that it is the world-to-come, and not the messianic age, that is the true telos of human action. In the *Mishneh Torah*, at *Hilkhot Teshuvah* (Laws of Repentance) 9:2,[33] Maimonides codifies the difference epigrammatically:

The ultimate and perfect reward, the final bliss which will suffer neither interruption nor diminution, is the life in the world to come. The Messianic era, on the other hand, will be realized in this world; which will continue in its normal course except that independent sovereignty will be restored to Israel. The ancient sages already said, "The only difference between the present and the Messianic era is that political oppression will then cease." (B. Sanhedrin 91b)

The Messianic Era is a corporate concept; the world-to-come is individualized. In *Pereq Heleq* – a section of the early *Commentary on the Mishnah* – Maimonides describes the world-to-come as the individual soul's bodiless participation in the "supernal fellowship...with the existence of God the Creator."[34] The calm and freedom from suffering that suffuses Maimonides' descriptions of the Messianic Era, however, is not an intrinsic good. It is instrumental; the Messianic Era is always the penultimate stage in Israel's hopes and aspirations. This is clear from passages in *Pereq Heleq* and *Hilkhot Melakhim* (Laws of Kings), the final section of the *Mishneh Torah*. In *Pereq Heleq*, Maimonides writes that the conditions of the Messianic Era "give powerful [assistance] for attaining the life of the world-to-come; the telos is the world-to-come, which one must strive to attain."[35] The *Mishneh Torah* passage reads similarly:

The sages and prophets did not long for the days of the Messiah that Israel might exercise dominion over the world, or rule over the heathens, or be exalted by the nations, or that it might eat and drink and rejoice. Their aspiration was that Israel be free to devote itself to the Law and its wisdom, with no one to oppress or disturb it, and thus be worthy of life in the world to come. (*Hilkhot Melakhim*, 12:4)

---

33 Translation by M. Hyamson, reproduced in *A Maimonides Reader*, 83.   34 Ibid., 412.

35 Translation from *Ethical Writings of Maimonides*, 167. Arnold Wolf (in *A Maimonides Reader*, 416) translates: "Thus [through the fulfillment of the messianic promise, described in the previous paragraph] men will achieve the world to come. The world to come is the ultimate end to which all our effort ought to be devoted."

The Messianic Era thus has no intrinsic value; it is no more than (but, of course, no less than) a time for unfettered halakhic contemplation.[36] Maimonides believes that this contemplation is dependent upon the restoration of national sovereignty, yet national sovereignty is only the last historical stage before the onset of the utopian world-to-come. Gershom Scholem's classic either/or typology of restorative versus utopian messianism – the renewal of a bygone Golden Age or the onset of an unfathomable new era – thus reveals itself to be inadequate. Scholem describes Maimonidean messianism as merely restorative.[37] Yet the fact that Maimonidean teleology places the world-to-come as the telos of the Messianic Era implies that utopianism cannot be excluded from the picture, by fiat, for the sake of an elegant binarism.[38] Hence Maimonidean messianism has been described by Amos Funkenstein as a "realistic utopianism."[39] Politics is surely important, but only as a means to a personal intellectual end: the rational perfection of the individual soul, aided by halakhic praxis that is useful toward this end.[40] As Aviezer Ravitzky has noted, the political aspect of messianic hopes is always subservient for Maimonides to the intellectual hope for the world-to-come.[41] The activity of Jews during the Messianic Era is intellectual; as Maimonides states at the end of the *Mishneh Torah,* during that time they "will attain an understanding of their Creator to the utmost human capacity, as it is written (Is. 11:9): 'For the earth shall be full of the knowledge of the Lord, as the waters cover the sea.'"[42]

Maimonides deploys the concept of the instrumentality of the Messianic Era curiously in the *Epistle to Yemen.* While on the surface, he supports the messianic longing of the Jews of Yemen in the face of Islamic power, his support is also couched in the rhetoric of his intellectualist proclivity. He seeks to assuage the sufferings of the Yemenites by neutralizing their messianic impulse through a call to rational perfection. The effect of this rhetoric is

---

[36] Cf. Joel L. Kraemer, "On Maimonides' Messianic Posture," in *Studies in Medieval Jewish History and Literature,* ed. Isadore Twersky (Cambridge, Mass.: Harvard University Press, 1984), 2:109–42, esp. 113–14.

[37] Gershom Scholem, "Towards an Understanding of the Messianic Idea in Judaism," in *The Messianic Idea in Judaism* (New York: Schocken, 1971), 1–36, esp. 24ff.

[38] To be sure, Scholem states that in Maimonides, "a utopian content of this vision is preserved, since in the Messianic age ... the contemplative knowledge of God will become everyone's principal concern" (24). Nevertheless, Scholem minimizes the importance of the utopian in Maimonides and certainly does not see it as the overriding telos that it is.

[39] Amos Funkenstein, "Law, Philosophy, and Historical Awareness," in Funkenstein, *Perspectives of Jewish History* (Berkeley: University of California Press, 1993), 131–68, esp. 147–55. For a mediation between the views of Scholem and Funkenstein, see Aviezer Ravitzky's article "'To the Utmost Human Capacity': Maimonides on the Days of the Messiah," in Ravitzky, *History and Faith: Studies in Jewish Philosophy* (Amsterdam: J. C. Gieben, 1996), 73–112.

[40] *Guide* III:27 (G 507): "the multitude of the Sages believe that there is indubitably a cause for them [the Commandments], I mean to say a useful end."

[41] Ravitzky, 105.   [42] *Hilkhot Melakhim* 12:5; translation from *A Maimonides Reader,* 226.

to extirpate the messianic passions of his audience. I therefore take issue with David Hartman's claim that the *Epistle to Yemen* "totally ignores the instrumental interpretation of messianism expounded in [*Pereq*] *Heleq* and the *Mishneh Torah*."[43] It is true that the rhetoric of messianism in the *Epistle to Yemen* differs from that found in the *Mishneh Torah*, as the epistle is written to a community in a determinate context. Nevertheless, the instrumental interpretation of messianism is equally present in both texts.

Addressed to Jacob b. Nathaniel al-Fayyumi, the leader of the Jewish community in Yemen, Maimonides' *Epistle to Yemen* was written in 1172, at a time when the Yemenite community was besieged by proselytizing efforts on the part of the Shi'ite community there, which included Jewish apostates. These efforts had risen to the point that the leader of the Shi'ite community, 'Abd al-Nabi' ibn Mahdi, "decreed forced apostasy on Israel" (EY 101). Maimonides' immediate response is to declare that "these are surely messianic travails from the seeing and experiencing of which the sages, peace be upon them, sought God's protection" (EY 102). This response inaugurates a strategy of consolation in which Maimonides argues that the current tribulations of the Yemenites foreshadow the approaching end of those travails. This strategy is parental, as the first response of a parent to a child in pain is to assure the child that respite from pain is on its way, that "it will be over soon." Likewise, Maimonides leads his audience to believe that the Messianic Era, and hence their freedom from forced apostasy, is imminent: "it has become clear from all that Daniel and Isaiah say and from all that the sages mentioned, that he [the Messiah] would only arise when the Roman and the Arab empires have spread over the earth, as it is today" (EY 124). Belief in the imminence of the Messianic Era is thus presented as the best coping mechanism for the messianic travails. This strategy culminates in Maimonides' transmission of a remarkable family tradition which claims that the return of prophecy to Israel (and hence the imminence of the Messianic Era) will occur in fewer than forty years, in 1210 C.E. (EY 124).[44] The power of this family tradition to assuage the Yemenite community comes to the fore in

---

43 David Hartman, "Discussion of *The Epistle to Yemen*," in *Crisis and Leadership: Epistles of Maimonides*, ed. Abraham Halkin and David Hartman (Philadelphia: Jewish Publication Society, 1985), 190.

44 Maimonides' argument is rooted in a midrash on Balaam's prophecy at Numbers 23:23 ("Jacob is told at once/Yea Israel, what God has planned"). The "at once" (*ka' et*) is retranslated literally as "a like period of time," and the whole verse is interpreted to mean that prophecy will return to Israel in a like period of time as that from creation to Balaam's utterance (2,485 years). Kraemer, 119, notes that Maimonides does not actually calculate the year but instead leaves it to the reader to perform the difficult mathematical operation of doubling 2,485. Thus Maimonides protects himself from violating the halakhah (in B. Sanhedrin 97b) against calculating the date of the onset of the Messianic Era. Both Kraemer and Halkin (at *Crisis and Leadership* 145n. 223) note that Maimonides' purported family tradition is in fact rooted in Y. Shabbat VI, 9.

the following paragraph, in which Maimonides introduces evidence against other calculations of the onset of the Messianic Era, presumably to bolster his own. Lastly, in the final pages of the epistle, Maimonides responds to reports of messianic pretenders by stressing that "the prophets have predicted and instructed us, as I have told you, that pretenders and simulators will appear in great numbers at the time when the advent of the true Messiah will draw nigh" (EY 130). Here, Maimonides seems to be engaged in a fine-tuned perception of the particular needs of the Yemenite community and its leaders, and he responds in a correspondingly attuned matter.

Nevertheless, there is another strategy of consolation, which appears less frequently in the *Epistle to Yemen*,[45] and may be more ethically troublesome. Here, Maimonides appears as the sort of teacher who tells a student that he is an underachiever who can solve his problems simply by applying himself. Directly following the claim early in the epistle that the Yemenites are no doubt experiencing the prophesied messianic travails, Maimonides continues by summarizing Jacob's reports of apostasy among some members of his community and also linking this apostasy to prophetic writings, particularly in Daniel. But these prophecies are no longer linked to messianic expectation. Rather, Maimonides' response follows another rhetorical path entirely. Maimonides telescopes his argument vehemently.

And now, O our brethren, all of you must listen and consider what I am presenting to you. Instill it in the youths, children, and women, so that their weakened and unsettled faith may be made firm and that unremitting certainty may be planted in their souls. This is – may God save us and you – the true and valid religion, revealed to us by [Moses]. (EY 102)

Within the narrative structure of the epistle, it appears that the solution to the apostasy of certain Yemenites is simply to stress the (rational) *truth* of Judaism – not only to the elite but also to the masses – and the place of halakhic observance within the true life. Thus, Maimonides is no longer saying that the solution to the Yemenites' problems lies in religious ritual and will come to those who patiently wait; the solution to the difficulty of the Yemenite situation takes place in the arena of truth and reason, not in that of halakhic observance alone. Apostasy can be prevented only by stressing the *philosophical* value of the halakhic life.

Here Maimonides makes claims about the utilitarian value of Torah that will appear again thirteen years later in the *Guide*. Basing his argument on a belief that apostasy is facilitated by an understanding of all religions as formally similar and hence equal – the commandments of the Torah are

---

[45] Leo Strauss proposed that, when faced with two mutually exclusive trains of thought in Maimonides, that which appears less frequently reflects Maimonides' true position. Cf. Strauss, "The Literary Character of the *Guide of the Perplexed*," in Strauss, *Persecution and the Art of Writing* (Glencoe, Ill.: Free Press, 1952), 73.

fungible with the commandments of Islam – the insertion of a teleological element into the halakhic life becomes the wedge between Judaism and the other monotheisms.

> Were he [the Jew tempted by apostasy] to understand the inner meaning, he would recognize that the entire wisdom of the true divine Law is in its inner meaning. There is no positive or negative command save that its inner meaning contains things that bring benefit in human perfection and remove any impediments to the achievement of that perfection; and that induce ethical and rational virtues among the many according to their capacity and among the elite according to their apprehension. And through these the divine community becomes preeminent, attaining both perfections: I mean the first perfection, which is his continued existence in the world under the best conditions befitting a human being, and the second perfection, which is apprehending the intelligibles as they are in accordance with human capacity. (EY 105)

The deeper meaning of the mitzvot is their teleological role.[46] By being useful in striving after excellence, the mitzvot reveal themselves to be true and divine. By contrast, the other monotheisms are atelic simulacra of Judaism, aimed at present self-satisfaction and nothing more (EY 106). Teleology is the criterion by which the truth of religion is judged. And since the goal of teleology is broadly understood as intellectual perfection, training in speculative matters also becomes a criterion of whether or not a putatively revealed way of life is divine or not. As Maimonides writes in *Guide* II:40, a law that does not contain "attention . . . directed towards speculative matters" cannot be God-given (G 383).

At the surface of the text, Maimonides tells the Yemenite community to turn back (or at least turn with a renewed vigor) to Torah-observance. But at a deeper level, at least in certain passages of the *Epistle to Yemen,* the reason lying behind this exhortation has little to do with fostering hope in the political stability concomitant with the advent of the Messianic Era and much to do with increasing the intellectual capacity of the community. Their rational perfection will lead them to attain the knowledge of God that is itself redemptive.[47] Nowhere in the epistle is this more apparent than the

---

[46] Isadore Twersky cites this passage as a summation made for a popular audience of the viewpoint found on numerous occasions – at least 30, with Twersky's cross-references to at least as many other passages – in the *Mishneh Torah.* Twersky, *Introduction to the Code of Maimonides (Mishneh Torah)* (New Haven, Conn.: Yale University Press, 1980), 417–30.

[47] Likewise, Maimonides differentiates between living the life of Torah on the basis of knowledge of its ability to lead one to true knowledge of God and living the life of Torah on the basis of heteronomous religious authority (*taqlid*). For Maimonides, Job exemplifies the difference in these two ways of living:

> [Job] said all that he did say as long as he had no true knowledge and knew the deity only because of his acceptance of authority, just as the multitude adhering to a Law know it. But when he knew God with a certain knowledge, he admitted that true happiness, which is the

broad strokes by which Maimonides inculcates the value of skepticism in his audience. The majority of the final three chapters of the epistle consist of brief lesson plans for identifying pretenders to divine knowledge. Instructions for identifying prophets – no prophet will abrogate the Torah, he will be an Israelite, he will perform a miracle as corroboration of his prophetic testimony – constitute the second chapter of the epistle. Instructions for identifying false calculations of the onset of the Messianic Era constitute the third chapter. Instructions for identifying the Messiah – he will be the most superior of prophets, and his status is independent of familial lineage – constitute the majority of the fourth and final chapter. What Maimonides is doing, then, is arming the Yemenite community with a hermeneutics of suspicion and, by extension, with the rational facility that comes with being able to identify astrological miscalculations and theological misinterpretations. As Funkenstein writes, "skepticism is not a mark of disbelief in the coming of the Messiah, but rather the foremost duty of the learned."[48] The hermeneutics of suspicion is not merely rooted in proper interpretation of the Bible and in realizing that Torah-observance is now and will be in the messianic future the central element of Jewish life. In the third chapter, Maimonides makes it clear that this suspicion is also rooted in knowledge of the natural sciences.

It appears from Maimonides' comments (EY 120ff.) that the leaders of the Yemenite community believed that human affairs were subject to astrological convergences. Maimonides takes Joseph to task for this: "Remove all this from your mind. Purge your imagination of it as you would wash garments sullied with filth." Later, Maimonides urges Joseph and the other Yemenite elites to substitute true scientific knowledge for false astrological beliefs: "I see you saying that science in your country is scarce and that wisdom [philosophy] has ceased among you. And you attribute the cause of this to the conjunction being in the earthly trigon [of Taurus, Virgo, and Capricorn, during which elite culture allegedly is dormant]" (EY 121). Maimonides proceeds to outsmart Joseph in astrological and astronomical matters, coming to the conclusion that such calculations are of no use

knowledge of the deity, is guaranteed to all who know Him and that a human being cannot be troubled in it by any of all the misfortunes in question. While he had known God only through the traditional stories and not by the way of speculation, Job had imagined that the things thought to be happiness, such as health, wealth, and children, are the ultimate goal. For this reason he fell into such perplexity and said such things as he did. (II: 23; G 490–91)

The existence of this intellectualist rhetoric in both a supposedly elite text such as the *Guide* and a popular text such as the *Epistle to Yemen* should lead interpreters of Maimonides to question the assumption that Maimonides thinks it impossible for the masses to attain true knowledge of God.

[48] Funkenstein, 135.

in predicting the beginning of the Messianic Era. And Joseph is bluntly scolded: "You ought to know that these and similar statements are fraudulent and false. You should not consider its being written in books as proof of its validity" (EY 119). If Joseph himself cannot muster the rational resources against Muslim (or Christian) astrologers and other proselytizers, what hope is there for the masses that look to him for guidance? There can be no hope for the return of prophecy to Israel if its leaders do not perfect themselves intellectually, for the only possibility of perfection on the part of the masses is their receiving overflow from the elites of their community. If there is nothing to trickle down, according to Maimonides' supply-side model of social relations, all hope is lost.

Thus throughout the epistle, we see some evidence that the salvation of the Yemenites from their sociopolitical troubles will come not at the hands of a messianic king, but at the hands of their own rational powers, made possible through Torah-observance. The deep-seated desire for the arrival of the Messianic Era is thereby neutralized. For the concept of honing one's intellectual skills and aiming at intellectual excellence, as laid out in the *Mishneh Torah* and later in the *Guide of the Perplexed*, is associated with the world-to-come, not with the Messianic Era, which is important only for the political freedom it gives to develop one's rational faculties. If Maimonides is arguing that the best way to cope with messianic longing is to cultivate learning and science, he is also arguing that the best way to respond to messianic longing is to let go of yearning for the Messianic Era, extirpate the passion of that yearning, and keep one's heart focused on the world-to-come. In short, Maimonides addresses the concrete situation of the Yemenite community at the same time that his prescription for the community's healing seems to irrevocably suppress it. The prescription of striving after intellectual excellence to the best of one's capability is the same one that is given to all of Maimonides' patients.

This peculiar elision of messianic yearning is reinforced by a closer look at the so-called family tradition by which Maimonides predicts the renewal of prophecy among the sons and daughters of Israel to occur in 1210 C.E.[49] Notably, this calculation is only of a date when the "approach of the messianic era" will become known.[50] Yet the renewal of prophecy in Israel is dependent not upon exterior forces, but upon interior causes, specifically the intellectual perfection of the community (EY 126). "We ourselves stipulate of every prophet that he should have utmost wisdom, after which God causes him to

---

[49] The prooftext that Maimonides gives for his claim that the return of prophecy to Israel announces the imminence of the Messianic Era is Joel 3:1, "After that I will pour out My spirit upon all flesh; your sons and daughters shall prophesy," Hence, it seems that the eschatological return of prophecy is certainly not limited to the elite, but is found throughout the community. Here, the elitism found in the *Guide* is absent. The return of prophecy to Israel is contingent upon making philosophers out of the masses.

[50] For another interpretation, see Hartman, "Discussion of *The Epistle to Yemen*, 169ff.

prophesy."[51] This is curious. In the *Mishneh Torah*, Maimonides claims that the Messianic Era will be a time in which wisdom can be cultivated within the community. Yet in the *Epistle to Yemen*, Maimonides claims that the Messianic Era cannot even begin unless the community has already cultivated the intellectual perfection necessary for prophecy.[52] But if it has already done so, then the very function of the Messianic Era that Maimonides lays out in other writings is already accomplished. Reading the *Mishneh Torah* and the *Epistle to Yemen* together leads to the bizarre conclusion that the community will become worthy of the world-to-come without assistance from any outside messianic or kingly agency. *The members of the community will become their own Messiahs.* They will have freed themselves and awakened to the worship oriented toward the love of God; their intellects will become a conduit of the divine overflow and thus serve to make God manifest, just as the dwelling of the messianic king on Mount Zion (Ps. 2:6) serves to manifest divine rule and proximity to Israel.[53]

As such, the instrumentality of the Messianic Era is shown to be even more of a hortatory tool in the *Epistle to Yemen* than it is in the heavily instrumentalist accounts of the *Mishneh Torah* and the introduction to *Pereq Heleq*. It seems clear – contra the claim of Hartman – that it is certainly not given any intrinsic value.

To find such a heavily intellectualist Maimonides in a document generally regarded as "popular" is more than a little surprising. Traditionally, the *Epistle to Yemen* has been read as Maimonides' response to the call of a particularly troubled situation, in which he leaves his philosophical self behind in order to be a better source of consolation. While this is undoubtedly one strand of the epistle, it masks another strand that is a more straightforward application of the halakhic-philosophic model so apparent in other writings. All of Maimonides' rich and specific observations of the Yemenite

---

[51] This summary of B. Shabbat 92a is duplicated in both the seventh chapter of *Shemonah Peraqim* and chapter II:32 of the *Guide*. Cf. G 361–62 and *Ethical Writings of Maimonides*, trans. Butterworth, 81.

[52] There is one hint in the *Epistle to Yemen* that Maimonides subtly encourages the community to develop the perfection of the imagination as well (EY 104): "It is imperative, my fellow Jews, that you make this great spectacle of the revelation appeal to the imagination of your children. Proclaim at public gatherings its nobility and its momentousness." As Maimonides makes clear at *Guide* II:37 (G 374), perfection of both the intellectual and the imaginative faculties are necessary for prophecy. Those who have only one or the other perfection are either philosophers or politicians, not prophets.

[53] Therefore, it is by no means clear that messianism in Maimonides should be understood in light of Steven Schwarzschild's Cohen-inflected understanding of the penultimate of Maimonides' Thirteen Principles. (Cf. Schwarzschild, "On Jewish Eschatology," in *The Pursuit of the Ideal*, 211.) There is no reason to assume that Maimonides believes always and everywhere in an eternal delay of messianic arrival; indeed, one might assume that in certain texts, Maimonides appears to believe that messianic agency can be momentarily concentrated within the acts of a community.

situation must be analyzed in the context of the substantive advice he gives to the community. We find embedded in Maimonides' response to the tribulations of the Yemenite Jews the same model of intellectual perfection that is found elsewhere in his writings. His attentiveness to their suffering under the pressure for apostasy is pedagogically valuable, but the rhetoric of consolation is only a mode of wily graciousness by which Maimonides leads the Yemenite community to a life lived in accordance with his rigorously intellectual model of a teleological religious path. There is no difference between Maimonides' advice to Jacob in the *Epistle to Yemen* and the advice he gives to his student Joseph in the *Guide.* In short, the content of the epistle belies its outward formalism.

David Novak has recently critiqued Maimonides for such formalism, although not with respect to the *Epistle to Yemen.* On Novak's reading, Maimonides' God is incapable of relating to Israel throughout history and is thus closer to the God of Aristotle than to the God of Abraham.[54] Novak sees Maimonides' ethic as passionless, aimed at humanity as a whole, and hence as completely formal. One way to respond to both Novak and Maimonides would be to develop a picture of Jewish ethics as grounded in the emotions. But it is inaccurate to say that Maimonides' problem is his intellectualism or his Aristotelianism. Rather, Maimonides' dilemma is that his Neoplatonic background forces him to see *to mē on,* the world of privation around him, as evil. The individual's desire for God is grounded in revulsion at the world. What is needed is a reinterpretation of *to mē on* that values matter as the starting point that reveals the ethical/messianic path of nearing God. The desire concomitant with privation would thus have an aspect of intrinsic goodness. Hermann Cohen offers an interpretation of nonbeing that, in part, avoids this problem due to his interpretation of the Greek sources. As a result, the ethics that is part and parcel of Cohen's teleological arc comes closer to satisfying the criteria we find in Nussbaum's critique of Stoic ethics: the desire for a rich particular vision, one that takes joy in the world.

MEONTOLOGY IN COHEN'S *LOGIK DER REINEN ERKENNTNIS*

Secondary literature on Hermann Cohen within the discipline of philosophy of religion has rarely examined the methodology of neo-Kantian thinking that determines Cohen's religious thought. If little secondary literature has tried to amend this situation, it is due to the monumental nature of the task; Cohen was a very prolific writer.[55] Therefore, before turning to

---

[54] David Novak, *Natural Law in Judaism* (Cambridge: Cambridge University Press, 1998), 135.

[55] For attempts to read Cohen as a unified thinker, see Alexander Altmann, "Hermann Cohen's Begriff der Korrelation," in *In zwei Welten* (Tel Aviv: Verlag Bitaon, 1962), 377–99; Reinier Munk, "The Self and the Other in Cohen's Ethics and Works on Religion," in *Hermann*

Cohen's analysis of Maimonides in "Charakteristik der Ethik Maimunis," it is necessary to examine in some detail the context that Cohen has established for *to mē on* in his earlier *System der Philosophie*. By the time "Charakteristik" was published in 1908, the first two volumes of Cohen's system had already been published: the *Logik der reinen Erkenntnis* in 1902, and the *Ethik der reinen Willens* in 1904. The concept of *to mē on* appears explicitly in the second volume only briefly.[56] But the *Logik* shows *to mē on* to be a metanarrative in Cohen's methodology during this time. I will first summarize Cohen's explicit presentation of *to mē on* in the *Logik*, and then contextualize it within the text's larger project of elucidating a philosophy of origin (*Ursprung*).

Cohen's first mention of *to mē on* in the *Logik* is a brief account of its historical progeny. According to Cohen, the pre-Socratic atomist Democritus was the first thinker to depart radically from the Parmenidean doctrine that prohibits all speech about that which is not. It is in Democritus that being and nonbeing are both seen as principles of existence:

With the bravado of basic thinking, Democritus (using this particle [*mē*]) proclaimed nothing [*Nichts*] to be a fundamental term of the highest intrinsic value. And he put it on a par with something [*Etwas*] . . . "There is no more reason for the thing to be than the nothing." [*"Nicht mehr ist das Ichts als das Nichts"* (*mē mallon to den ē to mēden einai*).] (LRE 85)

The fragment of Democritus that Cohen cites is classic.[57] It radically undermines Parmenides by questioning whether there is indeed any sufficient reason for the Eleatics to believe that the existence of the nonexistent is impossible. This fragment also forms the basis of Aristotle's understanding of Democritus at *Metaphysics* A.4, where the language of nothing as *mēden* is transformed into an explicit meontological dictum: the atomists Leucippus and Democritus "say that what is [*to on*] is no more than what is not [*to mē on*], because the void is no less than body is."[58] Cohen's interpretation of Democritus is thus attested to even in the writings of his foe Aristotle. Whereas Aristotle argues (specifically in *Physics* Δ.7) against the Democritean pairing of being and nonbeing as principles, Cohen sees it as the first great philosophical advance. Being and nonbeing are the basic elements of the world in which we live; it is in the belonging together of being and nonbeing that the world is most clearly understood.

Cohen then supplies an argument for this claim, continuing with a brief elucidation of the *function* of this apparently counterintuitive dictum that

Cohen's Philosophy of Religion, 161–81, and Michael Zank, *The Idea of Atonement in the Philosophy of Hermann Cohen* (Providence, R.I.: Brown Judaic Studies, 2000).

56 Hermann Cohen, *Ethik der reinen Willens*, 5th ed. (Hildesheim: Georg Olms, 1981), 208.

57 In the Diels-Kranz classification of pre-Socratic fragments, this is DK 68B156. I have used the translation in Richard D. McKirahan, Jr., *Philosophy before Socrates: An Introduction with Texts and Commentary* (Indianapolis: Hackett, 1994), 314.

58 Aristotle, *Metaphysics* A.4, 985b7. This is DK 67A6; trans. McKirahan, 305.

pairs being and nonbeing as principles. It is not simply the case that Democritus is laughing in the face of Parmenides; rather, Democritus argues that the existence of nonbeing is necessary for good scientific work.

> Through these monstrous abstractions, he [Democritus] has defined his fundamental principles, which have been maintained in science throughout the centuries and have been steadily reduced to a smaller scale. This is especially true of *the void*, which he has placed alongside his atoms. And by defining the void as that which is not [*das Nichtseiende*] he has come across the expression of truth for beings themselves. The void is that which is not because it eludes perception, as do the atoms that are removed from it. But this is precisely the reason why the void and the atoms are, *in truth, being* (*eteē on*) [*sind das Leere und die Atome* das wahrhaft Seiende]. Thus, in Democritus that which is not is led to true being; the nothing is led to something. (LRE 85)

Democritus performs his critique of Parmenidean monism by theorizing that the world is composed of an unlimited (*apeiron*) number of eternal building blocks too small to be perceived, that is, atoms.[59] These atoms move about irregularly and combine in various ways to create perceptible objects. Yet there cannot be *only* atoms in the world; Democritus claims that without positing a void alongside the atoms, the challenge to monism fails. There cannot be many atoms unless there is some empty space between them that keeps the atoms separate, and hence many. If there were no void, there would be no space between the atoms, or more precisely, there would be no atoms at all but rather the Parmenidean One.[60] Furthermore, if there were no void, change and atomic motion would be impossible; there would be no place for the atoms to go. The void is a necessary condition for motion,[61] and for all generation, corruption, cohesion, and rearrangement on the part of the atoms. Thus one can say that the void *is*, insofar as it is a necessary condition for the appearance of objects within the empirical world. It serves as a mediating concept between the principle of the single atom at the base of reality, and the compounds that we see in our daily lives.

---

[59] The argument for the unlimited number of atoms can be found in Aristotle's *De Generatione et Corruptione* 315b9, DK 67A97, trans. McKirahan, 305. "Since they [the atomists] held that the truth is in the appearance, and appearances are opposite and unlimited, they made the shapes unlimited."

[60] Democritus posits an infinitesimal space between atoms even in compounds in order to solve this problem fully.

[61] Aristotle, *Physics* Q.9, 265b24: "They say that motion occurs on account of the void." There is some debate as to whether the void should be seen as the same as space. Aristotle defines the void as the "place" in which the atoms move (DK 68A37). McKirahan, 315, following D. Sedley, "Two Conceptions of Vacuum," *Phronesis* 27 (1982), 175–93, argues that both the atoms and the void exist in space, much as fish and the water in its fishbowl both take up space.

Nonetheless, the existence of the void is not existence in the sense of the existence of real beings, the atoms.[62] Democritus' pairing of the atoms and the void as the principles of existent things is equivalent to a pairing of being (*to on*) and nonbeing (*to mē on*) as principles, as stated by Aristotle at *Metaphysics* A.4. Thus, when Cohen writes "the void and atoms are, *in truth, being* [*sind das Leere und die Atome* das wahrhaft Seiende]," we should not understand this to mean that Cohen is arguing that the void is just as real as the atoms are. Rather, Cohen is simply recapitulating the Democritean dictum that there are both atoms and void in the world. In this manner, Democritus "leads" or guides the ordinary Parmenidean understanding of nonbeing as absolute nonbeing (that which does not exist) into an understanding of the being of nonbeing, as a void that must exist in order for compounds, or even atoms, to exist.

Cohen goes on to assert that Plato "displays the deepest relation with Democritus" (LRE 86), apparently because the *Sophist* also argues contra Parmenides for an account of nonbeing that involves a certain kind of being – in Plato's case, as otherness. Despite Cohen's misinterpretations of the Greeks (there is not a single mention of Democritus in Plato), he shows true insight in claiming a link between Democritus and Plato in terms of "the development of relationships [*Beziehungen*] among types of beings" (LRE 86). As seen in the previous chapter, the account of nonbeing in the *Sophist* assists in the larger epistemological project, insofar as justified true knowledge of a being X must necessarily involve knowledge of the other beings to which it is related. Seeing an object X in terms of its difference from other objects further determines its nature, and the concept of nonbeing is an important detour in this epistemological project. Likewise for Democritus, because nonbeing is a necessary condition for motion to occur and for compounds to exist, it is only through the concept of nonbeing that science can see the objects of the world as pluralities of atoms. For both Democritus and Plato, it is only through the development of the concept of nonbeing that objects can be seen as both one and many, as a single whole with many parts; only in this way can philosophy navigate between the Scylla and Charybdis of Parmenidean monism and Protagorean relativism. Nonbeing is a necessary step on the path toward knowledge of the whole qua knowledge of the reciprocal interrelations (Cohen's *Beziehungen*) of its parts. Epigrammatically, one might say that nonbeing lies on the path to *harmony*.

Democritus' philosophy was not successful; its metaphysics was hardly corroborated by empirical evidence, and this led to insuperable problems, especially when Democritus attempted to explain sensation and vision through postulating that atoms jumped off surface objects onto one's hands and

---

[62] Jonathan Barnes shows that the void "is" only in the sense of Frege's *Esgibtexistenz*, not in the sense of *Wirklichkeit*. Cf. Barnes, *The Presocratic Philosophers*, 2 vols. (London: Routledge, 1979), 2:101–3.

eyes.[63] But by Cohen's time, the atomistic worldview had become completely vindicated. With the rise of physical chemistry (LRE 33, 242, 322ff.), and particularly Michael Faraday's discovery of atomic energy (LRE 33, 442ff.), Democritus' description of atomic motion as random – what we now term "Brownian motion" – had become justified. For Cohen, the most resounding confirmation of a view of objects as composed of indivisible points of infinitesimal magnitude occurs within mathematics, with the rise of the infinitesimal calculus. According to Cohen, this mathematical revolution begins with Gottfried Leibniz (LRE 124–26). Leibniz, in the 1670s, was the first to adopt a simplified notation (still used by high school and college students today) that obviated the need for diagrams and tangent constructions when employing infinitesimal quantities to calculate areas and volumes.[64]

So if the science of Cohen's day justifies a return to Democritus, what function does the Democritean concept of *to mē on* – the void that separates infinitesimal qualities – serve in Cohen's *Logik*? I believe that it is the engine of the pansophist quest, the desire for universal knowledge. Such a hypothesis may strike the reader as strange. After all, Cohen is a neo-Kantian, and Kant hardly strove after universal knowledge. The ideas of reason – God, the world, the subject – are noumenal for Kant; they are limiting concepts with a merely regulative validity, "the function of which is to curb the pretensions of sensibility."[65] Especially with regard to the idea of the world, Cohen departs from Kant on this point. What separates Cohen's neo-Kantianism from the Kant of the *Critique of Pure Reason* is the status of the noumenal and ideal thing in-itself (*an sich*). For Kant, there is no intuition that can render the *an sich* intelligible; rather, the true nature of the object exists beyond the bounds of experience. Cohen, taking account of the new science of his day – Planck, Boltzmann, Hertz, Einstein (e.g., LRE 296–98) – had evidence of how mathematics and the natural sciences were able to transcend these allegedly impenetrable epistemological barriers. Hence, Cohen developed the view that logic could indeed determine the nature of objects. After all, if the world becomes intelligible through higher math and science, and if this science operates according to laws that are independent of sensible

[63] McKirahan, 330–33.

[64] For an account of this history in full detail, cf. Margaret Baron, *The Origins of the Infinitesimal Calculus* (Oxford: Pergamon, 1969). It is perhaps too specialized for those who are not mathematicians, but the account (270ff.) of how Leibniz, in 1672, was able to derive the sums of geometric series $(1/2 + 1/4 + 1/8...)$ from $A = A$ is exemplary.

In 1883, Cohen published *Das Prinzip der Infinitesimal-Methode und seine Geschichte*, in which he interpreted Leibniz's monadology in terms of Democritean atomism. Cf. Poma, 41. The philosophical appropriations of Leibnizian calculus in 1883 resonate through the end of Cohen's career, including the *Religion of Reason*.

[65] Kant, *Critique of Pure Reason*, B 311, trans. Norman Kemp Smith (New York: St. Martin's Press, 1929), 272.

intuition, then there is no longer any sufficient reason to remove the *an sich* from the realm of intelligibilia.[66] Scientific knowledge thus becomes the paradigm for *all* knowledge; what we can think is regarded as what we can experience. The a priori laws of mathematics in the end construct and produce *all* objects of experience. Since we can *think* the ideas of reason, we can therefore *know* them. The processes and rules of the subject's thought are thereby made into the source of objective validity. Cohen collapses the subject–object distinction as early as his very first published article (a psychologistic reading of the Platonic forms) in 1866.[67] In so doing, he also collapses the distinction between thinking and knowing that is paramount for Kant in the second preface to the first *Critique*.[68]

Cohen's Kantianism lies only in his apriorism and his belief in the primacy of practical reason; otherwise, his thought bears the marks of a pansophism that is more reminiscent of Leibniz, Comenius, and possibly the occult movements associated with Rosicrucianism and Kabbalah.[69]

This is not to argue that Cohen's Kantianism is somehow merely exoteric; it would be specious to claim that the Cohen of the *Logik* and earlier does not see himself in the shadow of Kant. Nevertheless, Cohen's return to Kant is not as pronounced as that called for by German philosophers of the 1850s such as Hermann von Helmholtz and Jürgen Bona Meyer.[70] For Cohen does not see Kant, or at least Kantian epistemology, as a novum in the history of thought. Kant is viewed through a Leibnizian lens.

Kant specified thought as *synthesis*. And through synthesis, he defined and formulated all his systematic concepts...And he differentiated types of syntheses. Therefore the objection was raised against him that he debased thinking to the level of mechanical assembly [*Zusammensetzung*]. Indeed the objection, in all its enormity, would not have become possible had one not ignored...the end [*Ziel*] in favor of the means. Assembling does not amount to synthesis; but the result of assembly should rather first mean synthesis. But this excludes every remotest appearance from assembly; it is unity. *Synthesis is synthesis of unity.* And it was not necessary to first learn from Kant that unity is the antithesis to every type of assembly; one could have learned this from Leibniz. (LRE 25–26)

In Kant's first *Critique*, the function of understanding (*Verstand*) is to put together the manifold of representations in an intuition, or to assemble

---

[66] This is the common understanding of neo-Kantianism; in the paragraphs following, we will trace this movement through the *Logik*. Cf. Thomas E. Willey, *Back to Kant: The Revival of Kantianism in German Social and Historical Thought, 1860–1914* (Detroit: Wayne State University Press, 1978), 108ff., and Köhnke, 180–97.

[67] Köhnke, 183.   [68] Kant, *Critique of Pure Reason*, B xxvi and n., trans. Kemp Smith, 27.

[69] For panlogism in Leibniz, cf. Donald Rutherford, *Leibniz and the Rational Order of Nature* (Cambridge: Cambridge University Press, 1995), 99–105. For an intriguing account of Leibniz's infatuation with occult and Christian-Kabbalistic thought, cf. Allison P. Coudert, *Leibniz and the Kabbalah* (Dordrecht: Kluwer Academic Publishers, 1995).

[70] Köhnke, 96ff.

concepts in the act of judgment. This is not simply an association of various aspects of the intuition or of various concepts. Kant is clear that the nature of the understanding reveals that the synthetic unity of the manifold (i.e., the a priori adherence of sense-intuitions to the categories of understanding) is not something that the understanding's judgment imposes upon intuitions; rather, the unity of the manifold is already the ground of the diverse representations and concepts that the understanding synthesizes.[71] Although Kant claims that this unity is not intelligible, Cohen seems to be arguing that with each conceptual advance, the understanding achieves this qualitative unity and is self-reflectively aware of it. Thus the result of the synthesis is more important than the act of understanding itself, since the result is what is transcendentally prior to the act of synthesizing and hence is of higher value. Cohen's reading of Kant marks a return to a Leibnizian epistemology in which "all knowledge, in any domain, can be regarded as the result of combinations of certain primitive concepts or ideas."[72] The act of philosophizing thus begins with the manifold of disorganized pieces of knowledge, and works back (for Cohen, through transcendental logic) to these basic concepts that are then shown (through formal logic) to govern the manifold of acquired knowledge.

The goal of synthesis is to resolve the perennial philosophical problem of the one and the many. The Leibnizian method of Cohen's *Logik* is again apparent.

Already by the early time of Greek mathematics ... two expressions for unity [*Einheit*] had developed: [numerical] unity (*hen*) and monad (*monas*). The first [sense of] unity is that of the beginning of the series of numbers; the other lies outside this ... The first type of unity continues to plurality [*Mehrheit*]. But each type of plurality and each individual within plurality must be a unity. For this, the other type of unity is obliged to make an entrance. How is this entrance to be understood? Is the concept of unity also to be extended to plurality? Or should plurality be simply taken as the precondition [*Voraussetzung*] of unity? But the case is the latter; therefore the difficult reflection, which arises against [the ordinary understanding of] synthesis: *synthesis certainly aims at unity, but it has plurality as its precondition.* (LRE 26)

In this passage (which contains the first mention in the *Logik* of the important concept of plurality), synthesis is seen as flowing in two opposing directions. The epistemological project operates teleologically; it binds together the plural objects given to the understanding in such a way as to discover the substantial form that is its basis. This approach departs from Kant. Experience is dependent upon given intuitions for Kant, yet the complexity of nineteenth-century mathematics demonstrates that thought can proceed upon pure intuition alone, without anything having to be given to it empirically. If mathematics is pure in the Kantian sense, that is, if it is

---

[71] Kant, *Critique of Pure Reason*, B 130–31, trans. Kemp Smith, 151–52.   [72] Rutherford, 100.

not derived from anything empirical,[73] and if mathematics exemplifies the nature of thought in general, then thought itself must always be pure, *pace* Kant. The Kantian rhetoric of givenness only "indicates the frailty through which Kant is connected to his English century [and] damages the innate independence of thought" (LRE 27).

Cohen then recasts the activity of thinking as *Erzeugung*, generating, producing, or bringing-forth (LRE 28). This bringing-forth must have a nonempirical origin (*Ursprung*), which perpetually fuels itself through its own action (*Tätigkeit*), leaping from concept to concept in the philosophical jungle. Cohen writes that the generative process aims only at furthering itself: "production itself is the product," and "thinking itself is the goal and the object of its activity" (LRE 29). Each moment of thinking engenders a new moment of thinking, which in turn engenders a new moment, and so on. Only in this manner, independent of all empirical givenness, can thinking have "creative sovereignty" (LRE 28). To translate *Ursprung* as "origin" is to miss the sense of activity inherent in Cohen's elucidation of thinking as an *Erzeugung*; Reinier Munk has captured this sense in his phrase "act of origination."[74]

This movement of thinking is the metaphilosophical interpretation of Democritean atomism and Leibnizian calculus. For Cohen, each moment of thinking is parallel to an infinitesimal point on a curve. This point has a conatus within it so that, in an instant (according to the Leibnizian gloss on Newton's $F = ma$),[75] it engenders the next point on the curve. According to the calculus, the magnitude of an area X is determined through the summation of an infinite number of infinitesimal points inside that area. In relation to the quantitative magnitude of a line or curve, the infinitesimal point is a nothing, a *mē on* that possesses its own kind of existence, even if it is without the quality and quantity that characterize actual objects. Cohen's interpretation of Democritus (LRE 84–85), in which a being is truly determined by being "led [*geführt*]" on a "detour [*Umweg*]" through nothingness,[76] is formally equivalent to the interpretation of the infinitesimal calculus in which the area of a plane surface is determined by being led through a detour through a series of infinitesimals (LRE 33). Yet this is the only way in which an entity can be truly determined. The immediacy of empiricism belies the spirit of mathematics, while the immediacy of speculative idealism collapses the difference between being and the nothing that is its precondition.

---

73 Kant, *Critique of Pure Reason*, B 3, trans. Kemp Smith, 43. Kant here explains how certain propositions can be a priori but not pure.
74 Munk, 166.   75 Rutherford, 246.
76 Cf. Munk, 168–69. Some of what follows is indebted to Munk's elucidation of the methodology operating in the *Logik*. Also cf. Poma, 94ff.

For Cohen, as for Maimonides, the essence of thinking/intellection is action. Yet what lies at the end of the teleological path? On the one hand, differential equations in the sciences have concrete answers; the volume of a sphere is $4/3$ of πr^3, and that's that. Cohen, on the other hand, claims that philosophical answers must always still be questions, or else the process of *Erzeugung* collapses.[77] To treat a philosophical answer with the self-sufficiency of a mathematical one is to treat thinking as if it were finished. So how is thinking different than a sphere? The progressive structure of *Erzeugung* – thought determining itself with gradually more exactitude – would imply that nothing except the *Ursprung* could be the goal of the thought process that it institutes. This is Reinier Munk's interpretation of the matter: origination is its own task.[78] Yet Cohen never explicitly states this in the *Logik*. When Cohen uses the phrase "bringing-forth of the origin [*Erzeugen des Ursprung*]" (LRE 53), it is impossible to tell at first glance whether this is an objective or a subjective genitive, whether one is bringing something *out* of the origin, or whether one is bringing the origin *itself* forth. An earlier passage (LRE 31) is not much more helpful. At one point, Cohen asserts that if the *Ursprung* "should be located beyond being," it must then exist in thought. Four sentences later, however, Cohen writes that "thinking can, thinking should discover being." These two sentences appear to be mutually exclusive. If thinking is thinking of the origin (LRE 36), and if this origin is located beyond being, then a statement that posits being as the goal of philosophy would also posit being in an undetermined form as the originating act of philosophy. Yet it is difficult to see how being could be the goal of philosophical discovery when the *Ursprung* simply does not truck with being, according to Cohen's own definition thereof. By common sense, being and that which is beyond being are completely disjunctive; either the *Ursprung* is beyond being, or it is being-itself. How can Cohen have it both ways?

Help for this puzzle arrives in Cohen's methodological meditations on the infinite and the infinite judgment. In alleging that Aristotle has misinterpreted the Platonic and Democritean concept of *to mē on*, Cohen at least realizes that there was nothing in his misinterpretation that was "irretrievable" (LRE 87). For the Aristotelian definition of nonbeing as simply indeterminate being has, in the history of philosophy,[79] given rise to the logical category of the infinite judgment. In the modern era, Alexander

---

[77] LRE 30: "Above all, it was the question-form, in which Socrates formulated the concept, which appealed to him and encouraged him. 'What is it?' (*ti esti*) This question, at the same time, was supposed to be the answer." LRE 84: "The question ... is the lever of origin ... It is the temporal starting-point [*Anfang*] of knowledge."

[78] Munk, 166.

[79] Most notably in Boethius; cf. Wolfson, "Infinite and Privative Judgments in Aristotle, Aremoes, and Kant," in *Studies in the History of Philosophy and Religion*, ed. Isidore Twersky and George H. Williams (Cambridge, Mass.: Harvard University Press, 1977), 2:542.

Baumgarten, Christian Wolff, and Kant defined the infinite judgment simply as a proposition that appears to be negative but is actually affirmative.[80] Kant's example in the first *Critique* is that of the soul: "by the proposition, 'the soul is nonmortal,' I have, so far as the logical form is concerned, really made an affirmation. I locate the soul in the unlimited sphere of non-mortal beings."[81] But in Cohen's Platonizing interpretation of Kant, what is important is not the grammatical structure of the proposition, but the fact that such propositions are in themselves evidence for the belonging-together of the infinite and the finite, of the unlimited (*apeiron*) and the limit (*peras*). Cohen interprets pre-Socratic thinking, in its deepest speculation, to claim that the infinite is already constituted with an orientation [*Richtung*] toward the limited finite.

For Cohen, this orientation originates in the infinite. As a result, there appears to be a conflation here between the infinite and the infinitesimal, similar to that which Rawidowicz observed in Maimonides. I make this claim because Cohen describes the various Greek conceptions of the infinite in the same language of origination that he describes Leibniz's and Democritus' conceptions of the infinitesimal. Cohen avers that Plato's first principle of the good that is beyond being (*epekeina tēs ousias*) comes to light through an authentic use of the infinite judgment and thereby grounds the determination of ethical principles (LRE 88). Since both the infinitesimal and the infinite are without the boundaries that would give them magnitude, the structure in both cases is parallel to the examples adduced earlier from the Greek texts and from Maimonides, in which the nothing qua *to mē on* is seen as the condition of the possibility of being. *To mē on* is here described as both above being and below it; what is important is the absence of quantity in either case.[82] The relation between the nonbeing within being and the nonbeing beyond being – the way in which the infinitesimal is grounded in the infinite – is revealed in the infinite judgment. The function of the infinite judgment is

> *to bring the originative-act* [Ursprung] *of the concept which forms the problem into definition.* Thus, the so-called *nothing* (but in no way to be understood as such) becomes the *operative means in every case* for bringing the uncertain something into its origin, and thereby really into generation and determination. (LRE 89)

Cohen's formulation recalls Plato's desire in the *Sophist* to determine being through its nexus of interrelations with various determinate other beings.

---

[80] Ibid., 554.   [81] Kant, *Critique of Pure Reason,* B 97, trans. Kemp Smith, 108.

[82] Hence, whereas Munk is correct to point out that Cohen's concept of nothing is privative and below being, this concept can also be infinite and above being. In the *Logik,* Cohen strictly differentiates between infinite and privative judgments in a way that neither Kant nor the Arabic Aristotelians did. Cf. Cohen's quotation of William of Ockham on this distinction at LRE 90, and Munk, 168–69.

Nevertheless, in both cases the function of the infinite judgment is not simply to lead philosophy upward toward the infinite. Rather, the function of the infinite judgment seems to be to lead philosophy upwards and outwards in order to show how the limit and the unlimited are related. Cohen's philosophy is a calculus of the world, in which the world's magnitude is seen in terms of the sum of the infinite series of its parts. In this mathematical belonging-together, the whole of being is brought to the fore, both as a monadic unit and as the entirety of the many interrelations it includes. Thinking does indeed discover being. But the being it discovers is seen in the light of the unbounded whole that conditions it and is hence "beyond being" in the sense that it stretches across the bounded one and the boundless many. The determinate being that is the goal of thinking is one that includes, in a highly intimate relationship, both being in its ordinary sense and the various nothings (void, infinitesimal, goodness) that are usually thought to be completely external to being.

One of Cohen's names for this intimate relationship, already in 1902, is *correlation*.[83] It allows for "the activity of pure thinking . . . to come to a clear determination" (LRE 60). It stands against a model of dialectic as the "exchange [*Wechsel*]" (LRE 61) of apparent opposites. Rather, correlation is described as a "preservation [*Erhaltung*]" of the apparent opposites. When thinking establishes a correlation between two contraries (something/nothing, unity/plurality), each contrary simultaneously remains separate from the other (maintaining plurality) and related to the other in a larger unity. Thinking demands

> that preservation maintain unity in plurality and plurality in unity. . . . [But] plurality should not collapse into unity. And unity should not separate itself [by being maintained] in plurality. Plurality should, indeed as unity, remain plurality. And unity should preserve itself as unity. And both should not rest next to each other, so much as overflow [*übergehen*] into each other. (LRE 62)

The first sentences of this quotation imply that this overflowing of the contraries is certainly not a complete merging of the two poles. Plurality is maintained, or else there is no real correlation. Correlation is indeed a

---

[83] Although this term is scattered throughout the *Logik*, and not yet codified as a Cohenian *Leitmotif*, it retains the same meaning that it will have in Cohen's late writings.

  Robert Gibbs, in his *Correlations in Rosenzweig and Levinas* (Princeton, N.J.: Princeton University Press, 1992), 17–18 and 86, doubts whether Cohen's use of this term is parallel to that of Paul Tillich. After all (86), "Cohen is claiming that . . . because any conceptual answer is complete, systematic thought is always a task, never a totality." Tillich's theology, on the other hand (18), possesses a "knowledge of the answers." While Gibbs's caution is certainly called for, Tillich does write that "God answers man's questions, and under the impact of God's answers man asks them . . . This is a circle which drives man to a point where question and answer are not separated." If this is a totality, it is certainly not one that leads to contentment or stability; and the equation of answer and question here is rather close to Cohen (cf. LRE 30). Cf. Tillich, *Systematic Theology*, 1:61.

synthesis of unity (LRE 26), but this philosophical concept of unity is aware of the plurality that was its precondition, and it respects that plurality by calling attention to the history of the development of its structure. No moment of unity, no moment of plurality is *aufgehoben* into a higher moment. In the later sections of the *Logik*, which apply the methodology of the opening ninety pages of the text to the history of math and science, Cohen claims that the typical example of the preservation of opposites is the mathematical concept of function, as expressed in the equation $y = f(x)$ (LRE 284). The relationship of function in Greek mathematics expressed the potency of the quantity x; in Leibniz, it signifies "the mutual dependence of two variable quantities" (LRE 277).

Cohen's understanding of correlation means that no moment of nonbeing is consumed in the process of the determination of something, and no infinitesimal is absorbed into the integrative calculation. The conatus of the infinitesimal perseveres throughout the various progressive developments of thinking that preserve the relationship between the one and the many. Thus, thinking sets itself up as a task that is always oriented toward the future and is not satisfied with the present, which for Cohen (LRE 62) "contains an illusion, an impulse toward error" and hence "must become future" (LRE 63) in the act of originative thinking. Like Maimonides, Cohen temporalizes the concept of nonbeing, so that nonbeing is seen to be the not-yet-integrated world. The present moment is always to be conceived as a not-yet. Thinking is future-oriented; at some point in the future, the correlation between unity and plurality will be brought into relief. Here (LRE 63–64), Cohen never uses the Hegelian language of sublating and dissolution (*aufheben*), but stays on its perimeter in his use of the verb *heben*. In this movement of elevation toward the ideal, opposites flow into each other and interpenetrate, without dissolving and producing something new.

Therefore, the goal of this interpenetration is not an attaining of the infinite by an act that would transcend the material finite world. Rather, it is the fully determined interpenetration of the infinite and the finite, the nothing and the something, the one and the many. Cohen calls this determinate interpenetration "totality [*Allheit*]"; and here the pansophist undercurrent of the *Logik* bursts into the open. In one of the many analyses of infinite number series in the *Logik* (LRE 182ff.), Cohen states that the value of an integral is "nothing else than the totality in which the infinite series is bound up with the infinitesimals." In this relation, "continuity flows through [these] discrete pluralities," and the movement of abstraction from plurality to unity neither leaves plurality behind nor depends upon these pluralities in any mode of empirical givenness. Through this continuity,[84]

---

[84] Cohen here is referring to Leibniz's law of continuity, which Rutherford characterizes as the rule that "the movement from any one element of a series to another must always occur through the smallest possible increment, with no abrupt changes of value. Changes of time,

the category of totality is established, along with the real possibility of giving
this totality determinate content. The infinitesimal sets forth the possibility
of totality. But since the laws of mathematics also serve as the ground rules
for thinking, one thereby gains the right to claim that nonbeing sets forth
the possibility of universal knowledge.

Cohen goes on to close the circle between totality and the infinitesimal,
between universal knowledge and nonbeing:[85] "The infinitesimal would not
have been invented, if not for the goal of totality. Thus totality is the true
goal and the true subject-matter [*Sache*] of the infinitesimal" (LRE 183).
According to the logic of the generation of originative thinking, the goal of
thinking is already included in its origin. Thinking has itself as its task. As a
result, one cannot with sincerity state that the totality and the infinitesimal
are different; totality is only the fullest abstraction from and determination
of the infinitesimal. But formally, they are the same. Totality is present in the
infinitesimal as that which is to be generated; it is a seed waiting to awaken
and come to fruition. The conative impulse with which Leibniz and Cohen
typify the infinitesimal, then, is totality in miniature. Certainly one would
have no right to say, according to the parameters of Cohen's thinking, that
totality is *exterior* to the infinitesimal. The task of thinking is to articulate it
in life and thereby bring it to actuality.

FROM TELEOLOGY TO MESSIANISM: COHEN'S INTERPRETATION OF MAIMONIDES

The argumentative path of Cohen's "Charakteristik der Ethik Maimunis"
does not turn away from the path of thinking laid out in the *Logik*. The
subject matter of ethics does not mark a turn away from the scientism of
the *Logik*. Rather, the method of *Erzeugung*, of generation (out) of the origin that Cohen develops in the *Logik*, is the operative method in all philosophical disciplines. In the *Logik*, Cohen therefore defines ethics as "the
logic of the human sciences" (LRE 253). Logic serves as the foundation of
ethics insofar as it lays down the method by which ethics searches for and
establishes laws (LRE 607). The data that ethics uses are not the scientifico-
mathematical data of the *Logik*, and thus ethics has independence as a field
of thought, although the method by which ethics analyzes its data is completely determined by logic. As shown earlier, this method is constructed
out of generalizations made from Leibnizian mathematics, specifically the
infinitesimal calculus. As a result, Cohen is able to epigrammatically state in

place, or motion are always 'continuous,' in the sense of occurring through an infinite series
of smaller gradations" (29). Also cf. LRE 90ff., in which Cohen amplifies Leibniz's law of
continuity into a general law of thinking, in accordance with the scientific method.

[85] For another geometry of Cohenian teleology that focuses on the concept of line, cf. Robert
Gibbs, "Lines, Circles, Points: Messianic Epistemology in Cohen, Rosenzweig and Benjamin,"
in *Toward the Millennium: Messianic Expectations from the Bible to Waco*, ed. Peter Schäfer and
Mark R. Cohen (Leiden: Brill, 1998), 363–82, esp. 364–70.

the "Charakteristik" essay that "idea links ethics and logic; the idea of good distinguishes ethics from logic" (CEM 227).

If ethics and logic share a common methodology for Cohen, one would expect that Cohen's analysis of Maimonides would lead to a view of the ethical life as a gradual and continual path that develops the origin of this ethical life into a completely determinate structure. It will be applied ethics, moving forward into analyses and prescriptions of determinate interpersonal and international structures. And it will also be philosophical ethics, doing the transcendental backstroke toward the first cause that serves as an exemplar for how applied ethics should model itself. This *Erzeugung* of the originative act into a totalized structure, as in the *Logik*, begins with the concept of the *mē on*.

As already seen, the concept of the *mē on* in the *Logik* serves a dual purpose as the nothing that transcendentally grounds something. On the one hand, it is the infinitesimal that serves as the basis upon which all areas and volumes are calculated – the nothing that is less than being. On the other hand, the example of the idea of the good in the *Logik*, arrived at through the infinite judgment, is nonbeing in a different manner. It is the nonfoundation (*Ungrundlegung*) that grounds those principles that are customarily taken as the rational foundations of thinking (LRE 88ff.; CEM 226).

In the "Charakteristik" essay, Cohen is slightly more explicit than he is in the *Logik* about the relationship between God, the infinite judgment, and nonbeing. This explicitness allows Cohen to flesh out the further consequences of the meontological starting point of his thought. Not only is the teleological arc of existence revealed, but here we can also read Cohen applying this teleology in two different arenas. First, there is the performance of this teleology in the *Erzeugung* of the community; this transforms teleology into ethics. Second, Cohen reconfigures the telos of human existence in light of the insight into God as the *Ursprung*; this transforms teleology into messianism.

Cohen realizes that to draw a strict dichotomy between intellectual and moral perfection in Maimonides is to think simplistically: "For Maimonides, [scientific] knowledge is the task and goal of religion and hence ethics" (CEM 245). The knowledge that is specifically the province of religion is knowledge of God, given in terms of the divine attributes. Cohen rightly points out that the divine attributes for Maimonides are attributes of action, not attributes that describe God's essence as substance (CEM 246). This is a straightforward reading of the close of *Guide* I:52 (G 118–19) and the first half of I:54 (G 124–25). Here Maimonides claims that his theology parallels the account of Ex. 33, in which God grants Moses' request to see the ways of God but refuses the request to see the glory. Cohen appears to be of two minds as to whether Maimonides is claiming that God is essentially action or not. Cohen writes, with apparent approbation, that Maimonides "concentrates and limits the concept of God to the ethical concept of God," thereby implying that there is some ineffable content to the concept of God that the discussion of attributes cannot reach. Humankind is denied knowledge of the attributes of God's substance, and the attributes of action are really only attributes in the sense that they "serve as standards for human action" (CEM 246). The real attributes, those of God's substance, are simply not touched. But if this were Cohen's opinion on the matter, Maimonides would indeed be a negative theologian in the classic sense. Nevertheless, Cohen refers to discussions of Maimonides' negative theology as discussions of "the *so-called* negative attributes" (CEM 248; emphasis mine). Indeed, Cohen writes of the attributes of action that they are "more positive, because they are more fruitful, than the positive [essential attributes]" (CEM 257). Action and ethics do not simply skim the surface of an unknowable God; they go right to God's basis (*Fundament*). Cohen is wary of stating that God is essentially morality and nothing more; this would reduce God to a simple limit-concept. The most one can explicitly gather from Cohen's interpretation of Maimonides is that the idea of morality is the basis of God *from the vantage point of our understanding* rather than being the objectively definable essence of God.

Yet to state that God appears to us only as the idea of morality, while God's true essence transcends this, will not do; such an account relies on the very opposition between appearance and things-in-themselves that Cohen's neo-Kantianism rejects. If we know God through the idea of morality, this must be what God is *an sich*.[86] This view is necessitated by the recontextualization of the following sentence of Cohen's within *Guide* I:54: "Therefore, knowledge [of God] can only be that in which and through which the human being [*Mensch*] can develop oneself toward one's ethical essence [*Wesen*], in imitating God – that is to say, the actions of God – in one's own actions" (CEM 247). Cohen's link between the attributes of action and *imitatio Dei* is authorized by Maimonides himself at the close of I:54 (G 128): "For the utmost virtue of man is to become like unto Him, may He be exalted, as far as he is able; which means that we should make our actions like unto

---

[86] On the other hand, cf. Cohen's following remark in the posthumously published *Religion of Reason Out of the Sources of Judaism*, trans. Simon Kaplan (New York: Frederick Ungar, 1972), 95: "these norms [the *middot*, the qualities of God that for Maimonides are the same as the attributes of action] are encompassed by the essence of God, but it is impossible to imagine that they could exhaust this essence: they could have been conceived for man only, could be valid for the actions of man only." Cohen cites *Guide* I:54 on Exodus 33 at this point; yet this statement is more Kantian than anything that Cohen says more than a decade earlier in CEM.

For David Novak, this is the one passage of Cohen that could possibly allow for a rehabilitation of Cohen's God-idea in terms of the covenant over and above the Kantian regulative ideal; yet as it is only one sentence in the thousands of pages Cohen wrote on God, Novak reads it as an exception to the rule. Cf. Novak, *The Election of Israel* (Cambridge: Cambridge University Press, 1995), 59n. 30. Undoubtedly, the entire legacy of neo-Kantianism and the issue of a "turn" in Cohen's thought from the philosophical system to the later writings on religion rests on this single sentence.

His, as the Sages made clear when interpreting the verse, 'Ye shall be holy [as I am holy]' (Lev. 19:2)." We can then construct the following series of inferences. If imitating God's actions brings out our ethical essence, and if this ethical essence makes us more like God, then God's essence must be ethical, actional.

For Cohen, the most interesting aspect of the section of the *Guide* on the divine attributes is not simply the claim of the primacy of practical reason, but the argument Maimonides makes to get there, an argument Cohen (mistakenly) associates with Plato. The negation in Maimonides of the essential attributes of God is for Cohen bound up with the infinite judgment (CEM 250), which, we have seen, Cohen associates with the particle *mē* as opposed to the simple negation of *ou*. In the "Charakteristik" essay, Cohen associates the infinite judgment not simply with Plato's procuring of the idea of the good as the nonfoundation beyond being but also with the Maimonidean concept of the "negation of privation," which procures a similar status for God. Meontology for Cohen is based upon "not a negation, but rather... an apparent negation" that is indeed ultrapositive.[87] It serves as the basis for a "true and firm standing [*Position*] for God," (CEM 250) for a rational theology of God as creator.

Therefore, although *to mē on* technically refers to the world as the realm of privation, Cohen's association of *mē* with the infinite judgment allows him to speak of God as an ultrapositive infinite, best characterized by privative prefixes (such as the "in" in "infinite."). But the fact that we speak of both God and the world in privative language does not make them equal. In discussing the nature of privation in the "Charakteristik" essay, Cohen writes that "privation must therefore be limited to those relationships which let lack [*Mangel*] appear not as a theft [*Beraubung*], but which let the absence of the predicate in question appear as grounded" (CEM 252). In other words, while on the surface Cohen's use of *mē* rolls around awkwardly between the privation of matter and the negation of that privation that is God, Cohenian meontology demonstrates a correlation of the two different kinds of negativity – a correlation that Maimonides (and Plotinus) could ground only in an empirical observation of the soul's desire for God. In Cohen's meontology, neither pole (world or God) has its full meaning without the other; it is only in the relation between them that each can be understood as fully

---

[87] Zvi Diesendruck, followed by Shubert Spero and Almut Sh. Bruckstein, has challenged Maimonides' and Cohen's use of the phrase "negation of privation," charging that "privation of privation" would be more reflective of the emphasis, in both Maimonides and Cohen, on the ultrapositivity of divine attributes. But "privation of privation" would technically mean that God is potentially potential, which is nonsense. Cf. Diesendruck, "Maimonides' Theory of the Negation of Privation," *Proceedings of the American Academy for Jewish Research* 6 (1934–35), 139–51, esp. 146–47; Spero, "Is the God of Maimonides Unknowable?" *Judaism* 22:1 (1973), 67–78, esp. 72–73; Bruckstein, "Hermann Cohen's 'Charakteristik der Ethik Maimunis,'" 26–29; Wolfson, "Infinite and Privative Judgments," 554.

as possible. The *mē on* described in the *Logik* calls out for a foundation that lies beyond being (what Cohen terms a nonfoundation, *Ungrundlegung*), but it too serves as the foundation for a more exact understanding of its (non)foundation. In Democritus, the void both is grounded in an understanding of the atom (because there must be something besides atoms) and is the ground of a more sophisticated understanding of the atom. In Leibniz, the point on the curve is grounded in a simple understanding of the point as a part of the whole curve, but it also grounds a fuller understanding of the magnitude under the curve through the infinitesimal calculus. For Cohen, as with these other authors, the concept *mē* always operates in both directions simultaneously. *Meontology speaks to the belonging-together of the infinite and the infinitesimal.*

Thus, it is not simply the case that Cohen uses Maimonides to explain how meontology works; rather, Cohen uses meontology to explain how Maimonides works. For without meontology, Maimonides would not work for Cohen; there would be no resolution between the transcendence of God's nature and the immanence that is necessary for God to be imitated by humans. The relation Maimonides institutes between humankind and God in *imitatio Dei* is a correlation in the Cohenian sense. The understanding of meontology from Democritus and Leibniz is used in the "Charakteristik" essay to claim that relation is the central point of the *Guide* – that every privation is necessarily predicated upon a nonfoundational ground that is its negation, a ground that is completely without lack and without potential. The deep intimacy between God and humankind is expressed almost heretically by Cohen at one point in the "Charakteristik" essay, as he writes that the God of Judaism "must think men, insofar as he thinks himself; but indeed he must think them from within, out of himself [*aus sich selbst heraus*], and by no means out of the essence of humankind" (CEM 253).

The actualization of this intimacy is ethical. If humans are "part" of God in some way, as Cohen's quote implies, then God becomes the standard-bearer for human conduct, the role model for the true self to be actualized in *imitatio Dei.*

Thus, the love of man originates in the love of God: the love of the neighbor, of the stranger, and thereby of man. And the love of man radiates back into the love of God, for God is the exemplar of man. To love God means to foster ethics, which constitutes the essence of God. (CEM 240–41)

Cohen's argument for an essence of God that is active and ethical means that the path of *Erzeugung* will be an ethical one; it posits God as the telos of the ethico-religious life. But how does the interpenetration of unity and plurality occur in the ethical life, along the teleological path toward God? For Cohen, this is through the constitution of the ethical community. The fostering of ethics is not simply the cultivation of virtues, as in Aristotle, but the humble placing of oneself into relationships with others, in accordance with the Talmudic concept of *lifnim mishurat ha-din* (CEM 269), tradition-ally understood by the rabbis as a principle of supererogation (equivalent to "beyond the limits of the law") and by Cohen as a principle of justice and fairness.[88] Cohen writes that Maimonides is "never so moving" as when he describes humility (CEM 270), and claims that Maimonides places it at the center of the ethical life. Yet because of Cohen's interpretation of the at-tributes of action as exemplary for humankind, Cohen is forced to claim that human humility must be an imitation of divine humility. Hence, humility must be one of the attributes of action, although Maimonides never men-tions it as such in the *Guide*. Cohen does not attempt to interpret a section of Maimonides to bolster his interpretation. Here, despite his opposition to rabbinics elsewhere in the "Charakteristik" essay (CEM 249), Cohen's source for such a view is an *aggada* from the Talmud that "expounds upon the humility of God and its coherence with God's magnitude [*Größe*], just as if it were the grounding of greatness through humility."[89] Cohen finally gives the true, philosophical, reasoning behind this: "Because man is obliged to think humility through and carry it out, realize it [*durchführen*]; for that reason alone must God be, as it were, humbled with this attribute" (CEM 271).[90]

The philosophical framework of a gradual realization of a task – exem-plified through both the *Erzeugung* motif of the *Logik* and the earlier ex-pression of the moral law as a process of creating ethics, defined as "the relation [*Verhältnis*] between man and man" (CEM 268)[91] – casts the ethi-cal path as a path of ontological nearing. Cohen describes it with specific reference to the figure of a line (CEM 275) as one of an act of making oneself complete (*Selbstvervollkommnung*).[92] We have seen that in ethics, the individual makes herself whole, makes herself infinite in the pre-Socratic sense of the word *apeiron*. Cohen imagines individuals as points on a surface. Ethics develops itself along this surface, through the interpretation of all the

---

[88] Cohen's willingness to read Maimonides' discussions of supererogatory ethics in *Hilkhot Deʿot* in terms of the modern discourse of justice and emancipation is striking. Indeed, the passage that Cohen cites as evidence for his conclusion (1:1), does not even mention the concept of *lifnim mishurat ha-din*. The reader again has to do outside work to attempt to justify Cohen's conclusions: cf. *Hilkhot Avadim* 9:8, in which Maimonides concludes that supererogation is incumbent upon Jews so that Jewish and Gentile slaves can be treated equally. Cf. *A Maimonides Reader*, 177. For a Kantian link between justice and humility, cf. Kant, *Metaphysics of Morals*, trans. Mary Gregor (Cambridge: Cambridge University Press, 1991), 230–31.

[89] B. Megillah 31a: "In the place you find God's greatness, there you find God's humility."

[90] Cohen seems to be deducing the attributes of God from the categorical imperative.

[91] Cohen uses the scientific-mathematical word for "relation" here, and not the term *Beziehung*, "relationship," laden with emotional content. Cf. Novak, *The Election of Israel*, prefatory pages.

[92] I translate this word as "self-completion" and not "self-perfection" to show the resonances with Greek thought and mathematics, alongside the resonances with Maimonides and Judaism, that are Cohen's primary purpose in the "Charakteristik" essay.

points along it as interrelated: the unified line/group is a plurality of unitary points/individuals. Placing his own Maimonidean conception of ethics over and against Aristotelian eudaemonia, Cohen argues:

> It is an engaging illusion [to think] that the solitary thinker in his eudaemonia could most certainly mature to selfhood [*zum Selbst*]. To the contrary, we know that this lonesome self of thought can not be the ethical self, because the ethical self is the self of action. For this self, there can be no I without a You. The other person is called *rēa* [the Hebrew word used in "Love your neighbor as yourself"]; he is like you, he is the You for the I. The self is the result of the eternal relation [*Verhältnis*] between I and You; the infinite ideal of this eternal relation. The ideal, to be sure, remains ideal; the task remains task. But the ideal is only ideal insofar as it demands emulation, and hence makes nearing feasible. (CEM 275)

These sentences are a brief summary of a more extended passage in Cohen's 1904 *Ethik des reinen Willens*.[93] As for every X there is a not-X, so for every I there is a not-I, a You.[94] Just as Cohen interpreted the nonbeing of the void as the ground of the fuller concept of the atom in Democritus, Cohen sees the ethical You as the ground of the more fully determined concept of the I, its relative *Ursprung* who in turn is grounded in the absolute *Ursprung* that is God.[95] In this way the unity of God that serves as the original unity transmits itself down a chain of thought into the quest to establish the unity of humankind (*Menschheit*). Yet as in the *Logik*, this process of integration stretches in two directions simultaneously, both in the direction of unity and in that of plurality. Thus the task is infinite, since the act of unifying cannot go so far as to be at the expense of plurality, and the task of recognizing plurality cannot simply fall into irredeemable Protagorean diversity. As soon as one moves in one direction, a move must again be made backwards, and vice versa. Progress is certainly made, but the whole surface is not yet determined, and hence the task of producing the surface in the light of its simultaneous unity and plurality is an infinite one. Nevertheless, it would be false to charge Cohen with completely imposing the Leibnizian epistemology of neo-Kantianism onto Maimonides. At one point, Cohen equates self-perfection or self-completion with *tzedaqah*, the traditional concept of righteousness that Maimonides places as one of the suprarational virtues at the close of the *Guide*. Although Cohen cites no passage in Maimonides to bolster his claim, Maimonides' aphoristic summation of the meaning of *tzedaqah* at the close of III:53 does move toward Cohen's conceptualization of the issue: "*tzedaqah* [is applied] to every good action performed by you because of a moral virtue with which you perfect your soul" (G 631). Maimonides' view of the responsible life as ethical teleology

---

93 Cohen, *Ethik*, 218ff. contains the explicit biblical reference; the entire argument for Cohen's mathematical conception of interpersonal ethics and its consequences for political identity stretches from 201 to 257.
94 Ibid., 208.   95 Ibid., 212.

and self-perfection is undeniable; Cohen undertakes the difficult task of systematizing it.

In the closing pages of the "Charakteristik" essay, Cohen makes a transition from a somewhat demythologized description of life as a process of nearing God to a more determinate description of this demythologization as messianism. Cohen's conceptualization of the Messianic Era serves a heuristic function similar to that in Maimonides, insofar as the idea of such a time serves as a stimulant for the increase of human intellectual capacity. In other words, the Messianic Era is a heuristic code for intellectual perfection, as in Maimonides' use of the concept in the *Epistle to Yemen*. We have seen that intellectual perfection for Cohen is always an ethical concept, and hence messianic anticipation becomes the narrative by which my drive for ethical perfection gains cosmic meaning. As such, for Cohen messianism is not about the Messiah, but about selfhood. With each of my ethical acts in this world, I perform one of an infinite number of integral summations. In other words, redemption is placed into my hands and heart, and insofar as I hasten it through my actions, I am the Messiah.

In the "Charakteristik" essay, Cohen sets the stage for this vision by deploying various ideas derived from Maimonides, ideas that he will organize more deftly in the *Religion of Reason*. For Cohen, the Messiah is always and everywhere a this-worldly concept and has nothing to do with the world to come: "The Messiah is not the redeemer of humankind in the beyond, but the redeemer of humankind in this world" (CEM 281). Yet Cohen departs from the Maimonides of the *Mishneh Torah* who insists that the Messianic Era will be led by a messianic king. Everywhere after the preceding passage, Cohen refers to the messianic idea, and never again to the messianic person, except when quoting Maimonides. Yet messianism is not totally reduced to an idea existing in the philosophical stratosphere; it is reduced only to an idea that encompasses human action:

> Maimonides could make use of [the concept of] the beyond (ethicized onto the shore of self-completion) for the messianic age insofar as he converted the messianic age into the precondition for that beyond. Realizing and recognizing [*erkennen*] the idea of the Messiah means anticipating this preparation and ensuring of self-perfection. (CEM 284)

This latter sentence is somewhat obscure. At least it is clear that the final genitive is objective: since self-perfection has already been defined as a task – the self is to be created through the I–You relationship (CEM 280) – the concept of preparing for a task seems rather nonsensical. What we are anticipating, then, is the self-perfection that is itself a preparation for universal knowledge of God (CEM 286), perceived as ethical humanitarian action (CEM 287) on the part of a unified humankind (CEM 288), an ethical totality. It is less clear from this sentence alone whether the messianic idea refers to this telos of a completely integrated humanism, or whether it means that the

messianic idea is realized now insofar as one anticipates that telos. Yet insofar as Cohen appropriates Maimonides' instrumental concept of messianism
in the previous sentence ("the precondition for that beyond"), it seems that
the latter possibility must be the case. Messianism is thus anticipation of
the world-to-come; the idea of the Messiah serves as the impetus for my
ethical action by postulating the real possibility of the unity of humankind,
otherwise understood as the immortality of the human (CEM 288).

The teleological arc of human knowledge of God, which Cohen has
opened up through his analysis of Maimonides' attributes of action in terms
of nonbeing and the infinite judgment, can proceed only through interpersonal relationships. The penetration of the infinite into the finite is actualized through an infinite task of interactions with other beings. Yet even in
this age of CNN and real-time hyperlinks, I cannot form relationships with
individuals on the other side of the globe. The community into which I integrate myself is necessarily limited, by neighborhood or formal and informal
rules governing association. Nevertheless, there are means of further integrating these communities: municipal organizations, councils, and larger
representatives of the state. For Cohen, these are necessary pit stops on the
ethical-teleological path:

the human individual can only ripen in a precise nexus with the ethical development
of the human race. State and law [*Recht*] must lead [the way] to this self-completion
of humanity, but in their isolated historical materializations, they can only bode
nearings to this goal of theirs. (CEM 284)

Here serious questions arise. Exactly how much power should the individual
hand over to the state in order to accomplish an ever-closer nearing to
Cohen's humanistic goal? To what extent are concrete individuals preserved
in his maddeningly brief vision of the state? What is the relationship between
the state of which I am a member and the universal human community?
These questions are not answered in the "Charakteristik" essay. But they
must be answered, for if Cohen in the end absorbs the individual into the
state, there can be no richly particular vision, and Cohen's claim to have
constructed an ethical system of philosophy is met with a serious challenge.
Therefore, it is necessary to turn to Cohen's most detailed examination of
communal relationships in the light of the God-idea, to be found in the
posthumously published *Religion of Reason out of the Sources of Judaism*.

THE INTEGRATION OF THE COMMUNITY: *RELIGION OF REASON*

If the *Logik* introduces the *mē on* as the foundation of the teleological arc
of human life, while the "Charakteristik" essay serves to apply this arc to the
concepts of ethics and messianism, then the *Religion of Reason* brings the
dialectical interplay between the divine and the human to the forefront of

the discussion. This occurs in two places: (1) the discussion of privation and the attributes of action in the "Creation" chapter, and (2) the discussion of ethics in the light of the individual's love for God. With these situations fleshed out, one can then move to an examination of the place that a rich particular vision, as described by Martha Nussbaum, may or may not play in Cohen's thought.

The primary difference between the account of the *mē on* in the *Religion* and in the earlier writings lies in the end to which it is put. In the "Charakteristik" essay (CEM 257), Cohen only briefly mentions Maimonides' statement in *Guide* I:58 that "the meaning of our saying that He is not powerless [inert] is to signify that His existence suffices for the bringing into existence of things other than He" (G 136). Within his Leibnizian-Kantian framework, Cohen interprets this to mean that God is the *Ursprung* of all existent things. This example reads as part of a long list of infinite judgments that Cohen believes Maimonides to be making. It is definitely *not* the case here that Cohen views this passage as proof for a concept of God as Creator; indeed, at this point in his thinking, Cohen believes creation to be a problematic concept for Maimonides (CEM 253). But by the time of the *Religion of Reason*, this sentence has become the benchmark citation for Cohen's account of Maimonides' doctrine of attributes; it is a "signpost" (RV 73/63) for all discussion of divine attributes. This is due to its demonstration of the correctness of the biblical narrative of creation, and its alleged falsification of Aristotelian arguments for the eternity of the world.

> Creation can no longer be in contradiction to reason. In this logic the religion of creation itself has become reason. God is not inert; this means: God is the prime cause [*Urgrund*] of activity. God is the creator. His being can be determined in no other way than by the immanence of creation in his uniqueness. Creation is not a heterogeneous concept in – or in addition to – God's being. (RV 73–74/64)

Thus, it is not simply that meontology, through its place in infinite judgment, leads to an argument for the existence of God; it leads to an argument for the existence of God as Creator.

In addition, Cohen's arguments against Greek pantheism are more strident in this section of the *Religion* than in his earlier writings. Whereas the "Charakteristik" essay speaks of the "the ethical motif of pantheism" (CEM 234), Cohen is more explicit in the *Religion* that any such language threatens the very teleological project he is trying to establish: "if God were not creator, being and becoming would be the same; thus, nature itself would be God" (RV 77/67). If God is identical with the world, there is no longer any need to improve the world. It is already the embodiment of the All-Highest, and thus it is scandalized by any conception of ethics.

Yet with this stridency comes an equal measure of ambiguity. From the context of Maimonides, Plotinus, and Aristotle, we are able to parse each

of the words in the phrase "negation of privation." Privation refers to the
earthly material-potential world of coming-to-be and passing-away, whereas
its negation refers to the incorporeal noumenal realm that is fully actualized
in every respect. "Privation is totally foreign to God's essence."[96] As in his
earlier writings, Cohen shifts around on this issue on numerous occasions
in the "Creation" chapter of the *Religion*; at times privation is what is to be removed from the Godhead, while at other times it is the God-idea itself that
is characterized by privation. On the more orthodox Maimonidean side,
Cohen gives the standard interpretation of the doctrine of attributes when
he writes that predicating "not inert" of God is an operation that "negates
the negativity contained in a privation" (RV 73/64). This lies side-by-side
with more heterodox phrases, such as "logically, chaos is merely the undetermined, not the infinite, which is designated by privation" (RV 76/66).

Cohen continues this confusion when he claims that the doctrine of creation he has deduced from the infinite judgment is amenable to the biblical
account of *creatio ex nihilo*, insofar as it does not postulate the existence of
an eternal matter that is independent of God.

Assigning the concept of *Ursprung* for the divine being also settles [the issue of] the
Nothing, which is a stumbling block for the thought of creation. The Hebrew word
that seems to correspond to "nothing" (*'ayin*), in no way means merely nothing, but
rather the relative infinity of privation. Privation, however, is not situated within [*bei*]
becoming, within matter, within the desire for essence that characterizes primeval
substance [*dem Desiderat des Urstoffs*], but rather only within [*innerhalb*] the unique
being of God. (RV 76/66)

Here, the very privation that we find in Maimonides, and that elsewhere
in Cohen carefully distinguishes the God-idea, is now located within God.
Despite his protests to the contrary, Cohen here risks suggesting that God is
not a fully actualized being, as embodied beings are. Furthermore, Cohen
appears to have preemptively cut off any attempt at theodicy. For if there is
nothing external to God – that is, if Cohen does not, like Maimonides, try
to make the concept of nothingness into a thingless subsistence completely
deprived of being[97] – then God is responsible for having created all the
suffering within the world as well as all the good. No longer would one be
able to say, along with Cohen himself (RV 243/208), that God is *der Gute*,
"the Good one," a moral ideal. In short, once privation is included within
the Godhead, there is no longer any substantive difference between God
and the world that is also characterized by privation, and it does not take
long to hop over to a pantheistic worldview.

Nevertheless, in the *Religion* as in the earlier texts, there are philological, philosophical, and theological explanations for Cohen's vacillation on

---

[96] Ivry, 192.   [97] Ibid.

the nature of privation. At the level of philology, Cohen has every right to describe that which is "infinite" as a privation, since Latin grammar has assigned privative status to words beginning with "in" or "un" (LRE 87). To ascribe privation to God is to ascribe to God some lack before the moment of creation. It is to assert that the definition of God as infinite activity means not only that God *can* create ("his existence suffices for the bringing into existence of things other than He"), but that God *needs to* create. This does not mean that God's freedom is compromised; but just as humans have within them a conatus to create and are nevertheless free, so does God (understood essentially as activity) have a conatus to create.

This mutual conatus lies behind the God–human correlation in the *Religion*. "Correlation" is defined in the *Religion* as "a concept of exchange [*Wechselbegriff*]" (RV 101/86). This term describes the essence of the concepts involved in the correlation. In Cohen's systematic writings, correlation refers to the task of thinking the relata as preserved within one another. It is not simply that I need one pole to understand the other; correlation is not simply an epistemological concept. Its force goes as deep as being itself; I must somehow think the unitary object in terms of its differentia, its parts. I must think of the one object insofar as it is (in some respect) simultaneously many, not simply in terms of how it differs from an object. In his thinking of the concept of negation, Cohen here goes far beyond Plato, no doubt thanks to the influence of Leibnizian mathematics, which sees the single line as the sum of an infinite number of *ta mē onta*, relative nonbeings of infinitesimal magnitude.

To return to the relationship between God and humankind: if one is to think of the God–human relationship in terms of a correlation, one must look for that concept that expresses the essence shared by both of the relata. Later in the *Religion*, Cohen will name this shared essence "holy spirit," that which God has placed into human beings through revelation, which for Cohen is the gift of reason. Yet already in these early pages of the *Religion* Cohen is making a similar essential link through the meontological attribute of privation. Both God and humankind are lacking the complete determination (and hence, the fullness of being) that exists as the telos of the process of *Erzeugung*, insofar as neither has completely come into relation with plurality and differentiation. The unitary individual must see him- or herself within plurality and hence forge ethical relationships with others in order to become a true self. God must create and enter into relation with the multiple differentia of the finite world in order to become knowable, a God not simply in-itself but also a God for-others who is completely determined within the limits of human knowledge. Prior to this end point, both God and the individual are lacking, and both can be fairly described in terms of privation. Although God remains for Cohen completely transcendent, in this one respect God and the individual are similar.

The ethical encounter, for Cohen, is the site at which the individual actualizes his or her knowledge of God. It is where the individual and God meet, and each appears in actuality. In the "Charakteristik" essay, Cohen moves from the discussion of the attributes of God to the norms of human ethics as *imitatio Dei* without asking the important question of what it is within the human that allows *imitatio Dei* to occur at all. How do we know that ethics is not a ruse, a legal fiction imposed upon the singular individual by the state or other repositories of authority? In the *Religion*, Cohen solves this problem through the concept of the holy spirit, which he interprets as the essence of God (RV 117/101). The argumentative strategy here is not philosophical, but biblical. There is no proof for the existence of the holy spirit in the human being (a "sublime moral destiny," as Kant says); there are only prooftexts. It must be emphasized that the citation that Cohen most often uses here, Lev. 19:2 ("Be ye holy, as I am holy"; RV 111/96, 120/103, 239/205), is still an insufficient prooftext, for even this word of God does not give any evidence that holiness is potentially within human power now. From this verse alone, one might conclude that even if this is the word of God, it still might be the word of a sadistic God who issues commands that are impossible to obey. There is far more substance in Ps. 51:13, in which David, responding to God's anger over David's indirect murder of Uriah the Hittite (Ps. 51:1, cf. 2 Sam. 11–12), begs of God not to "cast me out of Your presence, or take Your holy spirit away from me." The very phrasing of the verse from Psalms within the 2 Samuel narrative implies that David possessed a holy spirit *at the very moment* he sent Uriah to the battlefront. Given the presupposition of the truth of prophetic texts, Cohen has every right to deduce from this that "I have Thy holy spirit; sin cannot frustrate it within me" (RV 119/103).

Individuals therefore *can* be ethical in the Cohenian sense and can near themselves to God through actualization of the divine spirit within. This holy spirit, being shared across God and the human, must therefore possess the same conative force within the human individual as it does within God. This conatus expresses itself through ethical action; the element that expresses the correlation between humankind and God actualizes itself in the inter-personal correlation (RV 133/114). The conception of history as *Erzeugung* means that it cannot be otherwise. If the singular individual were to aim at mystical union with God, the mystic would have ignored the fact that history is a series of mutual determinations of unity and plurality. In the intent for union between the one mystic and the one God, the category of plurality is completely elided. The religious concept of correlation thus guides the religious believer toward the existential instantiation of plurality (the social realm), and the task is to determine this plurality as a unity through the process of an ever-expanding formation of community. The unity of the holy spirit, split across both God and God's creatures, seeks the return of its unity through the integration of the community. This return begins through the individual's conversion of his vision of the other person as merely spatially adjacent (Cohen's category of "the next man" [*Nebenmensch*]) into a vision of the other person as already related to me (Cohen's category of the "fellow-man" [*Mitmensch*]). Insofar as Cohen refers to the categories of the *Logik* in the ethical sections of the *Religion* (RV 131/113), one can conclude that the interhuman correlation is the sociopolitical instantiation of the Leibnizian-Cohenian infinitesimal calculus. The other person is not discontinuous with myself, but I am related to him or her already in the same manner as two points on a curve, infinitesimal with respect to the infinite whole. As Cohen writes, echoing a passage from the "Charakteristik" essay quoted earlier:

Yet the I is only the I for a Thou . . . The I, as well as the Thou, are singular beings, but they are such only as members of a social plurality, or even totality, insofar as the latter can be established through social love . . . Only through the Thou can the I be generated [*zur Erzeugung kommen*]. (RV 192/165, 208/178)

Once I include the category of my plurality in my worldview, there is no logical resistance to the correlation between myself and any other individual. My detour through plurality allows me to more fully determine myself as an individual, as an *Etwas* in the terms of the *Logik*. Insofar as the social task is the creation and determination of the community (RV 164/141), the other person is formally similar to Cohen's earlier mathematical description of the infinitesimal *mē on* in the *Logik*. As such, the neighbor (*réa*) is like me insofar as she or he appears under the mark of the infinitesimal.

At this point, ethics seems to be just as easy as mathematics, with individuals reduced to elements in an infinite series. Yet it is essential to remember that the account of correlation in the *Logik* is one in which the parts are always preserved in the whole. Correlation is preservation (*Erhaltung*). The difference between the self and the other person can never be elided; in the sociopolitical realm, this difference is made manifest through the suffering of the other person and my sinfulness in this regard. The distance between self and other is what allows community to take place; if the self and the other person could both be sublated into the concept of the community, there would be no room for the reciprocal action (*Wechselwirkung*) in which "community is performed and realized" (RV 158/137). Community can be a telos only if there is suffering now, as a symbol of the mere plurality of fungible individuals. The observation of suffering is thus the first step to the determination of the I in the *Religion*. When I see someone suffering in poverty (perhaps financial or emotional), I may react with compassion, *Mitleid*, literally, "suffering with" (RV 160/138ff.). When I do this, I take responsibility for the other's suffering and realize my guilt. The ability to have the affect of compassion proves indeed that the other person is like me, that she is as infinitesimal as I. But the fact that I have only noticed this now means that I have neglected this formal similarity and neglected my own responsibility to integrate the community in this single case. I am guilty, not only insofar as I have abdicated my responsibility to make concrete the formal structure of humanity. Because the telos of community is the desire of the holy spirit that God has placed within me, my social guilt also has meaning within the religious sphere and is therefore sin. I atone for my sin through my cognitive recognition of it and my active suffering with the other person, for in this action I convert him or her from the next man into the fellowman, the person whom I exist *with*.[98] Yet this atonement is not permanent, for there are an indefinitely large number of situations that display evidence of my abdication of responsibility; as long as poverty and suffering exists, I am still a sinful being. Cohen cites Ps. 51:7 ("Indeed I was born with iniquity; with sin my mother conceived me") as a proof-text for the individual's constant sense of "innate feebleness and fragility" (RV 247/211). Moreover, Cohen sees suffering as what it is to be human: "suffering reveals itself to be the essence, as it were, of man . . . If you wish to know what man is, get to know his suffering" (RV 170/146). As such, the negativity of the Thou never recedes after I have confessed my sin against her and against God; my atonement is never a completed act, but part of a larger process of self-sanctification.

In this manner, the other person is always preserved in his or her otherness. One can see that for all of Cohen's misreading of the sources here, his misreadings make possible a view of the other person that allows her to be seen as intrinisically good, as having an identity over and above her role in my self-completion. For my self-completion is realized along with the completion of the community. The confession of sin and the redress of sin leads to social progress: "out of non-being a higher being is to come forth" (RV 286/244). This path from nonbeing to higher (i.e., more determined) being, which in the *Logik* is simply the mathematical process of an ever more exact determination of the correlative poles, is in the *Religion* (as in the "Charakteristik" essay), messianic ethics. Ethics must be messianic because it is situated along the path of *Erzeugung*; it is complete only when the unitary self sees him- or herself as part of a total community. As such, ethics is progressive; it "maintains the development of the human race" (RV 337/289) and places more worth in the value of the future over that of the present or the past. Ethics prophesies a perpetual peace for the future. Insofar as this prophetic voice is grounded in the analysis of the actional essence of God and the view of God as the standard-bearer of human moral conduct, this perpetual peace has a religious as well as an ethical meaning, and it can therefore be equated (in Cohen's view) with the classical descriptions of the Messianic Era.

Thus, ethical progress occurs through imitation of biblical descriptions of the Messiah. The messianic idea Cohen chooses out of the possibility of

---

[98] The previous four sentences are a summary of Chapters 8, 10, and 11 of the *Religion*.

ideologies at his disposal is, ironically enough, the concept of the suffering servant in Isaiah 53 (RV 329/283ff.), a biblical passage that had mini-
mal messianic overtones in ancient Judaism or even in early Christianity.[99]
What Cohen has done, then, is combine the messianic interpretation that
Christianity has assigned to this passage in Isaiah with the Jewish interpretation of the "servant psalms" in which the concept of the "servant of the
Lord" is seen to refer to the suffering of Israel as a nation. This has the effect
of simultaneously demythologizing the Christian understanding of messianism and lifting an idealized concept of the nation of Israel to the status of
Messiah: the idea of Israel as "holy remnant" serves the function of pro-
claiming a "messianic call, its elevation into one humankind [*Menschheit*]"
(RV 303/260). As the Messiah is the servant of God in Cohen's interpretation of Isaiah 53, so should "all Israel and finally all men become servants
of God" (RV 304/261).

How does the individual become a servant of God? Through *imitatio Dei*,
to be sure; yet Cohen more explicitly defines *imitatio Dei* in the *Religion* as
constant humility and taking on the suffering of the poor. By representing
in his own actions the suffering that essentially describes humankind, the
ethical self announces that the ideal community has no bounds, that it is
essentially as unbounded and infinite as the God-idea.

And while he suffers *about* [*um*] them, he suffers *for* them ... The humble man is
therefore the true sufferer; he is the representative of suffering. Only he is able to
undergo suffering in its moral essence. He is not only the representative of suffering
but even more the only true bearer of it ... The ideal man suffers. The Messiah is
seized by the distress of humankind in its entirety. (RV 310/265–66)

The idea of the Messiah is therefore, like the concept of God, an exemplar
for ethical action. Nevertheless, Cohen insists that the Messiah is not immanent in God, but immanent in humankind (RV 298/255). This undoubtedly
serves to safeguard a role for Judaism as a religion of reason, yet it also serves
to justify the evil of suffering. If the suffering of the ethical self, emulating
the messianic figure of Isaiah 53, is part and parcel of the progressive arc
of history, then this suffering has value from a cosmic perspective. The evil
of suffering for Cohen is not useless; it is itself the nonbeing from which a
higher being will emerge.

From the messianic point of view, a light of theodicy is cast even upon this riddle of
world history [the misery of the Jews] ... The messianic calling of Israel sheds another
light upon its own earthly history. As Israel suffers, according to the prophet, for the
pagan worshippers, so Israel to this very day suffers vicariously [*als Stellvertreter*] for
the faults and wrongs which still hinder the realization of monotheism. (RV 312–
13/268)

---

99 Cf. Alan F. Segal, *Rebecca's Children: Judaism and Christianity in the Roman World* (Cambridge,
    Mass.: Harvard University Press, 1986), 91–94. However, see also the discussion on p. 178.

At this point, the fact that the personal Messiah is demythologized as the suffering nation of Israel should be clear. The incorporation of the community is not performed by an exterior agent. It is achieved by the nation of Israel. Thus, as in Maimonides, Cohen argues for the redemptive capacity of the individual.

However, a problem arises with regard to the Messiah-idea in Cohen, one that gets to the heart of the issue of the ontological (or meontological) intimacy between the human and God, between the infinitesimal and the infinite, which we have been exploring throughout this chapter. For it is never clear in the *Religion* what the relation is between the figure of the Messiah and its actualization in history. Is the Messiah to come in the infinite future, or is the Messiah here in some shadowy form now? Let us review the presuppositions from the *Logik* that inform this question. From the description of the teleological arc inaugurated by the *Ursprung*, one would suppose that at each moment the infinitesimal bears a relationship with the infinite within its deepest recesses, the most intimate secrets of its crypts. Indeed, it should bear an indeterminate form of the infinite within itself, one that will become more determined over the course of the *Erzeugung* of the God–human correlation. Yet as we have seen, correlation means intimacy, not identity. The absence of attributes of essence in the Godhead is one example; the difference between the atoms and the void is another. God and man are irreconcilably different; God is uniquely being, whereas the human realm is the meontological realm of becoming (RV 53/46). When this is applied to messianism, Cohen's language becomes complex because this situation – intimacy without identity – cannot be easily expressed. For example, the omnipresence of suffering in the human world heightens the difference between God and the human, so that the intimacy is delayed until the end of time. As a result, certain of the references to the messianic idea in both Cohen's Jewish interpretation of philosophy and his philosophical interpretation of the Jewish sources are always references to an *idea*, to a *hope*, to a heuristic device. For example:

> The Messiah comes only at the end of the development of the soul, which is synonymous with immortality. In fact his coming is not an actual end, but means merely the infinity of his coming, which in turn means the infinity of development... the Messiah represents the time of the future, that is, the infinite development of the concept of the human soul. (RV 366/314)

The Messiah is here the result of the integration of the community, the ethical task that marks the development of the soul. The phrase that "his coming... means merely the infinity of his coming" may imply that the idea of the Messiah represents the entirety of the ethical process and is thus stretched across the historical bow. Yet even if this is the case, the fact remains that the range across which the Messiah is integrated is from zero to infinity. The Messiah is always to-come, for the integrative operation is not complete in the here and now. Even if I act ethically now, even if I have incorporated the suffering others into the social community (in its religious or political instantiations), I am not even close to being adequate to the messianic idea. This would seem to be a corollary of Cohen's Platonic premise that the idea supersedes historical appearance; history can be appropriate to the idea (as the ethical self can be near to God), but "adequation is indeed impossible to establish" (RV 427/367). Yet the definition of the Messiah as the "infinity of his coming" is more radical; it states that history cannot even be appropriate to the idea, that the soul on the developmental path is not appropriate to the idea of the Messiah.

This interpretation, however, has the consequence of equating the Messiah and God. For the Messiah is here defined as the end point of the process of *Erzeugung;* it is the result of history's development. Cohen claims in the *Logik* that the telos of the *Erzeugung* is the same as its *Ursprung;* according to Cohen's Platonic-Leibnizian account there, the process of dialectic serves to make the indeterminate origin fully determinate within the order of the real. Additionally, Cohen insists constantly in the opening chapters of the *Religion* and from the sections of the "Charakteristik" essay on Maimonides' account of divine attributes that the *Ursprung* can be nothing other than God; this is the meaning of the infinite judgment. In sum: if the Messiah is the telos, and if the telos is the *Ursprung,* and if the *Ursprung* is God, then one can equate the Messiah and God simply through the transitive laws of logic.

This is the Messiah to-come. But as is evident from the socialist tone of Cohen's messianic writings, this is not the *only* messianic figure about which Cohen writes. The Messiah is also immanent in humankind here and now, even with shadowy or undetermined content.

The Messiah is equated with the pious man. This is what we have previously said...Not only do the poor become the pious, but only through the mediation of humility, which is expressed in the poor, is piety manifested in them. Hence, humility becomes the foundation of messianic mankind. (RV 495/427)

Here, every humble act, every pious act, every moment of ethics is equated with messianism, with a deep relation toward the messianic idea. The Messianic idea is not simply in the far-off future, but is actualized in some shadowy status through my proleptic anticipation. This is more than messianism existing merely as potential; my humility is completely actualized. True enough, this moment of intimacy with the Messiah is fleeting; a single act of humility on my part is never sufficient to engender a permanently unified and just human community. Yet this does not make the act any less actual. The argument in the passage just quoted in which Cohen finds theodicy in Jewish suffering is predicated upon the premise that Jewish suffering is evidence of Jews' participation in messianic ethics. It is Jews' piety here and now that renders Jews instantiations of the messianic idea, that makes them the Messiah before the inauguration of the single human community. Insofar as they engender, even in part, the integration of the community, they fulfill the function of the messianic concept.

However, this strange intimacy between the human and divine is nothing new within the framework of the *Religion*. It is the motor of everyday religious acts such as prayer: "So intimately does prayer connect me as an individual with my God, with the God who in this prayer more than ever becomes my God" (RV 440/378). It is also the origin of the religious life; divine–human intimacy is predicated in the description of the holy spirit that makes ethical action a genuine possibility for humankind. Every individual possesses, as a gift, God's holy spirit. This is a precondition for ethical action. As such, every ethical action is an actualization of this holy spirit. When I act ethically, I have *already* attained the "nearness to God" that Cohen posits to be the basic desire of the religious individual (RV 190/163). I have momentarily actualized holiness in my ethical action, even though holiness is also for Cohen the task of self-purification (RV 354–55/305). Holiness thus oddly becomes its own precondition; I cannot attain God's nearness unless I am already near to God. This should not be seen as hopelessly paradoxical. Although Cohen is not clear on the issue, the nearness that is the goal of the ethical task is qualitatively different from the nearness that is reflected in my ability to act ethically. The difference between the two kinds of nearness (or holiness, or Messiahs, or I's) is the same as that between the *Ursprung* at the beginning of the dialectical process and that at its end. As expressed in the *Logik*, this difference is one of determination. At the beginning of the thinking process, the *Ursprung* is simply a bare unity; at the end, it is seen in conjunction with its plural parts, it is measured out across the totality of the meontological points that constitute it.

If the telos of the ethical life is the formation of a total community, what is the status of the singular members of this community? Are they indeed sublated into the category of totality, as appears to be the case with Maimonides' advice to the Yemenites? The answer to this question is once again maddeningly twofold, because the philosophical method of the ethical life is at odds with the hortatory claims that Cohen wants to make to the audience of the *Religion*.

On the one hand, the *Logik* dictates that the determination of the *Ursprung* does not sacrifice plurality for the sake of unity; indeed, the difficulty of this task is part of what makes it infinite. In the *Religion*, this refusal to sacrifice the fellowman in the name of the community is expressed in the chapter on Yom Kippur. Redemption does occur on the Day of Atonement, but it is only an ephemeral redemption. It does not cancel the suffering that, for Cohen, dominates the present. Cohen's theodicy is formulaically expressed in the *Religion* as "no redemption without suffering." This has two senses: (1) there can be no final redemption without the temporally prior suffering of humankind, for it is in the taking on of suffering that nearness to God is achieved, and (2) in each and every temporal moment, redemption and suffering coexist. Redemption "clings to every moment of suffering, and constitutes in each moment of suffering a moment of redemption" (RV 274/235). The dyadic relationship between these two terms is yet another of these doubled descriptions of concepts in the *Religion*. Insofar as redemption is in every moment, the I is actual, here and now already free; insofar as it is always accompanied by suffering, the I has not yet fulfilled its task and has demonstrated only that sinlessness is a real possibility in the infinite future. The dialectic between the two poles is never fixed and is never resolved: "The feeling of joy in being liberated from suffering has its validity only as a moment. Such a moment is redemption . . . only for a moment does the I have stability" (RV 269/230). At each moment, I see more suffering for which I have not atoned, and I realize that the freedom that I have attained was only of instantaneous duration. Therefore, as long as suffering exists – and Cohen believes that suffering determines what it means to be human – I must continue in my conversion of the adjacent person into the fellowman, integrate him or her into the community at large. I must continue to observe and get to know his or her suffering, get to know the intrinsic worth of that person, determine how this *réa* is as myself (RV 138/119). This is the case even if all the evidence is to the contrary: if a gulf between myself and the other appears due to culture, class, politics, ethnicity, hygiene, disability, religion. In this way, the fellowman/*réa* raises a challenge for me to cultivate my skills of discernment in a manner that is certainly not contrary to Martha Nussbaum's vision of the moral life.

On the other hand, there are passages in Cohen that just as strongly testify to the merely instrumental value of ethics, as in Maimonides. Even as early as the "Charakteristik" essay, Cohen writes that the recognition of the correlation between the I and the You (which in this essay is described not as a correlation per se, but as an "eternal relation") is a means for me to "work on my self" (CEM 275–76), a means for me to near God. In the *Religion*, the act of atoning for my sin against the other person benefits only me in the short run, giving me a knowledge of my essence and task (RV 221/189). At his most blunt, Cohen writes that "the knowledge of man becomes a means to [*Mittel zur*] the knowledge of God" (RV 127/109). This knowledge is always individual, always *my* knowledge. I am integrating the community for my own sake. But the most macabre instrumentalization of ethics lies in the structure of the *Religion* as a whole. For hundreds of pages, Cohen has led the reader into a determination of ethical messianism as true religion and has shown that this identification is as rooted in the Jewish tradition as in the philosophical tradition, if not more so. The reader is led to the expectation of a grand messianic ending. But this expectation is shattered; instead, we get the grand telos of the text of the *Religion* as . . . a notion of death that is no longer quite as frightening as it might have been 500 pages earlier. In one of the most lyrical passages in the *Religion of Reason*, Cohen writes:

All the meaning, all the value of life is in peace. Peace is the unity of all vital powers, their equilibrium and the reconciliation of all their contradictions. Peace is the crown of life. Human life concludes in death. Death is not the end but a conclusion, a new beginning. It is significant for the Jewish consciousness that it also thinks of death as, and calls it, peace . . . Peace takes away from death its sting. It also gives a solution to the riddle of death. The man who is torn from life is not removed from peace, but rather brought nearer to it . . . Death is the world of peace. One cannot praise death better and more blissfully than by distinguishing it from the world of struggle . . . Life ought to seek peace; it finds it in death. Death is therefore not the actual end of human life but rather its goal, the trophy of life and all its striving. Whosoever loves peace cannot fear death. (RV 531–32/460)

While I cannot put myself in the place of an eminent philosopher during his final months, this passage appears anticlimactic; it marks a return from the rhetoric of community to the rhetoric of the individual. Cohen is more convincing in an earlier lyric about the immortality of humankind that conquers "tragic life and incurable death" (RV 312/268). This concept at least links the telos of life with the ethical process of community formation. In contrast, the closing sections of the *Religion* reduce the ethical life to a macabre selfishness; because my suffering has cosmic significance, I can die happy. I can even face martyrdom with courage, for my death will be "in the service of history" (RV 508/439). The fact that these teloi occupy the closing pages of the *Religion* gives them a literary significance that is only rarely supported by the philosophical arguments of the first two-thirds of the text.

CONCLUSION

The doubleness of nonbeing – as both privation and transcendence – has become more pronounced in the move from Maimonides to Cohen. Not only does the concept of privation ground the radical infinity of God (who, in Cohen, is thereby also characterized privatively, as infinite), but the temporalizing move in both thinkers, their reading of nonbeing as not-yet-being, instills a teleological arc to embodied existence (even if that arc seeks to extirpate the body) and institutes messianic ethics as a norm. These are the two primary shifts in the evolution of the concept of nonbeing from Plato to Cohen. Neither Maimonides nor Cohen can justify the place of ethics and messianism without appropriating the discourse of nonbeing from Plotinus and Democritus.

But there are metaphysical and ethical problems concomitant with this discourse. In reference to the metaphysical problem, Maimonides and Cohen agree that privation has an understanding of its goal within it, a conatus that leads it on its temporal path (either as emotional desire, or through the conatus of the infinitesimal toward integration). In some sense, privation is not completely deprived; it possesses its goal at least proleptically. And because this telos is also the origin (the One, or God), the telos shares the characteristic of nonbeing with the privative state that the cultivation of reason and ethics conquers. While Maimonides and Cohen are usually clear that "meontology" is always a term that is used to refer to existence and never to what lies beyond it, there is a strand in which both thinkers use meontological rhetoric to express the telos of human existence as well. God is without essential attributes as is sheer matter, the *Ursprung* of existence is also its *Ungrundlegung*, and thus other than being. Because there is no criterion to differentiate between two kinds of nonbeing, this leads to confusion. This is especially the case in Cohen, for whom the telos of human existence – which he describes as the messianic Age – is relegated to the far-off distance, and exists in the present moment of my ethical act. Yet again, this philosophical problem is not the result of carelessness; it expresses the truth of the correlation between the nonbeing above being (associated with critical meontology) and the nonbeing that characterizes the privative world (associated with dialectical meontology). Perhaps one might say that, like being and nonbeing in Plato and Husserl, these two accounts of nonbeing are non-independent. Yet the way in which a consciousness might come to know this correlation is unexpressed even in Cohen; the matter calls for a phenomenological answer that takes into account the intuition of the categorial in the sensuous (where here the category is one of nonbeing). The Jewish meontological tradition does not offer such an answer until Levinas, as will be seen in the next chapter.

In reference to the ethical problem, I have shown that the philosophical deduction of teleology from the concept of nonbeing leads to an instrumentalist ethic for both Maimonides and Cohen, although this ethic is more pronounced in Maimonides. The sociopolitical world of existence is the privative order that I am trying to transcend. An individual's philosophical analysis tells her that her redemption lies at the end of the teleological path, and that a cultivation of rational perfection (along with the ethical principles that are corollaries of this perfection) is the way to achieve this redemption. Ethics is a side effect of reason. The individual's cultivation of philosophy comes first; ethics comes thereafter. What is needed, and what is hinted at in Cohen's account of the interpersonal encounter, is a situation in which the cultivation of philosophy arises from the interpersonal scene. Ethics would not be the hysterical refusal of privation, nor would it arise from a *thinking* of privation. It would arise out of the glorious experience of privation, the everyday embodied sensing of matter. Once again, phenomenology will be of aid, since the sensuous world serves as the matrix from which all sense originates.

In the next chapter, I explore one proto-phenomenological and one phenomenological account of the relationship between nonbeing, teleology, ethics, and messianism. Rosenzweig will attempt (and, on my reading, fail) to give the world an essential role by viewing it as a stage in God's self-development, whereas Levinas turns to the body as the site of ambiguity, where nonbeing and being meet. In this carnal encounter – in which non-being does not simply show itself as the contrary or the contradictory concept of being but is cognized through the interpersonal encounter – one finally sees a resolution of the metaphysical problem of nonbeing that does not fall into ethical problems.

4

Nonbeing Ensouled, Nonbeing Embodied

Levinas versus Rosenzweig on the Role of the Other in Messianic Anticipation

It is by now a truism that the most dramatic development in American modern Jewish thought since the 1960s, and especially since the 1990s, has been the explosion of work on the writings of Franz Rosenzweig (1886–1929) – the interpretive secondary works, the new translations, the scores of conference papers.[1] Rosenzweig is an ideal standard-bearer for the task of formulating a Jewish philosophy for the postmodern era: his language evokes the texts of the Talmud, Kabbalah, and Maimonides and is ahead of its time insofar as it anticipates the rise of phenomenology in Continental philosophy as well as the linguistic turn of recent French thought and American pragmatism. The multiple "Rosenzweigs" apparent in a reading of the *Star of Redemption* (first published in 1921) parallel the text's multiple Judaisms: the extensive evocation of the concrete life of Jewish ritual liturgy in the third book, as well as a demythologized view of revelation and religious ethics in the second book. The *Star* is a book for everyone.

Indeed, Rosenzweig may be even better suited than Levinas for the task of providing an organic Jewish philosophy. Levinas is definitely implicated in both the Jewish and postmodern worlds by virtue of his ethical critique of the totalizing humanist systems that reduce the particular to the general, and by virtue of his verifying this critique through a return to Jewish texts, both from the Talmud and from the ethico-Kabbalistic texts of the Lithuanian *musar* movement.[2] Yet for all of the devotion Levinas shows to Jewish texts, and even for all the Torah-observance that Levinas showed in his personal life, it remains a question as to whether philosophy coexists with a thick and non-demythologized sense of ritual on completely equal terms in Levinas's

[1] For a history of this trend, see Peter Eli Gordon, "Rosenzweig Redux: The Reception of German-Jewish Thought," *Jewish Social Studies* 8:1 (2001), 1–57.
[2] On the relationship between Levinas and the *musar* texts of Vilna Jews, see Jacob Meskin, "Toward a New Understanding of the Work of Emmanuel Levinas," *Modern Judaism* 20:1 (2000), 78–102, especially the works cited in nn. 17, 18, and 21.

writings. It may be that the richness of concrete Jewish ritual as, for example, the life of the synagogue, can be trumped by the conversion of its content into philosophemes. In a 1972 reading of B. Berakhot 61a entitled "And God Created Woman," Levinas discusses the Talmud's enumeration of forgivable apostasies and concludes, "a person may rebel against the synagogue because of the unbearable burden [*fardeau*] he carries. Let us forgive this revolt!"[3] Yet when placed in the context of his philosophical writings, this vocabulary of burden and weight becomes amplified to surprising effect. For Levinas's discussions of ethical responsibility are often expressed in this vocabulary. The responsibility for the other person "is incumbent on me [*m'incombe*],"[4] pressing down upon me (as the Latin *incumbere* connotes). Levinas's conclusion about the nature of the self who takes on this ethical responsibility is that he or she "is under the weight [*sous le poids*] of the universe, responsible for everything" (AE 147/116). This cluster of weight-related concepts leads one to the conclusion that there is no ethical self who is *not* under a burden; the ethical agent gains the right to revolt against the synagogue. While Levinas does not contravene or ridicule Jewish ritual observance, the philosophical writings allow his readers to minimize the importance of observant life in his work. But for Rosenzweig such a conclusion is impossible. Ritual is not a sphere from which ethics is extruded in his work; it is, rather, the unsurpassable context in which ethical actions are *performed.*

An uncritical appropriation of Jewish life can be found in Levinas's writings only through reference back to Rosenzweig. Levinas does authorize this move himself in an oft-quoted sentence from *Totality and Infinity*: "We were impressed by the opposition to the idea of totality in Franz Rosenzweig's *Star of Redemption,* a work too often present in this book to be cited" (TI xvi/28). If Rosenzweig's work, including its emphasis on lived Jewish tradition, is everywhere present in Levinas, then a traditionalist reading of Levinas suddenly becomes possible. Scholars can use this single sentence – which is truly as enigmatic as the most difficult of sentences in Levinas – to forge links between the two authors that remain unspoken on the surface of their published work. Thus, to provide only one example, Robert Gibbs claims that the Levinasian corpus is a *midrash,* an interpretation or "adaptation" of the Rosenzweigian corpus into the language of phenomenology.[5] However, Gibbs also claims that in Levinas, "Rosenzweig is nonetheless not merely

3 Levinas, *Du sacré au saint* (Paris: Minuit, 1977), 147, translated by Annette Aronowicz in *Nine Talmudic Readings* ed. and trans. Annette Aronowitz (Bloomington: Indiana University Press, 1990), 176.

4 Levinas, *Éthique et Infini* (Paris: Fayard, 1982), 102, translated by Richard A. Cohen as *Ethics and Infinity* (Pittsburgh: Duquesne University Press, 1985), 96.

5 Robert Gibbs, *Correlations in Rosenzweig and Levinas* (Princeton, N.J.: Princeton University Press, 1992), 26–32.

presented in a new coat, nor is he simply dragged forward fifty years."[6] The implication of this sentence is that there is something that separates Levinas from Rosenzweig over and above the philosophical context of 1950s and 1960s France. There must be some critique. Indeed, this is what is at stake in the invocation of midrash. While midrash does amplify the biblical worldview through its narrative and philological inventiveness, it often does so at the expense of the literal meaning of biblical verses: "Read not X, but Y," where Y is a revocalization of the word X. Therefore, if the relationship between Levinas and Rosenzweig is truly to be midrashic, it is necessary to point out not only the moments of Levinas's direct adaptation of Rosenzweigian motifs but also the places in which the primary meaning of the Rosenzweigian base-text is denied by the Levinasian interpretation.

The Rosenzweigian and Levinasian dramas *sound* similar to the reader: they are narratives of ethical relation, of the ways in which transcendence is revealed, of the nature of the path to redemption. But making connections in terms of the content or plot of these narratives is far more tenuous, as tenuous as an argument that a midrashic text uncovers the intended meaning of a biblical text.

In this chapter, I will argue for both Levinas's similarity to and his critique of Rosenzweig. Both Rosenzweig and Levinas are meontological thinkers; they include the entire realm of existence under the sign of the "not-yet." Yet the narrative deployment of this theme differs in the two thinkers. It is helpful to return to the flitting reference to Rosenzweig in *Totality and Infinity* and put it in a slightly fuller context. Although every sentence in this paragraph (TI xvi–xvii/28–29) has important things to say about the limited parameters of the Levinas–Rosenzweig relationship, I have selected only a few of the neighboring sentences.[7]

The relation between the same and the other does not always amount to knowledge of the other by the same, nor even to the *revelation* of the other to the same, which is already fundamentally different from disclosure.

We were impressed by the opposition to the idea of totality in Franz Rosenzweig's *Star of Redemption*, a work too often present in this book to be cited. But the presentation and the development of the notions employed owe everything to the phenomenological method. Intentional analysis is the search for the concrete. [. . .]We shall deal with both [theory and ethics] as modes of metaphysical transcendence. The apparent confusion is deliberate and constitutes one of the theses of this book. Husserlian phenomenology has made possible this passage of ethics to metaphysical exteriority.

---

[6] Ibid., 32.

[7] For the limits of Levinas's appropriation of Rosenzweig, also cf. Levinas, "Philosophie, Justice, et Amour," in *Entre nous* (Paris: Bernard Grasset, 1991), 137, translated by Michael B. Smith as "Philosophy, Justice, and Love," in *Entre Nous*, trans. Michael B. Smith and Barbara Harshav (New York: Columbia University Press, 1997), 118.

When one views the ephemeral encomium to Rosenzweig in this context, it becomes quite puzzling. Why is Levinas suspicious of the category of revelation, a category that lies at the heart of Rosenzweig's *Star*, when discussing the same–other relation? Why does Levinas seem to be drawing a dichotomy between Rosenzweig's *Star* and the analysis of concrete structures? The final sentences of the previous quotation are in greatest tension with the encomium. Not only is Levinas here crediting Husserl, and not Rosenzweig, with the grounding of a viable ethical metaphysics, but the "passage" of which Levinas writes moves in a diametrically opposite direction from the passage of Rosenzweig's own thinking. Levinas's passage moves from the ethical interpersonal scene to its grounding in a quasi-theological metaphysics. As I shall illustrate, Rosenzweig moves in the opposite direction, from a posited theological ground to a construction of ideal ethical behavior.

The Levinas-Rosenzweig relationship is extremely complex, but there is more than enough room to articulate how the Levinasian adaptation of Rosenzweig includes a moment of critique. In this chapter, I shall focus on the issue of the place of the concrete in Levinas's method. On the basis of the two sentences directly following the encomium to Rosenzweig – "but the presentation and the development of the notions employed owe everything to the phenomenological method. Intentional analysis is the search for the concrete" – it is valid to make a hypothesis that the remainder of this chapter will verify. The ground for Levinas's opposition to totality differs from that found in Rosenzweig. Levinas believes thought to be transcendentally grounded in a concrete given (i.e., phenomenological intentionality is rooted in given concrete sensations). This type of grounding is completely lacking in Rosenzweig, for whom thought is grounded in a revelation whose origin is not the created world. Indeed, what Levinas has that Rosenzweig does not is the phenomenological method learned from Husserl. While Levinas does forsake much of Husserlian methodology in his writings, Levinas states, in a 1985 interview, his adherence to a basic principle of phenomenology, namely, that the "search for the concrete status" of the given object that grounds my intentional aims "seems to me to constitute phenomenology's fundamental teaching ... [the] privileged intelligibility of the concrete is developed as early as the third *Logical Investigation*, and the term 'concrete' keeps recurring in Husserl's phenomenological descriptions."[8]

The stakes here are large. On the one hand (what I hypothesize to be the Levinasian narrative), the move to the quasi-theological "metaphysical exteriority" begins with an analysis of human sensed life and then moves upward and outward to God. On the other hand (what I hypothesize to

---

[8] Levinas, "Sur la philosophie juive," in *A l'heure des nations* (Paris: Minuit, 1988), 212, translated by Michael B. Smith as "On Jewish Philosophy," in *In The Time of the Nations* (Bloomington: Indiana University Press, 1994), 180. Also cf. Richard A. Cohen, *Ethics, Exegesis, and Philosophy: Interpretation after Levinas* (Cambridge: Cambridge University Press, 2001), 99–119.

be the Rosenzweigian narrative), such a move does not need to be justified, since there is an immediate experience of God that then grounds
our intentional aims. Simply stating that there are experiences of transcendence in both authors does not help matters any. It still remains to pose a
fundamental question: *how* does the event of transcendence occur to human consciousness? For the event can be an immediate relationship with a
noumenal God who is hierarchically situated above and beyond the world
of appearances. Or it can pass through the vague sieve of a relationship with
a concrete and fleshy – sometimes nude – body, completely phenomenal
yet still possessing shards of divinity within. The role of the human body, insofar as it may mediate human interaction, becomes very important for the
narration of the experience of transcendence, and by extension for the narration of the Rosenzweig–Levinas relationship. For the first conception of
the event, the body is unnecessary, profane, and useful instrumentally only
as it sets the stage for the transformation of voice into idea in a contemplation without distraction. For the other conception of the event, the profane
nature of the concrete mechanism of the body still possesses elements of
intrinsic goodness.

The Rosenzweig–Levinas relationship thus enables us to pick apart the
strands of thought that led us to an uneasy discomfort with the rhetorical
oscillation about the instrumentality of ethics in Maimonides and Cohen,
seen in the previous chapter. In this chapter, I will associate Rosenzweig
with a thinking of transcendence as purely sacred, a mode of thinking that
in the end instrumentalizes ethical action. Levinas is able to get out of
this bind, I argue, via a phenomenological method that complicates the
sacred/profane distinction. Undoubtedly, both Rosenzweig and Levinas are
concerned with how humankind can engender the preconditions for eternal
truth (in Rosenzweig) or messianic triumph (in Levinas) through love of
neighbor. However, I will argue that Rosenzweig's nonembodied thinking
of the neighbor causes a severe ethical problem and that the fourth section
of *Totality and Infinity* (specifically the phenomenology of eros) and the
analysis of sensibility in *Otherwise than Being* can be understood to serve as a
corrective to the ethical danger that undergirds Rosenzweig's eschatology.
For Rosenzweig sees the neighbor only as an alter ego. This is the very
notion of otherness that Levinas critiques as insufficient in works as early
as *Time and the Other*: "The Other as Other is not only an alter ego: the
Other is what I myself am not. The Other is this . . . because of the Other's
very alterity," a property that, for Levinas, the Other possesses completely
independent of any reference to me.[9] By virtue of this eradication of the

9 Levinas, *Le temps et l'autre* (Paris: Presses Universitaires de France, 1989), 75, translated by
   Richard A. Cohen as *Time and the Other* (Pittsburgh: Duquesne University Press, 1994), 83. For
   a detailed account of this position as a critique of Husserl's theory of analogical apperception
   in the fifth of the *Cartesian Meditations*, cf. Edith Wyschogrod, *Emmanuel Levinas: The Problem
   of Ethical Metaphysics*, 2nd ed. (New York: Fordham University Press, 2000), 48–52.

alterity of the other person, one can claim that in the system of the *Star,* the neighbor serves only as a means to the end of the praying chorus of the Jewish community. My love of neighbor has nothing to do with the neighbor him- or herself; I am simply interested in making the voice of my congregation louder.[10]

Since it is phenomenology that enables Levinas to view the Other as intrinsically good, the argument that follows will involve somewhat lengthy sections of passages in Merleau-Ponty and Husserl. But the critical moment that I will articulate here will not be at the expense of the sizable extent of Levinas's adaptation of Rosenzweig, especially in the area of meontology. For in both the *Star* and *Totality and Infinity,* the structure of messianic or eschatological anticipation is described as existence in that which is "not-yet." For Rosenzweig, the not-yet is discovered through existence in the world (S 249/223); for Levinas, it is discovered through sensibility and the erotic caress (TI 235/258). Rosenzweig's genius is to appropriate the methodology of Schellingian idealism in order to argue that although the world has positive meaning as God's expressive act, it nonetheless bears a negative meaning to humankind until persons live in the world and transform it from the status of creature or substance to something subject, something "ensouled [*beseelt*]" (S 268/241). For Rosenzweig and Levinas, humans cannot but perceive the world to be unfinished; one can thereby say that the world, as it appears to me, has a meontological nature. Insofar as in *Totality and Infinity* and *Otherwise than Being* the separated self enjoys the objective world yet is called into question by the subjectivity of the Other's face and body, Levinas retains the meontological nature of the world, as well as the idealist form (if not the content) of the transition of the exterior from substance

---

[10] Rosenzweig's interest in the maximization of the religious community is, in my view, starkly opposed to the rhetoric of disinterestedness in Levinas; see "Dieu et la philosophie," in *De Dieu qui vient à l'idée,* 2nd ed. (Paris: Vrin, 1986), 111, translated by Bettina Bergo as "God and Philosophy," in *Of God Who Comes to Mind* (Stanford, Calif.: Stanford University Press, 1998), 67. Additionally, Rosenzweig's interest is always an interest in *my* religious community. The relations between Jews and Christians in the *Star* are only formal, not content-filled relationships *between* persons. Thus, I disagree with David Novak's view in *The Election of Israel* that Rosenzweig contradicts classical Judaism's view of the neighbor as one's fellow Jew. The voice of the community in the synagogue or church sings "We" (S 263–64/236–37), leaving all outside one's own house of worship to be dreadfully judged as "Ye," no matter how integral they may be to the appearance of divine truth in the world. It seems to me that Levinas himself likewise mistakes a formal symmetry between communities for a lived relationship when he writes in "The Philosophy of Franz Rosenzweig" that the *Star* argues for "the greatest intimacy between Christians and Jews, an intimacy centered around truth." Cf. "La philosophie de Franz Rosenzweig," in *A l'heure des nations,* 179, translated by Michael B. Smith in *In the Time of the Nations,* 154. For another critique of Novak's position, cf. Leora Batnitzky, "Dialogue as Judgment, Not Mutual Affirmation: A New Look at Franz Rosenzweig's Dialogical Philosophy," *Journal of Religion* 79:4 (1999), 523–44, esp. 537n. 40, and Batnitzky, *Idolatry and Representation: The Philosophy of Franz Rosenzweig Considered* (Princeton, N.J.: Princeton University Press, 2000), 145–68.

to subject.[11] But the concrete situation in Levinas is one of understanding tempered by critique by the other person, whereas Rosenzweig projects the understanding of the world gained in the private revelatory encounter onto the world.

The arguments of this chapter depend upon the temporalization of non-being analyzed in the previous chapter. In other words, this chapter assumes the validity of the transformation of the "not" into the "not-yet" found previously. The path of the argument of this chapter will proceed as follows. I begin with an explanation of the meontological perspective of Rosenzweig's *Star* by reference to its first book. From that point, I move to a presentation of the way in which the construction of meontology in the first book of the *Star* determines the construction of the neighbor within the arc of messianic anticipation in the second book, setting the stage for the instrumentalization of love that occurs within. The argument will then shift to a discussion of Levinas's work. First, I claim that in *Totality and Infinity*, eros qua the experience of the embodied Other *par excellence* justifies philosophical claims about the meontological, understood as that which has no essence and is hence other than being as it is traditionally described. Then, I will turn to the Husserlian heritage of *Otherwise than Being* – Husserl's understanding of body in *Ideas II* and the lectures on time consciousness – to show that Levinas here expands the analysis of eros from *Totality and Infinity* into an analysis of all sensibility in general. Sensibility, like eros in the earlier work, is linked with "the immediacy of enjoyment and its frustration" (AE 94/74). In the later work, the body is completely engaged in messianic ethics, over and above the predominantly biological sense of paternity in *Totality and Infinity*. However, in both works (and in other essays), Levinas continues to equate the ethically responsible self with the Messiah, and this ethics always respects the intrinsic goodness of the Other. Here lies the complete articulation of the belonging-together of the dialectical and critical concepts of meontology: my ability to ethically relate to another person in the social realm channels an agency that originates in that which lies beyond being.

THE SOUL, FAITHFUL IN PATHOS

The *Star of Redemption* announces its meontological journey near the beginning of its first book (S 23/21), when Rosenzweig explicitly links his methodology with Cohen's appropriation of the infinitesimal calculus: mathematics

---

[11] Cf. G. W. F. Hegel, *Phenomenology of Spirit*, trans. A. V. Miller (Oxford: Oxford University Press, 1977), pars. 18 and 803, amid many others. I certainly do not wish to deny the many differences between Hegel and Levinas, especially Levinas's theme of "my subjectivity" as accusative and "the Other's subjectivity" as nominative. For Levinas, "subject" is hardly synonymous with "I," but is rather always understood in the accusative. See AE 14/11.

reveals the origin of the objective realm in that which is not. Cohen does not attempt to use the language of the infinitesimal calculus directly in making theosophic postulations about the nature and history of God. But for Rosenzweig, this is part of the project of the opening book of the *Star*. Rosenzweig's source for supplementing Cohen in this regard is Schelling, specifically *Die Weltalter* (*The Ages of the World*), which Rosenzweig had with him as he wrote the opening sections of the *Star* on postcards to his mother while fighting at the front during the First World War.[12]

The *Weltalter* is a history of God – an account of God's becoming self-conscious as the precondition of creation and revelation. Schelling construes this path of becoming-conscious as a dialectical sequence of three potencies, each of which marks a successively further determination of the Godhead. The style of Schelling's thought bears at least a linguistic similarity, if not more, to the Cohenian motif of *Erzeugung*.[13] The *Weltalter* begins with the hypothesis that God is a dipolar entity and that the fullness of God lies in the historical process of dialectical movement between these two poles, necessary essence and free power. This hypothesis is not made completely out of thin air. Rather, Schelling believes that it is part of rigorous reasoning: "Movement is what is essential to knowledge. When this element of life is withdrawn, propositions die like fruit removed from the Tree of Life" (W 208/4). Movement must be dependent upon contradiction between poles, for "without contradiction, there would be no movement, no life, no progress. There would only be eternal stoppage, a deathly slumber of all forces" (W 219/12). Contradiction here appears to have the connotation of the perdurance of difference, as opposed to the logical category of contrariness. There can be no history without this movement between poles.[14] The relationship between the poles must be described in terms of potency or potential; if they were actualities satisfied in the fullness of their stasis, then

---

[12] The most complete presentations of Schelling's influence upon Rosenzweig are Else Rahel-Freund, *Franz Rosenzweig's Philosophy of Existence: An Analysis of* The Star of Redemption, trans. Stephen L. Weinstein and Robert Israel, ed. Paul Mendes-Flohr (The Hague: Martinus Nijhoff, 1979 [1933]), esp. 17–45, 105–11, and 138–40, and Michael Morgan's comments in Rosenzweig, *Philosophical and Theological Writings*, ed. Michael L. Morgan and Paul Franks (Indianapolis: Hackett, 2002), 25–47.

[13] For an account of the place of *Erzeugung* in Schelling, see Edward Allen Beach, *The Potencies of God(s): Schelling's Philosophy of Mythology* (Albany: State University of New York Press, 1994), 84–88. The question of whether Cohen's dialectic bears any explicit or implicit debts to Schelling is not one that I can answer at this time. If it could be answered in the affirmative, however, it would call for a serious re-visioning of the alleged antitheosophic nature of Cohen's *wissenschaftlich* way of thinking. Indeed, the rise of Kabbalist historiography with Gershom Scholem is currently seen as a revolt against Cohen's way of thinking. See David Biale, *Gershom Scholem, Kabbalah, and Counter-History* (Cambridge, Mass.: Harvard University Press, 1979), esp. 109–12.

[14] Cf. David Farrell Krell, "Trauma, Forgetting, and Narrative in F. W. J. Schelling's *Die Weltalter*," *Postmodern Culture* 11:2 (http://muse.jhu.edu/demo/pmc/11.2krell.html).

there would be no impulse to the dynamism that propels history. The first potency is the subjective pole of pure power, pure potentiality; the second potency is the objective pole of being, the "being as being" generated by this power (W 226/17–18).[15] Thus Schelling, like Plotinus and Maimonides in *Guide* I: 17, co-opts the ontological rhetoric of substance and attribute such as that found in Aristotle, and leaves this rhetoric in its philosophical privilege while folding it into a rhetoric of nonbeing understood as potentiality and privation. God is not (yet) before God is. Basing his reasoning on the claim that "what is posited as the beginning is precisely that which is subordinated afterwards," Schelling concludes that only "what inclines most to the nature of what does not have being can be posited at the beginning" (W 221/13). Since nonbeing includes within itself a conative impulse toward being, it is that which is subordinated.

The system of potencies is the theosophical coding of a journey in which God comes to manifest himself fully and wholly as "the one and many in intimate connection" (W 312/84), the full and complete determination that we saw in the last chapter as the end point of Cohen's theory of thinking as *Erzeugung*. Earlier in the *Weltalter*, Schelling describes this as "a progression from darkness into light and from death into life" (W 303/77). This latter phrase is well known to readers of the *Star* as the primary arc of its narrative, which begins with the words "from death [*vom Tode*]" and concludes with the words "into life [*ins Leben*]."[16] It is then not at all an exaggeration to say that Rosenzweig's appropriation of Schelling seeps through every page of the *Star*. To this reading I now turn, wishing to glean from this quick reading of Schelling the fact that the fullness of God is only meaningful for human consciousness through the construction of the system of potencies. Always and everywhere Schelling's goal is to imagine the dialectical turns that are necessary to bring the fullness of God's spiritual being into reality. Already from the point of view of the Levinasian approach, this appears odd. In Schelling (as in Maimonides), the experience of the fullness of being is our greatest desire.

Rosenzweig opens the *Star* with a phenomenology of death; this grounds his turn away from idealism. Death is not the mere fact of nothingness, of nonexistence. The fact of death also includes my intentional comportment of fear toward it "all that is mortal lives in this fear of death, and every new birth augments this fear by one new reason" (S 3/3). Rosenzweig claims that the history of philosophy from the pre-Socratics through Hegel has never wanted to think through this fear, but rather "plugs up its ears before the cry of terrorized humanity" (S 5/5). The empirical mistake that this "old"

---

[15] For a detailed account of the potencies with primary reference to Schelling's many works in the philosophy of mythology, see Beach, 111–46.

[16] For a fuller account of this architectonic, cf. Zachary Braiterman, in "'Into Life'??! Franz Rosenzweig and the Figure of Death," *AJS Review* 23:2 (1998), 203–21.

thinking makes is a blindness to the category of the singular, where thinking is always already situated. The fact of fear in the face of death means that the fearful subject cannot be reduced to the category of the human. Neither can this fear be bracketed away, since it is the environment in which all my epistemological endeavors are situated. In addition, the philosophical abstraction away from death ignores the time-bound nature of existence. Temporality, as exemplified in the ever-recurrent moment of my fearful cry, banishes knowledge of the single idea. This analysis marks the beginning of Rosenzweig's pushing the Kantian ideas back so that they sink away into the murky depths of the beyond, of the "meta."

But does Rosenzweig's argument force us into a Protagorean relativism? Is knowledge hopeless, and is my thinking always bound by my fearful interests? Here meontology comes to Rosenzweig's rescue. It is the dynamic nature of nonbeing, its containing its own telos hidden within itself, that justifies the epistemological quest. Temporality is the transcendental context for knowledge of being. Rosenzweig describes this in terms of Cohen's infinitesimal calculus; the "nonbeing of the differential" is not equivalent to the number zero, but "points to a something, its being; at the same time it is a being that still slumbers in the lap of nothing" (S 23/20). Thus, as with Maimonides and Cohen, but in opposition to Levinas's putative understanding of Rosenzweig, the *Star* is not an opposition to totality *tout court*, but a deferral of totality. The telos of the soul's spiritual journey – the vision of the face of God in the Star of David at the moment of death, akin to the rabbinic understanding of Moses' "death by God's kiss"[17] – is the "something" that we have every right to expect once we view nonbeing as not-yet-being (S 433/390). For Rosenzweig, nonbeing is always comported toward God as its full development and expression. (At the same time, Rosenzweig also, like Cohen, states that "God is the Nought" [S 434/390].) These arguments are not limited to the close of the *Star*. Near the end of its first part, Rosenzweig also appropriates the temporalization of nonbeing observed in the previous chapter: the All – the sum of the Kantian ideas – is "a secret . . . not yet manifest to us" (S 99/90).

The *Star* is thus oriented by both Schellingian and Cohenian rhetorics. This is not always an easy friendship. For while Cohen's process of divine *Erzeugung* is a determination of an object in comparison with its surrounding objects, Schelling's is a settling of accounts between two contrary impulses within the closed-off object of analysis. Although Rosenzweig's announced methodology is Cohenian, the content of the first book of the *Star* is clearly Schellingian in vocabulary. Rosenzweig in fact universalizes Schelling's theosophy by asserting that each of the Kantian ideas – God, world, and the subject-I ("man") – is structured as a dynamic

---

[17] Cf. B. Baba Bathra 17a.

interrelationship between two polarities. Insofar as these ideas, examined apart from the others, are claimed to be "irrational" (S 21/19), one might say that God, world, and the subject-I are all afflicted by a bipolar disorder.

In the case of God, Rosenzweig appropriates fully the concepts of the eternal Yes and the eternal No, the two poles of God according to Schelling's portrait in the *Weltalter*. There, the eternal Yes refers to the infinite essence of the divine, whereas the No refers to the power that forces this essence to contract and hide itself: the first potency is the configuration in which the negating power "shoves back the affirming essence and plants it within, inactive or in secret," while the eternal Yes also acts upon the power-pole and prohibits it from forcing itself upon any other sphere of action (W 215/9). Likewise, for Rosenzweig, the Yes refers to the infinite essence of God (S 31/29), while the No refers to the divine freedom that is completely other than this essence (S 32/30). These two poles govern the dynamic of the divine nonbeing. On the one hand, the Yes refers to the singularity of God, to the fact that God transcends any essential attributes that humans might ascribe to God, to the positing of God as a singular and transcendent idea. The No, on the other hand, refers to the potential of God for relation. Freedom itself is finite; it can aim at only one action out of many at any given moment. Yet it does aim; it "reaches beyond itself with unlimited power" (S 32–33/30). Nevertheless, there is nothing for it to aim at except for the Yes-pole of divine essence. The account of the bare potentiality of the Godhead that Rosenzweig develops here is again identical to that of Schelling. The essence-pole swallows up the power-pole.

But in approaching essence, the freedom of choice [*Willkür*] falls under the spell of essence's inert being. Without being [essence] emitting force upon freedom of choice, the latter feels its force ebbing. With every step that takes it closer to essence, the infinite power (of choice) senses a growing resistance, a resistance which would become infinite at the goal, at essence itself. (S 33/31).

Divine freedom, having no essence of its own, is always oriented externally. It desires something to act on. Yet the only "thing" that freedom has to act on is the divine essence that has already been defined as infinite and self-absorbed. It thus acts manically upon the divine essence, which is (as Cohen asserted, following Maimonides) inert, and attempts to draw it into itself, to control it in some way. Conversely, the essence-pole can also enfeeble the power-pole, moving it from euphoria to depression. Because the divine essence is completely inert, it cannot express any of the force that divine freedom wants to pass on to it. One could here draw an analogy from the classic example in introductory mechanics of billiard ball collisions: the divine essence would be akin to the fixed sides of the table that gradually sap the billiard balls of their kinetic energy. Yet at the same time, the divine essence gradually, through its relations with divine freedom, is able to amass and inhere energy within itself, which can eventually become self-expression in creation (S 125/113).[18]

Rosenzweig, unlike Schelling, continues by applying the Yes–No dipolarity in his analysis of the other two Kantian ideas: the world and the human. Rosenzweig describes the unknowability of the world, a "negative cosmology" (S 44/41) in terms of the reining in of its affirmative form- or essence-pole by its negating and determining finite content-pole. The Yes of the world is its form as *logos*, as the ordering of soul/form that exists within each object (S 46/43). Its No is the plenitude of content to which this *logos* is always applied. As with the idea of God, Rosenzweig's understanding of the idea of the world in the first book of the *Star* follows the structure of the first Schellingian potency: negation holds the affirmative essence of the idea in check, renders it passive, and prohibits it from expressing itself fully and independently; there is an "ever-renewed constriction of procreation and birth" (S 48/45). The *logos* of the world "is utterly universal and yet everywhere attached to the world, tied up in it" (S 47/44). In the first gaze at an object, there is no linkage between that object and other objects in the world. Every object appears as "particular [*besonderes*]" (S 49/45), as radically different from every other object in the world. The world appears simply as a panoply of things, not as the ordered emanation of an overarching concept that serves to bond objects to one another.

With respect to the third Kantian idea, the Yes-pole is the particular "peculiarity" of the particular person. Unlike the affirmative poles of the Godhead and the world, the human Yes-pole is not infinite in terms of space. Nevertheless, one can still describe it as apeirontic, "finite yet boundless" (S 69/64). Rosenzweig describes the *apeiron* of the peculiar individual as an ignorance of anything that exists outside of selfhood. As long as there is an "I think" that justifies and supports all of the operations of my understanding, I am unable to extricate myself from myself, and hence cannot gain the benefit of an exterior view that would lead to any justifiable knowledge-claims about myself. The negative pole of the human is expressed as free will, the determinate orientation of my freedom. Freedom has a negative force, insofar as "all negation posits something determined [and] finite" (S 71/66). In the act of willing, my particular and peculiar form is packaged into the content of a determinate and ephemeral object of my will. In each free act of volition, I am choosing between two or more alternatives, accepting one while rejecting and negating all the others.[19] Yet for Rosenzweig, that which is determined and negated is not simply an object of my will in the world, but is, rather, my very peculiarity itself. In other words, just as divine freedom repressed

---

[18] Compare with Rahel-Freund, 92–93.

[19] For an amplification of this Kantian account of volition, see John Silber, "The Ethical Significance of Kant's *Religion*," in Kant, *Religion Within the Limits of Reason Alone*, trans. T. M. Greene and H. H. Hudson (New York: Harper & Row, 1960), lxxix–cxxxiv, esp. lxxxvi–ciii.

and held back the divine essence, so does human freedom repress human distinctiveness: "the 'self' is what originates in this encroachment by free will upon peculiarity" (S 73/68). This is the construction of the defiant will. The defiant will does not make peculiar decisions that allow the subject's distinctiveness to develop, but wills the perseverance of the peculiarity that it already sees itself as being. The essence of the individual, distinctiveness, is thereby made passive, confined within its solitary way of life, turned "into the content of predications about something else" (S 75/69).

The descriptions of the Kantian ideas of God, world, and human subjectivity given in the first book of the *Star* are all versions of the repressive relationship narrated in Schelling's description of the first potency in the *Weltalter*. This repressive relationship is, also in accordance with Schelling, seen as meontological: the essence of each of the three ideas has not yet come to be. Rather, appearance shrouds the universal essence, so that one can truly speak of the idea as being something which-is-not. Most importantly, the structure of the ideas at this point is one of a relationship between two poles. Meaning is constructed by the interrelations of the poles within each idea, *not* by the interrelations of the ideas themselves.

There are brief hints in the first part of the *Star*, more clearly with reference to the world and God than to human subjectivity, in which Rosenzweig shows how the future configuration of the ideas will consist in a switching of the valences of the poles. No longer will the No-pole repress the Yes-pole, but the affirmative essence will be affirmed by the power-pole, which renders itself passive as it allows the essence of the idea to come to appearance. In the dynamic nature of the cosmos (S 97/88), the ideas are always in a process of conversion: "what converged as Yes will radiate forth as No; what entered as No will issue as Yes." In this conversion, which Rosenzweig associates with revelation and faith (contra philosophy), and which is patterned on the transition from the first to the second potency in Schelling's *Weltalter* (W 246–47/32–33) the three ideas come into relationship with each other. Rosenzweig describes revelation as "the self-emergence [*Aussichherausgehen*], conjunction [*Zueinandergehören*] and intersection [*Zueinanderkommen*] of the three 'real' [*tatsächlich*] elements of the All – God world man" (S 127/115).

The key question that the reader must pose to Rosenzweig's account of conversion is one of temporal order. What comes first – the switching of the valences of the poles of the ideas, or the meetings between the ideas? Does the meeting determine the reversal of the valences, or does the spontaneous reversal of the valences lead to the meeting? If the meeting determines the reversal of the valences, then there is room for alterity to be a constitutive factor in the development of the idea in question. The donation of essence that characterizes revelation will be prompted by the expression of the essence of another idea, Other in the richest of senses, within its concrete instantiations. But if the reverse is the case, then the interaction between the ideas will be only an application of a revelation-formula. That

which gives its essence will give it to a blank slate, a completely empty otherness, since the giving and affirmation associated with the Yes is magnetically
attracted to the inessential and determinate No. As I shall now show, the gift
of essence in Rosenzweig always occurs in accordance with the latter model.
At the end of the first part of the *Star*, God, world, and human subjectivity
are empty of all essence, still within the meontological structure of the not
or the not-yet. The move from emptiness to fullness must begin somewhere,
within one of the ideas, and then spread to the others. This beginning is
within God.

The transition from the protocosmic mystery of the first part of the *Star*
to the manifestation of each of the ideas of its second part is a pure miracle
(S 99/90), rooted in an act of free choice on the part of God (S 128/116).
Rosenzweig writes that in creation, power becomes an attribute of the subject, but not simply an attribute like other substantial attributes; rather, it is
"no longer isolated deed, no longer free choice, but essence. God the creator is essentially powerful" (S 125/113). The negative power-pole realizes
that it can further extend itself when it couples with essence; the positive
essence-pole realizes that it can finally express itself when it couples with
power. Here, there is a reversal of the Yes and the No on the part of the
poles within God. The power-pole now freely decides to affirm essence, by
creating new essences within the world; and essence now determines power,
by renewing the presence of essences in the world at every moment in an
apparently infinitely punctiform series. Nothing has forced God to make
this decision, although Rosenzweig does note that once the decision for
self-manifestation has been made, there is no turning back: "as 'manifest'
God he cannot do otherwise than to create" (S 128/116). Once God has
freely switched the valences of the poles that lie within him, creation and its
daily renewal (S 135/122) proceed, as it were, on automatic pilot. In other
words, God's creation provides the world, but establishes no relationship
between God and the world.

Moreover, God's act of creation does not even provide the world as an environment that houses objects composed of both form and content, essence
and concrete instantiation. It only authorizes the transition from the protocosmic world as "essenceless semblance" to a new conception of the world as
"unessential essence." This argument is one of the most difficult in the *Star*.
It might be theologically intuitive for some readers to assign a dimension of
fullness (although not complete fullness) to God's creation, a fullness that
includes both formal essence and concrete material. Yet Rosenzweig claims
that "the world has not yet come to an end through the once-and-for-all creative act of God" (S 132/119) and that "the world did not have to 'become'
something 'finished' in the divine creation" (S 133/120). These claims are
of paramount strategic importance in the *Star*. If the world could be thought
as having a uniform essence, always present and transparent, then the world
would be seen as only an emanation of the divine; one would not be justified

in speaking of redemption. Most importantly for Rosenzweig, this scenario would entail a knowledge of the world that (by virtue of the emanationist framework) could be amplified into a knowledge of God. With this knowledge, there would be no terror in the face of death. Therefore, *without* an incomplete creation, the empirical motor of Rosenzweig's thinking loses all of its power. Therefore, the argument deserves further unpacking.[20]

The shift of polar valences in the Godhead causes a parallel shift in the valences of the world. In accordance with the conversion of Yes into No and vice versa (S 97/88), the created world will mark the appearance of the infinite in the particular, as distinct from it. The *logos* of the world was, in the protocosmos, completely absorbed into the particular object; the object was saturated (*gefüllt*; S 54/50) with its own concept.[21] Creation, as a mechanism in which the universal does not attract its own repression, but freely gives its essence to the particular, shows the universal. In the pagan pantheistic worldview (what Rosenzweig terms the "protocosmos," equivalent to Schelling's first potency), the object plunges into the universal; in the created world the universal plunges into the "outside," externalizes itself in objects. This means that the universal in the end temporalizes itself, and this temporalization itself prevents the full externalization of the universal.

In the act of creation, worldly objects are preserved from moment to moment through the workings of divine causality. An occasionalist argument such as this is nicely explained in Descartes' third *Meditation*:

For a lifespan can be divided into countless parts, each completely independent of the others, so that it does not follow from the fact that I existed a little while ago that I must exist now, unless there is some cause which as it were creates me afresh at this moment – that is, which preserves me. For it is quite clear to anyone who attentively considers the nature of time that the same power and action are needed to preserve anything at each individual moment of its duration as would be required to create that thing anew if it were not yet in existence. Hence the distinction between preservation and creation is only a conceptual one.[22]

Rosenzweig is at the same time more and less sophisticated than Descartes on this matter. For Rosenzweig does not argue for occasionalism on the basis of the structure of time, and thus he does not demonstrate creation out of the structure of human existence. Rather, Rosenzweig has already demonstrated that God *must* manifest himself in the world through creation because of the

---

[20] There are further remarks on the incompleteness of creation in Stéphane Mosès, *System and Revelation: The Philosophy of Franz Rosenzweig*, trans. Catherine Tihanyi (Detroit: Wayne State University Press, 1992), 83–85.

[21] Compare Jean-Luc Marion, "The Saturated Phenomenon," *Philosophy Today* 40 (Spring 1996), 103–24.

[22] René Descartes, *Meditations on First Philosophy*, in *Selected Philosophical Writings*, trans. John Cottingham, Robert Stoothoff, and Dugald Murdoch (Cambridge: Cambridge University Press, 1988), 96.

dynamic of the system of potencies; this is more of a wager for creation than a proof of it. Rosenzweig's own claim that "creature-consciousness [is] the consciousness not of having once been created but of being everlastingly creature" (S 133/120) seems to be merely imaginative, less justified than anything in even Schelling, much less Descartes. But one can reconstruct Rosenzweig's train of thought from the previous sentence in the *Star*: "Seen from its [the world's] own point of view, its being-created would mean for it manifesting itself [*ihr Sich-Offenbaren*, lit., its self-revelation] as creature." This, I think, can be unpacked as follows. For creation to mean anything for human consciousness, creatureliness must be apparent to human consciousness at any moment at which an object is perceived. If this is not the case, then there is no revelation to human consciousness that occurs through the medium of creation or through any other medium. In addition, there could be no self-temporalization of the divine as necessitated by the infrapotency dynamic. Occasionalism is a clear and distinct idea in Rosenzweig because to contradict it means to contradict both the compulsion that drives the act of God's creation of the world and the ability of the individual to receive this revelation at any point in time (S 128/115–16). I cannot experience creation as a mode of revelation unless I experience the creatureliness of the objective world. And this must happen in the present moment; a postulation of the Creator of the world merely as a first cause who acted long long ago does not come close to approaching an experience of the Creator.

Thus, creation as revelation necessitates occasionalism. This means, for Rosenzweig, that the created object does not possess its essence as an "enduring essence" but possesses only "a momentary, infinitely renewed and yet universal essence" (S 133/120). For the created object to possess an essence that stretches across the punctiform instants of the temporal continuum is to deny what Rosenzweig sees as the necessary truth of occasionalism, which precludes the very notion of an enduring essence. Thus, the essence of the object must be given to it again from moment to moment in the divine preservation of the object. This marks the fundamental difference between the protocosmic world and the created world. In the protocosmic world the distinctive particularity of every object saturated it to the extent that it enveloped the *logos* at every moment. This is the meaning of Rosenzweig's description of this world as an "essenceless semblance" (S 134/121), in which the essence comes to appearance along with the object. This model is opposed to the modern configuration of the object, such as that of Kant in which the thing-in-itself is hidden behind semblant appearance. For Rosenzweig, the essential being of the phenomenal object is perceived to lie in a different temporal order, in an irrecoverable past: the world "has its proper being in back of it, or had it before it became creature, but that being stayed behind in the 'essenceless semblance' of the proto-cosmos" (S 134/121). In the created world, the phenomenon betrays its essence, but only partially; it also betrays "its constant need for renewal" and its desire for "being in order to gain stability and actuality" (S 134/121). The essence of the created object is thus both universal and ephemeral, and thus created existence is a fully antithetical structure, in need of resolution.

In short, the necessity of experiencing creation requires an occasionalism of the hidden God who renews the essence of the object from moment to moment. The object cannot provide for itself, cannot cause itself to exist in the next moment in time. Due to this inability, there is yet another antithesis between the essence-pole and the power-pole of the object. The essence-pole of the object is active and comes to presence albeit ephemerally; the power-pole is unable to engender the stability of an object that can cause itself to persevere from one moment to the next and is therefore completely passive. This reversal of the polar valences of the world leads to what Rosenzweig describes as an "unessential essence [*unwesenhaft Wesen*]," an essence that is intelligibly near yet sensibly far, never sinking down to reside at the level of the concrete.

The essence of the world which has stepped into the current of actuality is not "always and everywhere." At every moment, it emerges anew with the whole content of the particular which it includes . . . It [essence] is existence. Existence in contrast to Being means the universal which is full of the distinctive . . . herein infected by the distinctive, [it] must continually become new in order to maintain itself. (S 133–34/120–21).

Even at this level, the created world is still meontological, still written under the sign of the "not." For some readers, this argument might be counterintuitive. After all, Schelling's *Weltalter* describes the "not" solely as what exists at the beginning, and having moved from the protocosmos to the created world, we are no longer at the beginning. Nevertheless, the incompleteness of the created world, as evidenced by the antithetical nature of existence, simultaneously universal and distinctive, does not exhaust the energy of privation; rather, it perpetuates the conative impulse that lies at the heart of nonbeing. The objects of the created world are still determined by the privation of being and any concomitant stability, any cessation of the conative impulse. Rosenzweig, perhaps unintentionally, describes this privation along the same lines as the meontological structure of objects delineated in Plato's *Sophist*. In the created world, things are always essentially "for-others," and gain meaning only in their relationships with other objects.

The thing possesses no stability as long as it stands alone. It is certain of its singularity, its individuality, only in the multiplicity of things. It can only be displayed in connection with other things. Its definiteness is a space-time relationship [*Beziehung*] to other things in such a connection. Even as something definite, the thing has no essence of its own; it is not in itself but only in its relationships. (S 148/133)

The unessentially essential nature of the object means that what makes it appear as a certain thing to consciousness is not any property of the object abstracted from the world in a kind of *epoché* through which consciousness might become a "connoisseur" (S 276/248) of its individual details and see the essence of the object. The phenomenology of the created world is impossible for Rosenzweig, for the essence of the created object is, as shown earlier, hidden behind the object. Meaning occurs through the dialectic development of relational structures between objects, either in terms of the spatiotemporal matrix or in terms of the act of conceptualization: "such essence as it has is not within it but is the relationship which it has to its genus" (S 148/133).

The neediness of the created world is paralleled by the neediness of the individual after the experience of immediate revelation from God. For Rosenzweig, immediate divine revelation, defined as the ephemeral "experience [*Erlebnis*]" of divine love,[23] is necessary. For to view God only as the origin of the created world (as Hermann Cohen does) is to think God only as empty idea, and not to believe in a God who relates to life. Rosenzweig writes that "from out of the darkness of his concealment there must emerge something other than bare creative power . . . lest God should once more be able to retreat behind these acts into the Concealed" (S 179/160). If God's freedom to create expresses the temporalization of the divine in the past, then God's being in revelation expresses his temporalization in the present. Yet if God's love is communicated in the present, it *must* be meontological – not yet fully present, fleeting in every moment. To view the love of God as something that constantly exists throughout the world is to remove it from the presentness of the present, and to banish it to the realm of lifeless ideas. The idea of God's love, like any idea for Rosenzweig, is particularly deadly in stasis. Rosenzweig compares a static attribute of divine love to "the rigid mask which the sculptor lifts from the countenance of the dead." A reifying portrait "would freeze the visage [*Antlitz*] to death" (S 183/164). As present and divorced from any categorizability, divine love is determined in space and time. God's love is an act, not an attribute, and so must be always and everywhere particularized and limited.

Like the created object, the act of love has no ontological stability.

God always loves only whom and what he loves, but what distinguishes his love from an "all-love" is only a Not-yet: apart from what he already loves, God loves everything, only not yet. His love roams the world with an ever-fresh drive. It is always and wholly in today, but all the dead past and future will one day be devoured in this victorious today. (S 183/164)

As in the dynamic of creation, the repositioning of the valences of the dipolar structure of God that occurs in divine love given to the human individual

---

[23] As Stéphane Mosès correctly points out, "revelation" in Rosenzweig also has a broader meaning that refers to the development of the relationships between God, humankind, and the world. Cf. Mosès, 97.

institutes a correlate repositioning of the polar valences in the object of that love. But revelation is unlike creation, and its dynamic is completely unique within the second part of the *Star*'s system. In my view, the moment of revelation, in its transformation of the inward human self into a relational identity that Rosenzweig names "soul" (S 89/82), institutes not simply the exchange of valences but also the unifying of the poles insofar as the soul is not apeirontic, as the self is. The human individual is completed and brought to presence before either God or the world is; this marks *the* difference between Rosenzweig on the one hand and Cohen and Levinas on the other.

Like the act of creation, God's act of revelation is a determination, and hence negation, of the divine essence. The act of love "bursts forth into the manifest [*ins Offenbare*] as a No, as an eternally new self-denial" (S 178–79/160). This marks the end of repression. Divine essence takes on a negative valence, ending the repressive regime of divine power that typified the protocosmic God. Human essence also takes on a negative valence, ending the repression of the distinctive content of the individual by the defiant will that sees itself as the measure of all things. The content of the individual, the "I" that is the "No that has become audible" (S 194/174), is discovered through the encounter between the human and the divine. This happens in a sequence that one can reduce to three steps.

First, God issues the command "Love me!" As stated earlier, if love is not to be an eternal and deadened attribute but a singular relationship with an individual existing within the present moment, then it cannot take place in the indicative mood. "I love you," for Rosenzweig, is a rather pathetic little sentence: "like every declaration it always comes afterwards [*hinterher*] and thus, since the present time is the love of the lover, the declaration of love is truly continually belated" (S 197/176–77). There is always a gap between the moment at which love is felt and the moment at which love is communicated. As soon as it is heard, the declaration loses any truth-value it had at the moment it was uttered. The response that "I love you" prompts is always "Do you *still* love me, *now*?" It gives no security. One can paraphrase Rosenzweig's concern with the propositional declaration of love by stating that "I love you" is not a performative sentence. It does not seek to establish a relationship, but to communicate a state of affairs. At best, it serves as an inadequate reminder of the eternality of the feeling of love. When spoken at the outset of a relationship, the declaration usually is also a hidden request that love be returned. "I love you" can *always* be demythologized and decoded as "Won't you love me?" or "Do you love me?" The masking of the question underneath the affirmation is emotionally stunted, not to mention socially improper. The benefit of transferring this scene to the God–human relationship, for Rosenzweig, is that the transcendence of the divine lover means that he does not need to ask for love in return. The impropriety is shattered. Instead,

God can command love – "Love me!"[24] – in accordance with the biblical command to love God (Deut. 6:5; Matt. 22:37), and inaugurate the loving relationship in that manner.

Second, I respond to this love immediately, based on my fidelity to the commanding lover: "in the eternal loyalty of her love, the beloved opens her arms wide to take it in" (S 197/177). In the moment in which I hear the command, I am cognizant of myself as being loved by God, and have a stable identity as such. But this identity lasts only for the moment that the command is given. Afterward, the desire to make the moment endure takes over: "the beloved is conscious of wanting nothing in the future but to remain what she is: beloved" (S 199/179). The insertion of the experience of revelation into the temporal continuum involves not only a hope that the joy of being-loved in the present will persevere in the future but also a comparison with past moments in which I did not open myself up to this love and acknowledge it. The identity of the beloved again risks falling into repression; how can I vocalize this identity when I suddenly become aware that I have failed to live up to the love-commandment in the past? For Rosenzweig, at this moment shame washes over the beloved and mutes the ability to acknowledge divine love. Identity is strangulated at the same moment that it tantalizingly comes to presence.

At this point, the will serves to break the impasse of the inexpressible identity, in the third step of the individual's arrival at full presence. Now, he decides to admit, before God, his failure to live up to the commandment prior to his experience of it. This acknowledgment of sin is for Rosenzweig "already the full admission of love" (S 200/180). Thus the soul – the self who has now entered into relationship with the divine, having left behind its inward life – does not assert its love in propositional form either. God commands; the individual confesses. No one asserts. In the act of confession, the individual wills to experience its own identity, and attains complete self-consciousness, specular reflection mediated through God. It is only once shame is cast away in the confession of past sin (*Sünde*) that the believer can attain knowledge of his or her true essence as a beloved creature: "the soul ... attains being, a being visible to itself, only when it is loved" (S 201/182), and when it acknowledges that love by acknowledging its own past sins. In the union of defiant will and singular character that compose religious self-consciousness, there is also a union of limit and unlimitedness, *peras* and *apeiron*. I am still the measure of my own judgments; the will's defiant rejection of shame confirms that it is still completely autonomous and the measure of its own destiny. Yet in the passage from this defiance to the confession of sin (S 187/168), I have now placed bounds upon myself, and see myself as part of a larger God-governed world. Indeed, I see myself as

---

[24] One might dryly note that "Love me!" is hardly the most efficacious of inaugural romantic maneuvers.

possessed by God – for Rosenzweig, the beloved soul says to God, "I am yours" (S 204/183) – at the same time that I possess certainty of God's love for me.

In this certainty I become aware of the gap between my inner sense and my outer sense, the fact that the interior experience (*Erlebnis*) of the soul is not paralleled by the soul's empirical experience in the world (*Erfahrung*). But this gap between the private and the public spheres is part and parcel of Rosenzweigian self-consciousness. *I am, whereas the world is not-yet.* This gap threatens the bliss of the certainty of divine love. At the same time that this threat marks the pinnacle of the love-experience as a painful, antiorgasmic scream that "sobs beyond the proximity of the lover . . . into the gloaming of infinity" (S 206/185), it also calls me to enact my newly discovered essence for-myself. But this action must be for-others, in relation to the divine command to love the neighbor. Rosenzweig sees this command as the fulcrum of redemption. The treatment of the neighbor as myself, the treatment of others as having experienced the same divine love that I have, assists in engendering the actuality of the eschatological Kingdom of God (which divine revelation had only made possible). Human self-consciousness requires moral obligation. Rosenzweig speaks to this in the 1922 Lehrhaus lectures: the moment of revelation in which I free myself from being simply an unessential essence in the world, like any other object, "must have been so that this 'I' could come quite freely, quite momentarily, out of the person's mouth. Since this momentariness could only have been given to the person insofar as his being-alone was a being-alone with *God*, then this freedom was all the more an obligation."[25]

The way in which revelation demands redemption – on account of the failure of the outside world to correspond to my inner truth – introduces a Hegelian idiom that should rightly be foreign to Rosenzweig. After all, it is Hegel who marks the nadir of the philosophy of the All that ignored the reality of death (S 7/7). Yet the redemptive act, as I shall now demonstrate, is a mimicry of the Hegelian path of thinking in which the subject recognizes itself in the substance of culture. Indeed, insofar as the world is still written under the "not yet" sign of *to mē on*, the act of redemption is precisely parallel to the Hegelian "magical power" by which the act of tarrying with the negative converts it (in this case, the world) into being.[26] And because others are used as the medium through which I actualize my self-consciousness, the Hegelian method is at one with an instrumentalist ethics.

To reiterate the antithetical nature of revelation: in order to convert the presentness of the commandment into something eternal and enduring, the

---

[25] Rosenzweig, "Die Wissenschaft vom Menschen," in *Zweistromland* (The Hague: Martinus Nijhoff, 1984), 649, translated by Barbara E. Galli as "Science of Man," in *God, Man, and the World: Lectures and Essays* (Syracuse, N.Y.: Syracuse University Press, 1998), 73–74.

[26] Hegel, par. 32.

individual soul can do nothing but display its faithfulness to the commandment and continually acknowledge itself as loved. Yet this acknowledgment
of the commandment cannot remain within the God–soul relationship. It
must orient itself outside the fleeting instant. Now that the self is a soul, more
than a created object but recipient of the love of God, it must return to the
world to ground the experience of revelation in order to remain faithful to
the command of God. How can I enact my faithfulness to this command
when I have been taken out of my spatiotemporal location in the world by
the act of revelation? The task facing me is to ground my own faithfulness, to
once again become part of the world. Rosenzweig sees this task as analogous
to Adam's naming of the creatures in Genesis 2 (S 208–9/187). As Adam,
in naming the objects of the world, gives the world the content and individuality it lacked in creation, so I must endow the world with the content of
character, with the essence that lies behind the appearances of objects in the
world. In faithfulness, I demand and engender a correspondence between
created objects and my interior experience of revelation.

> One's own experience depends on one's own name; it therefore needs to be
> grounded in creation, that creation which we previously designated as the creation
> of revelation, as historical revelation. Because it is grounded in the world, it must
> therefore be grounded in space and time precisely in order to provide a ground
> for experience's absolute certainty of possessing its own space and its own time.
> (S 208–9/187)

How do I respond to the love given in revelation? I redeem. I convert the not-
yet into the now. Yet this grounding cannot be automatic. Even though the
world has begun on its own the process of creating organic life that already
moves objects from the level of appearance to that of being (S 248/222–
23), the being of phenomena are still hidden in the noumenal realm. The
inauguration of life does not mark the transition from the existence of
the world in space and time to its being in eternity, but only to beings of
the world in space and time. The world is still meontological:

> We sought a free-standing Infinite; we found all kinds of finites, indefinitely numer-
> ous. We found something finite which was finite in its very essence, for it attained
> its durability in resistance against something other... The finite life that we find is
> thus simply the not-yet-infinite. (S 248/222–23)

The universal and particular elements of the object are still in an unsynthe-
sized dialectic with each other. The creation of the world has supplied the
particular living organism; it is up to the redeeming individual to bring the
universal categorial form to presence. Simple biological growth is not sufficient to perform this synthesis for Rosenzweig. In a critique of Cohenian
asymptotic thinking, Rosenzweig claims that "in order to become revealed
form, the world requires an effect from without in addition to its own inner growth, the growth of life which is precarious because never certain of

enduring" (S 251/225). This effect is the human activity of redemption, which puts spatiotemporal form on the formless inner experience of revelation.

Whereas the world moves from universal to particular, the redeeming soul moves from particular to universal. It gives form to the objects that come before it. In so doing, it engenders their similarity to itself. I see the worldly object, or the other person, as neighbor and hence as part of the divinely governed world. Yet it is important to remember that if the soul encounters the world as not-yet-infinite in its search for the infinite, then any object that the soul comes across in its quest for naming is able to serve *only* as a representative of the universal infinite. Since the end of human action is the infinite, all finitude must necessarily be only a metaphor for that end:

> Now if a not-yet is written above every redemptive union, this can only lead to the conclusion that until the next moment [*zunächst*], the moment that just happens to be present stands in for the end. And until the next person [*zu-nächst*], the person who is the neighbor at any given time stands in for the universal and highest.[27] (S 261–62/234)

Although the *commandment* of God to love the neighbor is "clear and unambiguous in content" (S 239/214), the reader of the *Star* sees that the beloved neighbor is not. The object of love is seen as such only because of his or her spatial position. Rosenzweig states that the neighbor "is not loved for his own sake, nor for his beautiful eyes, but only because he just happens to be standing there, because he happens to be nearest to me" (S 243/218). And as such, the neighbor could be anyone; I do not pay attention to anything that makes her particularly concrete (such as her facial features, her gestures, her sense of humor, the list is potentially endless). *I do not sense her.* I heed only my desire to fulfill the commandment, to "bring about the Messiah before his time" (S 253/227). Thus the human lover in redemption "barely even sees the neighbor" and "feels only the overflowing craving for the act of love" (S 262/235). This is necessarily so for Rosenzweig; how can I love the concrete, particular neighbor when it is precisely this subjectivity that I am supposed to engender in the object of my love, when the neighbor is not the starting point of my love but the (unintended)[28] result of my love, since "the act of love fashions its object into a neighbor" (S 263/235)?

Rosenzweig's model of religious action sets itself up for a critique that the neighbor is no more than a stepping stone to God. For at the moment of revelation, only the I is definite. God has said "You are mine." I am no

---

[27] My thanks to Barbara Galli for assistance in translating this difficult sentence of the *Star*. Responsibility for the shortcomings and inelegance of my rendering of the German pun is solely mine.

[28] Rosenzweig is clear that the only motive for love of world is the desire to be faithful to God; thus, any result that may spring from the act of love is purely accidental. See S 239/214–15.

longer a self taking up space; I am God's. In my love of neighbor, I see that
the neighbor is God's as well, that he is like me. As such, the philosophical
move is this: my identity is not expropriated from me to the neighbor, but
I appropriate the neighbor's identity (and God appropriates my identity).
Thus, the words "I," "neighbor," and "world" are seen in the light of redemption to be synonymous in their nature of being possessed by God. This is a
fundamentally Hegelian move, for the otherness of the other person is interpreted by the act of love only in terms of the soul's identity. Rosenzweig's
description of the loving relation between the soul and the neighbor is as
follows:

> Out of the endless chaos of the world, one nighest thing, his neighbor, is placed
> before his soul, and concerning this one and, until the next person [*zu-nächst*], only
> concerning this one he is told: he is like you. "Like you," and thus not "you." You
> remain You and you are to remain just that. But he is not to remain a He for you,
> and thus a mere It for your You. Rather he is like You, like your You, a You like You,
> an I – soul. (S 267/240).

Compare this with the end of the "Morality" section in Hegel's *Phenomenology
of Spirit*, which describes the "forgiveness of evil" as the affirmation of the
similarity between self and other:

> The reconciling *Yea*, in which the two 'I's let go their antithetical *existence*, is the
> *existence* of the 'I' which has expanded into a duality [*Zweiheit*], and therein remains
> identical with itself, and, in its complete externalization and opposite, possesses the
> certainty of itself: it is God manifested in the midst of those who know themselves in
> the form of pure knowledge.[29]

In both passages, the I is already constituted *before* its encounter with the
neighbor, and its love (for Rosenzweig) or forgiveness (for Hegel) of the
other person is simply a recognition of itself in the other. This conflation of
universality and particularity – my particularity is also the other person's particularity which in turn is the universality of selfhood – is for both Rosenzweig
and Hegel the manifestation of a trilateral relationship between God, self,
and community. It can take place only through the encounter between two
persons, the temporary stage of the dual that Hegelian dialectic resolves
into the immanence of God in intersubjectivity, and that Rosenzweigian
dialectic resolves into the immanence of the *relationship* with God in the
world: "Where the dual has once applied, where someone or something has
become neighbor to a soul, there a piece of world has become something
which it was not previously: soul" (S 263/235). This difference between the
role of God in Hegelian dialectic and the role of the soul in Rosenzweigian
dialectic, I would argue, is not a qualitative one, for in both cases we see
the effect of love/forgiveness as the conversion of substance into subjective

---

[29] Hegel, par. 671.

ipseity. I do not only call my neighbor "You" (as Levinas is so fond of quoting in his hagiographies of Rosenzweig),[30] I call him "soul," I call him "I." The neighbor is part of the song of myself. After revelation, the soul is never called into question. Rather, by foisting its love upon the world, it ensures that it will never be critiqued by anyone or anything in the world, by any worldly form.[31]

The neighbor's quality of alter ego is the only aspect of the neighbor's neighborliness that matters. One can already hear the objection: but what is soul?[32] Is it not already the model for the expropriation of all egoistic notions of what "I" can be? Are not the words "I" and "soul" always in tension for Rosenzweig? If the neighbor and I are both soul, are we not already taken out of ourselves in a perpetual self-sacrifice for the greater good of the community? This is a strong argument, yet I am not sure whether this is an entirely Rosenzweigian view, or whether it is made with Levinasian hindsight. For what does the soul do in the *Star*? It tries to "live permanently in the love of God" (S 190/170). It sings "he is good" wherever it goes, before whoever is nearest to it, and in whatever it does. It gathers more voices for its song of praise to God. It prays for the coming of the kingdom (S 206/185). It does this in every situation. It does not know of irresolvable ethical questions. It does not know the tensions of deep friendship that threaten the universality of the categorical imperative. It certainly does not know the problem of theodicy. It does not know the concrete of the body, for it prays outside of the body as "ensouled [*beseelt*]" (S 267/240). Indeed, revelation serves as a way of relieving the antithetical nature of embodied existence for Rosenzweig. This is not to say that the soul is necessarily pietistic; Rosenzweig's critique of mystic experience (S 232/208) insures this. But neighbor-love in the *Star* is a metaphysical version of a flasher's exhibitionism, exposing soul instead of skin: the soul's journey toward redemption "merely brings into the view of everything living that which had previously taken place in authentic revelation as invisible occurrence in his own soul" (S 278/250). In its prayerful perception, the soul only verifies its own experience. The redemptive act is not concerned with the concrete content of the world – that was already the

---

[30] Cf. Levinas in Mosès, 15, and in *Difficult Freedom*, trans. Seán Hand (Baltimore: Johns Hopkins University Press, 1990), 192.

[31] One should note that it is not necessary to read Hegel in such a heterophagous and totalizing manner as I have done here. One can easily point to the careful distinction between Hegelian dialectic and Fichtean dialectic made by Robert R. Williams in his *Recognition: Fichte and Hegel on the Other* (Albany: State University of New York Press, 1992), and also to Williams's elucidation of Hegelian ethics in *Hegel's Ethic of Recognition* (Berkeley: University of California Press, 1997), in the interest of defending Hegel against the charge of ignoring alterity. Nevertheless, Rosenzweig's Hegel is a totalizing Hegel, as the opening pages of the *Star* make clear. Thus, any similarity in phrasing or language between Rosenzweig and Hegel is doubly interesting, and demonstrates that Rosenzweig cannot shake the specter of totality from his own thinking.

[32] I thank Leora Batnitzky for raising this objection to me.

revelation of creation – which might critique the soul. Rather, the soul exists "without there being a real doing" (S 267/240). Redemption as verifying perception is an act of *ap*propriation, not *ex*propriation. It is indeed the case that these acts occur in a communal context, in the cohortative song of the We (S 258/232). Yet they can never threaten the solitary experience of revelation that is always for Rosenzweig the bedrock of subjectivity, and through which all subsequent experience must be mediated. Outside of the relationship between God and the individual, all is formal.

If this is the only way in which, for Rosenzweig, I can genuinely relate to my neighbor, what kind of relation is this? Considering the fact that Rosenzweig defines the "We" as "the totality developed out of the dual," and as consisting of a "united" voice (S 264/236), never plural, one can infer that the relations between members of either religious community are simply formal relations (*Verhältnisse*), relations between perceived ideas predefined as part of the totality of revelation. For this relation to be a content-filled relationship, the I must be able to speak for itself outside of the voice of the We. You must be described as something over and above another soul equivalent to my own. Otherwise the interaction cannot produce anything new. But newness exists only in the relationship between the individual and God; the singular merely expands from I to We in the revelation of redemption, a mechanical reapplication of the revelation motif, without any critique of the adequacy of the solitary self's claim to experience divine love.

The way in which the formalism of the ethical relation in Rosenzweig lies opposed to what we will see in Levinas (for whom the Other is always concrete) is paralleled by an opposition on the issues of messianism and eschatology, the redemptive energy of which is fueled by the conative impulse of the not-yet. As we shall see, despite the self-descriptions of both thinkers as messianic, Rosenzweig and Levinas mean very different things by the term. For Rosenzweig, the "messianic" has nothing to do with the this-worldly messianism that the Bible transmits to us in Psalms 2, or that Maimonides transmits to us in *Hilkhot Melakhim*. Rosenzweig's messianism is linked not to any messianic figure, but to the cognition and experience of the eternal God in his being. Levinas, however, has little patience for the concept of eternity.

> But why eschatology? Why should we wish to reduce time to eternity? Time is the most profound relationship that man can have with God precisely as a going towards God. There is an excellence in time which would be lost in eternity. To desire eternity is to desire to perpetuate oneself, to go on living as oneself, to *be* always.[33]

But it is this shift of attention from time to eternity, from the historical to the ahistorical, that characterizes Rosenzweig's thought. The incorporation or

---

33 Levinas, "Ethics of the Infinite," in Richard Kearney, *Dialogues with Contemporary Continental Thinkers* (Manchester: Manchester University Press, 1984), 66.

the other person into the choral We of either the synagogue or the church is the conquering of time and the achievement of perdurance, buffeted from the risk of death or the possible bad fortune of life: "The We is eternal: death plunges into the Nought in the face of this triumphal shout of eternity. Life becomes immortal in redemption's eternal hymn of praise" (S 281/253). This is not an account of the expectation for a future redemption, or an argument for its real possibility, or an argument for existing "as if" the world were already redeemed. In the synagogue, or in church, the believer stands safe from harm, enveloped in the warm womb of an eternal love that never alters. The world has achieved the "and" characteristic of Schelling's third potency, in which both poles are brought into actuality (W 309/81). But this is at the cost of the very concreteness of the world itself. The world attains the third potency only when the individual has run away from it into the arms of eternity.

At this moment, meontology appears to be relieved by ontology. At the moment when the choir of the synagogue or church proclaims God as truth and verifies this truth through the construction of its communal ways of life, God is no longer not yet. Once God has made himself fully manifest in creation and revelation, and when this manifestation has been verified in human redemptive community-structures,

the First and the Last and the intimately present [*der Herzmittengegenwärtige*] burn into one in the God of Truth. And of this God in whom actual [*wirkliches*] past and actual present [*Ist*] and actual future crystallize, we may – now for the first time – say: He is.[34]

This is not a proleptic imagination of what the religious community will say at the moment of complete redemption of the world. It states that God becomes present – not simply in the sense that God is in the present moment, but that God's eternity becomes cognized by consciousness – in the performance of religious rituals. Faith enables a leap out of history and into eternity. The temporal continuum that underlies the world is denied, since Rosenzweig hopes that the readers of the *Star* will continue to verify God's existence and purify the mundane through sacralizing it, living "the day as the-All-within-the-everyday [*All-tag*]."[35] This is not a will toward eternity, as in Nietzsche's *Zarathustra*; it is a will that eternity has already come and that ritual only verifies and actualizes this fact.

These sentences from Rosenzweig's essay "The New Thinking" are perhaps not completely confirmed by the *Star*, some might say. After all, the message of the *Star* is that "God is the nothing" (S 434/390) and that God's self-manifestation still reveals nothing about his essence except that he is the

---

34 Rosenzweig, "Das neue Denken," in *Zweistromland*, 159–60, translated by Alan Udoff and Barbara E. Galli as "The New Thinking," in *Franz Rosenzweig's "The New Thinking,"* ed. Alan Udoff Barbara E. Galli (Syracuse, N.Y.: Syracuse University Press, 1999), 99–100.

35 Rosenzweig, "Das neue Denken," 160; "The New Thinking," 100.

transcendental condition of truth, that "truth is from God" (S 432/388). If
I can know and experience the eternal being of God, as Rosenzweig seems
to claim in "The New Thinking," might I not then use the *Star* to argue
that the claim of "The New Thinking" is vitiated by the realization that the
eternal being of God is fundamentally meontological, that God cannot be
defined in essentialist or ontological terms? This is the fundamental mystery of the *Star*. How much cognition does the believer have by the end of
Rosenzweig's recontextualization of idealism? Which word takes primacy in
the proposition "God is the nothing": "is" or "nothing"? What is the extent
of cognition here? One *must* side with the "is." Rosenzweig's "nothing" now
means exactly the *opposite* of what it did at the opening of the *Star*. There it
referred to that which was absolutely impenetrable and dark for human consciousness. But now, once the believer has had a quasi-mystical experience of
the face of God, the nothing is completely actualized, characterized by absolute light, "the mysterious [and] miraculous light of the divine sanctuary"
(S 472/424). As in Hegel's *Logic*, pure nothing and pure being are identical.
At the moment of the discovery of the truth of God as the nothing, the believing community of the We finds God "by our side, in immediate proximity,
as a man finds his friend" (S 434/390). Rosenzweig's language here evokes
Ex. 33:11: "The Lord used to speak to Moses face to face, just as a man speaks
to his friend." Thus, God *is* apprehended. If God is apprehended as "the
nothing," this means that the believing We apprehends God only in terms
of God's attributes of action, and not in terms of any essential attributes, for
once God has become manifest for Rosenzweig, "God's essence has melted
in his act, in his love" (S 434/390). Thus, although Rosenzweig seems to
limit the possibility of cognizing God when he writes that "He is beyond all
that might be a part of him [*was Teil werden mag*] . . . even above the Whole,
he is the One" (S 463/417), this language resembles Maimonides' description of the highest apprehension of God as ultimately simplex: "in every case
in which the demonstration that a certain thing [i.e., attribute referring to
God's essence] should be negated with reference to Him becomes clear to
you, you become more perfect" (G 139).

   What Rosenzweig, in effect, has done in the *Star* is democratize the eli-
tist accounts of prophecy characteristic of medieval Jewish philosophy. The
We of the synagogue, simply by taking on the everyday structures of Jewish
life and moving from time to eternity, attains the prophetic level of Moses!
While this egalitarian approach to Judaism has certain benefits, especially
for women in the synagogue, it also heightens the very problem of ethical
formalism highlighted earlier. For the prophet never sees the Other as concrete nor takes the time to note the particular situation of the Other. While
the prophet is certainly the leader of the community, passing on to the community the divine overflow that she or he has received from God (G 374),
the prophet has achieved universal knowledge: she or he "will see only God
and His angels, and will only be aware and achieve knowledge of matters

that constitute true opinions and general directives for the well-being of men in their relations with one another" (G 372). Indeed, the patriarchs are so attuned toward God that their bodies seem to act by rote, performing actions "with their limbs only, while their intellects were constantly in His presence" (G 624). Even if Rosenzweig's community is not quite at the level of the prophets or patriarchs, the emphasis on vision and proximity to God is the same. In the formalist approach to religious life, truth cannot be found in the historical world or the temporal continuum, no matter to what extent it is perceived as the creation of God. For Rosenzweig as for Maimonides, truth can only be found through turning away from the world and turning toward eternity.

But is it necessary for the meontological approach to philosophy to collapse in such a formalist ethics? Is it possible to have both a rich delineation of the relationship with God and a rich delineation of the intersubjective relationship? Perhaps one can extend the perpetual oscillation between the particular and the universal that takes place on every page of the *Star* to another area: the distinction between the holy and the profane. This revisioning of Hegelian dialectic would not simply refer to the soul's redemptive quest to recognize itself in substance. It would also refer to the quest to recognize the ultimate subject, God, in the substance of the world; it would enrich the Rosenzweigian argument for depicting creation in terms of revelation.

THE BODY, FAITHFUL IN EROS

As shown in the previous section, the Schellingian framework that underlies the dialectical turns of the *Star*, one in which concrete matter becomes no more than a vessel for the transcendent, prohibits Rosenzweig from seeing any intrinsic good in the concrete others who exist in our daily lives. In order to avoid an ethics in which a community uses others only instrumentally, for its own good, it is necessary to tarry with the phenomenal nature of personhood, to turn to the themes of embodiment and spatiotemporal comportment.[36] The theme of the body is completely missing in the *Star*, unless one wants to emphasize the brief reference to the community's understanding of redemption in terms of "the great allegory of marriage" (S 268/241). This blind spot in Rosenzweig calls out for bodily supplementation, and in this section, I shall argue that this is exactly Levinas's function in the Jewish meontological tradition. Levinas's analyses of embodiment and the finitude of knowledge within the spatiotemporal matrix lead to a view of the person as both intrinsically *and* instrumentally good. This serves

---

[36] Cf. Martha Nussbaum, "Saving Aristotle's Appearances," in *The Fragility of Goodness: Luck and Ethics in Greek Tragedy and Philosophy* (Cambridge: Cambridge University Press, 1986), 240–63.

to solve both the ethical and metaphysical problems of the meontological theories of Maimonides, Cohen, and Rosenzweig.

The structure of the argument of this half of the chapter will proceed as follows. First, I will set the phenomenological stage for Levinas's body philosophy by situating it in the context of Merleau-Ponty's appreciation of Husserl's phenomenological reflections in *Ideas II*. Second, I will lay out a brief overview of the Levinas–Husserl relationship and the development of Levinas's Husserlianism, paying special attention to Levinas's response to both Merleau-Ponty and Husserl in some technical phenomenological essays. With this context established, I will summarize the discussion of embodied eros in Levinas's *Totality and Infinity* and then show how this analysis is expanded in *Otherwise than Being* so that the body becomes the site at which the "dephasing" of time (with its concomitant ethical commands) is cognized by consciousness. Finally, I will show how these later analyses determine the Levinasian notions of prophecy and messianism, and in the context of one of Levinas's Talmudic readings, aid in the elucidation of a double selfhood: there is the ethically responsible self who *is* the Messiah, and the ethically responsible self who *awaits* the Messiah.

A philosophy of the body such as that of the French phenomenologist Maurice Merleau-Ponty is customarily interpreted as a turn away from the absolute idealism of the ego that suffuses the majority of Husserl's phenomenological writings.[37] For the body is not like other phenomena, insofar as consciousness has an ambiguous relation to it: "I am my body, at least wholly to the extent that I possess experience, and yet at the same time my body is as it were a 'natural' subject, a provisional outline of my total being."[38] If one cannot say what the body *is*, one must turn away from thought and into life in order to know the body, whether that body is mine or my neighbor's, and let go of any subjective claim that consciousness sees the essence of objects, that is, that objects are constituted by consciousness. Although Merleau-Ponty turns away from certain Husserlian concepts, he does not turn away from Husserlianism *tout court*. Rather, Merleau-Ponty's idea that consciousness is bodily ensconced in the world, and that thinking is always caught up in the structures and strictures of bodily existence,[39] is derived

---

37 On the critical relationship between Merleau-Ponty and Husserl, cf. the following: Remy Kwant, "Merleau-Ponty and Phenomenology" and "Merleau-Ponty's Criticism of Husserl's Eidetic Reduction," in *Phenomenology: The Philosophy of Edmund Husserl and Its Interpretation*, ed. Joseph J. Kockelmans (Garden City, N.Y.: Doubleday, 1967), 375–408, and to a far lesser extent James Schmidt, *Maurice Merleau-Ponty: Between Phenomenology and Structuralism* (London: Macmillan, 1985), 41–44. For Husserl on the transcendental ego, cf. Husserl, *Cartesian Meditations: An Introduction to Phenomenology*, trans. Dorion Cairns (The Hague: Martinus Nijhoff, 1960), §42–44.

38 Maurice Merleau-Ponty, *Phénoménologie de la perception* (Paris: Gallimard, 1945), 231, translated by Colin Smith as *Phenomenology of Perception* (London: Routledge, 1962), 198.

39 Merleau-Ponty, *Phénoménologie de la perception*, 235; *Phenomenology of Perception*, 203. Cf. Schmidt, 43.

from Husserlian works that were unpublished at the time that Merleau-Ponty was working on his manuscript (in part at the Husserl Archives in Louvain) during the Second World War, specifically the second volume of the *Ideas* (written during the First World War, but not officially published until 1952).[40] Merleau-Ponty's move toward voluntarism, based in an analysis of bodily comportment, depends upon a move in *Ideas II* that is critical of the primacy of theory. There, Husserl shows that the theoretical attitude that sees objects in the world as constituted by consciousness' intentional modes of comportment (desiring, detesting, doubting) – the claim of *Ideas I*[41] – depends upon bodily capabilities. The freedom of consciousness is unthinkable without kinesthetic freedom, since "the Body [*Leib*; lived-body as opposed to *Körper*, the thingly body of nature] is, in the first place, the medium of all perception . . . all that is thingly real in the I's surrounding world has its relation to the Body" (I2 56/61). There can be no thought without the ability "to freely move this Body and to perceive an external world by means of it" (I2 152/160).

The spontaneous comportments of the body lead to consciousness' ability to adequately describe objects. Sensation is not a challenge to the mind; rather, tactility (to take one example) as a necessary part of the meaning of an object is constituted via the discovery of more of its aspects (*Abschattungen*). Husserl describes the property of the object moving into the bodily organ that is sensing the object at the time:

My hand is lying on the table. I experience the table as something solid, cold, and smooth. Moving my hand over the table, I get an experience of it and its thingly determinations. At the same time, I can at any moment pay attention to my hand and find on it touch-sensations, sensations of smoothness and coldness, etc. In the interior of the hand, running parallel to the experienced movement, I find motion-sensations, etc. Lifting a thing, I experience its weight, but at the same time I have weight-sensations localized in my Body. (I2 146/153)

The shift from objective weight to subjective weight-sensations means that even if I were only to be dreaming of a table lying under me, I would still have touch-sensations on my back, perhaps going as far as to sense a splinter from a badly sanded table, even though no such splinter and no such table exist in objective reality. Without such kinesthetic sensations, I would be unable to describe the proper predicates of an object: "the touch-sensing is not a state of the material thing, hand, but is precisely the *hand itself*, which for us is more than a material thing, and the way in which it is mine entails that I, the 'subject of the Body,' can say that what belongs to the material thing is its, not mine" (I2 150/157). The body both receives sensations and constitutes their meaning, and therefore it lies on the borderline between the material and

---

[40] Cf. the translators' preface to the English edition of *Ideas II*, xvi.
[41] Husserl, *Ideas I* §27–28, 35–36.

the ideal. On the one hand, the lived body is "aesthesiological," the material organ for perception (*aisthesis*) of the surrounding material objects. On the other hand, the lived body is "for the will, the freely moving Body," which has its own reality insofar as it is the agency by which I can constitute the meaning of objects in the world, and do more than merely sense them. Husserl describes the Body as a "two-sided" reality (I2 284/297), and the relation between the two sides is difficult to delineate. They seem to be eternally correlated, but transcendentally, the aesthesiological stratum "is always a presupposition" for the possibility of any free movement, while empirically, it is free movement that makes this very knowledge possible.

It is this ambiguity in priority that Merleau-Ponty begins to manipulate in his rebellion against the perceived hegemony of the mind in Husserl, and that Levinas will then further manipulate in a rebellion against the hegemony of voluntarism in both Husserl *and* Merleau-Ponty. In 1960, Merleau-Ponty published *Signes*, a collection of essays that included a long summation of his view on Husserl, "The Philosopher and His Shadow."[42] The essay is exemplary insofar as it performs, in a simultaneous slavishness and criticism, the ambiguity that marks so many other aspects of Merleau-Ponty's thought. On the one hand, Husserl is for Merleau-Ponty always and everywhere correct – in *Ideas II*, that is. For it is in this text that Husserl moves away from the theoretical descriptions of the pure (i.e., transcendental) ego that has knowledge of being as thought, and from the position that the phenomenological attitude is always and everywhere superior to the natural one.

From *Ideas II* on it seems clear that reflection does not install us in a closed, transparent milieu, and that it does not take us (at least not immediately) from "objective" to "subjective," but that its function is rather to unveil a third dimension in which this distinction becomes problematic. . . . From *Ideas II* on Husserl's reflection escapes the tête-à-tête between pure subject and pure things.[43]

This third dimension is one situated as a bridge across the material and the mental. The embodiment of consciousness means that it is simply not the sum of mental processes by which consciousness is defined in *Ideas I*.[44] Rather, as already shown, Merleau-Ponty is drawn toward the structures of *Ideas II* that show phenomenology interrupting itself, insofar as they contest "the unidirectional relationship of the one who perceives to what he perceives."[45] When I rub my hand across a table, it is the roughness of the table that transfers itself into my hand in the act of sensation. Merleau-Ponty uses

---

[42] Merleau-Ponty, "Le philosophe et son ombre," in *Signes* (Paris: Gallimard, 1960), 201–28, translated by Richard McCleary in *Signs* (Evanston, Ill.: Northwestern University Press, 1964), 159–81.

[43] Merleau-Ponty, *Signes*, 205–6; *Signs*, 162–63.   [44] Husserl, *Ideas I* §36.

[45] Merleau-Ponty, *Signes*, 210; *Signs*, 166.

Husserl's example from *Ideas II* §36 of one hand touching another; here "the touched hand becomes the touching hand."[46] It becomes difficult to tell what is properly called subject and what is properly called object; the intentionality-structure of embodied consciousness blurs the difference between the two. Indeed, Merleau-Ponty goes on to hint that embodiment threatens the very noesis–noema distinction – the distinction between intentive form and hyletic data – upon which the model of intentionality in *Ideas I* is predicated.[47] The body is now more than something that must eat and sleep in order to avoid the fatigue that saps the mind; rather, the mind cannot be thought without the body, it thinks bodily.

For Merleau-Ponty and Husserl, embodiment is what solves the problem of other minds and grounds a sociality that avoids the solipsistic overtones of a structure of analogical projection of myself onto the other person. Concrete experience of another's body gives an immediate knowledge of that person, and the realization of an analogy between my embodied consciousness and that of the other person comes *after* this knowledge. When one hand touches another, there is no doubting the validity of my sensation of that hand *whether* it belongs to me or to someone else; and just as there is an immediate transfer of texture from one hand (or a table) to another hand, there is a similar transfer from one person to another. The analysis of sensibility leads Husserl and Merleau-Ponty to the conclusion that intersubjectivity underlies the constituting ego. And it does not matter whether I hug the other person or simply see him sauntering down the aisle; the analysis of the body shows that intersubjectivity is universally the matrix out of which the ego asserts its epistemic claims.

This does not mean that I know the other person completely. Husserl, and especially Merleau-Ponty, are clear that the immediacy of sociality only establishes the identity of the sensible field that the two share, and any positing of a mental identity over and above this is fraught with risk. Husserl writes that "to the seen Body there belongs a psychic life, just as there does to my Body," but says nothing about what kind of psychic life this is (I2 166/174). Merleau-Ponty draws out the limits of the Husserlian claim more efficiently: in a response to the objection that the constitution of an intersubjective embodiment will lead to the projection of an intersubjective mind, he emphasizes that the very phenomenology of the body in *Ideas II*, which upsets the relationship between constituting consciousness and constituted object, prohibits this kind of move. "The one who is constituting is as yet only animate flesh himself; nothing prevents us from reserving for the stage when he will speak and listen the advent of another person who also speaks and listens."[48] The analysis of sensibility only tells us that sociality

[46] Ibid.   [47] Merleau-Ponty, *Signes*, 211; *Signs*, 167. Cf. Husserl, *Ideas I* §85, 88.
[48] Merleau-Ponty, *Signes*, 213; *Signs*, 169.

is really possible and that this sociality is both indebted to and contrary to the transcendentalism of *Ideas I* because it deals with the "hither side [*en deçà*]"[49] of phenomena that lies beneath consciousness' activities and constitutes them as the precondition for any act of consciousness. Already in Merleau-Ponty and Husserl, we have the development of an account of a challenge to the mental processes of consciousness – bodily intersubjectivity, the realization that the touch of another is immediate and unimpeachable.

In the 1980s, Levinas published two brief articles on Merleau-Ponty's treatment of Husserl, both later reprinted in *Outside the Subject*.[50] While they endorse Merleau-Ponty's strategy of using *Ideas II* to critique the positions found in *Ideas I*, Levinas still finds that Merleau-Ponty's body philosophy does not go far enough. Although Levinas appreciates the emphasis on the role that bodily life plays in the mind's constitution of the meaning of objects, Merleau-Ponty's account still adheres to a cognitive prejudice: "we know far more about [things] in the natural attitude than the theoretical attitude can tell us – and above all we know it in a different way."[51] This different kind of knowing still involves a knowledge that the self and the other person are different modes of a primordial bodily intersubjectivity. Merleau-Ponty has given a more fully articulated account of *how* cognition comes about without critiquing the immediacy, and authority, of cognition. Therefore Levinas concludes that Merleau-Ponty does not see *Ideas II* as a challenge to the Husserlian model of consciousness, but as completing and bolstering its cognitivism: "sociality does not break the order of consciousness any more than does knowledge, which, uniting with the known [*s'unissant au su*], immediately coincides with whatever might have been foreign to it."[52] For Merleau-Ponty, any fact the body reveals is co-opted into the stream of mental processes and becomes a consolation for being unable to break through the solipsistic cage.

Nevertheless, Levinas's ethical critique of the egoism that perdures in Merleau-Ponty and Husserl is paired with a vibrant admiration for the two, especially for Husserlian thought, which "requires an attentive ear [*oreille aux aguets*] throughout, despite the apparent immobility or restating of the main theses."[53] In the latter of the two essays on Merleau-Ponty ("In Memory of Alphonse de Waelhens"), there is a strange paragraph that simultaneously

---

49 Merleau-Ponty, *Signes*, 228; *Signs*, 180. The phrase appears frequently in Levinas's later writings.

50 Levinas, "De l'intersubjectivité. Notes sur Merleau-Ponty" and "In memoriam Alphonse de Waelhens," in *Hors sujet* (Montpellier: Fata Morgana, 1987), 143–72, translated by Michael B. Smith as "On Intersubjectivity: Notes on Merleau-Ponty" and "In Memory of Alphonse de Waelhens," in *Outside the Subject* (Stanford, Calif.: Stanford University Press, 1994), 96–115.

51 Merleau-Ponty, *Signes*, 206; *Signs*, 163.

52 Levinas, "De l'intersubjectivité," 151; "On Intersubjectivity," 101.

53 Levinas, "De l'intersubjectivité," 148; "On Intersubjectivity," 98.

valorizes and dismisses the practical upshot of *Ideas II*'s ambiguous structure of knowledge. It is worth quoting in full.

Husserl's texts on empathy which appeared in *Ideas II*, present the meaning of this knowledge in a manner that is indeed particularly impressive in its phenomenological preciseness. These analyses, many years earlier than those of the fifth *Cartesian Meditation*, paradoxically seem to me richer than the latter. Specifically, I have in mind the whole of paragraph 56 of this dense but so very rich volume – and even more specifically the inimitable pages [I2 236–47/248–59] on the understanding of "spiritualized" objects (contrasted with our knowledge of all other meaningful objects): cultural and written ones. I have in mind the admirable effort to bring out, through the phenomenological analysis of appresentation, sociality and society in their height and preeminence in relation to the perception of objects simply endowed with "signification." Yet at no point in the course of that very beautiful analysis is the (ultimately or originally) cognitive structure of the lived put into question, in order to conceive of the cognitive accession to the objectivity of the other person on the basis of his or her proximity as neighbor, rather than founding the latter on the former.[54]

On the one hand, the Husserlian text finally falls prey to an analogical view of persons, in which the other person is seen in the light of my self-understanding; throughout his writings, Levinas associates this view with totality and the violation of the alterity of the other person. Yet on the other hand, Levinas does not find mistakes in Husserl's phenomenological investigations themselves; they are impressively precise. This gives the reader two options for interpretation: either Levinas is breaking with phenomenology, or Husserl is ignoring an element in his observations that would ground a more Levinasian ethics.

An interpretation of §56 and especially §56h (the section Levinas emphasizes in the previous quote) decides for the latter option. This section of Husserl gives the reader the social upshot of the discovery of consciousness as intentional. Earlier in *Ideas II*, Husserl demonstrated that sensibility prohibits the strict separation of subject and object, of the material and the mental. When Husserl turns to the constitution of other people in §56h, he analogizes from the co-presence of the material and mental in the stream of my conscious processes, to "introjectively posit" a similar unity in the other person (I2 228/240)[55] and claim that the other person is given to me as "one with [his or her] Body" (I2 233/245). But Husserl also realizes that in intersubjective situations, the other person confronts me bodily; my response to another person is contingent upon how the other person acts in relationship with me. The cause for Husserl still posits an order of

---

54 Levinas, "In memoriam," 168; "In Memory," 112–13.

55 For Husserl's use of "introjection" rooted in the writings of Richard Avenarius, cf. John Scanlon, "Objectivity and Introjection in *Ideas II*," in *Issues in Husserl's* Ideas II, ed. Thomas Nenon and Lester Embree (Dordrecht: Kluwer Academic Publishers, 1996), 213–22.

causality that he terms "motivation" (I2 229/241), in which the material-mental stream of the other person determines my response. Analogy is not the most fundamental stratum of the intersubjective experience:

> I hear the other speaking, see the pantomime of his face [*Mienenspiel*], attribute to him such and such conscious lived experiences and acts, and let myself be determined by them in this or that way. The pantomime is immediately a bearer of sense indicating the other's consciousness, e.g. his will which, in empathy, is characterized as the actual will of this person and as a will which addresses me in communication. The will characterized in this way . . . then motivates my counter-willing or my submission, etc. . . . The looks [*Miene*] of the other determine me (this is already a kind of motivation) to attach to them a sense within the other's consciousness . . . We are altogether outside the attitude required for grasping natural causality. (I2 235/247)

This is where the phenomenology of the Other stands at the beginning of §56h. Unlike the sensation of physical objects, which teach me about my own embodiment, the sensation of the Other expresses meaning to me, and this teaches me something about the Other's persona – an aspect of being-in-the-world that I have not yet constituted. In this manner, Husserl writes, other persons are like texts, in which the physical book is always animated by the sense of the words that are "fused" with the signifying words.[56] In the presentation of the other person's body, there is also a presentation of the other person's sense, or soul: "each movement of the body is full of soul – the coming and going, the standing and sitting, the running and dancing, etc." (I2 240/252). Moreover, because this presentation of the other person's soul is a presentation that I understand, it displays a stratum above and beyond body and soul, a stratum that is necessary for the *communication* of the body–soul duality to take place between two people. The belonging-together of two souls apparent in the presentation of the other person to me displays *spirit*, and this allows me to constitute a spiritual world of free persons over and above the natural world of mechanically determined objects.[57] Finally, the apperception of the other person as a "spiritualized" thing in turn leads to a new self-apperception as spiritualized, an apperception that is not available to the ego in any self-inspection but necessitates this detour through the Other. This leads to the constitution of the socioethical realm: "by means of this apprehension, with its complicated structure, I take my place in the family of humanity [*Menschheitsverband*], or rather, I create the constitutive possibility for the unity of this 'family'" (I2 242/254).

Of course, the ego comes first in Husserl; I constitute my own Body before I constitute anyone else's. Yet Levinas manipulates a tension between transcendental and empirical priority in these sections of *Ideas II* to make

---

[56] I2 320/333: "It is just like reading a newspaper: the paper imprinted with sensory and intuitive marks is unified with the sense expressed and understood in the word-signs."

[57] Cf. John J. Drummond, "The 'Spiritual' World: The Personal, the Social, and the Communal," in *Issues in Husserl's*, Ideas II, 237–54.

room for another narrative that emphasizes the radical alterity that serves as the transcendental condition for any constitution at all. For although the ego is empirically prior in the Husserlian narrative of the constitution of the Other, there is no guarantee that it is transcendentally prior. Just because I meet you for the first time does not mean that I have created you. And indeed Husserl says this explicitly in §56h, Levinas's favorite section of *Ideas II*.

It must be noticed, however, that the *unity of expression* is a *presupposition* for the constitution of the founded reality, but that it is not already in itself this reality. We could formulate it in this way: it is only by means of expression that the person of the other is there at all for the experiencing subject, and the person must necessarily be there first in order for him to be able to enter . . . into a real unity of a higher level [e.g., my constitution of him as soul or spirit] and indeed to do so together with that which serves as expression. (I2 245/257)

In other words, Husserl here is *retreating* from the correlation between the givenness of the object to consciousness and consciousness' intentional constitution of the object that *Ideas I* establishes, that is, the theory that objects are given to me as I constitute them and are thus fully dependent upon consciousness. Levinas himself had made this point in his 1930 dissertation on Husserl in claiming that things need consciousness in order to exist.[58] Yet the previous quote from *Ideas II* contradicts this. Here, it is not phenomena that depend upon consciousness, but consciousness that depends upon the phenomenon. The expressivity of the body is given from an I-know-not-where, conditioned by something unnamable. Moreover, this unnamable is necessary for my constitution of the other person as a spiritualized object. To be sure, this is always and everywhere *my* constitution of the other person *as* spiritualized; the spirit of the other person does not visit upon me from above and catch me by surprise. Yet even if my own ego is empirically prior to that of the Other, Husserl here seems to set out a possibility for the Other as transcendentally prior to the constituting self. The surprise of the priority of the Other comes in the phenomenological reflection upon how consciousness came to make sense of the Other as a spiritualized being.

I claim that it is this passage in *Ideas II* that serves as the locus of the Levinasian enigma *within* Husserl, and as the thematic discussion of the place where it becomes possible, within the bounds of a precise and rigorous phenomenology, to speak of "the other in the same" as Levinas does throughout *Otherwise than Being*. As Jacques Derrida has written about Levinas, the interruption of alterity into the soliloquy of consciousness occurs "on

[58] Levinas, *Théorie de l'intuition dans la phénoménologie de* Husserl (Paris: Alcan, 1930), 80, translated by André Orianne as *The Theory of Intuition in Husserl's Phenomenology*, 2nd ed. (Evanston, Ill.: Northwestern University Press, 1995), 48. However, Levinas does refer to the unpublished writings and the wrestlings with empathy there in the last paragraph of his text. Cf. *Théorie de l'intuition*, 215; *The Theory of Intuition*, 151.

the inside of phenomenology . . . phenomenology imposes this interruption upon itself, it interrupts itself."[59] Husserl's discourse in *Ideas II* §56h is enigmatic: there is "a simple equivocation in which two significations have equal chances and the same light," although "the exorbitant meaning is already effaced in [the very appearance of] its apparition."[60] Certainly, this effacing of the exorbitant aspect of the other person, the way in which she escapes the cognitivist and foundational claims of the ego, takes place in the *Ideas II* passage. For if the Other is transcendentally prior in this paragraph, then it is exactly here where Husserl's argument *should* but does not lead him to conclude that the cognitive access to the nature of the other person is grounded upon the Other's free expression, which has an intrinsic value before my deduction of any universal concept of a "family of humanity."

This inability to get behind the transcendental priority of the other person is a prime example of Levinasian *déphasage* (AE 44/34) – existence out of phase or out of joint, the lack of contemporaneity with one's own consciousness that describes the Levinasian self's difference-in-identity. In the penultimate section of a 1965 discussion of Husserlian phenomenology, "Intentionality and Sensation," Levinas turns to Husserl's analysis of the body in *Ideas II*.[61] For Levinas, the irreducible priority of the other person that Husserl demonstrates means that, although the qualities of an object are dependent upon the localized sensations of embodied consciousness, this still does not "convey an introspective given" that would bridge the gap between the interiority of my consciousness and the exteriority of the other person.[62] This does not leave the self completely powerless, however. The necessity of the gap between consciousness and the object grounds the freedom of the self to take up different bodily comportments with respect to the object, to have different interpretations of it. Moreover, this gap is the condition of the possibility of transcendence in the phenomenological sense – the ability for thought to leave behind the borders of its interior space and literally move over into the world that it perceives through bodily kinaestheses. The structure of the objects of the world are dependent upon me, and thus the *power of the self* to move necessitates for Levinas that a structure is never fixed, never simultaneous with itself: "The philosophy that announced the idea of

---

[59] Jacques Derrida, *Adieu à Emmanuel Levinas* (Paris: Galilée, 1997), 95–96, translated by Pascale-Anne Brault and Michael Naas as *Adieu: To Emmanuel Levinas* (Stanford, Calif.: Stanford University Press, 1999), 51.

[60] Levinas, "Enigme et phénomène," in *En découvrant l'existence avec Husserl et Heidegger*, 3rd ed. (Paris: Vrin, 1994), 209, translated by Alphonso Lingis, Robert Bernasconi, and Simon Critchley as "Enigma and Phenomenon," in *Basic Philosophical Writings*, ed. Adriaan T. Peperzak, Simon Critchley, and Robert Bernasconi in Levinas, (Bloomington: Indiana University Press, 1996), 71.

[61] Levinas, "Intentionalité et sensation," in *En découvrant l'existence*, 157, translated by Richard A. Cohen and Michael B. Smith as "Intentionality and Sensation," in *Discovering Existence in Husserl* (Evanston, Ill.: Northwestern University Press, 1998), 146.

[62] Ibid.

eidetic structures also results in radically denouncing the idea of structural fixity – its undephasable simultaneity – by introducing movement into the subjectivity of the subject."[63] But alongside this transcendence of the subject in movement is also the *collapse of the power of the self*, its inability to convert its intentional acts into pure representations of the essence of the object. The alterity of the world is never extirpated by the constituting acts of consciousness. The body that directly senses the content of worldly objects can do this only because it is an object, like those it senses. The body can take on the spatial contours of something it touches: for example, when keeping a hand on a rough object for a time leaves little red grooves on one's palm. Because this is the case, the spiritual apprehension that Husserl associates with intentionality becomes possible only as a metaphor and thus is not *really* possible. All objects possess an originary spatiality that cannot be recuperated by consciousness. Meaning thus oscillates between two kinds of loss: loss of meaning-for-consciousness within the physiological realm, and loss of the material content of that meaning in the psyche. In other words, although it is true to say along with Husserl that intention animates sensation and gives it meaning, this act is never performed without the death of the sensed content itself. And as Husserl admits in *Ideas II*, there is no resuscitation of materiality within consciousness: "only metaphorically are they [intentional acts] said to be related to the Body or to be in the Body" (I2 153/161). Thus, while consciousness transcends itself through its embodied being in the world, the worldliness of the world still transcends consciousness. Intentionality cannot transcend space itself, since its transcendence is in fact "a walking in the space of the subject constituting space."[64] This gap between the intentional aim and the hylomorphic intended object grounds the dephasing and iteration of the subject and the constitution of the meaning of another person as an alterity that critiques the subject's claim to power.

One might object, however, that the dephasing that is deduced from the relation between intentional consciousness and bodily comportment might be recuperated through an analysis of time. Perhaps, the argument might proceed, through an infinite sequence of embodied gazes upon an object, one might be able to gain essential knowledge. The metaphoricity of bodily intentionality could thus be conquered through prolonged examination of the object, since the object is always the selfsame object at all moments in time. (In film, we see this through the "bullet-time" technique – prominent in 1998 advertising campaigns by The Gap, popularized in the film *The Matrix*, and then ironized by various music videos and teen comedies – by which a director is able to give the viewer a 360-degree view around a still object by placing numerous cameras around it and using a computer to fill in the gaps in perspective.) Thus, the phenomenological grounding of

---

[63] Levinas, "Intentionalité et sensation," 159; "Intentionality and Sensation," 148.
[64] Levinas, "Intentionalité et sensation," 160; "Intentionality and Sensation," 148.

alterity in the dephasing between subject and object must make use of two arguments: one for the relation between the body and the space it occupies, and another for the relation between intentional consciousness and the temporal flow of impressions upon it. The first half of "Intentionality and Sensation" is an argument for this other kind of dephasing, and thus assures that objects, both in their spatial and temporal aspects, are constituted by consciousness as always already simulacra of their true essence. Levinas's argument in this 1965 essay is that not only space but also time is constituted as an iteration, in which the primordial impression (*Urimpression*) of an object is never apperceived by consciousness as such, but is copied at each moment.

The argument is rooted in Husserl's analysis of the constitution of time in the lectures *On the Phenomenology of the Consciousness of Internal Time*. Working through the challenge of coming up with an account of time-consciousness that allows something to be intuited in the present as something past without being mere imaginative representation, Husserl differentiates between two kinds of having-passed. On the one hand, there is the simple past that I recollect (e.g., "yesterday I put some water chestnuts in my shopping basket on my way to the checkout aisle"); on the other is the "just-passed" that characterizes the intuition of a temporally extended object, in which an aria or an essay endures while I listen or read, even though single notes and words elapse. In this latter case, Husserl develops a notion of time-consciousness in which each now-moment of a temporal flow is intuited as always running off into the past. Each now-point along a temporal continuum constitutes a "primary impression" (*Urimpression*) upon consciousness that then recedes into the past, yet is *still* present for consciousness *as* something past. Husserl calls the consciousness of this just-past moment "retentional consciousness" or "primary memory" (PIZ 31–32/29–30). For example, in a melody, my intuition of the fifth note of the primary motif includes within it an intuition of the onset of the theme that began four notes (and perhaps two beats) previously, as well as of the *entire* continuum of the melody up until the fifth note. In retention, the past is now, as the past that it is. The now-moment is always in flux as it travels in two directions: progressively along the temporal continuum and receding into the past of consciousness. All of this is rather unstably maintained in the present moment of intuition.

The "source-point" with which the "production" [*Erzeugung*] of the enduring object begins is a primal impression. This consciousness is in a state of constant change: the tone-now present "in person" [*leibhaft*] continuously changes into something that has been; an always new tone-now continuously takes over from the one that has passed over into modification. But when the consciousness of the tone-now, the primal impression, passes over into retention, this retention is itself once more a now, something actually existing. It is actually present itself (but not an actually present tone). (PIZ 30–31/29)

Husserl defines the *Urimpression* as the "absolutely unmodified primal source of all further consciousness and being . . . [that] has as its content that which the word 'now' signifies" (PIZ 67/70). The primal impression is absolutely punctiform; its temporal position individualizes it from the other primal impressions in the sequence. Nevertheless, Husserl also writes that "the moment of the original temporal position is naturally nothing by itself; the individuation is nothing in addition to what has individuation" (PIZ 67/70). This means that this primal impression that is the ground of all temporal consciousness must itself be retrospectively posited as part of this very consciousness. Just as in the discussion of the Body in *Ideas II*, in which the prior spatial expression of the Other was the precondition for consciousness' constitution of spatiality, here the theory of the sequence of retentive modifications of the originary *Urimpression* must serve as the modifications' own precondition. Thus phenomenology in both space and time retrospectively posits its own conclusions as exterior to itself, in the sense of Levinas's *déphasage*. There is no immediate contact with the primal impression; this is the synthetic work of intentional consciousness.

The whole now-point, the whole original impression, undergoes [*erfährt*] the modification of the past; and only by means of this modification have we exhausted the complete concept of the now, since it is a relative concept and refers to a "past," just as "past" refers to the "now." (PIZ 68/70)

The *Urimpression* has no meaning outside of its running off into the series of retentions. The punctiform series of nows that are "before" and "after" one another has meaning only through the act of consciousness that stretches this very punctiformity.

This leads to a firm divorce between the impression of the temporally extended object and the object itself. Husserl is extremely blunt about this in one of the sketches that served as the material for Edith Stein's assembling of the transcript of the "1905" lectures. Here, temporal consciousness of the retentional chain is completely opposed to objective time: "*the consciousness of the now is not itself now*. The retention that exists 'together' with the consciousness of the now is not 'now,' is *not simultaneous* with the now, and it would make no sense to say that it is" (PIZ 333/345). This now, which Husserl elsewhere terms an "ideal limit" (PIZ 40/42), is completely exterior to consciousness, because it never coincides with itself in the intentional aim, meaning that it never has meaning until it has passed and time has flowed on to a new now. This retrospective positing of the now, this process in which it has meaning only through becoming past and not-now, is for Levinas, another example of dephasing:

The *Urimpression* already errs from that needlepoint where it matures absolutely *present*, and through this deviation *presents itself*, retained, before a new punctual present... [This] deviation of the *Urimpression* is the event, in itself primary, of the deviation of dephasing.[65]

The impressional nature of consciousness displays the exteriority of objective time, in which the present moment runs off into a past dimension that is completely other and completely irrecuperable. Since all objects are temporally extended, one is forced to conclude that all sensation, as opposed to giving knowledge, is actually contingent upon a prior alterity. The temporal aspect of the material *Urimpression* demonstrates that the realm of the ego-consciousness has no meaning without an always already prior otherness that cannot be contained within the meaning-structure of consciousness (indeed, it "runs off" from it), and is hence, according to Cartesian principles, infinite. As with the analysis of *Ideas II*, we find that phenomenology presents a picture of the epistemological powerlessness of consciousness. Yet also as in *Ideas II*, this is not the entirety of the narrative. The gap between objective time and internal time-consciousness grounds the freedom to select an orientation toward a temporally extended object and constitute it through the mental act of stretching the now-moment out through a variety of retentions and protentions. Consciousness can recognize its own constituting power, and Husserl defines this to be "absolute subjectivity" (PIZ 74/79).[66]

Although Levinas is traditionally, and for good reason, perceived as a philosopher of a radical passivity, these Husserlian tensions between power and powerlessness exist in Levinas's phenomenology of the body and sensibility and in the elucidation of the phenomenological attitude to sensibility as a prophetic or messianic moment. The body is first mentioned in *Totality and Infinity* in the section on the dwelling as the form of self-sufficiency: "*To be a body* is on the one hand *to stand*, to be master of oneself, and, on the other hand, to stand on the earth, to be in the *other* [the elemental], and thus to be encumbered by one's body" (TI 138/164). This tension between the subjectivity of the body and its dependence upon the elemental, between the "pure passivity" of labor as bodily dependence and the "distance" from the world that allows one to master the elemental by building a dwelling that is "a perpetual postponement of the expiration in which life risks drowning" (TI 139/165), is Levinas's own description of the ambiguity of bodily existence. Yet my ability to form a dwelling involves as a precondition my ability to represent the objects as distant from myself. The interiority of being at home with oneself, giving myself the time that I need to combat the alienation of the elemental environment that both possesses me and gives me enjoyment, implies "a new event; I must have been in relation

[65] Levinas, "Intentionalité et sensation," 153–54; "Intentionality and Sensation," 142–43.
[66] Cf. James G. Hart, "Phenomenological Time: Its Religious Significance," in *Time and Religion*, ed. A. N. Balslev and J. N. Mohanty (Leiden: Brill, 1993), 17–45, esp. 22–23.

with something I do not live from" (TI 145/170). The representation of the object by which the body attempts to negotiate its ambiguity is also an endowing of the object with subjectivity, with an essence that has nothing to do with me. I separate the object from myself, and in so doing prove that I have the ability to set into motion a chain of events in which my very subjectivity can be put into question. Separation – the hypostasis of the I – is at the same time (from the point of view of the separating subject) an act of donation of essence to the object (TI 145/171). And once I see the object as having an aspect that is in-itself, it immediately becomes transcendent. I can no longer completely possess it, for I have fundamentally defined it as not-me in my act of hypostasizing myself in the dwelling. Thus, this act dialectically undoes itself and becomes a calling into question of myself by the object. This shift is one act in four stages: I take a position, I name the object, I see the object as having an essence, I realize that it transcends me.[67] And in this realization, I also realize that I *can* be called into question, and that I *can* be ethically for-others. For how can I sacrifice myself if I have not already constructed myself as apart from the world? How can I give bread to another if I do not already have it and realize that bread is something enjoyable? As in Husserl, the analysis of the body reveals the possibility of my practical acts, and this possibility – including the possibility of the priority of the world and its expressions – is in both Levinas and Husserl something that I constitute: "Alterity is only possible starting from me [*de moi*]" (TI 10/40). This "*moi*" here is the ego who stands accused and questioned by the other person, but it is also – at the same time – *le Moi*, the ego: "It is in order that alterity occur [*se produise*] in being that a 'thought' is necessary, and that an ego [*un Moi*] is necessary" (TI 10/39).

The distancing of the self from the object, although necessary as an act of self-positioning as a free subject, means that the self exists only in its selfhood completely detached from the objective world of nature, and is thereby constituted in part by the privation of objectivity, and thus as *mē on*. Levinas describes the self's hovering over itself in the ethical potency of interiority as the intersection of subjectivity and meontology, the articulation of subjectivity in terms of the not-yet:

In order that objective distance be hollowed out, it is necessary that while in being the subject not yet take part in being, that in a certain sense it be not yet born – that it not be in nature. If the subject capable of objectivity *is* not yet completely, this "not yet," this state of potency relative to act, does not denote a less than being, but denotes time. (TI 185/209)

---

[67] "In order that I be able to see things in themselves, that is, represent them to myself, refuse both enjoyment and possession, I must know how *to give* what I possess. Only thus could I situate my self absolutely above my engagement in the non-I. But for this I must encounter the indiscreet face of the Other that calls me into question" (TI 145/171).

The constructing of relationships, in fulfilling my desire to transcend the finitude of meontological subjectivity,[68] has only reversed my status as object to a new existential subject-status. In order for the desire to fulfill itself, I must ethically relate to the Other: I must have the power to give to someone, but the constitution of the Other as another person with an essence independent from my own is necessary before any act of donation. My power presupposes that the world is simultaneously something that belongs to me – the field of possible acts in which I can leave my own traces – and something that is completely alien to me on the intersubjective level, since I have constituted the world as the arena of my power on the basis of my body's own sensings without having constituted the other persons in that world, without having prepared for the possibility that others can express themselves to me and come into my apperceptive field without my hand running across them.

The constitution of the world as the sphere of my acts cannot be divorced from the subject's consciousness of time. For Husserl, acts "constitute a temporal being and in this regard are originarily giving" of impressions to consciousness at the same time as consciousness restores their objectivity through intentionality (I2 119/126). For Levinas, the significance of the ability to stretch my practical acts over a temporal frame inverts itself when reconceived at a higher phenomenological stratum (TI 140/166). Levinas claims that the relation to the world found in work and praxis is itself grounded in the possibility of the future as conquering death in the future's very nature as pure and transcendent possibility:

Time is precisely the fact that the whole existence of the mortal being – exposed to [*offert à*] violence – is not being for death, but the 'not yet' which is a way of being against death, a retreat with regard to death in the midst of its inexorable approach. (TI 199/224)

The support for this claim, I think, cannot be fully explained in *Totality and Infinity* without the fourth section of the book, which deals with the nature of eros. Only this section demonstrates why an infinite futurity – which renders the finality of death only relative, and not absolute – is embedded in the intersubjective relation.

It is key to read Levinas's account of eros and the caress (TI 233–44/256–266) not as a model of gender relations – the phenomenology of the caress does not depend on the gender of the caresser or the caressee – but as an argument for the real possibility of redemption. It is an account of how eros can engender "messianic triumph" (TI 261/285). For Levinas, eros is redemptive precisely because it is constantly oriented toward the future; one can never love the beloved-in-itself. The other whom I touch has always already disappeared: "The caress consists in catching hold of nothing, in soliciting

---

[68] Levinas defines the desire for infinity as the fundamental human desire at the beginning of the first section (TI 3/33).

what ceaselessly escapes its form toward a future never future enough, in soliciting what slips away as though it *were not yet*" (TI 235/257–8). This is very
difficult; one does not intuitively say that when I touch the person I love, I
am not touching anything at all. Yet this must be the case. The key sentence
in Levinas's meontological description of the erotic scene is that "in the
caress...in the carnal given to tenderness, the body quits the status of an
existent" (TI 236/258). The existent in Levinas is defined as that which is
exterior to being, which exists not as *a* being, but delights in its possession of
the world as its sphere (TI 92/119). For the erotic to leave this behind does
not mean that the erotic Other is fungible or becomes an implement for my
use, a piece of paraphernalia. The issue of fungibility never enters the picture. The touch of the erotic Other is not the same as the touch of a rough
surface in Husserl. The caress depends upon the Other's prior expression
of his erotic self, literally his disrobing. This expression, however, should not
be understood in the sense that the face expresses itself. The face expresses
itself linguistically and manifests itself (TI 174/200), leaving a trace of its
cry that I can capture at later points in time. The expression of the body,
however, iterates itself between the moment of disrobing (or the moment at
which he gives me the look that invites me to disrobe him) and the moment
of my touch.[69] The erotic embrace is temporally situated in a way that the
scene of manifestation (although not the scene of ethics itself) is not. As
an always *prior* expression of the sort detailed by Husserl in *Ideas II* §56h,
it is irrecuperable, just as any other *Urimpression* would be. Thus, the move
to fulfill the desire to truly know another person "in the biblical sense," is
doomed to failure. My constitution of the Other's self-expression is merely
a retention of the actual expression itself, and as a result, no determinate
form of the Other himself is given to consciousness in the erotic scene. The
erotic Other is given only materially. One might object that even a stone's
roughness and its other properties formally present themselves in the act of
my touching the stone, and that this can lead to an understanding of the
stone in such a way that it is valid for all values of the variable We, in accord
with my intentional aim. Yet the erotic touch gives no properties outside of
dermality, and as such contests my intentional aim in the erotic caress. For
reasons similar to these, I think, Levinas describes the erotic Other as "an

[69] The reader will note that I write little here about the face of the Other, which for Levinas
    issues the command that proscribes my violence and calls me to be responsible for and to
    the neighbor. I do this because the secondary literature treats this topic extensively, but
    also because the face is a modification of a more phenomenologically primordial erotic
    experience. The face shows itself, in its manifestation, to be a "phenomenon" (in scare
    quotes) that cannot sate human needs as the world can (TI 154–55/79–80). The result for
    the subject is that, as Edith Wyschogrod writes, "the hunger experienced in the presence of
    the Other feeds upon itself" and becomes ever greater. This is already the erotic mania, the
    "sublime madness," of Plato's *Phaedrus*. Cf. E. Wyschogrod, *Emmanuel Levinas: The Problem of
    Ethical Metaphysics*, 89.

exorbitant ultra-materiality" (TI 233/256). The object of my desire must always remain desire. Neither the essence nor the appearance of the Other can ever be signified in the erotic scene – "'Being not yet' is not a this or a that" (TI 234/257). Eros does not allow for reification. In a sense, then, the erotic Other who has always expressed himself before I touch him cannot be violated, and Levinas accordingly describes the object of erotic desire as always virginal (TI 236/258).

Yet why does Levinas temporalize the erotic Other? Why is the virgin "not-yet" and not simply "not"? Here a return to Husserl's language in *Ideas II* is useful. There is something in the Other's disrobing – the pantomime of his face – that motivates my desire. I can constitute the Other as the source of my eros; my eros is not blindly directed, but directed at someone who expresses himself to me. Yet the object of my desire is not graspable, not cognizable, despite the fact that I can posit *that* he exists (and even assign some sense to those come-hither looks). His fundamental priority leads me to defer the moment of complete cognitive grasp. The only option for the modality in which the erotic Other exists is future, as not yet. The object of desire is always that which is about to come. It situates itself always behind the veil of the Other's flesh as "the night of the hidden, the clandestine, the mysterious, land of the virgin, simultaneously uncovered by eros and refusing eros" (TI 236/258–59), and not even the parts of the Other's naked body can hint at the nature of the essence of alterity. Yet since alterity is the object of our desire, it always exists in meontological potential.

Since the erotic project necessarily fails, it dialectically collapses into he-donistic sensual pleasure (*volupté*, usually translated as "voluptuosity") in which the Other is turned into a sum of profane fleshy parts. And I enjoy this concupiscent relationship. Therefore, the erotic relation can be de-scribed as taking place on two levels. On the level of voluptuosity, the erotic relation is one of need and is fundamentally egoistic. On the other level, the failure of my attempt to relate to the essential alterity of the Other means that I can only discover the absence of that for which I search (TI 237/260): this obscure object of desire "hides while uncovering, says and silences the inexpressible" and as such "marks precisely the *force* of this absence, this *not yet*, this less than nothing" (TI 242/264). Thus Levinas is able to ar-gue that "eros goes beyond the face" and trace the path of sexual fecundity that engenders the perpetuity of subjectivity in time – again, the distance between myself and the object of my desire is what confirms my separa-tion from the exterior world, my utter singularity, and the independence of my subjectivity. It is this perpetuity, the inability to bring the two phases of my subjectivity (constituting and constituted, powerful and powerless) together at any moment in time, that makes it impossible for time ever to be rendered complete, for there ever to be an end of history. This necessary incompletion of time, the infinity of its future, is the precondition for the real possibility of what Levinas describes as "truth," "efficacious goodness," and "messianic triumph" on the closing pages of the fourth section. (If history were to come to an end, if might come to an end before the Messiah comes.)

Can one argue that this relation of redemption exhibits the concreteness that Levinas promises in his vision of phenomenology? Can one say that the Other of eros is more than the instrument of my fecundity, necessary for the anticipation of truth-telling? There are parts of the fourth section that lead one to believe that Levinas has made no advance upon the Rosenzweigian notion of love, in which the neighbor is only a stopping point on the route to truth. Levinas writes that love is "pleasure and egoism for two" (TI 44/66), and his descriptions of love collapsing into a relation of need can only echo the description of need given earlier in *Totality and Infinity* as a violent exploitation (TI 88/115–16) and should make the reader worry whether the erotic Other is simply a dermal object, an opportunity for orgasmic joy to punctuate the seemingly interminable wait for the Messiah. Yet it must be remembered that love is always ambiguous. Like all phenomena that have to do with the body, it always both is rooted in the sensual and transcends the sensual. The two cannot be separated.

Let us return to the description of pleasure. It is a scene of apolitical solitude. It does not know the state, it is "supremely nonpublic." The erotic couple is alone in the world yet completely abstracted from it, and in the light of profanation, the dialectic between the body I exploit in the production of a child (and the child's future) and the essence that I desire has become supremely complicated.

> The non-sociality of sensual pleasure is, positively, the community of sensing and sensed: the other is not only a sensed, but in the sensed asserts itself as sensing, as though one same sentiment were substantially common to me and to the other. Sensual pleasure is inward and yet intersubjectively structured, *not simplifying itself into consciousness that is one.* In pleasure, the other is me and separated from me. (TI 243/265)

Although the erotic Other qua separate from me is unknowable and ideal, this fact necessitates that she also be *intrinsically good*, that she have a value that is completely independent of all my thoughts and acts, and that is more than simply a spatiotemporal status. In this sense, the erotic Other is always undefinable and cannot be incorporated into any preexisting totality. This condition satisfies any "secular" ethical requirement to treat the other person as an end in himself. Yet one must admit that this does not mean that there is no instrumental dimension to the intersubjective encounter here. To the extent that the erotic Other is me in the child in which we stake our couplehood, he is instrumentally valuable as a means of my fecundity (and likewise, I am a means of his fecundity) and thereby, in this dimension of the relation, completely devoid of content. In Levinas's description of the me-ontological not-yet, there is a strange yet valid simultaneity of interpersonal

identification and its impossibility. In every erotic act, there is both powerlessness in the face of the holy (the beloved who cannot be defined),
and power over the profane (the beloved through whom I find sensual
pleasure).

Levinas argues that precisely because eros fails in its attempt to fulfill its
desire, it and only it can fulfill the precondition for messianic triumph. Levinas describes the difference between friendship qua ethics and love qua
eros as a difference in object: "friendship goes unto others [*autrui*]; love
seeks what does not have the structure of the existent, but [of] the infinitely
future, what is to be engendered" (TI 244/266). As opposed to the mutuality that someone such as Aristotle associates with friendship (*philia*),[70]
eros is a one-way street of devotion to the other person. Only in eros, in
the equivocation of the body, can I work toward bridging the gap of separation between myself and the Other. Without any erotic act that perdures
infinitely in its desire to bridge that gap in desirous communication with the
other person, there is no move into the future, to the "effectuation of time"
(TI 225/47) in any intersubjective scene. Friendship, for Levinas, aims at
the surface of the Other; its telos has an end. Love, however, aims at that
which is underneath the beloved's exterior appearance, at that which is to
me completely invisible, at the abyss of identity itself.

In loving the *body* of the Other, I can relate only to the *idea* of the Other.
Thus eros as sensual pleasure can only be "pleasure of pleasure, love of the
love of the other." For Levinas, what gives me pleasure in the erotic scene is
not you, but your display of pleasure. My desire for you has been frustrated,
ratcheting up the intensity of my sensual (and metaphysical) desire for you.
At this profane level, there is a certain kind of parallelism, a "substantially
common sentiment." My pleasure is your pleasure, as I read it on your face. If
I am not looking for signs of your pleasure, then my pleasure is an act of self-
deception. Nevertheless, this biologically common feeling is not constituted
in a psychologically equivalent way by both lovers, since my pleasure must
be as different from my beloved's pleasure as my body is from his. Identity
and difference coexist in eros, and it is this coexistence (*not* the valorization
of sheer powerlessness) that marks the path to transcendence: "in this un-
paralleled conjuncture of identification, in this *trans-substantiation*, the same
and the other are not united but precisely – beyond every possible project,
beyond every meaningful and intelligent power – engender the child"
(TI 266). The desire to unmask the hidden nature of the Other naturally
leads to the procreative act, which of course cannot occur without voluptuosity and the failure of eros. And my relationship with my child (or my
student, or my teacher – potentially with anyone with whom friendship is

---

[70] *Nicomachean Ethics* 115b27–35. If Levinas is indeed referring to Aristotle here, I am not
convinced that his evaluation is fair. For an account of *philia* that approaches Levinas's
account of love, cf. Martha Nussbaum, *The Fragility of Goodness*, 354–72, esp. 365ff.

perceived not as a mutual exchange, but as a taking on of the friend's desires as my own)[71] is my "relationship with the absolute future" in which I am able to outlive my own death and transcend myself (TI 246/268).

Having seen the conjunction of discourses of the instrumental and intrinsic goodness of the Other in Levinas as a piece with the general conjunction of the discourses of power and powerlessness in *Totality and Infinity*, it remains to show that for Levinas, as for Maimonides and the other thinkers in the meontological tradition, the "messianic triumph" that is made possible by eros not only describes a really possible future event, but at the same time is demythologized into a trope for the responsible self. The obvious text to cite here is one of Levinas's first Talmudic readings, delivered in 1961 and published two years later in *Difficile liberté* as the second half of the essay "Messianic Texts." Here it becomes clear that the production of time in teaching, procreating, or loving is not only a way to ensure that time will still exist at the moment when the Messiah decides to come. Rather, the production of time in touch, in caress, is already a production of messianic triumph in the here and now.

The Talmudic passage under discussion, and Levinas's commentary on it, read as follows:

> R. Nachman said: If he [the Messiah] is among those living, it might be one like myself, as it is written: "And his chieftain shall be one of his own [lit., from him], and his ruler [*moshlo*] will come out of his innermost [places]." (Jer. 30:21)

> Jeremiah's text concerns an age in which sovereignty will return to Israel. The Messiah is ... the absolute interiority of government. Is there a more radical interiority than the one in which the ego masters itself [*commande à lui-même*]? ... The Messiah is the King who no longer commands from outside – this idea of Jeremiah's is brought by R. Nachman to its logical conclusion: The Messiah is myself [*Moi*]; to be myself is to be the Messiah.[72]

This passage is usually understood as signifying that the Messiah, like R. Nachman, will come from Davidic stock. Levinas's interpretation, which links messianic sovereignty with personal autonomy, is not immediately

---

[71] Levinas himself states (TI 254/277) that the concept of fecundity "delineates a structure that goes beyond the biologically empirical." He is clearer in an interview entitled "The Paradox of Morality": "The father-son relationship, can exist between beings who, biologically, are not father and son. Paternity and filiality, the feeling that the other is not simply someone I've met, but that he is, in a certain sense, my prolongation, my ego, that his possibilities are mine – the idea of responsibility for the other can go that far." Levinas, "The Paradox of Morality," in *The Provocation of Levinas*, ed. Robert Bernasconi and David Wood (London: Routledge, 1988), 179–80. Also see Adriaan T. Peperzak, *To the Other: An Introduction to the Philosophy of Emmanuel Levinas* (West Lafayette, Ind.: Purdue University Press, 1993), 196.

[72] Levinas, "Textes messianiques," in *Difficile liberté*, 3rd ed. (Paris: Livre de poche, 1984), 119–20, translated by Seán Hand as "Messianic Texts," in *Difficult Freedom* (Baltimore: Johns Hopkins University Press, 1990), 88–89.

justified by the text – he himself admits it to be "audacious." But there
are two other axes of Levinas's interpretation that make the audacity worth-
while. First, Nachman's thoughts on the identity of the Messiah follow a citation of Is. 53:4 that affirms, in the rabbis' understanding, that the Messiah
does indeed vicariously suffer for others. Thus, the wisdom of political rule
is expressed through care for the subjects of the kingdom in their individual afflictions. The sphere of the world in which the king enacts his powers
serves as a giving up of those powers for the relief of the subjects' unbearable suffering. Second, the biblical verse that this Talmudic passage cites
is easily associated with the thematics of touch and caress that one finds
earlier in *Totality and Infinity*. Jer. 30:21 could easily have used another word
as an example of the Hebrew Bible's royal ideology of messianism (either
melekh, "king," or even *nasi'*, "prince"; indeed, Rav responds to R. Nachman
by hypothesizing that if the Messiah does live, he will be Judah ha-Nasi, the
codifier of the Mishnah). But instead, it uses *moshel*, "ruler" or "governor."
This is a nominalization of the verb *mashal*, "to touch" or "to handle"; the
ruler, so the thinking goes, is one who can manage and handle everything
well. (A *mashal*, or "allusive tale" – another nominalization of the verb – is
thus a technique by which Torah is made tangible or comprehensible to
the reader.) Thus, this section of the Talmud proclaims the Messiah to be
someone who literally touches – dare one say caresses? – from the depths
of his or her interior spaces. The erotic scene, generalized from the bedroom to the polis, is the scene of mastery . . . and also the scene of mastery's
failure. Mastery must turn into responsibility for the person whom I caress,
since that person has already expressed herself before I can constitute her
as someone whose suffering I can take on. My consciousness comes onto
the scene only after the event of expression. The phenomenological analysis of the scene shows that I have the freedom – the power – to stand up to
the transcendence of the Other and to give him or her an essence within
the sociopolitical sphere – to guarantee justice and the radical fungibility of
persons that it assumes – as a pale but necessary substitute for the priority
(and nonfungibility) of the other person.

Levinas continues in this essay by stating that "messianism is no more than
this torsion of the ego upon itself . . . and in concrete terms this means that
everyone must act as if he were the Messiah."[73] The figure of the torsion –
the iteration of the self in its practical power of freedom that is at the
same time an epistemological powerlessness – should now be familiar from
the complex dimensions of the phenomenological analysis of the sense of
touch. But exactly how does this torsion accomplish messianism? The failure of consciousness to give anything objective to itself in the caress returns
as success, for two reasons. It is the temporal distance of the expression
from consciousness (the gap between the *Urimpression* and consciousness'

---

[73] Levinas, "Textes messianiques," 120; "Messianic Texts," 90.

conception thereof), hidden underneath the immediacy of dermal contact, which makes possible the obsessive multiplication of erotic desire in the face of failure; desire multiplies because the desired person never comes to presence to fulfill my desire. Second, this ratcheting up of desire imparts a command to give resources and subjectivity to the Other, that is, to my performance of messianism in the here and now.

The language of torsion is almost omnipresent in Levinas's second magnum opus, *Otherwise than Being*. Yet the language of messianism is nowhere to be found there. Likewise, it is in *Otherwise than Being* that Levinas describes his project as meontological; yet the language of not yet does not appear. For all the thematic continuities between the two magna opera,[74] this discontinuity seems to be unbridgeable.

In the remainder of this chapter, I shall argue that the Husserlian background of Levinas in *Otherwise than Being* serves only to heighten messianic discourse. For prophecy in this text does not mean simply being a spokesperson for God.[75] Indeed, prophecy in Levinas is not about rousing the audience's desire to return to God through threats about the wages of sin, although certain texts from Ezekiel, such as those used as the epigrams to *Otherwise than Being*, do refer to this topos. Rather, Levinas adds a political dimension to this act of rousing. The Levinasian prophet ensures political sovereignty for the Other. As such, the prophet is no different from the description of the Messiah figure in *Difficult Freedom*. Prophecy has a redemptive function insofar as it announces or witnesses to God as origin, God as the unthematizable referent of my thinking. It announces me as God's agent, with the power to act ethically and create political institutions that reflect that power. Prophecy announces the possibility of all persons being the Messiah (the possibility of giving up my own possibilities for others).

But how do I realize that this is possible? How do I come to this insight? It is certainly not through a command from above, much less one that states "Love me!" Rather, it is through a command from below, *en deça*, "on the hither side."[76] I hear the command through doing phenomenology, through foraging for the concrete. The command is heard in the realization that the object's self-expression to consciousness is always out of phase with intentionality's giving meaning to the object. This dephasing is known

---

74 Cf. Adriaan Peperzak, "Through Being to the Anarchy of Transcendence: A Commentary on the First Chapter of *Otherwise than Being*," in *Beyond: The Philosophy of Emmanuel Levinas* (Evanston, Ill.: Northwestern University Press, 1997), 72–120. For a different account, cf. Bettina Bergo, *Levinas Between Ethics and Politics: For the Beauty that Adorns the Earth* (Dordrecht: Kluwer Academic Publishers, 1999), 132–47.

75 Cf. Michael Fishbane, "Biblical Prophecy as Religious Phenomenon," in *Jewish Spirituality I: From the Bible through the Middle Ages*, ed. Arthur Green (New York: Crossroad, 1986), 62–81.

76 John Llewelyn briefly notes this point while making the claim that there is no systematic boundary between the hither side and the beyond in *Otherwise than Being*. Cf. Llewelyn, *Emmanuel Levinas: The Genealogy of Ethics* (New York: Routledge, 1995), 155–56.

through sensation, through a tarrying with matter that is never found in Rosenzweig's writings on revelation.

> This beyond is said and is conveyed [*traduit*] in discourse by a saying out of breath or retaining its breath, the extreme possibility of the spirit, its very *epochη*, by which it *says* before resting in its own theme and therein allowing itself to be absorbed by essence. This breakup of identity, this breaking of the voice of being in signification, is the subject's subjectivity, or its subjection to everything, its susceptibility, its vulnerability, that is, its sensibility. (AE 17/14)

The vulnerability of sensibility that Levinas uses as the ground of the possibility of ethics is an extension of the model of eros. In the erotic scene, I am vulnerable as well to the erotic Other in the inability to recuperate him in consciousness, due to the dephasing of time. What is in *Totality and Infinity* the simultaneity of orgasm and its frustration is broadened in the later work to include the simultaneity of power and the breakup of power in every sensible experience.

To draw this out, it is first necessary to show Levinas's dependence in *Otherwise than Being* on Husserl's lectures on internal time-consciousness and then show how they connect with the writings on sensibility in the second and third chapters of the text. Near the beginning of the pages on the Husserlian notion of time in *Otherwise than Being*, Levinas claims that the lectures on internal time-consciousness are about the project of recuperating time (AE 41/32). In other words, the dephasing of the present in retention and protention, this "differing within identity, modifying itself without changing," is still a glow of consciousness, in which one is able to shed light on the faraway world that, as matter, is totally other than my own essence as mind. Yet Levinas then repeats the argument from "Intentionality and Sensation" that the *Urimpression* is the transcendental condition of its own constitution. Consciousness is thus, before it is perceived as consciousness *of* anything, fundamentally passive. If the Levinasian phrase "a passivity more passive than all passivity" (AE 64/50) means more than mere hyperbole, it refers to this insight into mental operations. Consciousness, onto which events are impressed, cannot make a decision to become passive; it simply is (on every page of its narrative) passive, and then represses this fundamental passivity in the face of the material world in its active attempt to remember this impression. In the attempt to remember how memory works, the phenomenologist seems to step outside of being.

> Though it be a rehabilitation of the "sensible given" of empiricist sensualism, the *Urimpression* recovers its power to surprise, in the context of intentionality (which remains imperious in Husserl) or after Hegelian negativity. Consciousness producing itself and being produced [*se produisant*] outside of all negativity in Being which still operates in the temporality of retention and protention. (AE 42/33)

In this passage it is difficult to tell whether the prepositional phrase "in Being" is part of the larger clause "outside of all negativity" or not. I here want to claim that Levinas wants to have it both ways. One should say that consciousness produces itself in the ontological framework of internal time-consciousness but is also passively produced meontologically, outside of being, by the weight of the sheer materiality of matter. Levinas supports this reading by viewing the realization of the exteriority of the *Urimpression* as a combination of two supposedly incommensurable orders: "Nothing introduces itself [*Rien ne s'introduit*] incognito into the same, to interrupt the flow of time" (AE 42/33). The nothing that lies outside of being would appear to be nonbeing, in the dual sense that was laid out in Chapter 2. This nothing (*rien*) is not sheer nothingness (*néant*); Levinas seems to recognize the validity of the Hegelian argument that pure being and nothingness are identical (AE 221/175). The Levinasian *rien* inserts itself between these identical poles, appearing within the order of that which is essentially cognizable (the same) as that which is exterior to it. As such, it is *to mē on* in the Platonic sense, cognizable as different from the retained impression. But this *rien* is also *to mē on* in the sense that Levinas means to use the Greek phrase in the Kearney interview I analyzed in the first chapter of this book. It is not cognizable in itself; rather, it exhibits the dephasing of time, the inability to capture the presence of the present, that Levinas terms "diachrony," "senescence," and "aging" (AE 67/52).

In *Otherwise than Being*, this thematics of time-consciousness is linked to the topos of corporeality. Levinas denies in the later work that the new link between corporeality and consciousness of time has anything to do with eros (AE 68/53), although eros was a ground and means of creating time and resisting death in *Totality and Infinity*. Yet Levinas also makes a link here between "the disorder of caresses" and the larger topics of vulnerability, sensibility, and the contestation of intentionality (AE 114/90). One should reconcile this contradiction, I think, through an argument that the model of the caress in the earlier work, in which the lover both penetrates and is penetrated by the beloved, now becomes a trope for phenomenology as such. Levinas moves away from the language of eros and back to the model of work in *Existence and Existents* (as analyzed in Chapter 1) in the interest of showing the way in which the body not only finds the fulfillment of its erotic desires unfulfillable but also expresses this lack of completion in its pain. While pain existed in *Totality and Infinity* only as a thematized extraction from the analysis of eros, in *Otherwise than Being* the correlation between sense and material that was the upshot of the earlier analysis is now inscribed throughout. Yet this does not mean that *jouissance* has disappeared from Levinas's analysis. Indeed, joy is a disclosive phenomenon for Levinas: "enjoyment is an ineluctable moment of sensibility" (AE 91/72). Moreover, joy has a dialectical meaning insofar as without the ego-reinforcing moments found in the satisfaction that underlies joy, "suffering would not have any sense" (AE 93/73).

The ambiguity of the mood of sensibility is written on the body, and this ambiguity is the expression of the primordial ambiguity of time-consciousness, as seen in the example of the *Urimpression.* Levinas sums up his phenomenology of the body, defined by its capacity to sense, as follows:

> Under the species of corporeality are united the traits we have enumerated: for the other, despite oneself, starting with oneself, the pain of labor in the patience of aging, in the duty to give to the other even the bread out of one's own mouth and the coat from one's shoulders. [As] passivity in the paining of the presently felt pain, sensibility is vulnerability, pain coming to interrupt an enjoyment in its very isolation, and thus coming to tear me from myself. (AE 71/55)

Each of these clauses refers to the dephasing of time, and only through this reference do they refer to any sociopolitical situation. For example, the "despite oneself," the title of the subsection of Levinas's argument directly preceding the section on corporeality, does not refer to any contestation of my will by a worldly incarnate force to which one could point in the natural attitude: "the passivity [of the 'despite'] expresses a sense in which no reference, positive or negative, to a prior will enters" (AE 65/51). This is not an argument about the face of a real live person who might occupy my bed or my monitor. Rather, the "despite" that refers to the inability to contest the "passivity more passive than any passivity" only "signifies in the 'passive' synthesis of its temporality" (AE 66/51). After this sentence, Levinas continues by again summarizing his interpretation of the way in which Husserl's lectures on time-consciousness disclose a transcendental exteriority. What does this have to do with the body? There are two answers to this question. One has to do with Levinas's return to the analysis of fatigue and lassitude from *Existence and Existents;* without openly referring to the Husserlian lectures on time-consciousness, Levinas uncovers this same structure of dephasing with respect to terms of bodily expression. The fatigued body is a time lag (EE 50/35; AE 70/54) in which the I's positing of its own present follows upon the irrecuperable present that weighs it down and that it immediately intuits. If the body expresses time – if time is spatialized in the way that skin hangs on bones – then dephasing announces itself in matter.

> This being torn up from oneself in the core [*sein*] of one's unity, this absolute non-coinciding, this diachrony of the instant, signifies in the form of the one penetrated-by-the-other. The pain, this underside of skin, is a nudity more naked than all destitution . . . a denuding beyond the skin. (AE 64/49)

The inability to gather consciousness into the plenitude of presence announces consciousness as radically impressional in its origin. If Husserl argued in *Ideas II* that the body is an extension of consciousness insofar as sensings are localized in the skin of the hand or in bodily comportment, Levinas here takes Husserl's point further by noting that this argument has the effect of making all consciousness, not only the skin, into a tabula rasa. Another body expresses itself and bursts into my consciousness, pricks the border of my skin, which guards my interior space and keeps it safe from attack, and then I sew myself up again in the constitution of that object. And this happens over and over again; the body is a tissue of scars. The borders of my self burst, spilling out "like a hemophiliac's hemorrhage" (AE 117/92). This bursting of the other body in my consciousness is not the pleasurable union of two naked bodies. This is the realization that for all my violation of the Other in our erotic entanglings, his immunity to this erotic desire that defines me at this moment is an attack on the way that I constitute myself as I lie with him. His skin, once silky, suddenly grows thorns. This is pain on the phenomenological level – meaning collapses when I realize that my constitution of the world relies upon the world's non-sensical unconstitutability, its constant running-off into the past – and the ground of the possibility of "real" pain. For if consciousness were completely enclosed, a windowless monad, then there could be no pain. Where would I have left myself open to attack? Why would my touch suddenly turn back on itself?

As in Maimonides and Cohen, the analysis of meontological subjectivity carries ethical consequences for Levinas. Since subjectivity is constituted by its vulnerability to the material world that it needs for its acts of making meaning, and since this meaning can never be fully made in the dephasing of time, the objects of the world – and particularly the other person with whom I exist in community – transcend me. In the phenomenology of the material world, I can see myself only as the object of that which I seek to objectify. This serves as a reversal of the idealistic movement seen in Rosenzweig. Objects do not exist for me, with an unessential essence from which I am to redeem them; rather, I exist for the objects of the world in responsibility, in the sense that I am responsible to him or her for the very sense of self that I have. Subjectivity is a gift from the Other. In both the idealistic/Rosenzweigian and Levinasian view of the relationship between the self and the Other, the Other exists within the self. Yet whereas idealism interprets this state of being as the self's cognizing and heterophagous control of the Other, Levinas shows that this control is a fiction grounded in the Other's piercing through the permeable and vulnerable boundaries of subjectivity. The Other has rendered me passive before I have even taken note of it, and in this sense I am a hostage to his or her supplications. This idealist narrative is not completely false; I have no sense of my existence in time without my stretching of the present impression into time-consciousness, and this violence of the givenness of the *Urimpression* is phenomenologically necessary to explain subjectivity. Thus, "I exist through [*par*] the other" at the same time that "I exist for the other" (AE 146/114).[77] Responsibility can never totally extricate itself from the knot of subjectivity that includes the necessary protoviolence of the operation of consciousness. The command to hearken to the Other's call is thus inexhaustible, and as I continue in my life committing more conscious acts, the need to atone for this violence and hearken to the Other who lies in my pierced skin (AE 146/115) or localized on my skin in the caress only multiplies toward infinity (AE 181/142).

If the meontological analysis of space and time leads to a hyperbolic ethics that is certainly more attuned to the materiality of the Other than in the earlier representatives of the meontological tradition, it appears to lead to a more attenuated messianism in *Otherwise than Being* than that which we have seen in those earlier texts. Indeed, as noted earlier, messianism is not even mentioned, and *Otherwise than Being* seems to mark a shift from the earlier theorizings of messianism as the apex of ethical action. It would be incorrect to take this conclusion at its surface level. What Levinas refers to as prophecy is nothing less than a sacrifice of the self to (or a fulfillment of the self as) the path of divine agency that ends up effecting political autonomy for all – in other words, the Maimonidean concept of the Messiah seen in the previous chapter.

The dephasing of time that reveals my vulnerability to the objects of the world before consciousness constitutes them and represses this vulnerability is a sign of the Other occupying the space of the self. Insofar as alterity is the transcendental condition for my being able to constitute anything at all, one can say that I am literally inspired by the Other. The Other is the source of my own breath and breathes in me as this source (AE 188/148). Yet although the other person expresses herself prior to my mental acts, and is thus intrinsically good, the Other does not decide to inspire me. This is not a contest of wills, and the phenomenology of subjectivity does not lead me to commit idolatry in worship of the Other. For the Other is himself, in the createdness of his very skin, also a vessel in which another agency communicates. Yet this communication takes place nowhere outside

---

[77] Levinas asserts the duality of these orders in other essays as well, again usually through an ambivalence about Husserl. For example, in "Philosophy and Transcendence," Levinas writes at one point "Does not Husserl's analysis of time come down to expressing time in terms of presence and simultaneity?" while further on, asserting "a reduced consciousness . . . also remains, as if supplementarily, non-intentional consciousness." Cf. Levinas, *Altérité et transcendance* (Montpellier: Fata Morgana, 1995), 35 and 39–40, translated by Michael B. Smith as *Alterity and Transcendence* (New York: Columbia University Press, 1999), 12 and 17. But this nonintentional aspect of consciousness can be accomplished only through the phenomenological reduction; I cannot exist for the other unless I exist through the other. The ontological order and the meontological order here follow the same vector and are distinguishable only through phenomenology. Additionally, Levinas reminds the reader in "Diachrony and Representation" that "diachrony does not signify pure rupture." Cf. *Entre nous*, 195; translation at *Entre Nous*, 176.

my own ego and its disruption. This other agency is termed by Levinas "the glory of the Infinite." One cannot stress enough that this does not refer to the Other; the glory of the Infinite refers to what is communicated by the responsible subject. The glory of the Infinite announces itself in temporal dephasing that confuses the labeling of the origin of conscious mental acts: "the glory of the Infinite is the anarchic identity of the subject flushed out without being able to slip away"[78] (AE 184/144).

This is a bizarre phrase. Levinas means it, I think, as an argument that the dephasing of time is predicated on an immemorial past that is absolutely irrecuperable to consciousness and thus radically transcendent, unable to be represented within the mind. To say that this radical transcendence can be named as "God," or even as "Infinite," is a theological abuse (AE 193/151), and Levinas chooses the term "glory" as a way of minimizing this violence of naming. Yet in Ex. 33:18–20, "glory" and "essence" or "presence" are synonyms; Moses asks to see God's glory and God refuses, saying that "no one can see My face and live." To escape this problem, it is best – or perhaps even necessary – to interpret Levinas's *gloire* not in its Western sense of honor or light, but in the literality of the Hebrew *kavod*, rooted in *k-b-d* "to be heavy, to weigh down." Glory is thus what Levinas refers to in this section of *Otherwise than Being* as "the weight [*poids*] that exceeds my capacity" (AE 187/146).

As this weight, the glory of the Infinite is an attributive phrase that refers to the accomplishing of a relation and never to a static attribute that would offer insight into the Infinite-itself.[79] The weight of glory weighs down *on me*, and not on some scale that would quantify its mass. When I discover this weight through my phenomenological insight, this exteriority becomes interiorized in a humble attunement to the ultimate uncognizability of the objects and persons of the world, and the pragmatic basis of human action.[80] This is my testimony to the glory of the Infinite: "the infinitely exterior becomes an 'inward' voice, but a voice bearing witness to the fission of inward secret" (AE 187/147). The Infinite does not reveal itself to consciousness and mark the irrelevance or the inessentiality of the lived world, but announces itself within that very realm of inessentiality. "The Infinite in its glory passes [*passe*] the finite, or takes place [*se passe*]" (AE 187/147): the Infinite happens and decays in consciousness (two possible meanings of the reflexive *se passe*) at

---

[78] Thus, Edith Wyschogrod writes that glory refers to "the suspension of the conatus to know or do." E. Wyschogrod, "Corporeality and the Glory of the Infinite in the Philosophy of Emmanuel Levinas," in *Incarnation*, ed. Marco M. Olivetti (Padua: CEDAM, 1999), 194.

[79] In other words, "glory" is an actional attribute in the Maimonidean sense. It is not strictly a relational attribute, since it does not posit any relationship between God's essence and the spatiotemporal order (G 117). Rather, it announces the incommensurability of these two orders within space and time.

[80] Cf. Robert Gibbs, *Why Ethics? Signs of Responsibilities* (Princeton, N.J.: Princeton University Press, 2000), 225ff.

the same time that it exceeds and crosses over (two possible meanings of the transitive *passe*) the finite.

In this crossing between the Infinite and the finite that occurs in the phenomenological insight of the fundamental humility and responsibility of consciousness, heteronomy and autonomy converge. I not only obey the command of the glory that tells me to assume the burden of the whole world that impresses itself upon my mind, I do this from within my own conceptual matrix, out of my own self. It is this conjunction of two orders that Levinas defines as prophecy.

We call prophecy this reverting in which the perception of an order coincides with the signification of this order made by [*faite par*] the person who obeys it. Prophecy would thus be . . . the other in the same, and all human spirituality – prophetic. (AE 190/149)

Prophecy is the coincidence of the heteronomous moment in which I intuit the fact that the world transcends me and the autonomous moment in which I act on this order freely and take on the suffering of others. What does this have to do with customary notions of the prophetic tradition? When speaking of mantic prophecy, absolutely nothing. When speaking of the biblical prophets' critique of hegemonic institutions, one gets closer. Cornel West writes succinctly that "the distinctive features of prophetic activity are Pascalian leaps of faith in the capacity of human beings to transform their circumstances, engage in relentless criticism and self-criticism, and project visions, analyses, and practices of social freedom."[81] All of this is true for Levinas, including the quasi-Heideggerean language of the projection of possibilities, as I shall show. What West leaves out – and although this is an obvious point, it needs to be said – is Levinas's notion that the critique is not made simply in the name of divine justice; the critique is actually a speaking out of the Infinite in which my agency is coupled with an infinite agency.[82] In my prophetic acts of critiquing the state, feeding the hungry, attending to the poor, I announce the Infinite. God (to abuse the term) is present in me – is the breath in my words – kerygmatically as the inspiration for my act.[83]

---

[81] Cornel West, "The Prophetic Tradition in Afro-America," in *Prophetic Fragments* (Grand Rapids, Mich.: Eerdmans, 1988), 38.

[82] Thus, in "God and Philosophy," Levinas writes that in the inspiration of prophecy, "I make myself the author of what I hear. . . . In this inspiration, or prophesying, I am the interpreter for what I utter." Levinas, "'Dieu et philosophie," in *De Dieu qui vient à l'idée*, 124; "God and Philosophy," in *Of God Who Comes to Mind*, 76.

[83] But no more than inspiration. God's presence in me is not the same as God coming to presence, especially since God comes to presence in the accusative "me," the self who wills to substitute him- or herself for others. Even so, the immanentist dimension of Levinas's language cannot be extirpated, although surely one cannot highlight this discourse at the expense of that of ultrapassivity, with which it is always coupled. A thinking of immanence underlies the expressions "alterity in the same" (AE 146/114) and "the relation with the

Prophecy also contains a futural push away from its own source. For I cannot live in the dephasing of time and space; the interruption of my consciousness can only be momentary. The customary work of consciousness is to resynthesize and gather the past impressions into the system of retentions and protentions, to represent objects. Here the political work of the prophetic tradition comes to the fore. For I need to adjudicate between the claims of different others, and for this "intentionality and the intellect...a system...essence as synchrony" is necessary (AE 200/157). Here a moment of universalizability – justice – becomes an imperative. But this does not mean that persons suddenly become interchangeable. Rather, as West writes, the pursuit of justice takes place through constant critique of the political system, or what Levinas refers to as "the periodic return of skepticism and its refutation" (AE 213/167). In the name of the Other, I challenge the tenets of the social group with various Pyrrhonistic arguments that reveal that the claims of the state to speak universally are fictive ones. This skepticism can only be ephemerally successful; as soon as I attempt to communicate my phenomenological arguments in natural language, I have lost sight of the dephasing and the cause becomes watered down, refuted. Here the path to redemption proceeds along a series of epicycles rotating between the voice of the state and the stiller smaller voice of those who are not included in its notion of justice.

Teleology seems to have disappeared in *Otherwise than Being*; there is no sense that we are on the way to anything resembling "messianic triumph." Instead, we are trapped in the oscillation between the State and those who critique it.[84] Yet there is another way of looking at the question. Once I have gained the phenomenological insight into my need, in the social realm, to carry the weight of the glory of the Infinite, can I not say that I have become the Messiah? I have made these ethical decisions autonomously out of my having been inspired by the Infinite, and thus I have achieved "the absolute interiority of government" with which Levinas associated the Messiah in *Difficult Freedom*. I have become myself and appropriated the reduction of the ego to vulnerable subjectivity. More importantly, this achieving of who I am – although always performed in light of realizing who I am not – ends up effecting political autonomy for those who are not included in the State's classification of autonomous citizens. As in the traditional Davidic ideology

Other as a relation with his/her transcendence introduces into me what was not in me" (TI 178/203). The immanence of God is both a betrayal and a revelation of God's transcendence.

[84] Robert Gibbs has raised a Habermasian objection to Levinas, arguing (62) that "for the question of the possibility of justice within a community, Habermas takes us further than Levinas." Cf. Gibbs, "Asymmetry and Mutuality: Habermas and Levinas," *Philosophy and Social Criticism* 23:6 (1997), 51–63, and the expansion of this argument in *Why Ethics?* 133–55. For a claim that the Jewish tradition associates justice with apocalypse, cf. David Novak, *Election*, 152–56.

of the Messiah (Ps. 2:6–7), my subjectivity is installed on (or inspired by) the divine agency of Zion. Even if this is only an irrecuperable memory, the origin of my consciousness in the having-passed of the Infinite still announces that I have been "fathered" by YHWH.

There is no denying the way in which meontological rhetoric – the not-yet in Rosenzweig and early Levinas, the *rien* in *Otherwise than Being* – is the motor of the development of ethical and messianic discourse in these two thinkers. Yet we have seen how the allegedly profane is essential to the Levinasian account of redemption. It is the body that announces a realm beyond meaning through its resistance to consciousness. It is the material impression of the object upon consciousness that announces the immemorial past that thrusts the weight of the world on me. In short, for Rosenzweig revelation comes from above. For Levinas the height of transcendence is found below, within the expression of matter, but not within materiality itself (that would be pantheism). For Rosenzweig, my selfhood is constituted before I constitute the world; for Levinas, the world must already be present before any act of my consciousness. The critique of totality in Levinas owes absolutely nothing in the form of its argument to Rosenzweig, but everything to Husserl's inability to render phenomenology a pure uncovering of the sense of the material world. If the expression of another person is the precondition for my being able to partake in any mental activity whatsoever, then the Other – mind and body – must be not only instrumentally good but also intrinsically good. The ancillary role of the body in Jewish philosophy, regnant at least since Maimonides' view of the body as only an instrument on the path to wisdom,[85] is now conquered. But in Rosenzweig's system, the hierarchization of the spiritual over the material leads to a model of hastening redemption in which others apparently serve only as voices in the chorus of "for he is good."

The main difference between Rosenzweig and Levinas lies in the relationship between the religious attitude and the natural attitude. For Rosenzweig, the religious attitude leaves nature behind completely and persuades me that nature is something that I can redeem from its fallen state of "unessential essence." But for Levinas, the two discourses are like flip sides of the same coin, or a Janus-face. It is only in the coexistence of the Other and the same, inside the order of the same that produces being through its temporal distensions, that one can say that the Infinite has taken place or passed by. What we find in Levinas, then, is a view of meontology that surprises us by revealing itself to be not at all distant from the writings of Emil Fackenheim, despite what I presented in Chapter 1 as the standard Levinasian response of suspicion to any positive view of Hegelian thinking. Both Levinas and

---

[85] Maimonides, *Hilkhot De'ot*, chapters 4 and 5, translated by Raymond Weiss in *Ethical Writings of Maimonides*, ed. and trans. Raymond L. Weiss, with Charles Butterworth (New York: New York University Press, 1975), 36–46.

Fackenheim, in the use of meontology, teach us that it is through the social realm that one comes to know God. It is in the realm of history that one can make metaphysical judgments and come to know the mystery of the otherness beyond being. One cannot separate the particular events of history from their transhistorical synthesis. Dialectical meontology and critical meontology cannot be understood apart from each other.

What does this mean for the reading of Levinas and Fackenheim? Using their (as we now see) common meontological approach to philosophy, what does each teach us about the other? Fackenheim shows us that Levinas is a Hegelian – certainly not that he is *only* a Hegelian, but that the Hegelian and idealist elements of his thinking are unavoidable. In prophecy, the finite aspect of the human individual is sublated into his or her infinite aspect (cf. MH 140). How could the infinite aspect of the human individual be any different from the infinity of God? How could it be possible to distinguish them – through finite qualities? The messianism at the heart of the Jewish meontological approach to the world makes a Hegelian argument; it suggests that the individual can, at moments, express that there is a transhistorical synthesis that is the condition of the possibility of there being any history at all and that this fact has ethical corollaries. To be sure, this argument does not invoke Hegel to the extent that one might speak of an absolute knowing in which God would rise to self-consciousness through incarnation in ethical subjectivity. Nevertheless, the Levinasian goal of the complete interpenetration of the Infinite and the finite – the glory of the Infinite in me that expresses itself through my appropriation of the burden of responsibility to the Other in my (ever-larger) community – is hardly anti-idealist. It is not necessarily anti-Hegelian either, for in prophecy the form of God gains content, in the persona of meontological subjectivity.[86]

With this realization of the intrigue of same and other, or of immanence and transcendence, we can return to the bizarre passage from Levinas's "A Man-God?" essay mentioned in the opening of Chapter 1. In this essay, Levinas refers to humility and poverty as a "bearing within being – an ontological (or meontological) mode,"[87] in apparently stark opposition to Levinas's other uses of "meontology" in the sense of "metaontology." Indeed, *Otherwise than Being* rewrites the occurrence of "meontology" in the original publication of the essay "Substitution" precisely to communicate this sense of utter transcendence. Is it then necessary to conclude that Levinas is being contradictory? Not at all. As the analyses of the Jewish meontological tradition have shown, it is *within* being – particularly these meontological modes, experiences of the privation of identity such as embodiment or humility – that the Infinite, beyond being, shows itself as the irrecuperable ground of privation. The finite and Infinite are, in a humble messianism, power and powerlessness interpenetrated, rolling around with

---

[86] Cf. Hegel, par. 798.   [87] Levinas, "A Man-God?" in *Entre nous*, 55.

each other as expressions of the necessary belonging-together of being and nonbeing, both moments of something that cannot come to presence in language.

All of this will appear to be a highly incarnationalist reading of Levinas and of the other thinkers analyzed in these pages; indeed, some might think it *too* incarnationalist, really more Christian than Jewish. This conclusion would be false: certainly, there is no argument in any of the thinkers in the Jewish meontological tradition that there is a unique site of an incarnation in history of that which lies beyond history. (That is not to say that there is not a privileged site. There is – the human realm broadly construed, as opposed to that of the animal or the nonpersonal aspects of nature.) Furthermore, to say that in certain privative modes of being the Infinite shows itself as the irrecuperable ground of that privation, or to say that the self can express the transhistorical realm in ethical acts, is not to say that the Infinite incarnates itself as something present. Rather, it is in a bearing of oneself in such a way that one both performs one's identity and sacrifices it for the other person (ethics) that one can enact, on a different plane, the having-passed of the Infinite that inspires all my worldly acts. This is not a classical notion of incarnation; it is a photographic negative of incarnation, an inversion of incarnation from light to shadow. On the plane of being, what inspires my acts (your flesh) exists apart from – in exile from – the Infinite who grounds that inspiration and remains invisible to presence.

But if this is the case, then two questions still arise. First, since the Jewish meontological tradition grounds its account of God in an account of the privative status of the world, would it not be the case that meontology reduces revelation to creation? This question is urgent and gets to the core issue of the liberal Jewish philosophical tradition. After all, if the philosophical portrait of the Jewish God is "the Infinite" whom I deduce only through an analysis of temporal flow, or of what it means for my hand to touch a table (or you), then this would seem to be fundamentally different from the portrait of God in the sacred texts of the Jewish tradition. Furthermore, the difference between Athens and Jerusalem would seem to be heightened by an account that charges the most biblically sensitive of these philosophers, Franz Rosenzweig, with an insensitivity to the intrinsic goodness of the other person. The response to this question, although difficult, must be to say that Athens gives Jerusalem a defense of its practices by articulating their meaning, and that the account of this meaning does not obviate those practices. Although one must say that I am already commanded by the infinite God before I touch anything, it still remains that I do not know this until I phenomenologically examine the faculty of touch. This means that I must retrospectively accede to a narrative framework that expresses the mutual implication of the transhistorical and the historical in a deep past, before I began my phenomenological explorations. I cannot simply posit a narrative, or else it is not a narrative about the deep past. But in acceding to this narrative, I can nevertheless understand it in the light of certain concepts that the analysis of nonbeing has shown me to be important: the openness or not-yet quality of historical time, ethics as enacting this openness, and the possibility that in certain acts, God's infinity is adumbrated in the acts of a group of individuals.[88]

The second question, in noting that the arguments about the force of meontological subjectivity depend primarily on a certain reading of Levinas, and not on any importing of Hegelian categories into Levinasian thought, asks why would it be necessary to turn to Hegel or Fackenheim at all. Here, the response must be that the realization that dialectical and critical accounts of meontology implicate each other is not a turn away from Levinas. Rather, it is a turn away from a certain misreading of Levinas, one that would argue, along with Gillian Rose, that "Levinas's Buddhist Judaism offers an extreme version of Athens versus Jerusalem."[89] As I have shown, in Levinas and the Jewish meontological tradition, it is the bringing together of Athens and Jerusalem that allows me to defend the validity of a religious life in which my acts can express both the immanence of divine glory and my yearning after divine transcendence, both divine self-realization in the world and human self-perfection. But while Fackenheim shows a more nuanced way of reading Levinas, it is Levinas who shows that it is inadequate for Fackenheim to leave his expression of the religious life so vague as to say only that the social realm points to the Other *par excellence* and even expresses it (MH 144), or that the actions of this Other are only apparent in a deeply felt but mysterious command to perdure. Levinas shows us that this Other *par excellence* has revealed himself and come to pass within the concrete human situation. It is not simply that human self-making is situated by the unique limitations of human finitude and that this finitude expresses a transcendent alterity as its ground. Rather, the unique limitations of human finitude express the *inaccessibility* of this transcendent alterity and lead the individual, in mourning this transcendent alterity, to inaugurate a movement in which he or she transcends the unbridgeable gulf between the self and that which lies beyond being by discovering shards of this transcendent alterity in the world. This worldly alterity, written on the bodies of others, commands the manically erotic behavior of ethical responsibility by which transcendence

---

[88] For another philosophical account of the dwelling of God with the people of Israel, cf. Michael Wyschogrod, *The Body of Faith: God in the People Israel*, 2nd ed. (Northvale, N.J.: Jason Aronson, 1996), 9–14. For an account of both the dwelling of God with the people of Israel as a whole and individual prophets, cf. Diana Lobel, "A Dwelling Place for the Shekhinah," *Jewish Quarterly Review* 90:1–2 (1999), 103–25. For an attempt to reconcile divine command and human autonomy that views submission to humanly constructed "divine commands" as pragmatic acts, see Martin Kavka and Randi Rashkover, "A Jewish Modified Divine Command Ethics," forthcoming in *Journal of Religious Ethics* 32:2 (Summer 2004).

[89] Gillian Rose, *Mourning Becomes the Law: Philosophy and Representation* (Cambridge: Cambridge University Press, 1996), 37.

can be recovered, but only in a moment as fleeting as a flash of lightning, in me.

At this point, the journey from Athens to Jerusalem is incomplete. What the arguments so far have shown is only that an account of nonbeing makes it possible for a religious life to be practiced in accord with these philosophical explanations of religion. What is still required is the task of finding narratives – at least one – that have the status in the tradition of arising from the deep past and in which the Jewish meontological tradition can begin to see a reflection of its insistence on the intimate relationship between the divine and the human, and between the act of self-perfection and God's redemption of the world. The pages of the conclusion are but one step in this process of allowing philosophy and text to come to recognize and love one another.

Conclusion

Deepening the Roots of the Jewish Meontological Tradition, or contra the Derridean "Messianic"

Rabbi,

In the last chapter, I extended through to Levinas a historical tradition that one could now call the "Jewish meontological tradition," in which the analysis of nonbeing serves to ensure that Jews have not been duped by the concept of messianic anticipation. Still, there is a question that is undoubtedly on your mind: *how* Jewish is this? There are several reasons for you to ask this question.

1. As I have shown in the last two chapters, for Maimonides, Cohen, and Levinas (and, to a lesser extent, Rosenzweig) the intellectually or ethically responsible individual is given redemptive power. Where is this in the texts of the tradition?
2. You will by now have noted that I argue that the accounts of nonbeing in those thinkers who have a rich sense of Jewish life and ritual (Maimonides and Rosenzweig) are not as defensible as the accounts in those thinkers for whom Jewish praxis is not an integral part of their philosophical system (Cohen and Levinas). Therefore, it appears that any identification of a "Jewish meontological tradition" might be better described as a tradition of philosophical accounts of nonbeing that flirt with Jewish concepts.

You have a right to be suspicious, especially of the modern thinkers I have treated. Cohen uses prophetic texts selectively insofar as they express Leibnizian or Kantian views, or adhere to his overarching narrative of historical progress. Rosenzweig uses scriptural and Kabbalistic motifs as a further application of Schelling's own earlier appropriations. And as I claimed in Chapters 1 and 4, Levinas's uses of Talmud are primarily expressions of his own postphenomenological arguments, and either authorize ethics as a possible (but not necessary) supersession of traditional Judaism or do not display an awareness of the coherence of the Talmud itself.[1] You therefore have every right to ask whether the thinkers treated here have to a large extent (either openly or secretly) disavowed the Jewish past. You have every right to ask whether it is possible to find premodern Jewish meontological texts. Indeed, you have every right to ask whether the preceding analyses have demonstrated only the correctness of Arthur Green's desire to steer Jewish thought toward a neo-Hasidic position.

Allow me to phrase these questions a bit more technically. You will also have noted that I have articulated Jewish meontology in what is at times quite a complex phenomenological discourse. In other words, this is not simply a discourse about objective reality, although I have emphasized the ethical stakes of a phenomenology in which the world outside me challenges my epistemic claims. It is also, at the same time, a discourse about a specific rational-messianic intentionality that a group of philosophers have aimed at the Jewish tradition. But you might think that a religious discourse is properly about objective facts, and not about our intentional relation to them. Specifically, you might think that messianic discourse is properly a discourse about a person other than me who transcends me, not a discourse about how my consciousness constitutes the Messiah. Therefore, you have a right to ask whether the influx of phenomenological language here raises too strong a challenge to a discourse on religion and revelation as natural facts, without any moment in the analysis in which my consciousness generates the sense of that revelation. You have a right to ask whether the previous analyses communicate not an attitude of faith in the facticity of a religious tradition's claims, but a faithfulness to the sentiment that Edmund Husserl expressed in a letter written to D. M. Feuling in 1933: "Genuine philosophy is *eo ipso* theology."[2] These are haunting questions, and the answer I will give here as I read Derridean phenomenology together with an ancient midrashic text will claim to deepen the roots of the Jewish meontological tradition beyond Maimonides.

I have taken on this issue because I hear your voice within me making these critiques, but I am unsure of the extent to which my response will bring an end to this haunting. Most likely, I will miss the mark. In order to respond to your voice in my head, my instinct is to share texts with you, as you have earlier shared texts with me. But in indulging this instinct, I cannot but turn away from you as I turn toward the texts. This is the dilemma, then: either I turn to you and absorb the claim that the Jewish meontological tradition imposes philosophy on the Jewish tradition, or I turn to the texts to respond to you and lose the force of your critique. Since I must respond – your voice within me is commanding me to respond – I must turn to these

---

[1] For an argument for the inappropriateness of the term "Jewish" for Levinas's understanding of religiosity, cf. Jill Robbins, *Altered Reading* (Chicago: University of Chicago Press, 1999).

[2] Cited in George Steiner, "Trusting in Reason," *Times Literary Supplement,* June 24, 1994.

texts (and to a more traditionally academic style of prose) and then wait for your response.

This question of the role of intentionality in religion has arisen recently in several of the texts of Jacques Derrida that over the past two decades have become more explicitly concerned with religion, especially the intersections between the Abrahamic religions.[3] In the midst of a return to the texts of this religious past, Derrida has articulated a murky religious existence – crossing as it does the boundaries separating Judaism, Christianity, and secular philosophy – that is something heretofore unthought in the history of philosophy. The theology that arises from Derridean phenomenology sees itself, I claim, as a new stage in religious thinking (but also as a return to its essence). For example, in *Specters of Marx*, the messianic is described as a "messianic without messianism" (SM 102/59), a difficult phrase that seeks to communicate an eschatological awaiting that nevertheless is "without identifiable content or Messiah" (SM 56/28) and therefore "absolutely undetermined" (SM 111/65). This serves to give the reader an image of "a structure of experience rather than a religion" (SM 266/168) as part of a rigorous phenomenology of faith, which "can only ever believe in the unbelievable" (SM 227/143); otherwise it would no longer be faith but something closer to natural science. These undetermined and pure notions of faith and the messianic are elements of Derrida's project of formulating the concept of "the event of a discourse in the philosophico-scientific form claiming to break with myth, religion, and the nationalist 'mystique,'" which therefore lies at a distance from dogmatic "forms of social organization" (SM 149/91).

It is in the category of the "messianic" that the greatest intersection lies between Derrida's thinking and the meontological accounts of messianic anticipation discussed in the previous two chapters. Yet despite the fact that the meontological tradition expresses an epistemology that lends urgency to messianic anticipation, Derrida explicitly disavows himself from the meontological tradition. In *Specters of Marx*, Derrida links the messianic with the concept of the specter. This term, which Derrida borrows from Marx (although it also has its own history in the writings of Derrida and Levinas), refers to that which is neither present nor absent, neither a determined hope (future present) nor a determined memory (past present). As such, its structure is formally similar to the messianic promise that for Derrida is always to-come, absolutely futural without any protension into the lived present, and therefore also divorced from the Heideggerean sense. Since

---

[3] Cf. John D. Caputo, *The Prayers and Tears of Jacques Derrida* (Bloomington: Indiana University Press, 1998); Gideon Ofrat, *The Jewish Derrida*, trans. Peretz Kidron (Syracuse, N.Y.: Syracuse University Press, 2001); and Gil Anidjar's revelatory reflections on Derrida as Arab Jew in the introduction to his edited volume of Derrida essays, *Acts of Religion* (New York: Routledge, 2002), 1–39.

the specter is situated between presence and absence, being and nonbeing, Derrida flatly asserts that it is *not* meontological (SM 236/148). Of course, neither is it ontological. Its structure must express in some way a position between two poles. But if the specter is not meontological, neither can the messianic be meontological. A strict boundary between Derrida and the tradition he inherits (Maimonides-Cohen-Rosenzweig-Levinas) comes into focus. This occurs despite the fact that Derrida uses the rhetoric of "not yet," which I have identified previously as signifying a temporalized understanding of *to mē on*, at key places in *Specters of Marx* (SM 15/xix, 160/97).

The position of the messianic between ontology and meontology is also a temporally diffused position; Derrida expresses the experience of the messianic as "in memory of the hope" (SM 111/65) for salvation. This experience between temporal extremes, as I will shortly show, bears a structural similarity to Derrida's phenomenology of mourning. The messianic mourns the hope for a future–present salvation. It mourns presence itself, as well as the presence–absence dialectic. "Mourning" is the fitting word for the mood that discloses and does justice to the concepts of self and time, in the between-structure briefly outlined earlier, which Derrida has explored in countless texts. The tool in these works has always been, either explicitly or implicitly, a radical use of the Husserlian concept of the phenomenological reduction, the *epochē* that discovers essences through the abstraction of content. As such, the most important criterion for judging whether an experience can or cannot be included among the authentically messianic is its adherence to this Husserlian structure. The concrete messianisms – the Abrahamic monotheisms – are excluded from the Derridean understanding of the messianic because (SM 102/59) "none of them can accept, of course, this *epochη* of the content, whereas we hold it here to be essential to the messianic in general, as thinking of the other and of the event to come" (SM 102/59).

Nevertheless, this claim – so new! so pure! – contains an implicit prejudice that the previous messianic movements and/or formulations of the messianic idea have never problematized the concept of the persona of the Messiah, have never atavistically thought along Husserlian lines, and have never linked the tropes of messianism and mourning. As it only takes the sight of one black swan to falsify the claim that all swans are white, so only one traditional example is needed to expose the falsity of Derrida's assertion that the messianic must always and necessarily be abstracted from any determinate religious life. To make this point (and to respond to your questions), I will introduce such an example in Pesikta Rabbati 34 (hereafter PesR 34), a rather undatable and unplaceable – 250 C.E.? 650 C.E.? 850 C.E.? Greece? Palestine? Italy? – rabbinic text[4] that articulates the messianic ideology of a

---

[4] English translations of this text will generally be from *Pesikta Rabbati*, 2 vols., trans. William Braude (New Haven: Yale University Press, 1968) (hereafter Braude). The original Hebrew

group who call themselves 'avelei tzion, the Mourners of Zion. (*Pesikta Rabbati* is a collection of sermons that one can assume are in the interest of this community.) In this text, there is a conceptual link between the Messiah and the mourning faithful that structurally parallels the category of the messianic that Derrida describes as new. While we cannot inherit the precise contours of a Levinasian model of ethics from PesR 34, this text does pass down to us a concept of the Messiah within a specific religious tradition that meets Derrida's criteria for the messianic and that can thus be enlarged to include the "thinking of the other" derived from Levinasian phenomenologies of the face, eros, and touch. In other words, I will argue here that PesR 34 is a historical example of a "messianism without content" – indeed, a disavowal of messianism[5] – because it recodes the term "Messiah" at the same time that it leaves intact the force of its traditional signification. Here, "Messiah" does not only have its usual signification as another person who rescues Israel and institutes an era of peace and emancipation, but it also refers to the responsible self. PesR 34 therefore fits in the Jewish meontological tradition outlined in the previous two chapters, which have shown how Greek meontology has been appropriated in Jewish philosophy for the purpose of demythologizing the concept of the Messiah as the ethically responsible self. Messiah will here be the metaphor of subjectivity itself, the drawing of the boundaries of the self.[6]

Thus, this conclusion proceeds on many levels. On one stratum, it claims that Derrida's position in *Specters of Marx*, which Derrida expresses as a rejection of meontology, is actually in line with the position of the Jewish meontological tradition on messianic anticipation that I have delineated in the previous chapters. On a second, it challenges Derrida's understanding of the content of the Jewish tradition. And on a third, it serves as a response to your urgent questions, by raising the possibility that the believer's intentional relationship toward the Messiah is part of one strand of Jewish faith, that the Messiah is more than just a natural fact that will occur in the future. Perhaps the reason for this is that the perdurance of messianic anticipation, century after century, might become traumatic and leave psychic traces. After explicating the relationship between mourning and messianism in

can be found in the second volume of Rivka Ulmer's critical edition of the text (Atlanta: Scholars Press, 1999), 816–21, as well as in Arnold Goldberg's *Erlösung durch Leiden: Drei rabbinischen Homilien über der Trauernden Zions und den leidenden Messias Efraim* (PesR 34, 36, 37) (Frankfurt am Main: Gesellschaft zur Förderung Judaistischer Studien, 1978), 394–99. On the dating and placing of this text, see Braude, 1:20–26, and Goldberg, 21–23 and 131–44.

5 For a broader account of the stakes of this disavowal (*Verleugnung*), cf. Martin Kavka, "The Absence Fetish," *Religious Studies Review* 29:3 (July 2003), 225–34.

6 Marcus Jastrow, in his *Dictionary of the Targumim, Talmud Bavli, Yerushalmi, and Midrashic Literature*, 2nd ed. (New York: Judaica Press, 1992), notes a use of the Hebrew *mashiach* in Yalqut Shimoni (a late homiletic text that quotes in part from PesR 34, 36, 37) to mean "to draw, measure."

the Derridean corpus, with specific attention to its psychoanalytic roots, I will outline the text and context of PesR 34 and draw out the meontological and Derridean elements of its conceptualization of the Messiah, which takes place within an intrainstitutional debate over the issues of law and covenant.

MOURNING BETWEEN INTROJECTION AND INCORPORATION

Like Heideggerean phenomenology, Derridean phenomenology looks to limit-experiences in order to uncover the structure of selfhood necessary to make such experiences possible. A sizable portion of the Derridean corpus has examined the phenomenon of mourning as one such limit-experience. The phenomenology of mourning, for Derrida, reveals the impossibility of the self's independent projection of its own tasks. Rather, the tasks of the self are given to it from outside, so that the self is shown to be always already fractured and/or infected by an other that is within. (There are resounding echoes here of the accounts of the constitution of alterity in Husserl and Levinas offered in the previous chapter.) Derrida's work on mourning began in 1976 with the publication of "Fors," his introduction to *The Wolf Man's Magic Word*, a reevaluation of Freud's "Wolf Man" case by the Hungarian-French psychoanalysts Nicolas Abraham (1919–1975) and Maria Torok (1925–1999).[7] Several remarks and footnotes in *Specters of Marx* (SM 160/97, 24n. 1/178n. 3) indicate to the reader that this essay is still operative for Derrida's arguments some seventeen years after its first appearance.

Abraham and Torok view the psychic life as an ongoing process of introjection, a term they borrow from Sandor Ferenczi, who defined it in 1909 as "an extension to the external world of the original autoerotic interests, by including its objects in the ego."[8] Yet Ferenczi himself never used the word in any uniform fashion, and appropriations of the term by Freud, Karl Abraham, Melanie Klein, and others only served to muddle the original sense of the

---

7 Jacques Derrida, "Fors: Les mots anglés de Nicolas Abraham et Maria Torok," in Nicolas Abraham and Maria Torok, *Cryptonymie: Le verbier de l'homme aux loups* (Paris: Aubier-Flammarion, 1976), 7–73, translated by Barbara Johnson as "*Fors*: The Anglish Words of Nicolas Abraham and Maria Torok," in Nicolas Abraham and Maria Torok, *The Wolf Man's Magic Word: A Cryptonomy* (Minneapolis: University of Minnesota Press, 1986), xi–xlviii.

8 Sandor Ferenczi, *Final Contributions to the Problems and Methods of Psycho-Analysis*, trans. Eric Mosbacher (New York: Brunner/Mazel, 1980), 316–17. Quoted in Torok, "The Illness of Mourning and the Fantasy of the Exquisite Corpse," at EN 235/112.

   Although references to *The Shell and the Kernel* are running in the text, preceding the book – especially in its English translation – is a collection of essays spanning several decades, and hence it is also necessary to distinguish among the essays of Abraham or Torok or both that one cites. The two essays cited most often in this chapter will be Torok's 1968 essay "Illness of Mourning," EN 229–51/107–24, and Abraham and Torok's 1972 essay "Mourning *or* Melancholia: Introjection *versus* Incorporation," EN 259–75/125–138. Other pages cited from *The Shell and the Kernel* will have explanatory notes attached.

term. Thus, in a 1968 essay, Torok elaborated the meaning of the term as follows:

> Like transference (that is, like its mode of action in therapy), introjection is defined as the process of including the Unconscious in the ego through objectal contacts. . . . Introjection does not tend toward compensation, but growth. By broadening and enriching the ego, introjection seeks to introduce into it the unconscious, nameless, or repressed libido . . . [I]ntrojection transforms instinctual promptings into desires and fantasies of desire, making them fit to receive a name and the right to exist and to unfold in the objectal sphere. (EN 236/113)

Thus, introjection is a process of self-creation within the continually changing contexts of one's life, an organic growth in which we see something new within (a desire, a feeling) or without (an event) and open ourselves to it, acquire it for ourselves, put ourselves into relation with it in a mode of love (EN 262/127) and self-awareness.

However, when the object of this erotic libido is lost, especially if lost in a traumatic or shameful manner, the possibility of the pathological response of incorporation appears. Incorporation is a consumption of the object into the self, and thus appears to be similar to the assimilative process of introjection. Yet for Abraham and Torok they could not be more different. Incorporation is incommunicable, and it thus belies an inability to decathect from the object, due to some sort of conflictual desire. Incorporation is "a refusal to acknowledge the full import of the loss" of the object of mourning (EN 261/127). As such, the psyche creates a fantasmic mechanism that resurrects the lost beloved within itself in order to hold on to the intimacy of which the psyche cannot, for various reasons, let go. And instead of introjection's process of including the world within the ego metaphorically as an object of desire, incorporation creates a topography within the psyche where the beloved is kept. For Abraham and Torok, the difference between the normality of introjection and the pathology of incorporation also manifests itself as a linguistic difference.

> The fantasy of incorporation merely simulates profound psychic transformation through magic; it does so by implementing literally something that has only figurative meaning. So in order not to have to "swallow" a loss, we fantasize swallowing (or having swallowed) that which has been lost, as if it were some kind of thing. Two interrelated procedures constitute the magic of incorporation: *demetaphorization* (taking literally what is meant figuratively) and *objectivation* (pretending that the suffering is not an injury to the subject but instead a loss sustained by the love object). The magical "cure" by incorporation exempts the subject from the painful process of reorganization. When, in the form of imaginary or real nourishment, we ingest the love-object we miss, this means that *we refuse to mourn*. (EN 261/126–27)

Introjection makes up for the absence of the world or the lost beloved inside the ego by giving it a linguistic shape, a metaphor that expresses the ego's cognizance of the absence of the love-object and its recognition of that object as an object of desire. The ego caresses its desire and nourishes it through figuration: "language acts and makes up for absence by representing, by *giving figurative shape* to presence" (EN 263/128). But incorporation manifests itself in either the inability to use figurative language or the use of language in acts or speech that prohibits figuration; Abraham and Torok cite coprophagy and "obscenities encouraging incest" as prime examples gleaned from their experience with patients. Incorporation thus destroys the metaphorical act of introjection (EN 268/132).

Incorporation erases the gap between the self and the lost beloved in an operation that Abraham and Torok describe as the creation of a *crypt*, within the self. Through this crypt, which serves as the psychic space in which the beloved is kept, the beloved continues to haunt the self, who disavows the existence of this very crypt because his or her mourning for the lost beloved cannot be expressed in any linguistic form. In this act "a whole world of unconscious fantasy is created . . . [and] sometimes in the dead of the night, when libidinal fulfillments have their way, the ghost of the crypt comes back to haunt the cemetery guard" (EN 266/130), causing varied neuroses and/or psychoses to manifest themselves. The creation of the secret tomb that is the crypt enables the ego to get beyond the traumatic loss by denying that it ever happened. For in his or her mind, the lost beloved always exists.

Nevertheless, as Derrida points out in "Fors," the logic of the crypt is paradoxical. The crypt is located not only within the self but also outside the self, since the inner forum is technically "a safe, an outcast outside inside the inside."[9] At first, this reads nonsensically. Yet Derrida is adequately expressing the fact that the cryptophore does not consciously know what she or he carries. When she or he discovers the crypt in the course of analysis, it is as if it were a sudden discovery of something in the outside world. From the Levinasian vantage point from which Derrida appears to be implicitly working in this essay, the crypt ironically obeys an imperative of alterity. Inside the crypt, the lost beloved is retained as Other qua Other in the mind of the analysand, although not in "reality." Introjection, however, would on this view deny the alterity of the Other since it sees the objects of the world only as extensions of the autoerotic impulse, in accordance with the original definition of the term by Ferenczi. Introjection would thus be for Derrida the mechanism of Hegelian heterophagy. (The section of Hegel's *Phenomenology of Spirit* on the "reconciling *Yea*," cited in the previous chapter, is introjection writ large.) Derrida's deconstruction of Abraham and Torok's distinction between introjection and incorporation results in the claim that an introjection of the lost object that seeks to respect his or her alterity (insofar as this is possible, given the limits of memory) cannot avoid the move of "pathological" incorporation. In mourning that is faithful to the otherness of the Other, the mourner situates him- or herself between

---

[9] Derrida, "Fors," in *Cryptonymie*, 12–13; "Fors," in *The Wolf Man's Magic Word*, xiv.

introjection and incorporation. It is necessary to incorporate the Other into the self, to attempt to eliminate all the metaphorical resonances of memory that mark the distance between the Other and the Other-whom-I-remember. Yet this experience is used for the introjective purposes of self-creation and self-transformation. What kind of self is the result of this process? The signification of the crypt robs the self of any claim to a unitary reality; after all, I am pregnant with the memory of another. In its place, the self instills a world that is both fantasmic (in accordance with Abraham and Torok's description of incorporation) and openly governed by desire (in accordance with their description of introjection), the desire to mourn authentically. For the responsibly mourning self, this virtual reality, both fantasmic and metaphorical in Abraham and Torok's use of the terms, is the only possible reality.[10]

The link between figurality, mourning, and incorporation appears almost a decade later in Derrida's lectures given in memory of Paul de Man, collected as *Mémoires*. Here, Derrida focuses on the nature of memory in the act of mourning, specifically the gap between the mourner's impossible desire to resurrect the beloved in memory and the impossible assertion that otherwise one would be mourning someone or something else besides the lost beloved. We want to mourn the beloved as she or he really was, with all the tangible overtones of this phrase. Yet the smiles, the tears, the kisses, and the lovable neurotic outbursts are, in mourning, now only mental concepts. We must supply the face that expresses these moods if mourning is to be successful. This great difference between the beloved *an sich* and the beloved as constituted by the mourner's imagination reveals that mourning is a figural act. The figure here is one of prosopopeia, face-giving; mourning gives a voice and a face to one who is no longer able to speak or express. Every time that, in mourning, I recall a conversation with the beloved, the structure by which memory constitutes this image inaugurates a subtle shift in which the mourned enters a no-man's-land between life and death. She or he is "really" dead, yet is resurrected in the fantasmatic realm of the imagination. As Derrida points out, it is not only the status of the beloved that shifts in the act of mourning. Since the beloved now resides in me, in *my* memory, this new intentional position shows that I have changed as well. The fact that I am able to take another person into myself through memory demonstrates that the self is not a bounded ipseity that is always staring at the objects of consciousness as if on the visitors' side of an athletic field. For Derrida, the

---

[10] In an essay from 1971 ("The Topography of Reality: Sketching a Metapsychology of Secrets"), Abraham and Torok shift their rhetoric slightly and thereby give the appearance that their position is actually the same as Derrida's position. Hence (EN 253/158): "To call desire by the very name of its prohibition is the law of hysteria's transparent opacity. *And that is fundamentally what we all do.*" (Emphasis mine.) Writing "Fors" in 1976, Derrida had both this essay and the essays on mourning that this passage contradicts in front of him – a situation calling for the formulation of the space between incorporation and introjection.

figuration of the mourner can be directly deduced from the figuration of
the mourned.

Derrida's claim *in nuce* can be found near the center of the opening
lecture in this series. In mourning

we are never *ourselves*, and between us, identical to us, an "ego" ["*moi*"] is never in
itself or identical to itself. This specular reflection never closes in on itself; it does not
appear *before* this *possibility* of mourning, before and outside this structure of allegory
and prosopopeia.[11]

This is a traditionally transcendental argument: the condition for the possibility of mourning (and thus of death and finitude) is the figurality of the
self. If persons were bounded and self-sufficient, death would not be painful.
But since death is painful, and the incorporation of the beloved is necessary,
the reality in which we mourn must be figural through and through. As a
result, what Freud would describe as "normal mourning" in the classic 1917
essay on "Mourning and Melancholia" – the prolongation of the existence
of the lost object in order to make time for the psychic work of detaching
from the beloved and realigning oneself with reality[12] – is nothing less than
a denial of pain and a denial of finitude. For here, the prolonged lost object
is nothing more than the beloved seen strictly and only as for-me. If put
into practice, one would end up as tragically sad as Marcel in his mourning
of Albertine in *Remembrance of Things Past*: here Albertine is reduced to "no
more than a memory, insignificant and full of charm."[13] But for Derrida
contra Freud, it is the weight of the Other's alterity, felt in the trauma of
death, which is significant above any other signifier. The fact that I *can* have
such an intentional relation to the Other in the limit-experiences of mourning means that, in other experiences well within the limit – experience of
objects, dead or alive, in general, *my* experience – I *must* have this same
figural intentionality. Experience always takes place in an environment that
can best be named by the sublimely ironic phrase "virtual reality."

The only option for responsible mourning, then, is to be hijacked by the
beloved, as the mourner's own ego disappears and ethical schizophrenia
takes its place. If I want to honor my attachment to the beloved, mourning
must become pathological. I must honor the rupture in me that the figu-
ralizing memory of the beloved has instituted. We are here neither wholly

[11] Derrida, "Mnemosyne," in *Mémoires pour Paul de Man* (Paris: Galilée, 1988), 49, translated by
Cecile Lindsay as "Mnemosyne," in *Mémoires for Paul de Man*, 2nd ed., trans. Cecile Lindsay,
Jonathan Culler, Eduardo Cadava, and Peggy Kamuf (New York: Columbia University Press,
1989), 28.
[12] Sigmund Freud, "Mourning and Melancholia," in *The Standard Edition of the Complete Psychological Works of Sigmund Freud*, ed. James Strachey (London: Hogarth Press, 1953–74),
14:245.
[13] Marcel Proust, *Remembrance of Things Past*, trans. C. K. Scott Moncrieff, T. Kilmartin, and
A. Mayor (New York: Vintage, 1982), 3:545.

in the realm of introjection nor in that of incorporation. In Derrida's account, the mourner is certainly expressing his or her loss, and hence introjecting the lost love-object. Yet the full expression of this loss forbids introjection: to include the other in the ego, while mourning, would only be to mourn an idealized, whitewashed version of the beloved, without the ambiguities in which the erotic attachment had been crystallized in the first place. Introjection hence becomes incorporation as soon as it expresses itself.

The mourning self has created and assented to an imaginary universe in which the lost beloved calls to me from inside me, not so kindly informing me that it has taken me hostage. But this act of the imagination is obeying a law that dictates that there is a point at which any analogy between myself and other persons must fail. There is necessarily a point at which the actions of others can surprise me and catch me, my various intentions and desires, off guard. As I obey this law by incorporating the Other into myself, I leave myself open ("this specular reflection never closes on itself") and transformed by my imaginative response to the dilemma of alterity. As I incorporate/introject the Other into myself, I realize that the ego has its transcendental roots in the other person. In and via the consciousness of mourning, others are part of what it means to say "I am X," as well as of the condition of being able to say that. Therefore, Derrida speaks of the "other who always speaks in me before me."[14] The Other speaks in me because I remember her; the Other speaks before me because I cannot adequately respond to the limit-event of mourning without having already incorporated others into my ego and punctured the ipseist myth. Alterity is something that can never be introjected into the self; rather, it takes the self over, impoverishing its aspirations and projections of a closed specular reflection – the state of pure autoeroticism. Because the figurality of the Other determines the figurality of the self, and because mourning discloses this situation, Derrida is able to claim that the mourning-consciousness in its relation with others "already carries, always, the signature of *memoirs-from-beyond-the-grave* [mémoires d'outre-tombe, lit., posthumous memoirs],"[15] the no-man's-land of resurrection.

How is the deconstruction of the opposition between introjection and incorporation related to messianism? The rupture of the self shows itself also to be a temporal rupture. For Derrida, the responsible mourner's incorporation of the Other into itself, done in faithfulness to the Other's singularity, takes the structure of a promise: "the self has that [quasi-narcissistic incorporative] relation to itself only *through* [depuis] the other, through the promise (for the future, as trace of the future) made to the other as an absolute past, and thus *through* this absolute past."[16] This sentence calls for parsing. The first clause (up to "through the other") is a restatement of the previous argument, namely, that mourning and its necessary pathology demonstrates the chiasm of identity and alterity as I constitute the meaning of the beloved whom I mourn. The second clause is far more difficult. Mourning promises to keep the lost beloved as unique in memory as the beloved was in life – it promises to erect a psychic space that resurrects the beloved and protects him or her from the elements. But the pathology of this crypt building renders this past (with the beloved "really" alive) inaccessible for the work of mourning. Ironically, the mourner is thus given freedom to focus on future activity as a way of honoring the singularity of the Other. The comportment of the mourner to the absolute past suddenly changes direction midstream and becomes involved in making singularity endure. The world becomes the locus of my desire to mourn; incorporation, in expressing itself, becomes introjection. A passage from an essay of Paul de Man's (quoted by Derrida) on the Proustean project of conquering anomie through literary production is helpful here:

> The power of memory does not reside in its capacity to resurrect a situation or a feeling that actually existed, but it is a constitutive act of the mind bound to its own present and oriented toward the future of its own elaboration. The past intervenes only as a purely formal element, as a reference or a leverage that can be used because it is different and distant rather than because it is familiar and near.[17]

For Derrida and de Man, it is through memory that one creates the time in which one can honor one's promise to be faithful to unconditioned alterity, the promise that was inherent in the desire to mourn truly and authentically. Note that this involves a turn to universalist rhetoric; at the same time it presses forward in the rhetoric of singularity that began Derrida's deconstruction of the introjection–incorporation opposition. But *this* universalist rhetoric is shrouded in negativity. I exchange the beloved to whom I promised singularity for the others with whom I will deal in the future because alterity is a universal characteristic of persons. Others are not like me because we share something such as reason or religion, but because we are all exterior to whatever our essence might be, and thus we are exterior to each other.

Yet in what manner can one say that the promise to the Other is a trace of the future? In the surface meaning of this phrase, a certain kind of future – one in which the singularity of all individuals will not be subsumed into

---

[16] Derrida, "L'art de *Mémoires*," in *Mémoires pour Paul de Man*, 77, translated by Jonathan Culler as "The Art of *Mémoires*," in *Mémoires for Paul de Man*, 66.

[17] Paul de Man, "The Literary Self as Origin: The Work of Georges Poulet," in *Blindness and Insight*, 2nd ed. (Minneapolis: University of Minnesota Press, 1983), 92. Quoted by Derrida in "L'art de *Mémoires*," in *Mémoires pour Paul de Man*, 72; "The Art of *Mémoires*," in *Mémoires for Paul de Man*, 59.

the various ego-mechanisms of institutions (i.e., justice as fairness regardless of political status) – has already been subtly posited as being the goal of thinking. Derrida at one point in *Mémoires* states that this is an "act of faith."[18] Faith here is a hope that the universal structures underlying experience will at some point correlate to the ways in which people actually behave, a hope that I will be able to keep my promise to remember the mourned beloved as he or she actually existed.[19] From the phenomenology of mourning, the values of the singularity of the individual and the transcendental precedence of the Other have come into focus. And so I hope that the values I see will empirically become true; I hope that life will correspond to phenomenology. This hope is uncertain, since it comes only from my intentional relation to the lost beloved. It is simply *not* an Aristotelian-style teleology in which people act for the sake of a certain state of affairs. For in the Aristotelian model, the telos is still capable of being grasped by the imagination as universal happiness, in which the nature of others' happiness is imagined in an analogical substitution of the self for the Other. This teleology can describe only a world in which there does not exist the kind of pleasure that one receives in noticing or experiencing something for the first time, in which one is carried by the mysteriousness of the object. There is nothing mysterious in a preanticipated telos. But when one is touched by death, the desire to be faithful to the alterity of the Other necessitates that the future for which I am acting be completely different from anything that I could possibly imagine. It must take me by surprise, or else it would not be other than myself. Hence one must classify it as eschatological and not as teleological.

In *Specters of Marx*, mourning takes on the general definition of the failed attempt to ontologize remains, to protend them into the present (SM 30/9). As the analyses of the earlier essays show, mourning speaks to a dislocation, a disjointing, a dephasing of time. The past becomes the future in an elision of the present, or at least in an elision of presence seen as constitutive of being, of the "what X is." The elision of presence is thus also an elision of content. For this reason, the Derridean eschatology organized around the concept of the "messianic" in *Specters* cannot have any content whatsoever. If the nature of mourning implies giving the lost beloved a status "in me" between presence and absence, in order to be as faithful as possible to his or her alterity, so then the status of the eschaton must be equally as vague as this otherness, with its memoirs of the shadowy place beyond the grave.

[18] Derrida, "Actes: Le sens d'un mot donné," in *Mémoires pour Paul de Man*, 143, translated by Eduardo Cadava as "Acts: The Meaning of a Given Word," in *Mémoires for Paul de Man*, 150.

[19] Cf. Derrida, "Foi et savoir: Les deux sources de la 'religion' aux limites de la simple raison," in *La Religion*, ed. Jacques Derrida and Gianni Vattimo (Paris: Seuil, 1996), 28, translated by Samuel Weber as "Faith and Knowledge: The Two Sources of 'Religion' at the Limits of Reason Alone," in *On Religion*, ed. Jacques Derrida and Gianni Vattimo (Stanford, Calif.: Stanford University Press, 1998), 18, reprinted in *Acts of Religion*, 56.

To claim otherwise, and to give the eschaton a certain content, either with miraculous creations or miraculous destructions, is already an imaginative taking-over of the future that deadens it. In speaking of the absolute nature of the eschatological event, Derrida stresses the necessity of thinking of it in absolutely formal terms:

> The event cannot be reduced to the fact that something arrives [*arrive*, "happens"]. It may rain this evening or it may not, but this will not be an absolute event because I know what rain is; so it is not an absolutely different singularity . . . If I am sure there will be an event, it will not be an event.[20]

The messianic (the eschaton seen through the lens of the alterity of persons) cannot belong to anything that I know or of which I can be sure.

So what is to be done? Derrida's solution in *Specters of Marx* is a formulation of a "New International" (SM 141–43/84–87) that acts in the name of a radical hospitality that sees every individual as singular, exterior to any class that would claim to swallow it. This hospitality to the stranger (SM 273/172) is grounded, however, in the realization that there is already a stranger encrypted within me that issues a call to me. Derrida, like Cohen, envisions this task as an infinite process (SM 143/86), and indeed Derrida's description of the New International as a link of "affinity, suffering, and hope" is strikingly Cohenian. This ethics and politics, then, are hardly postmodern in the sense of a departure from modern Enlightenment scientific modes of thinking. Rather, they suggest a rigorous and radical reading of the modern. One hastens the era of ethics by acting as if one were already bringing it to the world at every moment (as is the case for Rosenzweig).

In summary, the Derridean analysis of mourning naturally has an eschatological component to it. Yet in honoring the memory of the Other in his or her singularity, the mourner also engenders the future, and so becomes part of the very eschatological move to which he or she is responding. What Derrida refers to as the *epochē* of the content of the messianic (SM 102/59) in the end enacts itself as a doubleness regarding the issue of precisely who is acting messianically or Messiah-like. On the one hand, the coming of the Other in his or her absolute singularity marks a futural break at the site of the limits of the ego's imagination. At the same time and on the other hand, the relation of singularity is what marks the messianic, and it is this relation that I intentionally constitute in *my* act of mourning and in *my* radical hospitality to the Other; I am myself part of the messianic. Levinas argues similarly in his exegesis of B. Sanhedrin 99, in which he describes messianism as "my power to bear the suffering of all . . . the moment when I recognize this

---

[20] Derrida, "The Deconstruction of Actuality," translated by Elizabeth Rottenberg, in *Negotiations: Interventions and Interviews, 1971–2001*, ed. Elizabeth Rottenberg (Stanford, Calif.: Stanford University Press, 2002), 96.

power and my universal responsibility."[21] Yet Derrida must see himself as saying more than this, or else (one might surmise) he would not be so quick to distance himself from the meontological tradition. Perhaps the statement "I am the Messiah," even with all the ambiguities inherent in this statement, is too much knowledge, too much identity. But Derrida's suspicion of the meontological tradition also ends up *expressing* the very belonging-together of meontology and ontology that we have seen throughout this work from Democritus through Levinas. To say "I am the Messiah" means *also* to put myself at/in the hands of the singular Other. This person saves me, *and* I save myself. Or, when I decide to save myself, I let others save me, I let the Other within save me. The name "Messiah" is stretched across subject and object, lying somewhere in the between-space that should by all means make Derrida happy. Thus, the Messiah is both within and without, both myself and the Other. This name, this title, lies in the crypt that I build for the Other; there is no hope for future salvation without this labor. But, in messianic anticipation, who is this Other? God? And why am I mourning God?

THE MOURNERS OF ZION, *HADOMIM LO*

In the Jewish tradition, the term "mourners of Zion" first appears in the Bible at Is. 61:1–9, in one of the so-called suffering servant songs. Here, the rhetoric of anointing in the opening verse already establishes a context that links mourning with messianism. Because of the centrality of the imagery of Isaiah 61 to the text of PesR 34, I quote in full:

(v. 1) The Spirit of YHWH God is upon me because YHWH has anointed me to bring good tidings to the afflicted; he has sent me to bind up the brokenhearted, to proclaim liberty to the captives, and the opening of the prison to those who are bound;

(v. 2) to proclaim the year of YHWH's favor and the day of vengeance of our God; to comfort all who mourn;

(v. 3) to grant to the mourners of Zion – to give them a garland instead of ashes, the oil of gladness instead of mourning, the mantle of praise instead of a faint spirit that they may be called oaks of righteousness, the planting of YHWH, blessed be He.

(v. 4) They shall build up the ancient ruins, they shall raise up the former devastations; they shall repair the ruined cities, the devastations of many generations.

(v. 5) Aliens shall stand and feed your flocks, foreigners shall be your plowmen and vine-dressers;

(v. 6) but you shall be called the priests of YHWH men shall speak of you as the servants of our God; you shall eat the wealth of the nations, and in their riches you shall glory.

---

[21] Levinas, "Textes messianiques," in *Difficile liberté,* 3rd ed. (Paris: Livre de poche, 1984), 120, translated by Seán Hand as "Messianic Texts," in *Difficult Freedom* (Baltimore: Johns Hopkins University Press), 90.

(v. 7) Instead of your shame you shall have a double portion, instead of dishonor they shall rejoice in their lot; therefore in their land they shall possess a double portion; theirs shall be everlasting joy.

(v. 8) For I the Lord love justice, I hate robbery with a burnt offering; I will faithfully give them their recompense, and I will make an everlasting covenant with them.

(v. 9) Their descendants shall be known among the nations, and their offspring in the midst of the peoples; all who see them shall acknowledge them, that they are a people whom YHWH has blessed.

The first midrashic reference to a group of Jews who appropriated this name for themselves is in Pesikta Rabbati 34. Given the late date that interpreters over the last century have, by and large, assigned to this text, this is somewhat surprising. One might suppose that after the destruction of the Second Temple, these verses should have been an obvious source for rabbis to express messianic yearning. But they were not. It took some centuries for the rabbinic tradition to appropriate these verses in a messianic context or for a sect to refer to themselves as "the mourners of Zion" – exactly how many is not, and perhaps cannot, be known – and even when these verses were appropriated, the movement that arose was a highly heterodox one.

Before analyzing the text, it would be helpful to know something about the social context of the Mourners of Zion sect. But this historical reconstruction appears to be impossible. We *do* know that in the ninth and tenth centuries, Palestinian Karaites – Jews who rejected the rabbinic development of Oral Torah – identified themselves as mourners of Zion. The Karaite movement peaked approximately a century before the destruction of the Jewish settlement in Jerusalem in 1099. Since Karaism is generally linked to a wave of Jewish immigration into Jerusalem, the Karaite *'avelei tzion* are seen as ascetic fundamentalists who stressed immigration to the land of Israel as a precondition for redemption. One Karaite example of the connection between antirabbinism and self-identification as one of the *'avelei tzion* in Karaism is an epistle from a scholar who identifies himself as a Mourner of Zion and missionizes in the diaspora in order "to awaken the hearts of His people of Israel [and] turn them back to the [written] law of the Lord . . . and to warn them not to rely upon ordinances contrived by men and learned by rote." Only Israel's rejection of the rabbinic Oral Torah (the "ordinances contrived by men," which, in the eyes of this author, are not God-given and hence not Torah), will engender the fulfillment of the divine promise "to turn the ashes covering the heads of the mourners of Zion into an ornament of splendor."[22] This reference to Is. 61:3 suggests that it is a mass movement of mourning the absence of God that will cause God's return

---

[22] In *A Karaite Anthology: Excerpts from the Early Literature*, ed. and trans. Leon Nemoy (New Haven, Conn.: Yale University Press, 1952), 113–14.

to the people of Israel. The Karaite Mourners of Zion are also ascetics, in opposition to the rabbis who "vaunt their holiness and purity, but demand that the people bring them all kinds of sweetmeats and wine . . . so that they may eat and drink."[23] Finally, the Karaite *'avelei tzion* do not want the people of Israel simply to turn back to Written Torah alone, but to do so in the land of Israel. Barry Walfish has argued that the *'avelei tzion* movement is "an exclusively Karaite phenomenon" intended "to counteract the forces of assimilation in the Dispersion."[24] Walfish cites a letter generally attributed to the Jerusalem Karaite scholar Daniel al-Qumisi that uses Jer. 31:21 ("Return, Maiden Israel! Return to these towns of yours!") as a prooftext for his exhortation "prior to the ingathering of the Diaspora [to] come to Jerusalem and stand before the Lord in watches, day and night"; al-Qumisi interprets "return" and "these towns of yours" according to their surface meaning, as a call for immigration to the land of Israel.[25]

However, as Arnold Goldberg established, the dating of the Karaite *'avelei tzion* movement is not sufficient to date PesR 34 as originating in this period, as has been the dominant interpretation since Leopold Zunz and Heinrich Graetz first proffered it around the turn of the twentieth century.[26] If the text were a Karaite or proto-Karaite text, one would expect explicit references to Palestine or Jerusalem; there are none. If the text were from late antiquity, one would expect it to contain loan words from Aramaic or Greek, as can be found in other midrashic texts of the period; the text is written in a pure Hebrew. Nevertheless, if the text were to be dated earlier, one would expect frequent quotation of rabbinic sages. On the other hand, the text is equally absent of characteristics such as the frequent quotation of other rabbis. As a result of these textual difficulties, Goldberg concluded that "even now, no one can say for sure when and where this Hebrew was written."[27] The best conclusion one can make is that it seems most likely that PesR 34 represents a pre-Karaite period in the history of *'avelei tzion.* This homily is part of a series of commentaries on the passages from prophetic texts read

---

[23] Ibid., 115.

[24] Barry Walfish, "The Mourners of Zion: Karaite *Aliyah* Movement of the Early Arab Period," in *Eretz Israel, Israel and the Jewish Diaspora,* ed. Menachem Mor (Lanham, Md.: University Press of America, 1991), 47.

[25] Ibid., 44.

[26] Goldberg, 23. Also cf. Leopold Zunz, *Die gottesdienstlichen Vorträge der Juden* (Frankfurt: Hildesheim, 1966); Heinrich Graetz, *History of the Jews,* trans. Bella Löwy (Philadelphia: Jewish Publication Society, 1891). Braude agrees with a relatively late date for the text. Graetz believed PesR to be of Palestinian origin; Zunz argued that it was of Greek origin.

[27] Goldberg, 23. For other participants in the debate over dating these texts, cf. Bernard J. Bamberger, "A Messianic Document of the Seventh Century," *Hebrew Union College Annual* 15 (1940), 425–31; and Arthur Marmorstein, "Eine messianische Bewegung im dritten Jahrhundert," *Jeschurun* 13 (1926), 16–28, 171–86, 369–83. One should also note that Jacob Mann interpreted the *'avelei tzion* as a precursor to practical Kabbalah. Cf. his *The Jews in Egypt and Palestine under the Fatimid Caliphs* (Oxford: Oxford University Press, 1929), 1:47.

on the seven Sabbaths after the holy day Tisha B'Av (which commemorates
the destruction of the Jerusalem Temple); other texts in this series refer
primarily to a heartfelt yearning for redemption, not an activist hastening of
redemption through immigration.[28] It seems most likely that the "mourners
of Zion" described in this text are engaged not in a return to the letter of
the Written Torah, but in a reflection on the question of how to worship
God and conceptualize the Messiah after the destruction of the Temple.

The text of PesR 34 opens as follows:

"Rejoice greatly, Fair Zion! Raise a shout, Fair Jerusalem! Lo, your king is coming to
you. He is victorious and triumphant, yet humble, riding on an ass." (Zech. 9:9)
    This verse is to be considered in the light of what Isaiah was inspired by the
holy spirit to say: "Their descendants shall be known among the nations, and their
offspring in the midst of the peoples" (Is. 61:9). What did Isaiah have in mind when
he spoke this verse? He spoke it with a view to comforting the Mourners of Zion to
whom the Holy One, blessed be He, will give victory over their enemies, as it is said,
"Their offspring shall be known among the nations." Do not read "their offspring"
(*zar'am*) but "their arm" (*zero'am*). And who will stand by them with his arm? The Holy
One, blessed be He, will stand by them with His arm, in answer to the prayer "O Lord,
be gracious to us! It is to You we have looked. Be their arm every morning, also our
redemption in time of stress" (Is. 33:2). The phrase "every morning" alludes to those
who rise up every morning to beseech mercy, alludes particularly to the Mourners
of Zion who yearn for deliverance morning, evening, and noon.

PesR 34 presents itself as a series of midrashim rooted in Zech. 9:9. In the first
step of its analysis, rooted more in a thematic link of affliction in eschatological times than in a specific wordplay, the piska (chapter) connects Zech. 9:9
to Isaiah 61, a passage that portrays the material, spiritual, and political consolation of the Mourners of Zion. While there is no reason why the surface
meaning of the passage from Isaiah cannot be interpreted to refer to Israel at
large, the author sees this as impossible. More precisely, the author takes this
as an opportunity to resolve a surface irregularity in another verse in Is. 33:2.
In this verse, there is a sudden grammatical shift from the first-person plural
(*ḥanenu*, "be gracious to us") to the third-person plural (*zero'am*, "their arm"),
and then back again to the first-person plural (*yeshu'atenu*, "our redemption"
or "our deliverance"). This immediately raises the questions of who the
"they" of "their arm" might be, and why one should pray to God for strength
on behalf of this "they" when one could just as easily pray for the entire "we."
Indeed, the passage is so strange that the Revised Standard Version translation of the Bible chooses to elide the difficulty completely and translates
the verse as "be our arm every morning." But the divine word can make no
such mistakes. The verse necessarily implies that whereas God will eventually
redeem all Israel, God's immediate power actually lies behind, and God's

---

[28] For example, "it is still required that sighing for Jerusalem continue in our hearts until the
Holy One, blessed be He, returns to Jerusalem." PesR 31:1; Braude, 2:600.

agency lies immediately within, some smaller community, a subgroup that is a "they" with respect to the majority community who is actually uttering the prayer here in Isaiah 33. From this conclusion, the midrashist returns from Is. 33:2 to Is. 61:9 and decides to read "their offspring" (*zar'am*) as a shortened version of "their arm" (*zero'am*), the word that appears in Is. 33:2. Since the parameters of midrashic interpretation allow a reader to unfold a further dimension of meaning by assuming that identical words in different biblical verses have the same referent, the author of the PesR 34 is able to claim that the subgroup – the "they" of Is. 33:2 – is identical to the "their arm/offspring" described in Is. 61:9, namely, the Mourners of Zion. Indeed, the "at morning" in the Isaiah 33 verse is understood by the midrashist to allude "particularly to the Mourners [of Zion] who desire [*she-ḥamdu*] deliverance [every] morning, evening, and noon."[29]

The messianic figure who narrates Isaiah 61 provides only for the "mourners of Zion" (61:3). In the context of PesR 34, this means that the sect of the Mourners of Zion is closer to God than the rest of the people of Israel. The mourners, alone among the people of Israel, are the only persons who are comforted in the messianic "day of vengeance of our God" described in Is. 61:2. It is therefore apparent, from the midrashist's perspective, that if one truly desires redemption and messianic consolation, one should become a member of this group. Only in the context of mourning and identification as a Mourner of Zion can one be sure that the messianic prophecy of Zech. 9:9 is truly imminent. The midrashist feels that he has unpacked the essence of revelation, and revelation is always and everywhere revelation to the *'avelei tzion*. In speaking to them, the messianic voice of the narrator supersedes the covenant as it has been passed down through the rabbinic tradition. The text of PesR 34 continues by prophesying the future of those who remain apart from the sect of *'avelei tzion*:

Now the Mourners of Zion suffered great distress because it was the children of Israel who both mocked and scorned them. But when these children of Israel see the afflictions decreed by God for the years immediately preceding that extraordinary year in which the Messiah is to appear amidst Israel, and when they see that the afflictions follow one upon the other without ceasing, then at last they will understand that it was because of the unending prayers of the Mourners of Zion that the Messiah will appear . . .

In the seven-year period [preceding the arrival of the Messiah, the children of Israel] will find themselves so punished that they will have faces as black as the bottom of a pot. And wherewith will they be punished? With famine. Once the stubborn will of Israel is broken – and it is broken only by means of famine – then the righteous men of the generation will stand up and [in mourning] remove their tefillin, lay them upon the ground and say to Him: "Master of the universe, we have not acted rightly all these years – like sheep we have gone astray." The Holy One, blessed be

---

[29] One should not ignore the erotic overtones of carnal desire in the use of the Hebrew verb *ḥamad* here.

He, will say: "Your straying is forgiven you." Then he will kiss them and put back the garland [i.e., tefillin, cf. Is. 61:3] upon them. Thus he who has the merit of knowledge of Torah will find it standing by him; but he who has not the merit of knowledge of Torah, what can stand by him? . . .

"All who see them shall acknowledge them" (Is. 61:9) – all will acknowledge the Mourners of Zion with whom the Holy One, blessed be He, will specially concern himself. For during the time immediately preceding the appearance of the Messiah, the Holy One, blessed be He, will increase the number of the angels of destruction hovering over His world, and these will take their toll of those children of Israel who scorned the possibility of redemption. In that time the Mourners of Zion will walk among and beside the angels of destruction like a man visiting with his fellow man, for the angels of destruction will do no harm to the Mourners of Zion.

What is the possible source for this conflict between the Mourners of Zion and the rest of the people of Israel? The *'avelei tzion* are heteroprax or anti-nomian about certain divine commands. Because they identify as mourners, they are claiming that the laws pertaining to mourning – or, precisely, since God is not a body who can be buried, the laws pertaining to *'aninut*, the pre-burial phase of mourning when the observance of positive commandments is suspended, including the commandment to wear tefillin (phylacteries) during prayer – must be observed at all times by the entire community after the destruction of the Second Temple. They mourn the loss of God's presence in the Temple as a child mourns the loss of a parent; their halakhic practice relies upon a resolutely nonmetaphorical reading of the numerous biblical descriptions of God's parental relationship with Israel. Existence without the Temple necessitates an according shift in ritual praxis, a shift that will appear heretical and deserving of scorn by others in the community. Redemption will occur only when the entire community recognizes the truth of the mourners' interpretation of Isaiah 61.

The conflict between the *'avelei tzion* and the children of Israel is not simply one between two understandings of ritual. The conflict is theological. What PesR 34 reflects is a debate over the interior mood or stance that should accompany ritual praxis during the time of exile, whether or not the hope for redemption expressed through mourning the destruction of the Temple should become the central motif of Judaism and determine ritual life. As a passage I shall soon quote demonstrates, the crux of the issue is teleology: is Torah-observance its own telos, or does the unredeemed nature of the world in which Jews observe Torah disclose a higher telos that determines the framework in which one lives a Jewish life? The narrator of PesR 34 describes the children of Israel as having "scorned the possibility of redemption." Instead, they adhere to the Torah for its own sake, believing it to be eternally sufficient for maintaining Israel's covenantal obligations, despite the contingent events of Jewish history. From the perspective of the mourners, this is insufficient, as it fails to take into account the reality of exile and the necessity of positing the hope for redemption as the essential ground of halakhic praxis. This point is stressed in the text's following prophecy of a speech by God to the *tzadiqe hador,* the righteous members of the generation:

O righteous men of the world, even though words of Torah are sweet and necessary for me [and will be rewarded], you only attend to my Torah – you do not wait for My kingship. Hence I have declared on oath that for him who waits for My kingship I myself shall bear witness in his behalf, as is said (Zeph. 3:8) "Therefore wait for me, says the Lord, until the day that I rise up to witness [*le'ed*]." Those who have waited for Me are the Mourners of Zion who grieved [suffered pain] with me because of my house which is destroyed and because of my temple which is desolate. Now I bear witness for them, each of whom Scripture describes in the verse (Is. 57:15) "with one that is of a contrite and humble spirit." Do not read "with one that is of a contrite and humble spirit"; read rather "he that is of a contrite and humble spirit grieves with Me." Such are the Mourners of Zion who humbled their spirits, listened meekly to those who reviled them, keeping silent the while, and yet did not consider themselves particularly virtuous therefore.[30]

One does not relate to God through Torah alone; the text states that there is another dimension of the Godhead – God's kingship to come – which stands beside Torah and is of equal importance, if not even the center of Torah that gives it its efficacy. Attending to Torah is an act that recreates the

---

[30] This is my emended version of Braude's translation at 665–66. The text is difficult at many levels, owing to differences in manuscripts. The sentence I have translated as "words of Torah are sweet and necessary for me" reflects the *editio princeps'* reading of *she-divre torah tzerikhim* ("necessary") *hem 'alay* and the Parma manuscript's reading of *she-divre torah 'arivin* ("sweet, pleasing") *hem 'alay.* In addition, I have changed the meaning of the first two sentences in the quotation to reflect what in my opinion must be the original motive for the citation from Zephaniah. The use of "wait for" (*ḥiku*) in the verse should be paralleled by a similar use of the root *ḥet-kaf-he* in the sentences before. But instead, both the *editio princeps* and the Parma manuscript use corrupt forms of the root *ḥet-bet-bet,* "to love, honor." Thus the verse should read, "you only love my Torah, you do not love my kingship," and this is how Michael Fishbane interprets the text. Similarly, the Parma manuscript reads "I have declared an oath for him who loves my kingship," whereas the *editio princeps* uses the nonsensical root *kaf-ḥet-he,* which is most likely based on a scribal error that switched the first two letters of the root. But if the midrashist means the text to be about the love of God, there is no reason for the text to cite the verse from Zephaniah. It may be that the orthographic similarity between the two words led to the corruption of extant manuscripts. In addition, a lost manuscript may have contained the odd phrase "*sheḥikitem letorati,*" which means literally "you wait for my Torah." This makes little sense, since the Torah has already been given and there would be no reason to wait for it. Jastrow remarks that the verb here can also mean "to be anxious for," which I have emended to "to attend to." In Friedmann's critical edition, he notes that medieval commentators on the text interpreted the verb as *ḥet-kaf-he,* although they also understood the Parma manuscript's use of *'arivin* to describe words of Torah to be synonymous with *ḥavivin,* "beloved," thus reinserting the surface meaning of the manuscript back into the text. My thanks to Diana Lobel for discussing these manuscript issues with me.

Cf. Michael Fishbane, "Midrashic Theologies of Messianic Suffering," in *The Exegetical Imagination: On Jewish Thought and Theology* (Cambridge, Mass.: Harvard Unversity Press, 1998), 78; *Pesikta Rabbati,* ed. Meir Friedmann (Tel Aviv, 1962 [1880]), 276. A selection of all the manuscripts of this text can be found at Ulmer, 819.

past era in which God was present with Israel while the Temple stood. It sees no need to mourn the past, but is content to imagine it truly experiences the past in each present moment. In attending to Torah alone, one believes that one lives in eternity, but forgets that the destruction of the Temple marks an irrevocable breach between the present and the past.

Yet waiting upon kingship is an act that, according to Zephaniah, breaks from the past and awaits an era that is both like and unlike the present moment. In the era of exile, there is no place for God to make himself manifest ("my house . . . destroyed," "my temple . . . desolate"). This implies that the day of God's testifying to the devotion of the Mourners of Zion occurs in a time other than the present. The *'avelei tzion* await divine witness. Yet the rhetoric of the passage undergoes a striking shift as the prooftext moves from Zephaniah 3 to Isaiah 57. Suddenly God bears witness for the Mourners of Zion in the present ("Now I bear witness for them"), despite God's formal absence. Rather, the presence of God is manifest through the *'avelei tzion* themselves. The demeanor of mournful humility acts as a vector toward God. A shadowy and fantasmic presence – a trace, if you will, given the absence of the Temple and the concomitant impossibility of imagining divine presence – can be magically conjured up through the act of mourning.

PesR 34 itself shows how mourning renders the absent present, in its interpretation of Is. 57:15. A *yod* is added to the *'et* in the phrase *'et daka' ushefal ruach* ("with the contrite and lowly of spirit"), on the assumption that the *'et* is really a shortened form of *'itti*. This emendation of the text renders the text "and with *Me* [are] the contrite and humble of spirit."[31] In his translation, Braude adds "grieves" into this phrase ("he that is of a contrite and humble spirit grieves with Me") in order to explicitly tie the *derash* on Is. 57:15 back to the midrashist's earlier assertion that God grieves with the Mourners of Zion. Yet this is Braude's strong translation; the essential link between humility and the presence of God is actually more suggestive without this insertion. Indeed, Goldberg translates the passage in this more literal manner.

The addition of the *yod* into the text of Is. 57:15 argues that mourning is more than simply anticipation of the future. It is behaving as if the future of God's witness were now, since God makes himself present to the mourner in the very act of mourning. But *alongside* this, at the same time there is an awareness that this cannot be literally true; if it were, anticipation would no longer be necessary, and God would already be present. Thus, PesR 34 gives

---

[31] Friedmann's critical edition reads the reemended text to include *'itti*, and Braude and Goldberg translate accordingly. However, the *editio princeps* manuscript that both Goldberg and Ulmer produce reads *'oto*, which would lead the text to be translated as "and with Him . . ." Since this sentence takes place within God's speech to the *tzadiqe hador*, the shift in pronouns makes little sense, and Friedmann seems to have corrected the text accordingly. The Parma manuscript reads *'al dakah*, which is corrupt.

the reader a picture of a belief system in which what has become normative is the projection onto the real world of an imagined utopia. The type of existence that characterizes PesR 34's description of authentic faith is located somewhere on the threshold between imagination and reality. Only in reality can one hear the command to wait for God, but only in imagination can one obey it. To taste and see the goodness of the Lord, is to taste and see the future, and to rip oneself out of the present through an act of mourning that is dispersed in two directions at once. Mourning Zion is engaging in a memory of the lost past. But it is also oriented, in a moment of hope, toward a radical futurity in which this past is restored in fulfillment of the divine promise. Only by dispersing in both of these directions at once does an image of divine presence become possible. It is thus the gathering of time in the imaginative topos of mourning that replaces the literal topos of the Temple as a means of engendering the presence of God alongside the people of Israel. Yet again, the sense of the presence of God in the declaration "with Me are the contrite and lowly of spirit" is denied at the surface reading of the text, which always and everywhere imagines a scene of redemption that is always in the future. Divine presence is simultaneously appropriated and expropriated in the text. Mourning both engenders redemption now and awaits messianic redemption in the future. The "messianic" (era, person, group?) exists in a modality between that of presence and absence, as in Derrida's *Specters of Marx,* Maimonides's *Epistle to Yemen,* Cohen's *Religion of Reason,* and multiple Levinas texts.

In its final paragraphs, PesR 34 distills this double-sided temporality of the nature of *'avelei tzion'*s mourning. At first, this section seems like an afterthought to the previous discourse on *'avelei tzion,* the interpolation of another tradition for purely thematic reasons. While it shares its base-text, Zech. 9:9, with the rest of the homily, it never once explicitly mentions *'avelei tzion* and is concerned instead with the nature of the Messiah.

"Submissive, and delivering salvation" (Zech. 9:9) describes the Messiah, for when they laughed at him while he sat in prison, he submitted for the sake of Israel to the judgment imposed upon him, and is therefore properly called submissive. Why is he spoken of as "delivering salvation"? Because after submitting to the judgment for their sake, he said: "All of you deserve extermination; nevertheless, you will be saved, every one of you, by the mercy of the Holy One, blessed be He."

"Humble, afflicted ['ani], riding on an ass" (Zech. 9:9) describes the Messiah. And why is he called "afflicted"? Because he was afflicted during all his years in prison while transgressors in Israel laughed at him.

The author of these lines rereads the Masoretic text of this verse, *tzaddiq ve-nosha'* "victorious and delivering salvation," as *tzideq ve-nosha'* "submitting to judgment and delivering salvation." This midrashic rereading of the verse is not necessitated by a grammatical irregularity in the verse itself, as was the case in the earlier analysis of Is. 33:2. It is therefore natural to conclude that this is not *only* a discourse about the Messiah. Rather, this analysis of Zech. 9:9 has the effect of bolstering the status of the *'avelei tzion* in their community, by emphasizing the similarities between the current status of the Mourners of Zion and that of the Messiah. These similarities are inescapable. The Messiah is laughed at by Jews who transgress the Law; the Mourners of Zion are mocked and scorned by the "children of Israel" who refuse to adhere to laws of mourning that, in the sect's view, are necessary after the destruction of the Temple. The Messiah calmly submits to his sufferings; the Mourners of Zion "listened meekly to those who rented them, keeping silent the while." The Messiah redeems his antagonists; the narrative voice of the *'avelei tzion* has God forgive the sins of the "righteous members of the generation" who take off their tefillin upon realization that the Mourners of Zion are interpreting halakha correctly.

PesR 34 closes with a dramatic yet brief discussion of a messianic passage in the Bible that has not been discussed earlier in the homily. I quote the biblical passage, Ps. 132:17–18 here, and then the final section of PesR 34.

(v. 17) There I will make a horn sprout for David; I have prepared a lamp for My anointed one.
(v. 18) I will clothe his enemies in disgrace, And on him [*ve'alav*] his crown shall sparkle.

"His enemies" – those who dispute with him – "I will clothe with disgrace." "And on him his crown shall sparkle" – the "and" at the beginning of this clause indicates that his crown will shine upon himself, and also upon those who are at one with him.

The linguistic point of interest in Ps. 132:18 is why the second half of the verse begins with "and." Certainly the "and" is not necessary; Ps. 132:17 is easily comprehensible without a conjunction between the two halves of the verse. Again, the divine word cannot be spoken on a whim, and so the author of PesR 34 suggests that the "and" is not superfluous at all. Instead, the *ve'alav* is a brief signal for a longer phrase, *'alav ve'al hadomim lo*, which might be translated "upon himself and upon those who resemble him." Braude emphasizes the aspect of similarity in the Hebrew verb *damah*, by translating *hadomim lo* as "those who are at one with him"; Goldberg captures the nuance perfectly with the German verb *gleichen*, which communicates both the element of difference and likeness in the relationship between the Messiah and the others who have come on the scene. It is impossible to read this sentence as not persuading the audience that it is the sect of *'avelei tzion* who are the referent of "*hadomim lo*." Like earlier parts of the homily, the analysis of Ps. 132:18 serves to bolster the authority of the *'avelei tzion* in their surrounding community.

This last sentence marks the pinnacle of the remarkable externalization of the self-image of the *'avelei tzion*, one that perhaps justifies Braude's stretching the lexical limits of *hadomim lo*. The entire piska has undergone a shocking shift from juxtaposing the Mourners of Zion with the consoled mourners of Isaiah 61 to juxtaposing them with the Messiah himself, inviting a reading of the identity between the Messiah and *'avelei tzion* at the same time that the surface sense of the text insists that the Messiah is someone other than the Mourners of Zion. After all, the mourners are not consoled simply by God, as in Isaiah 61. They console themselves; their mourning actually inaugurates redemption, the moment when all Israel will come to "understand that it was because of the unending prayers of the Mourners of Zion that the Messiah will appear." And PesR 34 is strangely silent about what the Messiah actually does; the descriptions of him are to be understood as representing the situation of the *'avelei tzion*. But this symbolism is never expressed as such on the surface of the text; there is no reason to believe that the Mourners of Zion have ceased to believe in an external transcendent Messiah. As a result, messianic agency lies both inside and outside the mourner, as the expression of mourning and as the anticipated result of it. The mourner both is and is not the Messiah. The Messiah has been encrypted.

SWALLOWING TEARS

Obviously, a demonstration that PesR 34 displays in the personae of the *'avelei tzion* a portrait of meontological subjectivity cannot rest on any references in this text to Plato, Aristotle, or Plotinus. Yet the previous two chapters have shown that the Jewish meontological tradition uses the concept of *to mē on* to express three concepts: (1) a combination of a teleological arc of existence and the momentary manifestation of that telos in the present, (2) a notion of ethics centered around humility and/or the taking on of suffering for the sake of the community or world, and (3) an identity confusion between the responsible self (whether ethically, rationally, or scripturally) and the Messiah. PesR 34 exhibits the first and third of these concepts; the encrypting of the Messiah testifies both to an anticipated future and to the incarnation of that future in the *'avelei tzion* themselves. With that being said, it is important to recognize that PesR 34 and the Jewish meontological tradition are not immediately interchangeable; there is not a radical thinking of the Other in the rabbinic text as there is in Derrida. There is a certain epistemological righteousness to the Mourners of Zion as they protest their treatment at the hands of the children of Israel. The prophetic account of the children of Israel's suffering in the years before the arrival of the Messiah is hardly amenable to postmodern accounts of "ethics as first philosophy," or to the account of heeding another's suffering in the writing of Hermann Cohen. Nevertheless, the citation of Is. 57:15 in PesR 34 tempers this epistemological righteousness. It is only in humility and contrition that the divine comes to be present in the world; humility is a necessary precondition for effective mourning. This is a start to contemporary interpretations of PesR 34 that might broaden the horizon of what alterity might mean in this rabbinic text. These interpretations might also turn to the confusion in the *'avelei tzion*'s self-image, in which it is undecided at the surface of the text whether they are a group who are redeemed or a group who redeem. It is certainly the case that this confusion is self-aggrandizing for the beleaguered group in its social context. But in terms of its scriptural analysis, PesR 34 also manifests a sacrifice of ego, and thus it marks the beginning of a path of religious thinking that is certainly not averse to these phenomenological models of alterity. There is nothing preventing current readers of PesR 34 from valuing its discussion of the meaning of "waiting on kingship" over and above the narrative of the mourners' cavorting with angels of destruction. The text's notion that I carry the Messiah within myself means that I must imagine the future into the now; it means that I must work for emancipation in and through the work of mourning. Humility is a necessary element of this work, and the others before whom I humble myself include even those who mock me for believing that Torah-observance is insufficient for maintaining my covenantal responsibilities.

In this questioning of the simple objectivity of the Messiah, PesR stakes out, within the sphere of institutionalized religion, a meontological space in which the Derridean understanding of the messianic and mourning can dwell. But PesR 34 does more than simply make space for Derrida in the Jewish tradition; in so doing, it calls attention to the weakness of Derrida's account. For PesR 34 displays the two fundamental traits that Derrida refuses to associate with meontology in his apparent belief that meontology is merely otherworldliness. PesR displays an intrainstitutional *epochē* of the concept of the messianic, that is, a bracketing of the world in which the idea of the Messiah is given, without leaving Judaism behind. It also reveals a concept of mourning that is between introjection and incorporation. Let me develop these two points further.

PesR 34's account of the *'avelei tzion* manifests a phenomenological reduction of the concept of the Messiah. As Husserl states in numerous texts, the phenomenological reduction exposes the intentionality-structure of consciousness, namely that consciousness is always consciousness of something.[32] The intuition of essences that is the result of the phenomenological reduction is an intuition of the essence of the object *in terms of* the subject's intentional comportment. In the correlation between subject and object, perception of an object is seen as contingent upon the determinate position of the subject. Likewise, in the Pesikta Rabbati text, the mourners have an intentional relation to the messianic future. The Mourners of Zion do not simply wait for the Messiah; they engender redemption through the act of mourning and thus take messianic agency into themselves. The mourner, as she waits for a redeemer who is someone else, is also an agent that engenders the very future that she anticipates. As such, the mourning subject

---

[32] For example, cf. Husserl, *The Idea of Phenomenology*, trans. William P. Alston and George Nakhnikhian (The Hague: Martinus Nijhoff, 1973), 37–44.

of PesR 34 *intends* the future in a sense that the believer who "attends to Torah" does not.

This intentional comportment toward the messianic future is paired with an intentional comportment toward the persona of the Messiah. Like the future, the Messiah in PesR 34 is more than an object; the Messiah also stretches back into the subject, as the similarities between the Messiah and the '*avelei tzion* demonstrate – without reducing the Messiah to a mere symbol, a code for the subject's aspirations. The essence of the Messiah is seen in terms of the mourners' desire for the future. Their intentional relation to the messianic future grounds the account of the Messiah in PesR 34, and the Messiah is hence phenomenologically reduced, abstracted away from the coronation narratives of the Hebrew Bible and the priestly figures of the Second Temple period. However, because the '*avelei tzion* never threaten to secede from their community and do not turn away from their belief toward something purer (as Derrida has), their *epochē* of the messianic idea and the messianic persona is always intrainstitutional. The Mourners of Zion are able to do what Derrida (and Maimonides, Cohen, and Levinas) do, without leaving Judaism – indeed, with a halakhic justification for their ritual heteropraxis.

Moreover, the rhetoric of swallowing that Abraham and Torok use in their essays on mourning is not foreign to the Hebrew Bible.[33] The prophet Isaiah describes the eschatological future as a time when God "will swallow up death forever" (25:8). Another homily from *Pesikta Rabbati*, PesR 36, shifts the meaning of this passage toward messianic agency by interpreting this verse as a fictionalized assertion by Satan that "the Messiah will cause me and all the counterparts in heaven of the princes of the earth's nations to be swallowed up in Gehenna."[34] As the Messiah swallows death, so do the Mourners of Zion swallow the Messiah. But is this an act of introjection or incorporation? Clearly, it is introjection insofar as it openly expresses an eros for the future as an autoerotic impulse. The mourners wear their messianic libido on their sleeve;[35] it is their basic instinct, the most fundamental drive of their psychic lives. The concept of the Messiah, and the concept of divine proximity associated with it, lies within the potential for authentic selfhood.

[33] Indeed, it is essential to the passages from Ezekiel on the dedicatory page of Levinas's *Otherwise than Being*. For analyses of the significance of Ezekiel's swallowing the words he has been commanded to prophesy, cf. Bettina Bergo, *Levinas Between Ethics and Politics* (Dordrecht: Kluwer Academic Publishers, 1999), 73–81; Martin C. Srajek, *In the Margins of Deconstruction: Jewish Conceptions of Ethics in Emmanuel Levinas and Jacques Derrida* (Dordrecht: Kluwer Academic Publishers, 1998), 89–95; James L. Kugel, "Early Interpretation: The Common Background of Late Forms of Biblical Exegesis," in *Early Biblical Interpretation*, ed. James L. Kugel and Rowan A. Greer (Philadelphia: Westminster, 1986), 17–19.

[34] Braude, 678.

[35] As stated in n. 29 above, the language of messianic yearning for the '*avelei tzion* has erotic and libidinal overtones.

One waits for God through waiting for the Messiah; one waits for the Messiah through awaiting the universal conversion of Israel to the ideology of the *'avelei tzion*. The reader of the text is exhorted by the text to take on this messianic agency by taking on the stance of mourning him- or herself. Thus, the libidinal desire for God's return is expressed through love of self and hope for the redemption of its suffering; messianism has become a tool for self-making. As Ferenczi wrote in his original definition of introjection, "in principle, man can love only himself; if he loves an object he takes it into his ego" (EN 235/112). In the rhetorical slippages between the Messiah and the *'avelei tzion*, PesR 34 exemplifies a demythologizing impulse that does not completely divorce itself from myth.

Yet at the same time, this shift from love of God to love of the self, visible on the surface of the text of PesR 34, is written in a context of a mourning that cannot be normalized. Here, after the loss of the Temple, it is God who is the lost beloved. The death of a parent is natural; the death of a sibling or even a child can be explained, if only on the basest of biological strata, by the mortality that all humanity shares. However, God cannot be lost in the same sense that persons can. As a result, introjection, vis-à-vis God, cannot function, since God is not like other objects of erotic cathexis. To introject God would be more than to simply admit that God is no longer present. It would be to admit that God was never present in the first place, that all the instincts toward and arguments for God and the covenantal relationship are and were for nought, that the memories that console in other mourning processes are not memories at all, but myths. This only adds additional trauma to the original loss. Who could possibly admit this, when it is easier (and more important, still valid) to create new stories and interpretations of halakha that serve to explain the perdurance of the disjunction between worldly time and the God of history?

Thus, the mourners are unable to admit the loss, much less communicate it. This failure to communicate (in accordance with Abraham and Torok's clinical research) marks the transition from introjection to incorporation. Hence, the redeemer who symbolizes God's strength, presence, and "arm" is literally swallowed – encrypted – by the *'avelei tzion*, in order for them to magically resuscitate the divine-aided agency of the Messiah within themselves (which they then take as proof of the Messiah's imminence). Nevertheless, the rest of the community does not recognize the legality of their resulting actions. This points to the central irony of PesR 34. The Mourners of Zion are, in the context of modern psychoanalytic descriptions of mourning, *refusing* to mourn. Their actions are in *no* sense a decathexis from the beloved God. Rather, this cathexis becomes the central aspect of their identity. The *'avelei tzion*, through their humility, have realized divine agency within themselves.

In their spirit, the Jewish meontological tradition has disavowed the surface meaning of tradition, has moved away from viewing messianism only as a natural fact of revelation. Alongside a discourse of the future that has not yet come to pass, Jewish meontological thinkers have developed a rhetoric of the present moment, the now, in which consciousness constitutes redemption in its acts of ethics, humility, mourning, perfecting the self and the world, and so forth. In the privation of stability and identity, the sensing of having been constituted by one's environment, the transcendence beyond being has come to pass as a mode of being itself.

Now – in the time between the present moment in which I remember the passing of transcendence and the not-yet moment in which the promise of transcendence passing will become actualized, in the time between my writing this letter and the moment when you respond and your transcendence will flash before me – is the time of faith.

Works Cited

This list does not include works cited in the List of Abbreviations that appears in the front matter of this book.

Ackrill, J. L. "Plato and the Copula: *Sophist* 251–59." In *Plato I: Metaphysics and Epistemology*. Edited by Gregory Vlastos. New York: Anchor, 1971: 210–22.

Altmann, Alexander. *In zwei Welten.* Tel Aviv: Verlag Bitaon, 1962.

— *Studies in Religious Philosophy and Mysticism.* Ithaca, N.Y.: Cornell University Press, 1969.

— *Von der mittelalterlichen zur modernen Aufklärung.* Tübingen: J. C. B. Mohr, 1987.

Annas, Julia. *An Introduction to Plato's Republic.* Oxford: Clarendon, 1981.

Aristotle. *Metaphysics.* Translated by Hippocrates G. Apostle. Bloomington: Indiana University Press, 1966.

— *Metaphysics.* Translated by Hugh Tredennick. Cambridge, Mass.: Harvard University Press, 1933.

— *Nicomachean Ethics.* Translated by H. Rackham. Cambridge, Mass.: Harvard University Press, 1926.

— *On Sophistical Refutations. On Coming-to-be and Passing Away. On the Cosmos.* Translated by E. S. Forster and D. J. Furley. Cambridge, Mass.: Harvard University Press, 1955.

— *Physics.* Translated by Hippocrates G. Apostle. Bloomington: Indiana University Press, 1969.

— *Physics.* Translated by P. H. Wicksteed and F. M. Cornford. Cambridge, Mass.: Harvard University Press, 1929–34.

Bamberger, Bernard J. "A Messianic Document of the Seventh Century." *Hebrew Union College Annual* 15 (1940): 425–31.

Barnes, Jonathan. *The Presocratic Philosophers.* 2 vols. London: Routledge, 1979.

Baron, Margaret. *The Origin of the Infinitesimal Calculus.* Oxford: Pergamon, 1969.

Batnitzky, Leora. "Dialogue as Judgment, Not Mutual Affirmation: A New Look at Franz Rosenzweig's Dialogical Philosophy." *Journal of Religion* 79, no. 4 (1999): 523–44.

— *Idolatry and Representation: The Philosophy of Franz Rosenzweig Considered.* Princeton, N.J.: Princeton University Press, 2000.

Beach, Edward Allen. *The Potencies of God(s): Schelling's Philosophy of Mythology.* Albany: State University of New York Press, 1994.

Benjamin, Walter. *Illuminations.* Edited by Hannah Arendt. Translated by Harry Zohn. New York: Schocken, 1968.

Bergo, Bettina. *Levinas Between Ethics and Politics: For the Beauty that Adorns the Earth.* Phænomenologica 152. Dordrecht: Kluwer Academic Publishers, 1999.

Biale, David. *Gershom Scholem, Kabbalah, and Counter-History.* Cambridge, Mass.: Harvard University Press, 1979.

Bostock, David. "Plato on 'Is Not.'" *Oxford Studies in Ancient Philosophy* 2 (1984): 89–119.

Braiterman, Zachary. *(God) After Auschwitz: Tradition and Change in Post-Holocaust Jewish Thought.* Princeton, N.J.: Princeton University Press, 1998.

———. "'Into Life'??! Franz Rosenzweig and the Figure of Death." *Association for Jewish Studies Review* 23, no. 2 (1998): 203–21.

Brown, Lesley. "Being in the *Sophist:* A Syntactical Inquiry." *Oxford Studies in Ancient Philosophy* 4 (1986): 49–70.

Brown, Robert F. *The Later Philosophy of Schelling.* Lewisburg, Pa.: Bucknell University Press, 1977.

Bruckstein, Almut Sh. "Hermann Cohen's 'Charakteristik der Ethik Maimunis': A Reconstructive Reading of Maimonides' Ethics." Ph.D. diss., Temple University, 1992.

———. "Joining the Narrators: A Philosophy of Talmudic Hermeneutics." In *Reasoning after Revelation.* Edited by Peter Ochs, Robert Gibbs, and Steven Kepnes. Boulder, Colo.: Westview Press, 1998: 105–21.

———. "On Jewish Hermeneutics: Maimonides and Bachya as Vectors in Cohen's Philosophy of Origin." In *Hermann Cohen's Philosophy of Religion.* Edited by Stéphane Mosès and Hartwig Wiedebach. Hildesheim: Olms, 1997: 35–50

Burbidge, John. "Reason and Existence in Schelling and Fackenheim." In *Fackenheim: German Philosophy and Jewish Thought.* Edited by Louis Greenspan and Graeme Nicholson. Toronto: University of Toronto Press, 1992: 90–117.

Caputo, John D. *The Prayers and Tears of Jacques Derrida: Religion without Religion.* Bloomington: Indiana University Press, 1998.

Carlson, Thomas. *Indiscretion: Finitude and the Naming of God.* Chicago: University of Chicago Press, 1999.

Cohen, Hermann. *Ethik der reinen Willens.* 5th ed. Hildesheim: Georg Olms, 1981.

Cohen, Richard A. *Ethics, Exegesis, and Philosophy: Interpretation after Levinas.* Cambridge: Cambridge University Press, 2001.

Cohen, S. Marc. "The Logic of the Third Man." In *Plato: Critical Assessments,* vol. 4. Edited by Nicholas D. Smith. London: Routledge, 1998: 28–50.

Cornford, Francis M. *Plato's Theory of Knowledge.* New York: Harcourt Brace & Co., 1935.

Coudert, Allison P. *Leibniz and the Kabbalah.* Dordrecht: Kluwer Academic Publishers, 1995.

Daly, Mary. *Pure Lust.* Boston: Beacon Press, 1984.

Dancy, R. M. *Two Studies in the Early Acacdemy.* Albany: State University of New York Press, 1991.

Davidson, Herbert A. "The Middle Way in Maimonides' Ethics." *Proceedings of the American Academy for Jewish Research* 54 (1987): 31–72.

"The Study of Philosophy as a Religious Obligation." In *Religion in a Religious Age*. Edited by S. D. Goitein. Cambridge, Mass.: Association for Jewish Studies, 1974: 53–68.

de Man, Paul. *Blindness and Insight: Essays in the Rhetoric of Contemporary Criticism*. 2nd ed. Minneapolis: University of Minnesota Press, 1983.

Derrida, Jacques. *Acts of Religion*. Edited by Gil Anidjar. New York: Routledge, 2002.

Adieu à Emmanuel Levinas. Paris: Galilée, 1997.

Adieu: To Emmanuel Levinas. Translated by Pascale-Anne Brault and Michael Naas. Stanford, Calif.: Stanford University Press, 1999.

Edmund Husserl's Origin of Geometry: *An Introduction*. Translated by John P. Leavey, Jr. Lincoln: University of Nebraska Press, 1989.

"Faith and Knowledge: The Two Sources of 'Religion' at the Limits of Reason Alone." Translated by Sam Weber. In *On Religion*. Edited by Jacques Derrida and Gianni Vattimo. Stanford, Calif.: Stanford University Press, 1998: 1–78.

"Foi et Savoir: Les deux sources de la 'religion' aux limites de la simple raison." In *La Religion*. Edited by Jacques Derrida and Gianni Vattimo. Paris: Seuil, 1996.

"Fors: Les mots anglés de Nicolas Abraham et Maria Torok." In Nicolas Abraham and Maria Torok, *Cryptonymie: Le verbier de l'homme aux loups*. Paris: Aubier-Flammarion, 1976: 7–73.

"*Fors:* The Anglish Words of Nicolas Abraham and Maria Torok." Translated by Barbara Johnson. In Nicolas Abraham and Maria Torok, *The Wolf Man's Magic Word: A Cryptonymy*. Minneapolis: University of Minnesota Press, 1986: xi–xlviii.

"How to Avoid Speaking: Denials." Translated by Ken Frieden. In *Derrida and Negative Theology*. Edited by Harold Coward and Toby Foshay. Albany: State University of New York Press, 1992: 73–142.

Mémoires for Paul de Man. 2nd ed. Translated by Cecile Lindsay, Jonathan Culler, Eduardo Cadava, and Peggy Kamuf. New York: Columbia University Press, 1989.

Mémoires pour Paul de Man. Paris: Galilée, 1988.

Negotations: Interventions and Interviews, 1971–2001. Edited by Elizabeth Rottenberg. Stanford, Calif.: Stanford University Press, 2002.

Psyché: Inventions de l'autre. Paris: Galilée, 1987.

Writing and Difference. Translated by Alan Bass. Chicago: University of Chicago Press, 1978.

Descartes, René. *Selected Philosophical Writings*. Translated by John Cottingham, Robert Stoothoff, and Dugald Murdoch. Cambridge: Cambridge University Press, 1988.

Diesendruck, Zvi. "Maimonides' Theory of the Negation of Privation." *Proceedings of the American Academy for Jewish Research* 6 (1934–35): 139–51.

Dray, W. H. "Historicity, Historicism, and Self-Making." In *Fackenheim: German Philosophy and Jewish Thought*. Edited by Louis Greenspan and Graeme Nicholson. Toronto: Universty of Toronto Press, 1992: 118–37.

Drummond, John J. "The 'Spiritual' World: The Personal, the Social, and the Communal." In *Issues in Husserl's* Ideas II. Edited by Thomas Nenon and Lester Embree. Dordrecht: Kluwer Academic Publishers, 1996: 237–54.

Fackenheim, Emil. *God's Presence in History: Jewish Affirmations and Philosophical Reflections*. New York: Harper & Row, 1970.

Jewish Philosophers and Jewish Philosophy. Edited by Michael L. Morgan. Bloomington: Indiana University Press, 1996.

The Jewish Thought of Emil Fackenheim. Edited by Michael L. Morgan. Detroit: Wayne State University Press, 1987.

The Religious Dimension in Hegel's Thought. Bloomington: Indiana University Press, 1967.

"A Reply to My Critics: A Testament of Thought." In *Fackenheim: German Philosophy and Jewish Thought.* Edited by Louis Greenspan and Graeme Nicholson. Toronto: University of Toronto Press, 1992: 251–300.

To Mend the World: Foundations of Post-Holocaust Jewish Thought. New York: Schocken, 1982.

Ferenczi, Sandor. *Final Contributions to the Problems and Methods of Psycho-Analysis.* Translated by Eric Mosbacher. New York: Brunner/Mazel, 1980.

Fichte, J. G. *Science of Knowledge.* Translated by Peter Heath and John Lachs. Cambridge: Cambridge University Press, 1982.

Fine, Gail. "Knowledge and Belief in *Republic* V–VII," In *Plato: Critical Assessments,* vol. 2. Edited by Nicholas D. Smith. London: Routledge, 1998: 235–65.

Fishbane, Michael. "Biblical Prophecy as Religious Phenomenon." In *Jewish Spirituality I: From the Bible through the Middle Ages.* Edited by Arthur Green. New York: Crossroad, 1986: 62–81.

The Exegetical Imagination: On Jewish Thought and Theology. Cambridge, Mass.: Harvard University Press, 1998.

Forster, Michael N. *Hegel's Idea of a Phenomenology of Spirit.* Chicago: University of Chicago Press, 1998.

Fox, Marvin. *Interpreting Maimonides: Studies in Methodology, Metaphysics, and Moral Philosophy.* Chicago: University of Chicago Press, 1990.

Frank, Daniel. "Humility as a Virtue: A Maimonidean Critique of Aristotle's Ethics." In *Moses Maimonides and His Time.* Edited by Eric L. Ormsby. Washington, D.C.: Catholic University of America Press, 1989: 89–99.

Frede, Michael. "Plato's *Sophist* on False Statements." In *The Cambridge Companion to Plato.* Edited by Richard Kraut. Cambridge: Cambridge University Press, 1992: 397–424.

Freud, Sigmund. "Mourning and Melancholia." In *The Standard Edition of the Complete Psychological Works of Sigmund Freud,* vol. 14. Edited by James Strachey. London: Hogarth Press, 1963: 239–58.

Funkenstein, Amos. *Perspectives of Jewish History.* Berkeley: University of California Press, 1993.

Gerson, Lloyd. "A Distinction in Plato's *Sophist.*" In *Plato: Critical Assessments,* vol. 4. Edited by Nicholas D. Smith. London: Routledge, 1998: 125–41.

Gibbs, Robert. "Asymmetry and Mutuality: Habermas and Levinas." *Philosophy and Social Criticism* 23, no. 6 (1997): 51–63.

Correlations in Rosenzweig and Levinas. Princeton, N.J.: Princeton University Press, 1992.

"Lines, Circles, Points: Messianic Epistemology in Cohen, Rosenzweig and Benjamin." In *Toward the Millennium: Messianic Expectations from the Bible to Waco.* Edited by Peter Schäfer and Mark R. Cohen. Leiden: Brill, 1998: 363–82.

Why Ethics? Signs of Responsibilities. Princeton, N.J.: Princeton University Press, 2000.

Goldberg, Arnold. *Erlösung durch Leiden: Drei rabbinischen Homilien über der Trauernden Zions und den leidenden Messias Efraim (PesR 34, 36, 37).* Frankfurt am Main: Gesellschaft zur Förderung Judaistischer Studien, 1978.

Gordon, Peter Eli. "Rosenzweig Redux: The Reception of German-Jewish Thought."
  Jewish Social Studies 8, no. 1 (2001): 1–57.
Graetz, Heinrich. *History of the Jews.* Translated by Bella Löwy. Philadelphia: Jewish
  Publication Society, 1891.
Green, Arthur. "New Directions in Jewish Theology in America." In *Contemporary
  Jewish Theology.* Edited by Elliot N. Dorff and Louis E. Newman. Oxford: Oxford
  University Press, 1999: 486–93.
Handelman, Susan. *Fragments of Redemption: Jewish Thought and Literary Theory in
  Benjamin, Scholem, and Levinas.* Bloomington: Indiana University Press, 1991.
Hart, James G. "Phenomenological Time: Its Religious Significance." In *Time and
  Religion.* Edited by A. N. Balslev and J. N. Mohanty. Leiden: Brill, 1993:
  17–45.
Hegel, G. W. F. *Phenomenology of Spirit.* Translated by A. V. Miller. Oxford: Oxford
  University Press, 1977.
Heidegger, Martin. *Being and Time.* Translated by John McQuarrie and Edward Robin-
  son. San Francisco: Harper & Row, 1962.
History of the Concept of Time. Translated by Theodore Kisiel. Bloomington: Indiana
  University Press, 1985.
On Time and Being. Translated by Joan Stambaugh. New York: Harper & Row, 1972.
Platon: Sophistes. Frankfurt am Main: Vittorio Klostermann, 1992.
Plato's Sophist. Translated by André Schuwer and Richard Rojcewicz. Bloom-
  ington: Indiana University Press, 1997.
Prolegomena zur Geschichte des Zeitbegriffs. Frankfurt am Main: Vittorio Klostermann,
  1979.
Zur Sache des Denkens. Tübingen: Niemeyer, 1969.
Heschel, Abraham Joshua. *God in Search of Man.* New York: Noonday, 1955.
Husserl, Edmund. *Cartesian Meditations: An Introduction to Phenomenology.* Translated
  by Dorion Cairns. The Hague: Martinus Nijhoff, 1960.
The Idea of Phenomenology. Translated by William P. Alston and George Nakhnikhian.
  The Hague: Martinus Nijhoff, 1973.
*Ideas Pertaining to a Pure Phenomenology and to a Phenomenological Philosophy. First Book:
  General Introduction to a Pure Phenomenology.* Translated by F. Kersten. Dordrecht:
  Kluwer Academic Publishers, 1989.
Hyman, Arthur. "Maimonides on Religious Language." In *Perspectives on Maimonides:
  Philosophical and Historical Studies.* Edited by Joel L. Kraemer. Oxford: Oxford
  University Press, 1991: 175–91.
Ivry, Alfred L. "Maimonides on Creation." In *Creation and the End of Days: Judaism and
  Scientific Cosmology.* Edited by David Novak and Norbert Samuelson. Lanham,
  Md.: University Press of America, 1986: 185–213.
Jastrow, Marcus. *Dictionary of the Targumim, Talmud Bavli, Yerushalmi, and Midrashic
  Literature.* 2nd ed. New York: Judaica Press, 1992.
Jonte-Pace, Diane. "Situating Kristeva Differently." In *Body/Text in Julia Kristeva: Reli-
  gion, Women, Psychoanalysis.* Edited by David Crownfield. Albany: State University
  of New York Press, 1992: 1–22.
Kant, Immanuel. *Critique of Pure Reason.* Translated by Norman Kemp Smith. New
  York: St. Martin's Press, 1929.
Metaphysics of Morals. Translated by Mary Gregor. Cambridge: Cambridge Univer-
  sity Press, 1991.

Religion Within the Limits of Reason Alone. Translated by T. M. Greene and H. H. Hudson. New York: Harper & Row, 1960.

Kavka, Martin. "The Absence Fetish." *Religious Studies Review* 29, no. 3 (July 2003): 225–34.

Kavka, Martin, and Randi Rashkover. "A Jewish Modified Divine Command Ethics." *Journal of Religious Ethics* 32, no. 2 (Summer 2004).

Kearney, Richard. "Dialogue with Emmanuel Lévinas." In *Face to Face with Levinas.* Edited by Richard A. Cohen. Albany: State University of New York Press, 1986: 13–33.

Dialogues with Contemporary Continental Thinkers: The Phenomenological Heritage. Manchester: Manchester University Press, 1984.

States of Mind. Manchester: Manchester University Press, 1995.

Kellner, Menachem. *Maimonides on Human Perfection.* Atlanta: Scholars Press, 1990.

Köhnke, Klaus. *The Rise of Neo-Kantianism: German Academic Philosophy between Idealism and Positivism.* Translated by R. J. Hollingdale. Cambridge: Cambridge University Press, 1991.

Kraemer, Joel L. "On Maimonides' Messianic Posture." In *Studies in Medieval Jewish History and Literature,* vol. 2. Edited by Isadore Twersky. Cambridge, Mass.: Harvard University Press, 1984: 109–42.

Krell, David Farrell. "Trauma, Forgetting and Narrative in F. W. J. Schelling's *Die Weltalter.*" *Postmodern Culture* 11, no. 2 (http://muse.jhu.edu/demo/pmc/11.2krell.html).

Kugel, James L. "Early Interpretation: The Common Background of Late Forms of Biblical Exegeisis." In *Early Biblical Interpretation.* Edited by James L. Kugel and Rowan A. Greer. Philadelphia: Westminster, 1986: 11–106.

Kwant, Remy. "Merleau-Ponty and Phenomenology." In *Phenomenology: The Philosophy of Edmund Husserl and Its Interpretation.* Edited by Joseph J. Kockelmans. Garden City, N.Y.: Doubleday, 1967: 375–92.

"Merleau-Ponty's Criticism of Husserl's Eidetic Reduction." In *Phenomenology: The Philosophy of Edmund Husserl and Its Interpretation.* Edited by Joseph J. Kockelmans. Garden City, N.Y.: Doubleday, 1967: 393–408.

Lane, Edward William. *Lexicon of the Arabic Language.* Cambridge: Islam Texts Society, 1984.

Levinas, Emmanuel. *A l'heure des nations.* Paris: Minuit, 1988.

Altérité et transcendance. Montpellier: Fata Morgana, 1995.

Alterity and Transcendence. Translated by Michael B. Smith. New York: Columbia University Press, 1999.

Basic Philosophical Writings. Edited by Adriaan T. Peperzak, Simon Critchley, and Robert Bernasconi. Bloomington: Indiana University Press, 1996.

Collected Philosophical Papers. Translated by Alphonso Lingis. Dordrecht: Martinus Nijhoff, 1987.

De Dieu qui vient à l'idée. 2nd ed. Paris: Vrin, 1986.

Difficile liberté. 3rd ed. Paris: Livre de poche, 1984.

Difficult Freedom: Essays on Judaism. Translated by Seán Hand. Baltimore: Johns Hopkins University Press, 1990.

Discovering Existence in Husserl. Translated by Richard A. Cohen and Michael B. Smith. Evanston, Ill.: Northwestern University Press, 1998.

Du sacré au saint. Paris: Minuit, 1977.

En découvrant l'existence avec Husserl et Heidegger. 3rd ed. Paris: Vrin, 1994.

Entre nous: Essais sur le penser-à-l'autre. Paris: Bernard Grasset, 1991.

Entre Nous: On Thinking-of-the-Other. Translated by Michael B. Smith and Barbara Harshav. New York: Columbia University Press, 1998.

Ethics and Infinity: Conversations with Philippe Nemo. Translated by Richard A. Cohen. Pittsburgh: Duquesne University Press, 1985.

Éthique et Infini. Paris: Fayard, 1982.

Hors sujet. Montpellier: Fata Morgana, 1987.

Humanisme de l'autre homme. Montpellier: Fata Morgana, 1972.

In the Time of the Nations. Translated by Michael B. Smith. Bloomington: Indiana University Press, 1994.

"Martin Heidegger and Ontology." Translated by the Committee of Public Safety. *diacritics* 26, no. 1 (1996): 11–32.

Nine Talmudic Readings. Edited and translated by Annette Aronowicz. Bloomington: Indiana University Press, 1990.

Of God Who Comes to Mind. Translated by Bettina Bergo. Stanford, Calif.: Stanford University Press, 1998.

Outside the Subject. Translated by Michael B. Smith. Stanford, Calif.: Stanford University Press, 1994.

"The Paradox of Morality." In *The Provocation of Levinas.* Edited by Robert Bernasconi and David Wood. London: Routledge, 1988: 168–80.

Quatre lectures talmudiques. Paris: Minuit, 1968.

"La réalité et son ombre." *Les temps modernes* 38 (1948): 771–89.

"Substitution." *Revue philosophique de Louvain* 66 (1968): 487–508.

Le temps et l'autre. Paris: Presses Universitaires de France, 1989.

La théorie de l'intuition dans la phenomenology de Husserl. Paris: Alcan, 1930.

The Theory of Intuition in Husserl's Phenomenology. 2nd ed. With foreword by Richard A. Cohen. Translated by André Orianne. Evanston, Ill.: Northwestern University Press, 1995.

Time and the Other. Translated by Richard A. Cohen. Pittsburgh: Duquesne University Press, 1985.

Liddell, Henry, and Robert Scott. *Greek-English Lexicon.* Abr. ed. Oxford: Oxford University Press, 1994.

Lilla, Mark. "A Battle for Religion." *The New York Review of Books* 49, no. 19 (December 5, 2002): 60–65.

Llewellyn, John. *Emmanuel Levinas: The Genealogy of Ethics.* New York: Routledge, 1995.

Lobel, Diana. "A Dwelling Place for the Shekhinah." *Jewish Quarterly Review* 90, nos. 1–2 (1999): 103–25.

"'Silence Is Praise to You': Maimonides on Negative Theology, Looseness of Expression, and Religious Experience." *American Catholic Philosophical Quarterly* 76, no. 1 (2002): 25–49.

MacIntyre, Alasdair. *After Virtue.* 2nd ed. Notre Dame, Ind.: University of Notre Dame Press, 1984.

Malcolm, John. "Plato's Analysis of *to on* and *to me on* in the *Sophist.*" *Phronesis* 12 (1967): 130–45.

Manekin, Charles. "Belief, Certainty, and Divine Attributes in the *Guide of the Perplexed.*" *Maimonidean Studies* 1 (1990): 117–41.

Mann, Jacob. *The Jews in Egypt and Palestine under the Fatimid Caliphs*, vol. 1. Oxford: Oxford University Press, 1929.

Marion, Jean-Luc. "The Saturated Phenomenon." *Philosophy Today* 40 (Spring 1996): 103– 24.

Marmorstein, Arthur. "Eine messianische Bewegung im dritten Jahrhundert." *Jeschurun* 13 (1926): 16–28, 171–86, 369–83.

McKirahan, Richard D., Jr. *Philosophy before Socrates: An Introduction with Texts and Commentary*. Indianapolis: Hackett, 1994.

Meinwald, Constance. "Good-bye to the Third Man." In *The Cambridge Companion to Plato*. Edited by Richard Kraut. Cambridge: Cambridge University Press, 1992: 365–96.

Plato's Parmenides. Oxford: Oxford University Press, 1991.

Mendelssohn, Moses. *Jerusalem, or On Religious Power and Judaism*. Translated by Allan Arkush. Hanover, N.H.: Brandeis University Press, 1983.

Mendes-Flohr, Paul, and Jehuda Reinharz, eds. *The Jew in the Modern World: A Documentary History*. 2nd ed. Oxford: Oxford University Press, 1995.

Merleau-Ponty, Maurice. *Phénomenologie de la perception*. Paris: Gallimard, 1945.

Phenomenology of Perception. Translated by Colin Smith. London: Routledge, 1962.

Signes. Paris: Gallimard, 1960.

Signs. Translated by Richard McCleary. Evanston, Ill.: Northwestern University Press, 1964.

Meskin, Jacob. "Toward a New Understanding of the Work of Emmanuel Levinas." *Modern Judaism* 20, no. 1 (2000): 78–102.

Milbank, John. "The Ethics of Self-Sacrifice." *First Things* 91 (March 1999): 33–38.

Morgan, Michael. *Dilemmas in Modern Jewish Thought*. Bloomington: Indiana University Press, 1992.

Mosès, Stéphane. *System and Revelation: The Philosophy of Franz Rosenzweig*. Translated by Catherine Tihanyi. Detroit: Wayne State University Press, 1992.

Moses ben Maimon (Maimonides). *Crisis and Leadership*. Edited by Abraham Halkin and David Hartman. Philadelphia: Jewish Publication Society, 1985.

Ethical Writings of Maimonides. Edited and translated by Raymond L. Weiss, with Charles Butterworth. New York: New York University Press, 1975.

A Maimonides Reader. Edited by Isadore Twersky. West Orange, N.J.: Behrman House, 1972.

Munk, Reinier. "The Self and Other in Cohen's Ethics and Works on Religion." In *Hermann Cohen's Philosophy of Religion*. Edited by Stéphane Mosès and Hartwig Wiedebach. Hildesheim: Olms, 1997: 161–81.

Nehamas, Alexander. "*Episteme* and *Logos* in Plato's Later Thought." *Archiv für Geschichte der Philosophie* 66 (1984): 11–36.

Nemoy, Leon, ed. and trans. *A Karaite Anthology: Excerpts from the Early Literature*. New Haven, Conn.: Yale University Press, 1952.

Novak, David. *The Election of Israel: The Idea of the Chosen People*. Cambridge: Cambridge University Press, 1995.

Natural Law in Judaism. Cambridge: Cambridge University Press, 1998.

Nussbaum, Martha C. *The Fragility of Goodness: Luck and Ethics in Greek Tragedy and Philosophy*. Cambridge: Cambridge University Press, 1986.

Love's Knowledge: Essays on Philosophy and Literature. Oxford: Oxford University Press, 1990.

The Therapy of Desire: Theory and Practice in Hellenistic Ethics. Princeton, N.J.: Princeton University Press, 1994.

Upheavals of Thought: The Intelligence of Emotions. Cambridge: Cambridge University Press, 2001.

O'Brien, Denis. *Le Non-Être: Deux Études sur le* Sophiste *de Platon.* Sankt Augustin: Academia Verlag, 1995.

Ofrat, Gideon. *The Jewish Derrida.* Translated by Peretz Kidron. Syracuse, N.Y.: Syracuse University Press, 2001.

Owen, G. E. L. "Plato on Not-Being." In *Plato I: Metaphysics and Epistemology.* Edited by Gregory Vlastos. New York: Anchor, 1971: 223–67.

Peperzak, Adriaan Theodoor. *Beyond: The Philosophy of Emmanuel Levinas.* Evanston, Ill.: Northwestern University, Press, 1997.

Platonic Transformations: With and After Hegel, Heidegger and Levinas. Lanham, Md.: Rowman & Littlefield, 1997.

To the Other: An Introduction to the Philosophy of Emmanuel Levinas. West Lafayette, Ind.: Purdue University Press, 1993.

Pesikta Rabbati. Edited by Meir Friedmann. Vienna: Joseph Kaiser, 1880.

Pesikta Rabbati. 2 vols. Translated by William Braude. New Haven, Conn.: Yale University Press, 1968.

Pesiqta Rabbati: A Synoptic Edition of Pesiqta Rabbati Based upon All Extent Manuscripts and the Editio Princeps. 2 vols. Edited by Rivka Ulmer. Atlanta: Scholars Press, 1997–99.

Pines, Shlomo. "The Limitations of Human Knowledge According to al-Farabi, ibn Bajja, and Maimonides." In *Studies in Medieval Jewish History and Literature.* Edited by Isadore Twersky. Cambridge, Mass.: Harvard University Press, 1979: 82–109.

Plato. *Complete Works.* Edited by John M. Cooper. Indianapolis: Hackett, 1997.

Plotinus. *Enneads.* 7 vols. Translated by A. H. Armstrong. Cambridge, Mass.: Harvard University Press, 1966–88.

Poma, Andrea. *The Critical Philosophy of Hermann Cohen.* Translated by John Denton. Albany: State University of New York Press, 1997.

Prior, William J. *Unity and Development in Plato's Metaphysics.* La Salle, Ill.: Open Court, 1985.

Proust, Marcel. *Remembrance of Things Past.* 3 vols. Translated by C. K. Scott Moncrieff, T. Kilmartin, and A. Mayor. New York: Vintage, 1982.

Rahel-Freund, Elsa. *Franz Rosenzweig's Philosophy of Existence: An Analysis of* The Star of Redemption. Translated by Stephen L. Weinstein and Robert Israel. Edited by Paul Mendes-Flohr. The Hague: Martinus Nijhoff, 1979.

Ravitzky, Aviezer. *History and Faith: Studies in Jewish Philosophy.* Amsterdam: J. C. Gieben, 1996.

Rawidowicz, Simon. *Studies in Jewish Thought.* Edited by Nahum Glatzer. Philadelphia: Jewish Publication Society, 1974.

Rickless, Samuel C. "How Parmenides Saved the Theory of Forms." *The Philosophical Review* 107, no. 4 (1998): 501–54.

Robbins, Jill. *Altered Reading: Levinas and Literature.* Chicago: University of Chicago Press, 1999.

Prodigal Son/Elder Brother: Interpretation and Alterity in Augustine, Petrarch, Kafka, Levinas. Chicago: University of Chicago Press, 1991.

Rose, Gillian. *Mourning Becomes the Law.* Cambridge: Cambridge University Press, 1996.

Rosen, Stanley. *Plato's Sophist: The Drama of Original and Image.* New Haven, Conn.: Yale University Press, 1983.

Rosenzweig, Franz. *Franz Rosenzweig's "The New Thinking."* Translated and edited by Alan Udoff and Barbara E. Galli. Syracuse, N.Y.: Syracuse University Press, 1999.

God, Man, and the World: Lectures and Essays. Edited and translated by Barbara E. Galli. Syracuse, N.Y.: Syracuse University Press, 1998.

Philosophical and Theological Writings. Edited by Michael L. Morgan and Paul Franks. Indianapolis: Hackett, 2002.

Zweistromland. The Hague: Martinus Nijhoff, 1984.

Rubenstein, Richard L. *After Auschwitz: History, Theology, and Contemporary Judaism.* 2nd ed. Baltimore: Johns Hopkins University Press, 1992.

Rutherford, Donald. *Leibniz and the Rational Order of Nature.* Cambridge: Cambridge University Press, 1995.

Sayre, Kenneth M. *Parmenides' Lesson.* Notre Dame, Ind.: University of Notre Dame Press, 1996.

Plato's Late Ontology. Princeton, N.J.: Princeton University Press, 1983.

"The Role of the *Timaeus* in the Development of Plato's Late Ontology." *Ancient Philosophy* 18 (1998): 93–124.

Scanlon, John. "Objectivity and Introjection in *Ideas II.*" In *Issues in Husserl's Ideas II.* Edited by Thomas Nenon and Lester Embree. Dordrecht: Kluwer Academic Publishers, 1996: 213–22.

Schäfer, Peter. *Rivalität zwischen Engeln und Menschen.* New York: de Gruyter, 1975.

Schmidt, James. *Maurice Merleau-Ponty: Between Phenomenology and Structuralism.* London: Macmillan, 1985.

Scholem, Gershom. *The Messianic Idea in Judaism.* New York: Schocken, 1971.

Schwarzschild, Steven S. *The Pursuit of the Ideal.* Edited by Menachem Kellner. Albany: State University of New York Press, 1990.

Sedley, D. "Two Conceptions of Vacuum." *Phronesis* 27 (1982): 175–93.

Seeskin, Kenneth. *Searching for a Distant God: The Legacy of Maimonides.* Oxford: Oxford University Press, 2000.

Segal, Alan. *Rebecca's Children: Judaism and Christianity in the Roman World.* Cambridge, Mass.: Harvard University Press, 1986.

Sokolowski, Robert. *Husserlian Meditations.* Evanston, Ill.: Northwestern University Press, 1974.

Spero, Shubert. "Is the God of Maimonides Unknowable?" *Judaism* 22, no. 1 (1973): 67–78.

Srajek, Martin C. *In the Margins of Deconstruction: Jewish Conceptions of Ethics in Emmanuel Levinas and Jacques Derrida.* Dordrecht: Kluwer Academic Publishers, 1998.

Stapleton, Timothy J. *Husserl and Heidegger: The Question of a Phenomenological Beginning.* Albany: State University of New York Press, 1983.

Steiner, George. "Trusting in Reason." *Times Literary Supplement,* June 24, 1994.

Stern, Josef. "Maimonides' Demonstrations: Principles and Practice." *Medieval Philosophy and Theology* 10 (2001): 47–84.

"Maimonides on Language and the Science of Language." In *Maimonides and the Sciences.* Edited by R. S. Cohen and H. Levine. Dordrecht: Kluwer Academic Publishers, 2000: 173–226.

Strauss, Leo. *Persecution and the Art of Writing.* Glencoe, Ill.: Free Press, 1952.

Taminiaux, Jacques. *Dialectic and Difference: Modern Thought and the Sense of Human Limits.* Atlantic Highlands, N.J.: Humanities Press, 1990.

    Heidegger and the Project of Fundamental Ontology. Albany: State University of New York Press, 1991.

Tertullian. "On the Prescription Against Heretics." In *The Writings of Quintus Sept. Flor. Tertullianus,* vol. II (*Ante-Nicene Christian Library,* vol. XV). Translated by Peter Holmes. Edinburgh: T & T Clark, 1870: 243–65.

Tillich, Paul. *The Courage to Be.* New Haven, Conn.: Yale University Press, 1952.

    Systematic Theology, vol. 1. Chicago: University of Chicago Press, 1951.

Twersky, Isadore. *Introduction to the Code of Maimonides (Mishneh Torah).* New Haven, Conn.: Yale University Press, 1980.

Vlastos, Gregory. "Degrees of Reality in Plato." In *Plato: Critical Assessments,* vol. 2. Edited by Nicholas D. Smith. London: Routledge, 1998.

Walfish, Barry. "The Mourners of Zion: Karaite *Aliyah* Movement of the Early Arab Period." In *Eretz Israel, Israel and the Jewish Diaspora.* Edited by Menachem Mor. Lanham, Md.: University Press of America, 1991: 42–52.

Welch, Sharon. *A Feminist Ethic of Risk.* Minneapolis: Fortress Press, 1990.

    "Sporting Power: American Feminism, French Feminisms, and an Ethic of Conflict." In *Transfigurations: Theology and the French Feminists.* Edited by C. W. Maggie Kim, Susan M. St. Ville, and Susan M. Simonaitis. Minneapolis: Fortress Press, 1993: 171–98.

West, Cornel. *Prophetic Fragments.* Grand Rapids, Mich.: Eerdmans, 1988.

Willey, Thomas E. *Back to Kant: The Revival of Kantianism in German Social and Historical Thought, 1860–1914.* Detroit: Wayne State University Press, 1978.

Williams, Robert R. *Hegel's Ethic of Recognition.* Berkeley: University of California Press, 1997.

    Recognition: Fichte and Hegel on the Other. Albany: State University of New York Press, 1992.

Wolfson, Harry A. *Philo: Foundations of Religious Philosophy in Judaism, Christianity, and Islam.* Cambridge, Mass.: Harvard University Press, 1947.

    Studies in the History of Philosophy and Religion. 2 vols. Edited by Isadore Twersky and George H. Williams. Cambridge, Mass.: Harvard University Press, 1973–77.

Wyschogrod, Edith. "Corporeality and the Glory of the Infinite in the Philosophy of Emmanuel Levinas." In *Incarnation.* Edited by Marco M. Olivetti. Padua: CEDAM, 1999: 113–26.

    Emmanuel Levinas: The Problem of Ethical Metaphysics. 2nd ed. New York: Fordham University Press, 2000.

    An Ethics of Remembering: History, Heterology, and the Nameless Others. Chicago: University of Chicago Press, 1998.

Wyschogrod, Michael. *The Body of Faith: God in the People Israel.* 2nd ed. Northvale, N.J.: Jason Aronson, 1996.

    "Faith and the Holocaust: A Review Essay of Emil Fackenheim's *God's Presence in History.*" *Judaism* 20, no. 3 (1971): 286–94.

Zank, Michael. *The Idea of Atonement in the Philosophy of Hermann Cohen.* Providence, R.I.: Brown Judaic Studies, 2000.

Zunz, Leopold. *Die gottesdienstlichen Vorträge der Juden.* Frankfurt: Hildesheim, 1966.

Index